*THE AMERICAN HISTORY SERIES*

# THE MIDDLE PERIOD

1817-1858

BY

JOHN W. BURGESS, Ph.D., LL.D.

PROFESSOR OF POLITICAL SCIENCE AND CONSTITUTIONAL LAW, AND DEAN OF
THE FACULTY OF POLITICAL SCIENCE, IN COLUMBIA UNIVERSITY
IN THE CITY OF NEW YORK

*WITH MAPS*

NEW YORK        CHICAGO        BOSTON

Copyright, 1897, by
CHARLES SCRIBNER'S SONS

To the memory

of

my former teacher, colleague, and friend,

JULIUS HAWLEY SEELYE,

philosopher, theologian, statesman, and educator,

this volume is reverently

and affectionately

inscribed

# PREFACE

THERE is no more serious and delicate task in literature and morals than that of writing the history of the United States from 1816 to 1860. The periods which precede this may be treated without fear of arousing passion, prejudice, and resentment, and with little danger of being misunderstood. Even the immaculateness of Washington may be attacked without exciting anything worse than a sort of uncomfortable admiration for the reckless courage of the assailant. But when we pass the year 1820, and especially when we approach the year 1860, we find ourselves in a different world. We find ourselves in the midst of the ideas, the motives, and the occurrences which, and of the men who, have, in large degree, produced the animosities, the friendships, and the relations between parties and sections which prevail to-day.

Serious and delicate as the task is, however, the time has arrived when it should be undertaken in a thoroughly impartial spirit. The continued misunderstanding between the North and the South is an ever present menace to the welfare of both sections and of the entire nation. It makes it almost impossible to decide any question of our politics upon its merits. It offers an almost insuperable obstacle to the development of a national opinion upon the fundamental principles of our polity. If we would clear up this confusion in the common consciousness, we must do something to dispel this misunderstanding; and I know of no means of accomplishing this, save the rewriting of our history from 1816 to 1860, with an open mind and a willing spirit to see and to represent truth and error, and right and wrong, without regard to the men or the sections in whom or where they may appear.

I am by no means certain that I am able to do this. I am old enough to have been a witness of the great struggle of 1861–65, and to have participated, in a small way, in it. My early years were embittered by the political hatreds which then prevailed. I learned before my majority to regard secession as an abomination, and its chief cause, slavery, as a great evil; and I cannot say that these feelings have been much modified, if any at all, by longer experiences and maturer thought. I have, therefore, undertaken this work with many misgivings.

Keenly conscious of my own prejudices, I have exerted my imagination to the utmost to create a picture in my own mind of the environment of those who held the opposite opinion upon these fundamental subjects, and to appreciate the processes of their reasoning under the influences of their own particular situation. And I have with sedulous care avoided all the histories written immediately after the close of the great contest of arms, and all rehashes of them of later date. In fact I have made it an invariable rule to use no secondary material; that is, no material in which original matter is mingled with somebody's interpretation of its meaning. If, therefore, the facts in my narration are twisted by prejudices and preconceptions, I think I can assure my readers that they have suffered only one twist. I have also endeavored to approach my subject in a reverent spirit, and to deal with the characters who made our history, in this almost tragic period, as serious and sincere men having a most perplexing and momentous problem to solve, a problem not of their own making, but a fatal inheritance from their predecessors.

I have been especially repelled by the flippant superficiality of the foreign critics of this period of our history, and their evident delight in representing the professions and teachings of the "Free Republic" as canting hypocrisy. It has seemed to me a great misfortune that the present generation and future generations should be taught to regard so lightly the earnest efforts of wise, true, and honorable men to rescue the country from the great catastrophe which, for so long, impended over it. The passionate onesidedness of our own writers is hardly more harmful, and is certainly less repulsive.

I recently heard a distinguished professor of history and politics say that he thought the history of the United States, in this period, could be truthfully written only by a Scotch-Irishman. I suppose he meant that the Scotch element in this ideal historian would take the Northern point of view, and the Irish element the Southern; but I could not see how this would produce anything more than another pair of narratives from the old contradictory points of view; and he did not explain how it would.

My opinion is, on the contrary, that this history must be written by an American and a Northerner, and from the Northern point of view—because an American best understands Americans, after all; because the victorious party can be and will be more liberal, generous, and sympathetic than the vanquished; and because the Northern view is, in the main, the correct view. It will not improve matters to concede that the South had right and the North might, or, even, that both were equally right and equally wrong. Such a doctrine can only work injury to both, and more injury to the South than to the North. Chewing the bitter cud of fancied wrong produces both spiritual misery and material adversity, and tempts to foolish and reckless action for righting the imagined injustice. Moreover, any such doctrine is false, and acquiescence in it, however kindly meant, is weak, and can have no other effect than the perpetuation of error and misunderstanding. The time has come when the men of the South should acknowledge that they were in error in their attempt to destroy the Union, and it is unmanly in them not to do so. When they appealed the great question from the decision at the ballot-box to the "trial by battle," their leaders declared, over and over again, in calling their followers to arms, that the "God of battles" would surely give the victory to the right. In the great movements of the world's history this is certainly a sound philosophy, and they should have held to it after their defeat. Their recourse to the crude notion that they had succumbed only to might was thus not only a bitter, false, and dangerous consolation, but it was a stultification of themselves when at their best as men and heroes.

While, therefore, great care has been taken, in the following pages, to attribute to the Southern leaders and the Southern people sincerity of purpose in their views and their acts, while their ideas and their reasoning have been, I think, duly appreciated, and patiently explained, while the right has been willingly acknowledged to them and honor accorded them whenever and wherever they have had the right and have merited honor, and while unbounded sympathy for personal suffering and misfortune has been expressed, still not one scintilla of justification for secession and rebellion must be expected. The South must acknowledge its error as well as its defeat in regard to these things, and that, too, not with lip service, but from the brain and the heart and the manly will, before any real concord in thought and feeling, any real national brotherhood, can be established. This is not too much to demand, simply because it is right, and nothing can be settled, as Mr. Lincoln said, until it is settled right. Any interpretation of this period of American history which does not demonstrate to the South its error will be worthless, simply because it will not be true; and unless we are men enough to hear and accept and stand upon the truth, it is useless to endeavor to find a bond of real union between us. In a word, the conviction of the South of its error in secession and rebellion is absolutely indispensable to the establishment of national cordiality; and the history of this period which fails to do this will fail in accomplishing one of the highest works of history, the reconciliation of men to the plans of Providence for their perfection.

I have not, in the following pages, undertaken to treat *all* of the events of our experience from 1816 to 1860. The space allowed me would not admit of that. And even if it had, I still would have selected only those events which, in my opinion, are significant of our progress in civilization, and, as I am writing a political history, only those which are significant of our progress in political civilization. The truthful record, connection, and interpretation of such events is what I call history in the highest sense, as distinguished from chronology, narrative, and romance. Both necessity and philosophy have confined me to these.

I cannot close these prefatory sentences without a word of grateful acknowledgment to my friend and colleague, Dr. Harry A. Cushing, for the important services which he has rendered me in the preparation of this work.

JOHN W. BURGESS.

323 WEST FIFTY-SEVENTH STREET, NEW YORK CITY.
January 22, 1897.

# CONTENTS

### CHAPTER I.
                                                                    PAGE
THE NATIONALIZATION OF THE OLD REPUBLICAN PARTY, . 1

### CHAPTER II.
THE ACQUISITION OF FLORIDA, . . . . . . 19

### CHAPTER III.
SLAVERY IN THE UNITED STATES BEFORE 1820, . . 39

### CHAPTER IV.
THE CREATION OF THE COMMONWEALTH OF MISSOURI, . 61

### CHAPTER V.
THE BEGINNING OF THE PARTICULARISTIC REACTION, . 108

### CHAPTER VI.
THE PRESIDENTIAL ELECTION OF 1824, . . . . 131

## CHAPTER VII.

The Division of the Republican Party, . . . 145

## CHAPTER VIII.

Democratic Opposition to Internal Improvements and Protection, . . . . . . . . 166

## CHAPTER IX.

The United States Bank and the Presidential Contest of 1832, . . . . . . . . . 190

## CHAPTER X.

Nullification, . . . . . . . . . . 210

## CHAPTER XI.

Abolition, . . . . . . . . . . . 242

## CHAPTER XII.

The Bank, the Sub-Treasury, and Party Development between 1832 and 1842, . . . . . 278

## CHAPTER XIII.

Texas, . . . . . . . . . . . . 289

## CHAPTER XIV.

Oregon, . . . . . . . . . . . . 311

## CHAPTER XV.

THE "RE-ANNEXATION OF TEXAS AND THE RE-OCCUPATION OF OREGON,"  . . . . . . . . 318

## CHAPTER XVI.

THE WAR WITH MEXICO, . . . . . . . 327

## CHAPTER XVII.

THE ORGANIZATION OF OREGON TERRITORY AND THE COMPROMISE OF 1850, . . . . . . . . 340

## CHAPTER XVIII.

THE EXECUTION OF THE FUGITIVE SLAVE LAW, AND THE ELECTION OF 1852, . . . . . . . . 365

## CHAPTER XIX.

THE REPEAL OF THE MISSOURI COMPROMISE, . . . 380

## CHAPTER XX.

THE STRUGGLE FOR KANSAS, . . . . . . 407

## CHAPTER XXI.

THE DRED SCOTT CASE, . . . . . . . 449

## CHAPTER XXII.

THE STRUGGLE FOR KANSAS CONCLUDED, . . . . 460

## APPENDIX I.

THE ELECTORAL VOTE IN DETAIL, 1820–1856, . . . 475

## APPENDIX II.

THE CABINETS OF MONROE, ADAMS, JACKSON, VAN BUREN, HARRISON, TYLER, POLK, TAYLOR, FILLMORE, PIERCE, AND BUCHANAN—1816–1858, . . . . . . 485

CHRONOLOGY, . . . . . . . . . 491

BIBLIOGRAPHY, . . . . . . . . . 497

INDEX, . . . . . . . . . . . 503

## LIST OF MAPS.

FACING PAGE

FLORIDA AT THE TIME OF ACQUISITION, . . . . 32

TEXAS AT THE TIME OF ANNEXATION, . . . . 296

OREGON AS DETERMINED BY THE TREATY OF 1846, . 312

CALIFORNIA AND NEW MEXICO IN 1850, . . . . 336

NEBRASKA AND KANSAS, 1854–1861, . . . . 468

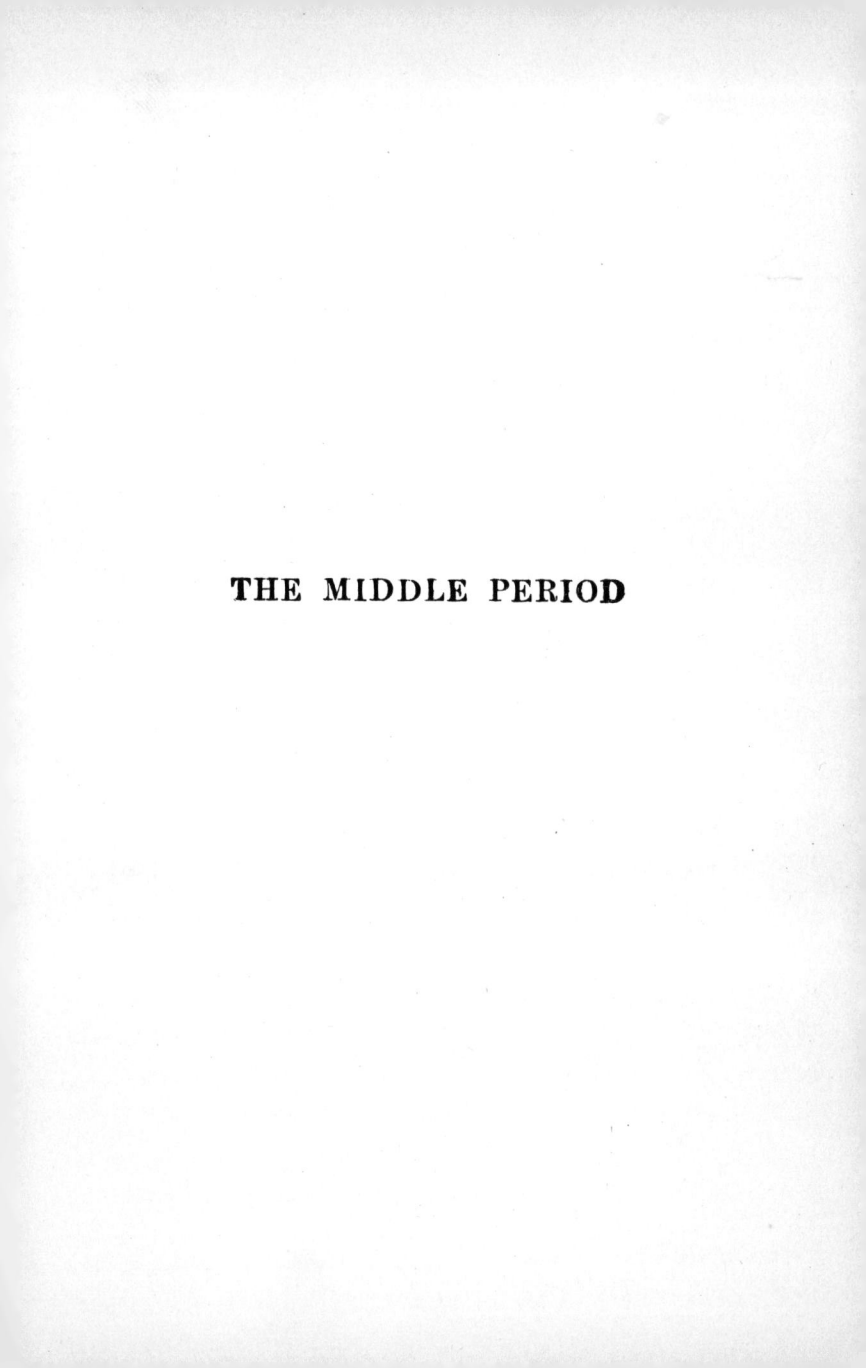

# THE MIDDLE PERIOD

# THE MIDDLE PERIOD

## CHAPTER I.

### THE NATIONALIZATION OF THE OLD REPUBLICAN PARTY

General Character of the Acts of the Fourteenth Congress—Madison's Message of December 5th, 1815—Change in the Principles of the Republican Party—The United States Bank Act of 1816—Report of the Bank Bill by Mr. Calhoun—Mr. Calhoun's Argument in Favor of the Bill—Webster's Objections to the Bank Bill—Mr. Clay's Support of the Bank Bill—Passage of the Bank Bill by the House of Representatives—The Passage of the Bank Bill by the Senate—The United States Bank of 1816 a Southern Measure—The Tariff Bill Framed by the Committee on Ways and Means—The Tariff Bill Reported—The Character of the Tariff Bill—Mr. Calhoun's Speech upon the Tariff Bill—The Passage of the Tariff Bill—The Army and Navy Bill—The Bill for National Improvements—Mr. Calhoun's Advocacy of this Bill—The Opposition to the Internal Improvements Bill—Passage of the Bill by Congress—Veto of the Bill by the President—The Failure of Congress to Override the Veto.

It is no part of my task to relate the events of the War of 1812-15. That has already been sufficiently done in the preceding volume of this series. I take up the threads of the narrative at the beginning of the year 1816, and my problem in this chapter will be to expound the acts and policies of the Fourteenth Congress in the light of the experiences of that War.

Those acts and policies were shaped and adopted under the influence of those experiences, and this influence was so predominant, at the moment, in the minds of the leading men in the Government and throughout the country as to exclude, or at least to overbalance, all other influences. This is especially manifest in the attitude of the statesmen of the slave-holding Commonwealths, and most especially in the attitude of their great leader, Mr. Calhoun, who was the chief champion of some of the most national measures voted by that Congress. A clear appreciation of his views and his acts at that period of his career will enable us far better than anything else to understand the terrible seriousness of the slavery question, which subsequently drove him into lines of thought and action so widely divergent from those upon which he set out in early life.

*General character of the acts of the Fourteenth Congress.*

It was the President himself, however, one of the chief founders of the "States' rights" party, Mr. Madison, who set the direction toward centralization in the Congressional legislation of 1815–17. In his annual message of December 5th, 1815, he recommended the increase and better organization of the army and the navy, the enlargement of the existing Military Academy and the founding of such academies in the different sections of the country, the creation of a national currency, the protection of manufactures, the construction of roads and canals, and the establishment of a national university.

*Madison's message of December 5th, 1815.*

This is a very different political creed from that promulgated by President Jefferson when the Republican party first gained possession of the Government at Washington. Then, decrease in all the elements of power in the hands of the central Government, and careful maintenance of all the rights and powers of the

## THE OLD REPUBLICAN PARTY

"States," were recommended and urged upon the attention of the national lawgivers.

From a "States'-sovereignty" party in 1801, the Republican party had manifestly become a strong national party in 1816; that is, if we are to take the two Presidential messages, to which we have referred, as containing the political principles of that party at these two periods of its existence. *Change in the principles of the Republican party.*

As the Congress of 1801 showed itself, in its legislation, to be in substantial accord with President Jefferson's views and sentiments, so did the Congress of 1815 manifest, in its legislation, the same general harmony with the views and sentiments of President Madison. In order that the latter part of this statement may be set down as an established fact of history, we will review with some particularity the two cardinal acts of this Congress—the United States Bank Act and the Tariff Act.

So soon as the reading of President Madison's message before the House of Representatives was completed, that body resolved to refer that part of the message which related to the establishment of an uniform national currency to a select committee. The committee chosen was composed of Mr. Calhoun, Mr. Macon, Mr. Pleasants, Mr. Tucker, Mr. Robertson, Mr. Hopkinson, and Mr. Pickering. The first five of these gentlemen were from Commonwealths south of the Pennsylvania line, and only two, therefore, from what began now to be called the "non-slave-holding States." In other words, it was a Southern committee, and the great South Carolinian was its chairman. It is, therefore, just to regard the bill which this committee brought in, and the arguments with which they supported it, as containing the views and the sentiments of the leading Southern Republicans in the House. *The United States Bank Act of 1816.*

This committee came speedily to the conclusion that the nationalization of the monetary system was the most pressing need of the country, and within a month from the date of the appointment of its members the chairman of the committee reported a bill for the creation of an United States Bank, a mammoth national banking corporation, which should have a capital of thirty-five millions of dollars; in which the central Government should own one-fifth of the stock and be represented by one-fifth of the directors; the president of which should always be selected from among the Government's directors; the demand notes and bills of which should be received in all payments to the United States; and the chartered privileges of which should be made a monopoly for twenty years.

*Report of the Bank Bill by Mr. Calhoun.*

In his great argument in support of the bill, delivered on February 26th, Mr. Calhoun dismissed at the outset any consideration of the constitutionality of the bill. That is, he simply assumed that Congress had the power to pass the bill, and declared that the public mind was entirely made up and settled upon that point.

*Mr. Calhoun's argument in favor of the Bill.*

Only five years before this, even the national-minded Clay had pronounced the dictum that Congress had no power to grant a national bank charter, and the fact that Congress then declined to grant such a charter is good evidence that the majority of the people of the country held the same view. There can be little question that the Republican party, down to 1812, regarded the establishment of an United States bank by Congress as an usurpation of power not granted by the Constitution.

Five years constitute a short period of time for the accomplishment of so important a change in the public opinion. Five years of ordinary experience would not have produced it. It was, without doubt, the strain brought upon the finances of the country by the necessities of the War that had developed a powerful national opinion upon the subject of the financial system of the country.

Mr. Calhoun also declined to discuss the question whether banks were favorable or unfavorable to "public liberty and prosperity." He assumed, here again, that public experience had settled that question, and said that such an inquiry was now purely metaphysical. This statement is certainly prime evidence that the practical experiences, made in conducting the Government under the pressure of war, had about knocked the metaphysics of the year 1800 out of the Republican party, and had led the party on to a much more positive stage of political opinion.

Mr. Calhoun furthermore dismissed the question whether a "national bank would be favorable to the administration of the finances of the Government," since there was not enough doubt, he said, in the public mind upon that point to warrant a discussion of it.

He declared, finally, that the only questions which demanded consideration were those relative to the existing disorders of the currency, and the efficiency of a national bank in working their cure. Upon these two points he was distinct, decided, and thoroughly national. He said that the Constitution had without doubt placed the monetary system of the country entirely within the control of Congress; that the "States" had usurped the power of making money by chartering banks of issue in the face of the constitutional provision forbidding the "States" to emit bills of credit; that the two hundred millions of dollars of irredeemable bank-notes, paper, and credits, issued by these banks, were the cause of the financial disorders of the country; and that the remedy for this condition of things was, in his opinion, to be found in a great specie-paying national bank, sustained by the power of the general Government in the work of bringing such a pressure upon these "State" banks as would force them either to pay specie or go into liquidation. This was clear, generous, and patriotic. No one made a fairer statement of the case, and no one advocated a more national remedy in its treatment.

On the other hand, it was Webster who, at this time, appeared narrow and particularistic. He objected to the large amount of the capital, and to the stock feature of the proposed bank, and expressed alarm at the proposition to place it under such strong governmental control. He thought that the bills and paper of the "State" banks would be good enough, if the general Government would only force them to redeem their currency in specie by refusing to accept for Government dues the bills of banks which did not pay specie on demand.

<small>Webster's objections to the Bank Bill.</small>

Whatever may be thought of Webster's attitude from the point of view of political economy, it was certainly, from the point of view of political science, the attitude of a "States'-rights" man rather than that of a nationalist. Webster did not, however, call the constitutionality of the bill in question. That was conceded upon all sides.

The friends of the measure felt more anxiety in regard to Mr. Clay. He had, only five years before, as we have seen, pronounced a similar bill unconstitutional in his opinion, and he was now the Speaker of the House, with all the power over the procedure in the House which that position involved. It was generally felt that the fate of the measure would be largely determined by his attitude toward it.

Mr. Clay did not leave the House long in doubt concerning his views. He quickly revealed and avowed that noted change of opinion upon this subject, which has been commonly accounted one of his greatest inconsistencies, but which may be very properly considered as simply manifesting that growth in patriotism and national spirit experienced by almost all the leading men of the country, outside of New England, in consequence of the vicissitudes of the period of war under which the nation suffered between the dates of Mr. Clay's two utterances. He frankly confessed that he had changed his opinion, and explained the change by saying that the power of Congress in respect to the matter was contained in the clause of the Constitution which conferred upon Congress the authority to make all laws necessary and proper for carrying the powers of the Government into operation; that, in the interpretation of the words "necessary and proper," reference must always be had to existing circumstances; that, when conditions change, the interpretation must be so modified as to meet and satisfy such change; and that the conditions obtaining in the country in 1816 were so changed from those obtaining in 1811 as to require the enlarged interpretation of the powers of Congress under this clause upon the subject of the monetary system of the country.

*Mr. Clay's support of the Bank Bill.*

The eloquence and the influence of Mr. Clay counted heavily in favor of the measure, and it was passed by a substantial majority of votes. In fact, the privileges of the proposed Bank had been increased by amendment during the progress of the bill through the House. The Bank and its branches were made the depositories of the funds of the Government. This great advantage was, at least, a substantial offset to the other modifications of the original bill, whereby the clauses requiring that the president of

*Passage of the Bank Bill by the House of Representatives.*

the Bank should always be chosen from among the Government directors, and reserving to Congress the power to permit a temporary suspension of specie payment by the Bank, were stricken out.

During the passage of the bill through the Senate only a single Senator expressed any doubts of its constitutionality, Mr. Wells, of Delaware. Mr. Wells did not deny the power of Congress to charter a national bank, but simply contended that the particular Bank proposed in the bill exceeded what was "necessary and proper" for carrying into effect the powers of Congress, and was therefore unconstitutional. On the other hand, Senators Barbour, of Virginia, Taylor, of South Carolina, and Bibb, of Georgia, supported the measure, both in principle and in details, and carried it with a larger relative majority through the Senate than it had received in the House.

*The passage of the Bank Bill through the Senate.*

The United States Bank of 1816 was thus a Southern measure, and Calhoun was its chief author. It was in principle a great national measure, and its creation by Congress is strong evidence of the great growth in national opinion and sentiment throughout the country, away from the national indifference of the Jeffersonian metapolitics of 1800.

*The United States Bank of 1816 a Southern measure.*

A review of the Tariff Act of 1816 will bring us to the same conclusions concerning the great nationalizing influence of the War.

*The Tariff of 1816.*

The rate of duty upon the principal articles of imported goods was, before the War, twelve and one-half per centum ad valorem. From a rate of five per centum upon these articles, imposed by the first Customs Act, that of July, 1789, the duty had been increased by about a dozen acts, passed by both Federal and Republican Congresses, until, in 1812, it had reached the above-mentioned per centum. Twelve and one-half per centum was, as a fact, nothing more than a revenue duty, and was intended for nothing more by the party in power at that date.

At the outbreak of the War double duties were imposed by the Act of July 1st, 1812, as a war measure, that is, as a measure for obtaining additional revenue for the prosecution of the War. It was not intended as a measure for the protection of manufacturers. This Act was to expire in one year, at the farthest, after the conclusion of peace with England.

The ratifications of the Treaty of Ghent were exchanged on February 17th, 1815. At the meeting of Congress, in December, 1815, the war duties were, therefore, still in force, but the Act establishing them would expire by its own limitation in less than three months. This Congress was obliged, therefore, to deal with the tariff anew.

The recommendations of the President in regard to the matter were referred to the committee of the House on Ways and Means, the regular revenue committee. At that moment this committee was composed of seven members, four from Commonwealths south of Maryland, and three from those north of Maryland. Mr. Lowndes, of South Carolina, was its chairman. It is fair, therefore, to call it a Southern committee, and to regard the bill which it produced as a Southern measure. *The Bill framed by the Committee on Ways and Means.*

The committee first asked for a continuation of the existing duties until the thirtieth day of the following June, in order to give proper time to mature the bill, which request was voted by both houses of Congress; and on March 20th, Mr. Lowndes announced that he was prepared to report the draft of the new Act. The measure contained virtually the continuation of the war tariff as the permanent rule and policy in time of peace. It was now manifestly a protective tariff, and it was in-

*The Tariff Bill reported.* tended to be such. Mr. Ingham of the committee said, at the beginning of the debate upon it, that "its great primary object was to make such a modification of duties upon the various articles of importation as would give the necessary and proper protection and support to the agriculture, manufactures, and commerce of the country." He went so far as to say that revenue considerations ought not to have any influence in the decision of the House upon the committee's propositions.

It is entirely evident, however, that the committee did not regard the bill as proposing advantages for the

*The character of the Tariff Bill.* manufacturers only, or as having for its principal aim the increase of the wages of the employees in the manufacturing establishments, but considered it a great national measure, a measure necessary to the industrial independence of the country. It is also evident that the bill was not thought by anybody to rest upon a perfect and permanent principle. Mr. Clay himself said of it, "that the object of protecting manufacturers was, that we might eventually get articles of necessity made as cheap at home as they could be imported, and thereby to produce an independence of foreign countries;" that "in three years we could judge of the ability of our establishments to furnish those articles as cheap as they were obtained from abroad, and could then legislate with the lights of experience;" and that "he believed that three years would be sufficient to place our manufacturers on this desirable footing."

It was Calhoun again, however, who surpassed them all in broadness of view and in patriotic devotion to the interests of the nation. The immediate occasion of his speech was a motion made by John Randolph, which seemed to Mr. Calhoun to attack the principle of the bill. He said, that so long as the debate had been confined to questions of detail he had refrained from joining in it; but now that the general policy of the measure had been attacked he felt obliged to come forward in support of that policy, which he could do with all the more grace and sincerity since his own private interests were primarily subserved by the advancement of agriculture, as were those of his section. He began his argument with the assertions that commerce and agriculture were the chief sources of the wealth of the country at the moment, almost the only sources, and that manufactures must be added to these in order to accomplish industrial independence. In proof of this latter proposition he referred to the well known effect of war between a maritime power and the United States upon the prosperity of the latter. He simply pointed to the historic facts that such a war destroyed the commerce of the country with foreign powers, and that the destruction of commerce caused the products of agriculture, usually exported to pay for manufactured goods imported from foreign countries, to perish in the hands of the producers. Domestic manufactures, he contended, would not only relieve us from dependence upon foreign countries for manufactured goods, but would create home markets for agricultural products. Encouragement to manufactures was, therefore, a sound national, a truly American, policy. As Mr. Calhoun proceeded in his speech, his strong patriotism became more manifest. He affirmed that the policy of protection to manufactures was calculated to bind more closely together the different parts of our widely extended country, since it would increase the mutual dependence of these different sections on each

*Mr. Calhoun's speech upon the Tariff Bill.*

other in proportion as it decreased their dependence on foreign markets. And he declared that he considered the production of this result to be the most fundamental of all our policies, for the reason that the absence of such mutual dependence would tend toward disunion, and disunion comprehended almost the sum and substance of our political dangers, against which, therefore, we ought to be perpetually guarded.

Calhoun was in his thirty-fifth year when he advanced these views. The sentiments which they revealed cannot, therefore, be ascribed to the enthusiasm of youth and inexperience. They rested upon the settled convictions of a mature man. They stand in need of no comment. They speak for themselves. We shall search the reports of the debate in vain for anything wiser, nobler, or more patriotic. In comparison with them the views pronounced by the New Englanders upon the subject appear narrow and selfish. They were willing to sacrifice the industrial independence of the nation to their own interests in the carrying trade upon the sea. Even the name of Webster is not to be found among those who voted for the final passage of the bill. The majority in its favor was, however, nearly two to one. In the Senate, the vote was nearly four to one for it. Though Southern in its immediate origin, it certainly had the support of the nation, and was regarded as a great measure of national independence. The opposition made to it by Randolph and Telfair, and by the remnant of the New England Federalists, was regarded as unnational and unpatriotic. It contributed to the complete disappearance of the Federal party from the arena of national politics.

*The passage of the Tariff Bill.*

This Congress gave, however, an even surer test of the growth of the national spirit among the people than either the Bank Act or the Tariff Act. It was the series of acts for the increase of the Army and the Navy, and for their thorough reorganization. The Republican doctrine of 1800 was, that there was no need of a national army; that the militias of the Commonwealths were a sufficient military force; and that a standing army was dangerous to liberty. By the Act of March 16th, 1802, Congress fixed the peace establishment at two regiments of infantry, and one regiment of artillerists, not more than thirty-five hundred men. No increase of this force had been permitted between 1802 and 1812.

<small>The Army and Navy Bills.</small>

During the War of 1812-15, the Commonwealths of Massachusetts, Rhode Island, and Connecticut taught the nation how much, or rather how little, reliance was to be placed upon the militias of the Commonwealths in the defence of the country against foreign attack. In spite of the plain provision of the Constitution, and the Act of Congress in accordance therewith, empowering the President to call the militias of the Commonwealths into the service of the United States, the Governors of Massachusetts and Connecticut disputed the President's authority in this respect and refused compliance with his orders. Well might the President complain that, even upon this most essential point, the military organization, the United States was not a nation. With such an experience as this, Congress and the people were thoroughly converted from the particularistic doctrinism of 1800, and now manifested their strong national spirit in the willingness to place a large standing military force in the hands of the central Government in times of peace.

By the Act of March 3rd, 1816, Congress fixed the peace footing of the Army at ten thousand men, excluding the corps of engineers; and by the Act of April 24th, of the same year, it reorganized, or rather recreated, the general staff, upon the principle that the staff should be as complete in time of peace as in time of war.

The Navy received similar attention and favor. By the Act of April 29th, 1816, Congress appropriated eight millions of dollars for the construction of nine seventy-four-gun ships, twelve forty-four-gun ships, and three steam batteries.

Evidently the fear that the President would, by virtue of his power as commander-in-chief of a large standing army and navy, declare himself emperor, and make the military and naval officers his dukes and counts, had vanished in the smoke of the burned Capitol, and, in place of this silly terror of crowns and diadems, a thoroughgoing confidence in the national Government had established itself in the brain and heart of the people and of their leaders.

These great national measures occupied the attention of Congress to such a degree, during the session of 1815-16, as to delay the consideration of the question of a system of national internal improvements to the second session, that of 1816-17.

At the opening of this session, Mr. Calhoun, again, came forward with a motion for the appointment of a committee, which should consider the question of setting aside the bonus to be paid by the United States Bank to the Government for its charter, and the net annual proceeds received by the Government upon its shares in the Bank, as a permanent fund for internal improvements. The motion was quickly carried, and the committee, consisting of two members from the North and two from the South, with Mr. Calhoun for chairman, was appointed. This was December 16th, 1816. In a week from this date the committee presented a bill providing for the setting

*The Bill for National Improvements.*

apart of the funds above indicated for the construction of roads and canals.

Mr. Calhoun opened the debate upon the bill, and his speech abounded with the same national ideas and patriotic sentiments which characterized his arguments in support of the Bank and Tariff measures. After asserting that the moment was most opportune for the consideration of the question, on account of the fact that all party and sectional feelings had given way to "a liberal and an enlightened regard for the general concerns of the nation," Mr. Calhoun again pronounced his warning concerning the greatest danger to which the country was exposed, namely, disunion, and declared it to be the highest duty of American statesmen so to form the policies of the Government as to counteract all tendencies toward sectionalism and disunion. He contended that from this point of view nothing could be more necessary or more advantageous than a large national system of internal improvements, establishing the great lines of commerce and intercourse for binding together all the parts of the country in interests, ideas, and sentiments.

*Mr. Calhoun's advocacy of this Bill.*

No part of his argument, however, is so instructive to the student of American constitutional history as the observations upon the question of the constitutionality of the bill. He said that he was no advocate of refined reasoning upon the Constitution; that "the instrument was not intended as a thesis for the logician to exercise his ingenuity on; that it ought to be construed with plain good sense; and that when so construed nothing could be more express than the Constitution upon this very point." The clause to which he referred was that which confers upon Congress the power "to levy and collect taxes, duties, imposts, and excises; to pay the

## 16  THE MIDDLE PERIOD

debts and provide for the common defence and general welfare of the United States." Mr. Calhoun claimed that these words were to be interpreted as vesting in Congress the power to appropriate money for the common defence and general welfare of the country at its own discretion, both as to object and amount. He insisted that a generous interpretation of the power to raise and appropriate money was absolutely required, in order to avoid the necessity of placing a forced construction upon other powers. It was all in his best strain, and showed Mr. Calhoun still as the chief advocate of national union and national development. No other person seemed to equal him in breadth of view and purity of patriotism.

The measure met, however, with more opposition than the Bank Bill or the Tariff Bill had experienced. Two years of peace had cooled the ardor of the national spirit somewhat, and the people were dropping back into the narrow spheres of ordinary life and business routine.

*The opposition to the Internal Improvements Bill.*

Moreover, the great hue and cry raised by the demagogues and the press over the bill, passed at the previous session, changing the pay of the members of Congress from a per diem of six dollars during attendance to an annual salary of fifteen hundred dollars, had made the members timid about the appropriation of money, and disinclined to obligate the Treasury to anything beyond absolutely necessary expenses.

Nevertheless, the great power and earnestness with which Mr. Calhoun addressed himself to the task of carrying the bill through its different stages were crowned with success. It finally passed both Houses, in a slightly modified form, during the last week of the Fourteenth Congress and of President Madison's second term.

*Passage of the Bill by Congress.*

To the great surprise of the friends of the measure, the President returned the bill to Congress on March 3rd, with his objections. These were, summed up in a single sentence, that there was no warrant in the Constitution for the exercise of the power by Congress to pass such a bill. The President held that Congress could appropriate money only to such objects as were placed by the Constitution under the jurisdiction of the general Government. He, therefore, repudiated Calhoun's latitudinarian view that Congress was referred to its own discretion merely in the appropriation of money for the advancement of the general welfare. He acknowledged the desirability of attaining the object contemplated by the bill, and indicated that an amendment to the Constitution, expressly conferring upon Congress the power in question, was the proper way to deal with the subject. He had, as we have seen, recommended the consideration of the question of internal improvements in both of his annual messages to the Fourteenth Congress, and it was chiefly for this reason that the veto was so unexpected. It is true that, in both of these messages, he had expressed some doubt in regard to the power of Congress over the subject, but it was supposed that this was only his cautious way of approaching a new thing, and that he would certainly defer to the views of the Congressional majority.

*Veto of the Bill by the President.*

It must be remembered, however, that Mr. Madison belonged to the first generation of the Republicans, and that the principle of the party, in the period of its origin, was strict construction of the Constitution in regard to the powers of the general Government. He had been driven by the younger men into the War, and into the national policies which it occasioned and produced, and it is at least intelligible that he returned to his earlier creed as the country settled down again into the humdrum of ordinary life.

The national Republicans looked upon his act, however, as an apostasy, and the House of Representatives repassed the bill by an increased majority and with considerable feeling. The majority was still, however, not sufficient to overcome the veto, and thus the first earnest attempt to commit the nation to a general system of internal improvements failed, failed through the resurrection of a spirit in the retiring President, which was destined soon to take possession of many who denounced it then as mean and narrow, and to lead the whole country back into those cramping tenets of particularism from which war and bloodshed alone could deliver it.

<small>The failure of Congress to override the veto.</small>

# CHAPTER II.

## THE ACQUISITION OF FLORIDA

The Influence of Physical Geography upon Political Development—Defect in the Southern Boundary of the United States before 1819—The Treaty of Paris of 1763—The Boundary between Louisiana and Florida—Occupation of Florida by the United States Forces during the War of 1812—The Hold of the Spaniards on Florida Weakened by the War of 1812—The British Troops in Florida during and after the War of 1812—Nicholls and his Buccaneer State in Florida—The British Government's Repulse of Nicholls' Advances—Destruction of the Nicholls Fort by the United States Forces.—The Seminole War—The Fight at Fowltown—The Seminole War Defensive—McGregor on Amelia Island—General Gaines sent to Amelia Island—General Jackson placed in Command in Florida—His Orders — Jackson's Letter to President Monroe — Jackson's Operations in Florida—The First Treaty for the Cession of Florida to the United States—Jackson's Popularity in consequence of the Seminole War—The Attempt in Congress to Censure Jackson — The same Attempt in the Cabinet—The Failure of the Attempt to Censure Jackson in Congress—Assumption of the Responsibility for Jackson's Acts by the Administration—Jackson Triumphant—The Treaty of Cession Attacked in Congress, but Ratified by the Senate—Rejection of the Treaty by the Spanish Government—Resumption of Negotiations—The New Treaty Ratified by the Senate and by the Spanish Government—Political Results of the Seminole War.

It was entirely natural that the quickening of the national spirit and the growth of the national consciousness throughout the United States, in the decade between 1810 and 1820, had, for one of their results, the extension of the territory of the United States, at some point or other, to its natural limits.

The element of physical geography always plays a large part in national political development. The natural territorial basis of a national state is a geographical unity. That is, it is a territory separated by broad bodies of water, or high mountain ranges, or broad belts of uninhabitable country, or climatic extremes, from other territory, and possessing a fair degree of coherence within. If a national state develops itself on any part of such a territory, it will inevitably tend to spread to the natural limits of the same. It will not become a completely national state until it shall have attained such boundaries, for a completely national state is the sovereign organization of a people having an ethnic unity upon a territory which is a geographic unity.

*The influence of physical geography upon political development.*

In the second decade of this century, and down to the latter part of it, the United States had not acquired the territory of the country as far as to the natural southern boundary east of Louisiana. This boundary was, of course, the Gulf of Mexico; but Spain held in quasi possession a broad strip, and then a long peninsula, of land along and within this boundary. In other words, the territory called Florida, or the Floridas, was, politically, a colony of Spain, but geographically a part of the United States. It was inhabited chiefly by Indian tribes. Spanish rule in this territory was, therefore, foreign rule, both from the geographical point of view and the ethnical. Indian rule was not to be thought of in the nineteenth century. There was but one natural solution of the question. It was that the United States should annex this territory and extend the jurisdiction of the general Government over it.

*Defect in the southern boundary of the United States before 1819.*

The Treaty of Paris of 1763 was the first great international agreement which gave a fair degree of definiteness to the claims of England, France, and Spain, upon the North American continent. In this Treaty, France surrendered Canada, Cape Breton, and all claims to territory east of the Mississippi River, from the source of the river to the point of confluence of the Iberville with it, to Great Britain. From this latter point, the boundary between the two powers was declared to be the middle line of the Iberville, and of the Lakes Maurepas and Pontchartrain, to the Gulf of Mexico. It is also expressly stated in this Treaty that France cedes the river and port of Mobile to Great Britain.

*The Treaty of Paris of 1763.*

In this same instrument, Spain surrendered to Great Britain Florida and every claim to territory east and southeast of the Mississippi.

The boundary between Louisiana and Florida had, to that time, been the River Perdido. After the cessions above mentioned to Great Britain, the British Government united the part of Louisiana received from France with Florida, and then divided Florida into two districts by the line of the River Appalachicola. That part lying to the west of this river was named West Florida, and the part east of it was called East Florida.

*The boundary between Louisiana and Florida.*

By a secret Treaty of the year 1762, which became known to the world some eighteen months later, but whose terms were not executed until 1769, France ceded Louisiana to Spain. After this, therefore, the North American continent was divided between Great Britain and Spain, and the line of division was, so far as it was fixed, the Mississippi River to the confluence of the Iberville with it, then the Iberville and the middle line of the Lakes Maurepas and Pontchartrain to the Gulf of Mexico.

The Treaty of 1762 between France and Spain, having been concluded before the Treaty of 1763 between France and Great Britain, gave Spain a certain show of title to the territory between the Mississippi and the Perdido; but the Treaty of 1763, in which France ceded this same territory to Great Britain, was, as we have just seen, known first, and was the Treaty which France executed in respect to this territory. The conflict of claims between Great Britain and Spain, which was thus engendered, continued to be waged for twenty years, and was settled in the year 1783, in so far as these two powers were concerned, by the recession of Florida to Spain.

In this same year, Great Britain recognized the independence of the United States, with a southern boundary extending from the point where the Mississippi River is intersected by the thirty-first parallel of latitude, along this parallel to the River Appalachicola, thence down the Appalachicola to its confluence with Flint River, thence on the line of shortest distance to the source of the River St. Mary, and thence by the course of this stream to the Atlantic. Spain thus held, as the result of these several treaties, all of the territory south of this line, unless England reserved in her recession of Florida that portion of Louisiana lying between the Iberville and the Perdido, ceded by France to Great Britain in the Treaty of 1763, and united by Great Britain with Florida. There is no evidence in the text of the Treaty of 1783 that Great Britain made any such reservation, or in the subsequent actions of the British Government.

By the Treaty of St. Ildefonso, of October 1st, 1800, also a secret treaty, Spain receded Louisiana to France. The description of the territory thus receded was very vague. It reads in the official translation of the treaty:

"His Catholic Majesty promises and engages, on his part, to cede to the French Republic, six months after the full and entire execution of the conditions and stipulations herein relative to his Royal Highness the Duke of Parma, the Colony or Province of Louisiana, with the same extent that it now has in the hands of Spain, and that it had when France possessed it ; and such as it should be after the treaties subsequently entered into between Spain and other states."

There was here certainly opportunity for a dispute between Spain and France as to the correct boundary between Louisiana and Florida. France could claim with some reason the Perdido as the eastern boundary of Louisiana, and Spain could meet this with a counter-claim that, after the cession in 1763 of all Louisiana east of the Iberville and the Lakes to Great Britain, and its union by Great Britain with Florida, the line of the Iberville and the Lakes Maurepas and Pontchartrain was the eastern boundary of Louisiana.

Before, however, any actual contest arose over the question, France sold Louisiana to the United States, with the same vague description of boundary contained in the cession of the territory from Spain to France by the Treaty of St. Ildefonso. The question of boundary became now one which must be settled between Spain and the United States.

The United States claimed at once that Louisiana reached to the Perdido. Spain disputed the claim, and held that Florida extended to the Iberville and the Lakes. Spain could make out the better abstract of title. Spain certainly did not intend to recede to France in 1800 anything more as Louisiana than France had ceded to her in 1762. But the United States had a show of legal title. It could be held that the ancient boundary of Louisiana was the one intended both in the Treaty of St. Ildefonso and in that of 1803, in which France passed the possession of Louisiana to the United States. The reasons of physical geography and of national development certainly favored the annexation of the whole of Florida to the United States; and with such forces to back the apparent legal claim to a large part of it, the result of the dispute could not well have been otherwise than it was.

The United States enforced its claim by military occupation of the disputed district before the close of the War of 1812.

During the course of the war, the British forces had occupied Pensacola. The Spanish governor either could not, or would not, prevent them from doing so. Florida became thus, in spite of its nominal neutral status, a base of operations for the enemy of the United States. No more convincing evidence of the necessity for its annexation to the United States could have been offered. It was thus seen that not only the geography and the national growth of the Union demanded it, but that the safety of the Union, in case of war with any power, required it. The sea is the natural boundary of the United States on the south, and it was the "manifest destiny" of the Union to reach it.

*Occupation of Florida by the United States forces during the War of 1812.*

The occupation of Florida would have been a sound and justifiable policy for the United States, had the Government commanded a sufficient military force for the purpose, when the British troops took possession of Pensacola. General Jackson did expel the British from Pensacola, but restored the place to the Spanish authorities, in order to avoid a conflict with Spain while engaged in war with Great Britain. We know now that the Congress of the United States had, by secret acts passed before the beginning of the War, authorized the

President to occupy Florida *east* of the Perdido temporarily. The President did not deem it wise, under the circumstances which prevailed, to make use of this power; but the readiness of the Congress to intrust the President with the authority to take possession of the territory of a friendly power certainly shows that a strong feeling existed among the representatives of the people that Florida must be acquired by the United States upon the first fair opportunity.

The occasion was destined soon to appear. The power of Spain upon the American continents was everywhere in rapid decline. At the close of the War of 1812, the Spanish occupation in Florida was confined substantially to three points—Pensacola, St. Mark's, and St. Augustine. The remainder of the province, by far the greater part of it, was a free zone, in which desperate adventurers of every race and land might congregate, from which they might make their raids for murder and pillage into the United States, and into which they might escape again with their prisoners and plunder.

*The hold of the Spaniards on Florida weakened by the War of 1812.*

We have noticed the occupation of Pensacola by the British troops during the War of 1812, and their expulsion by General Jackson from this position in November of 1814. After this, they concentrated upon the Appalachicola and established a fort some fifteen miles above the mouth of this stream for their head-quarters and base of operations. The British commander, one Colonel Nicholls, pursued from this point the policy which he had already inaugurated at Pensacola. This policy was the collection and organization of fugitive negroes, Indians, and adventurers of every character, and their employment in raids into the territory, and attacks upon the inhabitants, of the United States.

*The British troops in Florida during and after the War of 1812.*

It appears that Colonel Nicholls did not regard the Treaty between the United States and Great Britain concluding the War as putting an end necessarily to his hostile movements. He remained in command at his fort on the Appalachicola for several months after the ratification of the Treaty, and then went to London, taking with him the Indian priest Francis, for the purpose of securing a treaty of alliance between the British Government and his band of outlaws in Florida.

Before leaving the Appalachicola, he had incited the Indians and their negro auxiliaries to continue hos-
<small>Nicholls and his buccaneer state in Florida.</small> tilities against the United States, by represending to them that the ninth article of the Treaty of Ghent contained a pledge on the part of the United States to reinstate the Indians in all lands held by them in the year 1811. He represented to them that this provision restored to the Creeks the lands in southern Georgia surrendered by them to the United States in the Treaty between the Creeks and the United States made at Fort Jackson in August of 1814, although it was well understood by both of the high contracting parties to the Treaty of Ghent that only those lands were intended under this provision whose seizure by the United States had not been confirmed by an agreement with the Indians; and the pledge as to these only was conditioned upon the immediate cessation of hostilities on the part of the Indians when the Treaty of Ghent should be announced to them. This announcement had been made, and the actual continuation of hostilities, therefore, after the announcement, made this whole article nugatory.

Nicholls left the fort, with all its munitions, in the hands of the negroes and Indians. The garrison consisted of some three hundred negroes and about twenty Indians.

The British Government would not listen to Nicholls' proposition for an alliance between Great Britain and the buccaneering state which he was endeavoring to establish upon territory belonging politically to Spain.

*The British Government's repulse of Nicholls' advances.*

The United States Government waited a year and a half for the disbanding of this hostile force, or for its dispersion by the Spanish authorities, and then, when forbearance had ceased to be a virtue, did the work itself. The fort was destroyed by the explosion of its magazine, which was pierced by a red-hot shot from the batteries of the assailants, and almost the whole garrison perished. It was claimed that the attack was made by the United States forces with the consent of the Spanish authorities, whatever the significance of that may have been.

*Destruction of the Nicholls Fort by the United States forces.*

Professor von Holst, in his great work, has designated the expedition against the Nicholls Fort as a hunt by the United States army for fugitive slaves. He does not seem to have recognized the danger to the peace and civilization of the United States of the growth of a community of pirates and buccaneers upon its borders. It does not appear to have occurred to him that the most humane attitude toward the slaves of Georgia may have been to prevent them from being drawn into any such connection. He does not seem to have comprehended that any public interest was subserved by disposing of the negroes captured in this expedition in such a way as to prevent any future attempts on their part at co-operation with the Indians in their barbarous warfare upon the frontiers of the United States. In a sentence, he seems to have regarded the entire incident as a prostitution of the military power of the United States to the private greed of slave-hunters, and to have discovered in it a most convincing proof of the canting hypocrisy of the free Republic. In view of all the facts of the case, this certainly appears to be a very crude appreciation of the subject.

This same historian calls the attack upon the Nicholls Fort the beginning of the Seminole War. It appears, however, more like the termination of the War of 1812, so far as the negro outlaws of Florida were participant in that War, than like the beginning of a new war. Generals Gaines and Jackson and the War Department of the Government seem to have so comprehended the event.

*The Seminole War.*

After the destruction of the Nicholls Fort, or the Negro Fort, as it was then called, there was comparative peace, for a few months, on the frontier. With the beginning of the year 1817, however, hostilities were renewed. It is not known which party gave the first offence. Ex-Governor Mitchell of Georgia, then holding the office of Indian agent for these parts, thought both parties equally at fault. The point is a matter of little moment. The conflict between civilization and barbarism is irrepressible, and arises as often from the encroachments of civilization as from the onslaughts of barbarism.

In November of 1817, General Gaines endeavored to secure an interview with the chief of the hostile Indians, but the chief refused to visit the General, whereupon the General sent a detachment of soldiers to the chief's village, called Fowltown, to repeat his invitation, and to conduct the chief and his warriors to a parley-ground. The soldiers were fired upon by the Indians as they approached the village. They naturally returned the fire, and then seized and destroyed the village. A few Indians were killed in the conflict.

*The fight at Fowltown.*

The Indian agent, Mitchell, called this event the beginning of the Seminole War. It was certainly something more like it than was the capture of the Negro Fort. Still it will be more correct to consider it as being only the continuation of the War of 1812, in so far as the participation in that War of Great Britain's Indian allies on the southern border of the United States was concerned. They had never really resumed the status of peace after acting during that War, at the instigation of the British officers in Florida, against the United States.

Following the fight at Fowltown hostilities became much more active. Fowltown was situated north of the Florida line, upon territory ceded by the Creeks to the United States in the Treaty of Fort Jackson. If, therefore, the incident of November 20th was the beginning of the Seminole War, it stamps that War as defensive in its character. *The Seminole War defensive.* The troops of the United States were attacked upon the territory of the United States. If the further prosecution of the War should, in the judgment of the President, or of the officer whom he might vest with discretionary power in the execution of his will, require the crossing of the Florida line and the pursuit of the enemy upon Florida territory, the character of the War could not be changed thereby. This could not be regarded as making war on Spain. Spain could meet and satisfy the right of the United States to do this only by dispersing the Indians herself, and preventing Florida from becoming a base of hostile operations against the United States. Spain could claim the rights of neutrality for Florida only when she discharged these duties of neutrality. The general principles of international custom required that of her. When, now, we add to this the consideration that Spain had pledged herself in a specific agreement with the United States to do these very things, and that Florida, nevertheless, was actually a free zone, over which no civilized state had any efficient control, then it certainly appears that the right of the United States to pursue its enemy into Florida was clearly in keeping with the recognized law of nations. The President, therefore, ordered the pursuit of the enemy into Florida, under the qualification that if they took refuge in a Spanish fortification the fortress should not be attacked, but the situation should be reported to the War Department and further orders awaited. This order was issued on December 16th, 1817, to General Gaines, who was then in command of the forces on the Florida frontier.

Meanwhile an adventurer by the name of McGregor had, with a band of freebooters, taken possession of Amelia Island, which lies off the coast of Florida, just below the mouth of the St. Mary's River, and had, in the name of the Governments of Buenos Ayres and Venezuela, proclaimed the independence of Florida against Spain. They made the island an entrepôt for the smuggling of slaves into the United States, a storehouse for the results of their robberies, and head-quarters generally for piratical expeditions.

*McGregor on Amelia Island.*

By a secret act of the year 1811, the Congress of the United States had declared its unwillingness to have Florida, or any part of it, pass from the hands of Spain into those of any other power, and had authorized the President to prevent it. Acting upon this authority, the President instructed General Gaines to go to Amelia Island and take possession of it.

*General Gaines sent to Amelia Island.*

About ten days later, December 26th, 1817, the President assigned General Jackson to the command of the

# THE ACQUISITION OF FLORIDA 31

troops acting against the Indians. The day before the issue of the order to General Jackson, the War Department had received the news of the Indian attack upon Lieutenant Scott's boat while ascending the Appalachicola with supplies for the United States troops at Fort Scott. The cold-blooded massacre of almost the entire crew of the boat apparently moved the War Department to more energetic measures. The order to General Jackson, besides investing him with the command, empowered him to call on the Governors of the adjacent Commonwealths for such military forces as he might deem necessary, with those already in the field, to overcome the Indians, and informed him that General Gaines had been instructed "to penetrate from Amelia Island, through Florida, to the Seminole towns, if his force would justify his engaging in offensive operations." "With this view," the order to Jackson continues, "you may be prepared to concentrate your forces, and to adopt the necessary measures to terminate a conflict which it has ever been the desire of the President to avoid, but which is now made necessary by their settled hostilities."

*General Jackson placed in command in Florida. His orders.*

When Jackson received these orders he was in Tennessee. He wrote immediately to the President: "Let it be signified to me through any channel (say Mr. J. Rhea) that the possession of the Floridas would be desirable to the United States and in sixty days it will be accomplished." General Jackson naturally supposed that this letter was duly received and read by President Monroe, and that a subsequent order, giving him discretionary powers in the prosecution of the campaign, contained the answer to it. As we shall see, however, the President claimed later that he did not read Jackson's letter until a year after it was written and sent to him. It was certainly

*Jackson's letter to President Monroe.*

the President's fault if he did not. General Jackson certainly could not be held accountable for the President's strange negligence in examining official correspondence, and he had good reason to think, from the tone of the order issued to him after his letter had had due time to be received and read, that the Administration desired him to occupy Florida.

Upon taking command Jackson called his Tennessee veterans to him, and reached with them the Florida frontier in March of 1818.

When he advanced into Florida he found that the Spanish officials in Florida were in collusion with the Indians, and that the instigators of the hostilities were an Englishman, named Ambrister, and a Scotchman, named Arbuthnot, together with two Indian chiefs named Hillis Hajo and Himallemico.

*Jackson's operations in Florida.*

An order from the War Department, of January 16th, 1818, instructed the commander of the United States forces in Florida that the honor of the nation required a speedy termination of the War with the Seminoles, "with exemplary punishment for hostilities so unprovoked." Jackson naturally considered himself empowered to do speedy and thorough work. He felt it necessary to seize St. Mark's and Pensacola, in order to destroy the base of operations and the places of refuge of the enemy, and he caused the four ringleaders of the enemy to be executed. By the end of May (1818) the campaign was ended, and Florida was in the military possession of the United States. The President assumed the responsibility for Jackson's deeds, but offered to restore St. Mark's and Pensacola, and therewith the nominal possession of Florida, to Spain, so soon as Spain would garrison these points with forces able to maintain peace with the United States and dis-

# FLORIDA,
## at the Time of Acquisition.

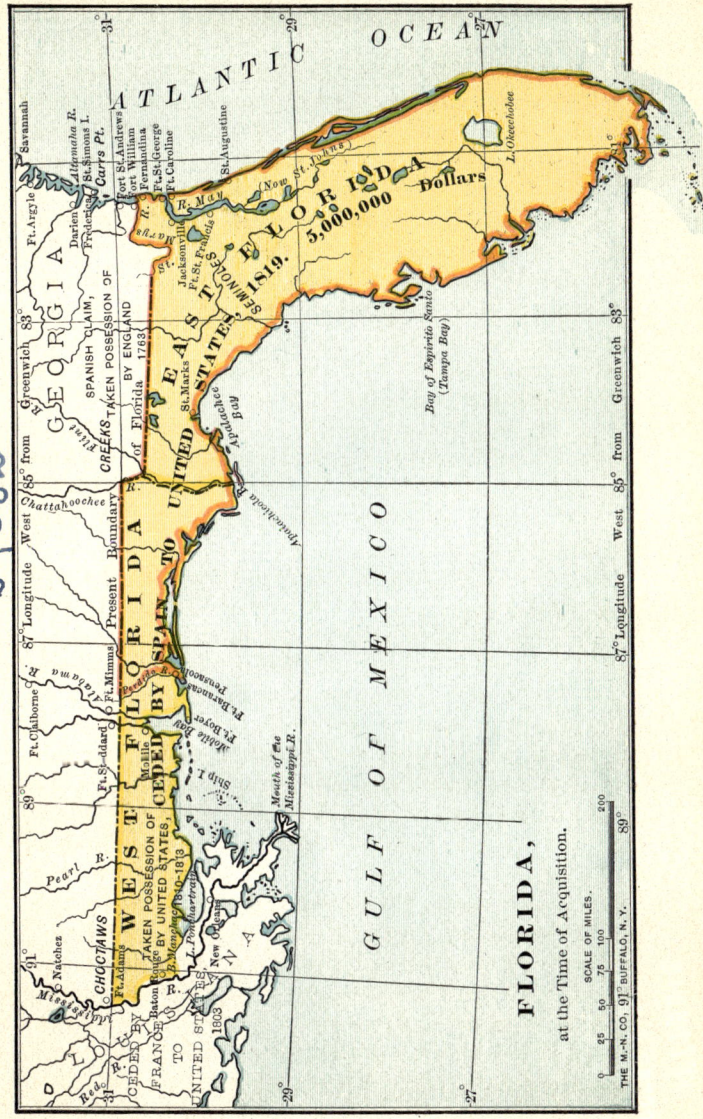

THE ACQUISITION OF FLORIDA 33

posed to do so. Spain accepted the offer, fulfilled in a way the conditions, and the places were restored to her jurisdiction.

It was now manifest to Spain, however, that she could not control Florida, and that her possession of the province was, and could be, only nominal. She now, therefore, agreed to cede it to the United States. The treaty bears date of February 22nd, 1819. Its important provisions are contained in the second and third articles. By these articles Spain ceded the Floridas, with the adjacent islands dependent thereon, to the United States; and agreed with the United States that the boundary between the two powers in North America should be the west bank of the Sabine River from its mouth to the thirty-second parallel of north latitude, thence the line of longitude to the Red River, thence up the course of the Red River to the one-hundredth parallel of longitude from London, or the twenty-third from Washington, thence the line of longitude to the Arkansas River, thence the south bank of the Arkansas to its source, thence the line of longitude to the forty-second parallel of north latitude, and thence this line of latitude to the South Sea.

*The first Treaty for the cession of Florida to the United States.*

This settlement of boundary included that of all other claims, of whatever character, of the Government, citizens, or subjects of either power against the Government, citizens, or subjects of the other. All such were mutually renounced.

The results of the Seminole War raised General Jackson to a still higher plane of popularity than he possessed as the hero of the War of 1812. It was evident that here was a character who would have to be reckoned with in future presidential contests. It is possible that Jackson's chief mentor, William B. Lewis, had con-

2

ceived, at this date, the idea of Jackson's candidacy for the highest place in the gift of the nation. And it is highly probable that the fears of all the existing aspirants for the presidency were excited by the appearance of this new and popular rival for public favor. It is difficult to explain upon any other theory the attempt made in Congress, during the session of 1818–19, to suppress Jackson by a vote of censure.

*Jackson's popularity in consequence of the Seminole War.*

This procedure certainly had no connection whatsoever with the question of slavery extension through the acquisition of Florida. When we find Tallmadge, of New York, the self-same person who introduced, at the same session, the proposition for restricting slavery in Missouri, defending Jackson's course in every particular, while Cobb, of Georgia, attacked it, and when we consider that John Quincy Adams, the life-long opponent of slavery, sustained Jackson in the cabinet, while Calhoun moved to bring him to account for disobedience to orders, we are bound to conclude that we have here nothing whatsoever to do with the question of slavery.

*The attempt in Congress to censure Jackson.*

Crawford, of Georgia, the Secretary of the Treasury, was the prime aspirant for presidential honors, after Monroe should have completed his two terms, and Cobb was Crawford's right-hand man. Clay was also working up his plans. These two men felt it necessary to discredit Jackson in every possible way. Clay made a great bugbear out of Jackson's military heroship, and so threatening did he make it appear to the principle of civil government and republican institutions that he really seemed frightened at it himself. Crawford set up the same strain, through Cobb, in a feebler key. Calhoun seems to have been animated rather by wrath at what he con-

*The same attempt in the Cabinet.*

THE ACQUISITION OF FLORIDA 35

ceived to be the violation of his orders, or, at least, the exceeding of his orders, than by jealousy of a presidential rival. His presidential fever had not, at that moment, reached a high degree. But what shall we say of Adams, who undoubtedly then considered himself a candidate for the successorship to Monroe, and who stood against the whole Cabinet in Jackson's defence, and carried the day against both Crawford and Calhoun combined. Of course it may be said that Adams thought his own turn would come before that of Jackson, and that he would gain Jackson's support by his attitude. But against such a supposition must stand the fact that the Cabinet pledged itself to secrecy in regard to all that was proposed on the subject, and that for ten years Jackson supposed that Calhoun was the friend in the Cabinet who had successfully defended him against the other members under the lead of Crawford. The attitude of Adams in the question was noble and disinterested, as well as patriotic, and had Jackson known of it in 1824, it is altogether probable that he would never have charged an unfair bargain with Clay upon Adams for his own defeat.

Clay and Cobb represented that every movement made by Jackson, from the moment of his appointment to the command of the expedition to the end of hostilities, was illegal and in defiance of the orders of the War Department. They said he had no right to call upon his old soldiers instead of asking the Governor of Tennessee for the militia. They claimed that he waged an offensive war upon his own responsibility against Spain, when the War Department had expressly forbidden him to attack the Spanish forts, and they accused him of murdering two prisoners of war. The House of Representatives showed what it thought of these accusations by voting

*The failure of the attempt to censure Jackson in Congress.*

down the resolutions which contained the censure by a majority of nearly two to one, while the resolutions of like effect introduced into the Senate were laid on the table and never taken up for consideration.

The Administration had, under the influence of the Secretary of State, Mr. Adams, already assumed the responsibility for Jackson's acts, had upheld their legality, and was even then bringing its negotiations with Spain, in regard to the cession of Florida, to a successful close; while the British Government had refrained from any interference on account of the treatment of Ambrister and Arbuthnot.

<small>Assumption of the responsibility for Jackson's acts by the Administration.</small>

The attempt to suppress Jackson broke down thus upon all sides, and he emerged from the assaults of his rivals with a greater popularity than he had ever before enjoyed, and with improved prospects as a presidential candidate. With the worship accorded to a hero he now enjoyed the sympathy extended to a martyr.

<small>Jackson triumphant.</small>

The Treaty itself, ceding the Floridas, did not escape attack. Adams regarded it as a great diplomatic triumph for the United States, but Clay expressed great disappointment with it, because it sacrificed, as he viewed it, the claims of the United States to the territory between the Sabine and the Rio del Norte. And Crawford, who was seizing every opportunity to discredit the Administration, by encouraging it to false measures from his place in the Cabinet, and then professing publicly his disapprobation of them, also saw in the point emphasized by Clay a prime occasion for making political capital.

<small>The Treaty of Cession attacked in Congress, but ratified by the Senate.</small>

The Senate showed what its members thought of such manœuvres by a speedy and unanimous vote in ratification of the Treaty.

# THE ACQUISITION OF FLORIDA

The Spanish Government, on the other hand, rejected the Treaty. Mr. Adams felt, at the moment, that this was a blow to his reputation as a diplomatist, and perhaps to his chances for the presidency. But it did not prove to be such. Had the Treaty been then ratified three large land grants made by the Spanish King to certain Spanish nobles, at a date earlier than Mr. Adams had supposed, would not have been extinguished by it. The rejection of the Treaty by the Spanish Government, which at the same time sent another Ambassador, General Vivês, to take the place of Don Onis, and to renew negotiations on the subject, gave Mr. Adams the opportunity to insist upon the cession of Florida with the extinguishment of the above mentioned grants.

*Rejection of the treaty by the Spanish Government.*

When the new Ambassador arrived, the country was in the midst of the excitement over the question of slavery extension in the Louisiana territory, the history of which will be related in a succeeding chapter. The effect of this agitation was to arouse some doubt in the minds of those opposed to the extension of slavery in regard to the expediency of any addition to the territory of the United States southward. Mr. Adams himself felt the influence of this doubt, and was prompted, in part at least, by it to assume an attitude of indifference toward the new propositions of the Spanish Ambassador. He gave the Ambassador to understand that Spain could make such a treaty with the United States in regard to the subject as would be satisfactory to the latter, or take the consequences of leaving things as they were. The unshakable determination of Mr. Adams won the day, and the old Treaty, with a new provision extinguishing the above mentioned land grants, was finally ratified by both Governments, two years after the date of

*Resumption of negotiations.*

the original agreement between Mr. Adams and Don Onis.

The vote of ratification by the Senate of the United States was again practically unanimous. Only four votes were recorded against it; and of these four one was cast by a brother-in-law of Mr. Clay, one by a subservient friend of the same gentleman, and one by a bitter personal enemy of General Jackson. The province was soon transferred to the United States and Jackson became its first territorial governor. With this the United States attained its natural boundary on the south, eastward from the mouth of the Mississippi, and a source of chronic irritation was removed.

*The new Treaty ratified by the Senate and by the Spanish Government.*

It was to be expected that this territory would be erected into a Commonwealth in which the institution of slavery would be legalized; but this did not deter the statesmen of the North from securing the great advantages just indicated. Radical abolitionism had not yet blinded them to the general and paramount interests of the Union. In fact, the results of the Seminole War and of the diplomacy of the Administration in connection with it had the immediate effect of diminishing the ultra-Southern influence in the Government. They brought Adams and Jackson to the front, and set Crawford and Calhoun back in the course of their careers. They had, indeed, much to do, as we shall see later, with the development of the era of personal politics, which prevailed from 1824 to 1832, and which terminated finally in the separation of the all-comprehending Republican party into the Whig party and the Democratic party.

*Political results of the Seminole War.*

# CHAPTER III.

## SLAVERY IN THE UNITED STATES BEFORE 1820

First Appearance of Slavery in the British North American Colonies—Early Theory of the Benefits of Slavery—The Earliest Legal Recognition of Slavery in the Colonies—Northern Colonies not well Adapted to Negro Labor—The Southern Colonies well Adapted to Negro Labor—Negro Slavery a Temporary Necessity in the South—Was Negro Slavery an Error and an Evil from the first ?—Slavery Legislation in the Southern Colonies—Partus Sequitur Ventrem—Definitions of the Slave Class—The Test of the Slave Status as Fixed by the Virginia Statute—The Legal Position of the Slave—Tendency Toward Serfage in the Code of 1705—Public Relations of the Slave System—The General Object of the Laws in respect to Slaves—Slavery and the Revolutionary Ideas of the Rights of Man—First Prohibition upon Slave Importation—Abolition of Slavery in the Northern Commonwealths after the Beginning of the Revolution—Slavery and the Constitution of 1787—Reaction against the Humanitarian Principles of the Revolution—Abolition of the Foreign Slave-trade by Congress—Cotton Culture and the Cotton-gin—The Effect of the Return to the Arts of Peace upon the Ideas Concerning Slavery — Slavery During the War of 1812, and the Years just before and just after this War—Slavery in the Louisiana Territory—Slavery in the territory West of North Carolina and Georgia—Slavery in Louisiana a Different Question from Slavery in the North Carolina and Georgia Cessions—Interest in Slavery in Maryland and Virginia Increased by the Acquisition of Louisiana—The Domestic Slave-trade—The Relation of Slavery to the Diplomacy of the United States.

IT is not easy to define the term slavery in the abstract without unfitting it for application to the great majority of the systems of servitude which have ever existed. Especially will it be difficult to gain a correct conception of the relation between the white man and the negro in North America previous to 1860 by means of such a definition.

The institution of negro slavery in the United States was an historical growth, which was in some respects unique. We shall, therefore, do better to follow the main stages of that development than to attempt at the outset any definition whatsoever. We may, in this manner, build up a true description of it, and escape the error frequently contained in the brevity of a definition and in the nature of an abstract proposition.

It began its existence, like most institutions and relations, as a social custom. Most of the historians record the appearance of a Dutch merchant ship at Jamestown, in the year 1619, having negroes on board, and inform us that twenty of them were sold to the colonists. What title the Dutch traders had to such property, exactly what they sold to the colonists, and what rights the colonists acquired in or over such property, were defined, guaranteed, and secured by no existing statutes. If any of the parties to the transaction reflected upon these subjects at all, they must have supposed that the right of possession and the freedom of contract covered the whole case. There is certainly no evidence that any of these parties, or anybody else, had the faintest conception that the law of any state, or any principle of natural justice, or of reason, was violated or impaired by the procedure or the results of the procedure. It was a firmly and universally established opinion of the time that the attachment of infidels to Christians in the relation of servant to master was vastly beneficial to the infidel, certainly so when

*Marginal notes:* First appearance of slavery in the British North American colonies. Early theory of the benefits of slavery.

the infidel was also a barbarian, and was taken out of slavery to a barbarian master, as was the case in respect to almost all of the negroes brought to the English colonies in North America.

We cannot dismiss this opinion as one of the errors of the dark ages. It lives to-day as a principle of modern political science and practical politics, under the form of statement that civilized people have the right and duty to impose civilization upon uncivilized populations by whatever means they may deem to be just and proper.

There can be no reasonable doubt that the negroes transferred from slavery in Africa to slavery in the English-American colonies themselves felt the amelioration of their condition, and were, in general, entirely contented with their new lot.

The relation was established in the Northern colonies, as well as in the Southern, in the early years of their existence, and it was in Massachusetts rather than in Virginia that it first received legal recognition, and began to be changed from a purely domestic institution by suffering governmental regulation. In the Massachusetts "Fundamentals," or "Body of Liberties," passed by the General Court in 1641, the slavery of negroes and Indians, and the slave-trade, were expressly legalized. In fact, so far as the colonists themselves were responsible for the introduction of negro slavery among them, the impartial historian must place the greater blame upon a Northern colony. Its citizens were first to develop commerce, and it was their ships which brought the slave cargoes from the coasts of Africa to all of the colonies.

*The earliest legal recognition of slavery in the colonies.*

The negroes were not, however, fitted for labor in the Northern colonies. In the first place, it was too cold for them to thrive there. A warm, moist air is the natural climate for the negro. In the second place, the work to be done in these sections was not suited to his capacity. The Northern colonies had not, indeed, at that early day, developed the finer forms of industry which have subsequently distinguished that part of the country. They were then, as to their internal pursuits, almost as completely agricultural as the colonies of the South. But their farming required a great deal more of intelligence, thrift, and industry in the laborer than the negro of that day possessed. The country was broken, the good soil was limited in amount, the weather was capricious, and the management of the crops demanded judgment and discretion. On the other hand, the vast level areas of good soil, the warm, uniform climate, and the simple crops of the Southern colonies furnished the conditions favorable to the employment of negro labor.

<small>Northern colonies not well adapted to negro labor.</small>

<small>The Southern colonies well adapted to negro labor.</small>

It is not easy to see how the rich swamp-lands of these colonies could ever have been reclaimed and made tributary to the civilization of the world in any way but by the employment of negro labor. And it is no easier to see how the pure negro could then have been brought to do this great work save through slavery to the white race, save by being forced to contribute the muscular effort, under the direction of the superior intelligence of the white race, to the realization of objects determined by that superior intelligence. The negro is proof against malaria, and thrives under the burning sun. The white man is destroyed by the former and greatly disabled by the latter. And the pure negro would not at that period of his development labor voluntarily. These were the elements of the problem which confronted those who undertook to subject the vast marshes of the Southern colonies to cultivation and to prepare them for the pro-

<small>Negro slavery a temporary necessity in the South.</small>

duction of their most valuable contributions to the comforts of civilized man. The solution of the problem was negro slavery.

We are most of us inclined, at this day, to hold that this was an erroneous solution, and that we could have discovered a better one; but it was the solution which was reached, and we shall be wiser if we seek to understand it clearly, instead of wasting our energies in its condemnation, remembering that many of the things of the past, which, from the point of view of the present, we are prone to regard as error, and even as sin, are only anachronisms. In fact, those who founded the colony of Georgia thought *then* that they had a better solution of the problem. They prohibited slavery at the outset from that colony. In fourteen years they came to regard this act as a great mistake, and the noblest spirits among them acknowledged themselves in error, and joined in the movement for the introduction of negro slave-labor.

*Was negro slavery an error and an evil from the first?*

The conditions above mentioned were undoubtedly the chief causes of the more rapid and pronounced development of negro slavery in the Southern colonies. And that more rapid and pronounced development directs us rather to the legislation of the Southern colonies than to that of the Northern, in following the legalization of the relation.

*Slavery legislation in the Southern colonies.*

Virginia naturally took the lead, and furnished the precedents for the others. The first question, both as to time and importance, which required legislative treatment, was the question of the status of the children of slaves. Where legalized marriage does not exist, the only certainty in respect to parentage is attained by regarding the mother. Rights and status in such a condition of society are, therefore, transmitted through the female line. *Partus sequitur ventrem* is the rule not only of the civil law, but of every system of law regulating the accidents of descent among people where the mingling of the sexes is not controlled by civilized marriage. Insuperable obstacles present themselves in the attempt to apply any other rule. It was no unusual or arbitrary enactment of the Virginia legislature which, in 1662, prescribed the rule that the status of the slave mother should determine that of her offspring. This rule was followed in all the colonies, and many of them enacted it into statute law.

<small>Partus sequitur ventrem.</small>

So long as the slaves were few in number and were not Christians the necessity for legislation defining the slave class was not felt; but so soon as the slave-trade became more active, and slaves began to receive Christian baptism, the old customary test in regard to this matter, that of infidelity or heathenism, would no longer suffice. The colonists of that day were too conscientious to cut the knot of this difficulty by denying Christian baptism to any one seeking it. They considered it their prime duty to lead the heathen to the knowledge of Christ. It is evident that their consciences were greatly troubled over the question of the effect of Christian baptism upon the slave status. The colonial legislatures, the Home Government, and the Bishop of London were appealed to for counsel in the dilemma. The answers received from all of these were to the effect that the status of the slave was not changed by Christian baptism or conversion.

<small>Definitions of the slave class.</small>

The test of the slave status was then necessarily fixed by legislation. The Virginia statute declared all servants brought into the country by land or sea, who were not Christians in their native country at the time when they were purchased or procured, nor free in

## SLAVERY IN THE STATES BEFORE 1820   45

England or some other Christian country, to be slaves. Exception was made of Turks and Moors in amity with the King. This statute, taken together with the rule *partus sequitur ventrem*, which rule was re-enacted, became the test of the slave class. At the same time heavy penalties were attached to the marriage or cohabitation of white women with slaves.

The test of the slave status as fixed by the Virginia statute.

Of course it very soon became necessary that the legal position of the slave should be definitely fixed. The legislature of Virginia again set the precedents. Concisely stated, this legislation provided that a slave could have no standing in the ordinary courts, either as party or witness; that a slave could own no property; that a slave owed obedience to the master, who might force the slave to labor, and chastise the slave even to the extreme of so injuring the slave that the slave might die in consequence thereof, without incurring the penalties of felony; that the slave could be sold or inherited as personal property; and that the offspring of the female slave belonged to the master owning her at the time of its birth.

The legal position of the slave.

The wilful killing of a slave by anyone, even the master, was accounted murder, and extraordinary tribunals, without a jury, were constituted for the protection of his person. The Code of 1705 even contained regulations which indicated that the trend of thought and of legislation, at that juncture, was toward attaching the slave to the soil, which would have been a step upward in a course, which, if consistently followed, would have made the slave a serf. But the still prevailing rules, which allowed the slave to be seized and sold for the debts of the master, and regulated the inheritance of slaves according to the

Tendency toward serfage in the Code of 1705.

law governing the descent of personal property, seem to have completely neutralized that tendency before the middle of the century had been reached.

Naturally the private law accidents of the relation were first developed and fixed, but very soon the rights and powers of the community in regard to the institution began to claim attention. The public peace and welfare must be safeguarded against the possible conduct of the slave, on the one hand, and of the master, on the other.

*Public relations of the slave system.*

The legislation of Virginia set the example in these respects also. That legislation provided that no slave should have, or carry arms, or go outside of the plantation of his master without a pass from his master, or lift his hand against a Christian; that a sheriff should arrest a runaway slave on the warrant of two justices, and might lawfully kill any slave who resisted arrest; and that no slave should be emancipated without the consent of the Governor and Council.

On the other hand, it provided that the master should be responsible for all damage done by his slave at any place where there was no Christian overseer, and required that any master giving freedom to his slave should pay the cost of his transportation out of the colony.

Such was substantially the law of negro slavery in all of the colonies at the beginning of the decade before the Revolution. It was perhaps more severe than this in South Carolina, and it was certainly less so in Massachusetts.

*The general object of the laws in respect to slaves.*

The objects which it had in view were to secure the master's property in the slave, to enable the master to hold the slave in obedience and force him, if necessary, to labor, and to protect the public peace and welfare against the abuse of the relation by the master, and against the vicious nature of the slave.

It does certainly appear that the century of law-making upon the subject had not ameliorated the condition of the slave. We must remember, however, that the first stages in the legalization of any relation sometimes make the situation appear worse than what obtained before the movement began, although it may not be worse in fact.

But the period of the Revolution brought with it a great change of view in regard to the morality of slavery, and this change of idea produced great modifications in the law of slavery, all of which tended not only toward an improvement of the condition of the slave, but also toward the ultimate extinction of slavery.

*Slavery and the Revolutionary ideas of the rights of man.*

When we regard the Revolution of the colonies against the motherland from the point of view of the present, we can easily see that its purpose was very different from that of the French Revolution. What it really sought and accomplished was national independence against foreign rule. Those, however, who formulated the creed of the Revolution sought its justification in the doctrine of human rights rather than in that of national rights. The philosophy of the eighteenth century was a humanitarian outburst. Politically and legally it is summed up in the very misleading propositions that all men are born equal and are endowed with freedom, and that the people have the right to change or abolish existing government at their pleasure. Whatever we may think of these doctrines now, our ancestors professed to believe in them, and there is no reason to doubt the sincerity of their profession, so far as their own consciousness went. They saw also the inconsistency of slavery with these doctrines, and quickly came to regard slavery as an evil which should be removed as soon as possible.

48                THE MIDDLE PERIOD

The Continental Congress took the first step in this direction. Two years before it declared independence
<small>First prohibition upon slave importation.</small> it prohibited any further importation of slaves, and repeated the prohibition two years later. These acts are good evidence that, at the moment, the question of slavery was regarded as a matter of national concern.

The Congress was, however, so occupied with the duties pertaining to the prosecution of the war, that it failed to go forward in this matter, as well as in many other matters of national concern ; and when the Confederate Congress succeeded the Continental Congress, it did so upon the basis of a written constitution, or rather articles of union, which vested no powers whatsoever in it over the subject of slavery.

The separate colonies, now become "States" by the theory of the Articles of Confederation, took up the
<small>Abolition of slavery in the Northern Commonwealths after the beginning of the Revolution.</small> question. Massachusetts abolished slavery substantially by her constitution of 1780. Pennsylvania provided for gradual emancipation by a statute of the same year. Rhode Island, Connecticut, and New Hampshire followed the example of Pennsylvania. And New York, New Jersey, Delaware, Maryland, and Virginia forbade any further importation of slaves.

Under such impulses and influences the Confederate Congress, in spite of the fact that no power in respect
<small>The Ordinance of 1787.</small> to slavery had been conferred upon it, assumed to pass the famous Ordinance of 1787, decreeing the free status exclusively in all of the territory then belonging to the United States north of the Ohio River. The power to enact the Ordinance could not even be derived by the most generous principles of implication from any provision in the Articles of Confederation. To justify the exercise of it by the Confederate

Congress it is necessary to go back to the general principle of political science that, as there was no government for this territory but the Confederate Congress, and as there were no limitations in the Articles of Confederation upon the powers of the Congress in this territory, the powers of that Congress must have extended in this territory to all subjects usually regulated by government.

The claim sometimes made that this Ordinance was a treaty between the "States" forming the Confederation, or between them and the "States" to be formed out of that territory in the future, is altogether untenable. It was nothing more nor less than a legislative act of the Congress.

It is an incontrovertible proof of the universality and intensity of the opposition to the farther spread of slavery that the common consciousness of the age acquiesced in this most latitudinarian construction of the powers of the Confederate Congress, and that the Congress itself voted the measure with but a single dissenting voice.

At the same moment that this measure was being considered in the Congress, the Constitutional Convention, sitting at Philadelphia, was framing the national Constitution of 1787. The attitude which the nation would assume in this new instrument of its organic law toward the subject of slavery was one of the most, if not the most, important of the questions which the Convention was called upon to consider.

*Slavery and the Constitution of 1787.*

There can be little doubt that the men of 1787 had come to regard the question of the rights of man a little more calmly than they did during the heat of the battle with the motherland. In Luther Martin's famous letter to the legislature of Maryland upon the work of the

Convention of 1787, a very significant passage concerning the existing views upon slavery occurs. He wrote: "At this time we do not generally hold this commerce" (the slave-trade) "in so great abhorrence as we have done. When our liberties were at stake we warmly felt for the common rights of men. The danger being thought to be past which threatened ourselves we are daily growing more insensible to those rights."

The Constitution of 1787 contains evidence of the correctness of this statement. Among its provisions were to be found three most important compromises with the slavery interest, three most important recognitions of slavery. The first was political in its nature. It counted the negro for three-fifths of the white man in the distribution of the representation in the House of Representatives and in the Presidential Electoral Colleges. The second was commercial in its nature. It forbade the Congress to prohibit, before the year 1808, the migration or importation of such persons as the existing "States" might see fit to admit. The third was a direct guarantee of slave property. It required the surrender to his master of an escaped slave wherever found in the United States. These were most momentous provisions. They secured slave property, increased slave property, and made slavery a vast political power in the hands of the slave-masters. There is no doubt that the clock of the ages was turned back full half a century in regard to this great question by the Constitution of 1787.

From 1787 to 1808 the reactionary course was pursued almost without a single break. Kentucky was made a Commonwealth with the slave status. The Congress accepted from North Carolina and Georgia cessions of the territory which lay to the west of them, and which they claimed as belonging to them, with a condition

## SLAVERY IN THE STATES BEFORE 1820 51

that slavery should not be forbidden therein by Congress. The slave Commonwealth of Tennessee was immediately formed out of a part of this territory. The vast territory of Louisiana, in which slavery existed wherever it was inhabited, was added to the domain of the Union. *Reaction against the humanitarian principles of the Revolution.* The District of Columbia, the seat of the general Government, was made a slave-holding community, through the adoption by Congress of the laws of Maryland as the code of the District. A fugitive slave-law was passed by Congress, which enabled any white man to seize, as his slave, any man of color, and bring him before any magistrate, and, upon proof satisfactory to the latter, to demand such papers and certificates as would legally warrant him in reclaiming the slave and transporting him to the place whence he was said to have escaped ; and petitions to Congress complaining of the abuse of this arbitrary power were laid aside without consideration. Even the Territory of Indiana prayed Congress to suspend for it that part of the Ordinance of 1787 which forbade slavery within its limits. And South Carolina abolished her law against the importation of slaves, and opened the way wide for a vast increase of the slave population.

These last acts seem to have aroused the consciousness of the Congress to the rapidity with which the whole country was becoming again subject to the slave-holding interests. The Congress resisted the importunities of the Indiana leaders, and after giving South Carolina a reasonable time to re-enact her law abolishing the foreign slave-trade, without effect, proceeded itself to abolish the trade from the first moment that the Constitution permitted this to be done, from January 1st, 1808. *Abolition of the foreign slave-trade by Congress.*

It has been customary to ascribe the great revulsion

of view in regard to slavery, which certainly manifested itself everywhere in the United States between 1790 and 1807, to cotton culture and the cotton-gin. The invention of the cotton-gin, in the first part of the last decade of the eighteenth century, and the increased demand for cotton fabrics throughout the world, had made the cultivation of cotton highly profitable. An increase in cotton culture was naturally encouraged by such enhanced profits, and this tendency produced an increased demand for negro labor and for new lands, since the cotton crop requires a warm climate and low lands, and exhausts the soil very rapidly. Those parts of the country adapted to cotton-raising felt, therefore, a renewed interest in the increase of negro labor and in territorial extension. And those parts not so adapted felt an indirect interest in the same, since the increased and still increasing profits of the cotton culture made a market for their slaves and a carrying trade for their shipowners. There is no doubt that such was the main cause of the great change of view in regard to the question of negro slavery which the country experienced between 1790 and 1810, but it was not the sole cause. It was inevitable that, when the men of that era passed out of the excited state of mind and feeling produced by the War with the motherland, and came to the task of re-establishing the relations of peace and every-day life and business, they should regain a calmness of judgment, a respect for vested rights, and a regard for customary relations, which placed the political philosophy of 1776 under many limitations and qualifications, some of which, certainly, were sound and valuable. It is only when we take all of these considerations together that we comprehend the reasoning of the men of the first decade of this century upon the great question. They saw a great interest developing which was bringing wealth and comfort into an impoverished country. They knew that it could be then sustained only by negro labor. They did not believe that the negro would work unless forced to it by the white man. They thought it was better for the negro himself to have food, clothing, and shelter, in slavery, than to starve, or become a robber, in liberty. They felt, on the other hand, that the slavery of one human being to another was an exceptional relation in a political system which rested its own right to independent existence upon the doctrine of human freedom. It was not, then, unnatural that they arrived at the conclusion that to prohibit further importations of the barbarians from Africa was the only remedy for which the time was ripe. They sincerely believed that they would place themselves and their slaves in a far more advantageous position for the gradual elevation of the latter by having to deal only with negroes born and reared amid civilized surroundings, and that freedom would finally be attained by all, as the result of a gradual advancement in intelligence, morals, and industry, and would be thus attained without any shock to the civilization and welfare of the country.

This appeared to the men of that day, both of the North and of the South, to be the only safe way to proceed in solving the question of the relation between the highly civilized Anglo-American race and the grossly barbaric negro race in the United States. We think now that they might have done better, and some of the more unsympathetic critics of our history affirm that they did nothing of any consequence, and that in what they did do they acted with a consciously deceptive purpose. There may have been a few to whom this criticism can be justly applied, but there is no sufficient evidence that the mass of them were insincere either in act or thought. The contention that they were is more partisan than truly historical.

The decade between 1807 and 1817 was filled with the questions of foreign relations, of foreign war, and of the results of foreign war. The suspension, and then the almost entire destruction, of foreign commerce by the British Orders in Council, the Napoleonic decrees, the Jeffersonian embargo, and the War of 1812, reduced the exportation in cotton from about fifty millions of pounds in 1807 to less than twenty millions of pounds in 1814. The pecuniary interest in the maintenance of slavery declined thus quite materially, and the majority of the leading men, both North and South, still regarded negro slavery as only a temporary status, which would be gradually modified in the direction of freedom.

*Slavery during the War of 1812, and the years just before and just after this war.*

Notwithstanding all this, however, the slavery interest was steadily waxing in influence and power throughout this period. First of all the existence and the extension of slavery in the vast territory purchased from France was secured. The custom of slave-holding had been introduced into this territory by the French and Spanish immigrants, while it was in the possession of France and Spain, before the year 1800. In that year Spain, as we have seen, receded it to France. Nine years before this date, slavery had been abolished in France by the National Assembly. It is certainly a question, then, whether the re-establishment of French supremacy over Louisiana in 1800 did not produce the abolition of slavery there. It will be remembered that France was at that moment subject to the consular government of Bonaparte, and that the Consul was not an enthusiast for the revolutionary ideals. He did not disturb the custom of slave-holding

*Slavery in the Louisiana territory.*

in Louisiana, and when he ceded this vast territory to the United States, in 1803, the custom existed in all its inhabited parts. The Treaty of cession contained a provision which pledged the Government of the United States to uphold the rights of property of the inhabitants of the province. It can be fairly said, therefore, that the United States Government obligated itself to France to maintain slavery within the territory ceded until it should be erected into a Commonwealth, or into Commonwealths, of the Union.

The United States Government might have violated the Treaty, if it had chosen to do so, and the question then raised would have been one of a purely diplomatic or international character. There would have been no question of constitutional power involved. The act of the United States Government breaking the Treaty would have been the law of the land for the inhabitants of this territory.

The United States Government, however, not only permitted the continuance of the custom of slave-holding in Louisiana, but when, in 1804, Congress divided this vast region into two parts by the thirty-third parallel of latitude, and organized the southern portion as the Territory of Orleans, and placed the northern portion under the jurisdiction of the Governor and judges of the Territory of Indiana, it, at the same time, authorized citizens of the United States immigrating into the Territory of Orleans, for the purpose of actual settlement, to take their slaves with them, and provided that the French laws in force at the date of the division should continue in the northern part until repealed or modified by the Governor and judges of Indiana Territory. Any danger to slavery in this district of Louisiana, which might be contained in the power vested by Congress in the Governor and judges of the Territory of Indiana to repeal or modify the French laws which Congress had allowed to continue in the district, was overcome, the following year, by the independent organization of this district as the Territory of Louisiana, and by a provision in the Act of Congress effecting this organization, which provided for the continuance in force of the laws of the district, until repealed or modified by the legislature of the Territory.

When, therefore, in 1812, the Territory of Orleans was erected into the Commonwealth of Louisiana, and the name of the Territory of Louisiana was changed to Missouri, there was no question about the status of the new Commonwealth. It was, both in fact and in law, a slave-holding Commonwealth; and the custom of slave-holding was perpetuated in the newly named Territory by the provision in the Act of Congress that the laws and regulations of the Territory of Louisiana should remain in force in the Territory of Missouri until repealed or modified by the legislature of the Territory of Missouri.

The Government of the United States had entered into obligations with North Carolina and Georgia, as we have seen, not to prohibit slavery in the territory ceded by them to the United States. Whatever we may think of the binding force of any such agreement from a legal point of view, certainly from an ethical point of view it could have been urged that the Government would have broken faith with some of the citizens of the United States had the Congress disregarded this understanding.

*Slavery in the territory west of North Carolina and Georgia.*

It cannot, however, be contended that there was any obligation, legal or moral, resting upon the Government of the United States toward any of the citizens of the United States, or any of the Commonwealths, to maintain slavery in the province of Louisiana and in the

## SLAVERY IN THE STATES BEFORE 1820

Territories carved out of it. There was, as we have seen, a provision in the Treaty of cession of 1803, by which the United States Government obligated itself to France to protect the property of the inhabitants of the province. But the Government of the United States was under no obligation to any citizen of the United States, or to any Commonwealth of the Union, to keep this Treaty inviolate. It may be affirmed, then, that the United States Government had, in the case of Louisiana, for the first time, permitted and maintained slavery in territory where it was perfectly free to act in regard to this subject as it would, in so far as its own citizens were concerned. This certainly manifested a great increase in the power of the slave-holders over the general Government.

*Slavery in Louisiana a different question from slavery in the North Carolina and Georgia cessions.*

In consequence of this vast territorial extension of slavery the interest of the more Northern of the old slave-holding Commonwealths in slavery was, during this period, greatly re-enlivened. Maryland and Virginia were already, in 1807, overstocked with slaves. The opening up of the virgin lands of the Southwest to the immigration of masters and slaves from the older Commonwealths, and the abolition of the foreign slave-trade, now made the Southwest an excellent market for the surplus slave population of these older Commonwealths.

*Interest in slavery in Maryland and Virginia increased by the acquisition of Louisiana.*

The domestic slave-trade began now to be one of the chief sources of the wealth of Maryland and Virginia especially. Those who participated in this traffic justified it by the claim that it was better for the slaves themselves to be removed to new homes, where they could be better supported, than to be kept in their old homes and suffer for the want of the necessaries of life, and that the distribution of the slave

*The domestic slave-trade.*

population over a larger area would make future emancipation easier, and less dangerous to the supremacy of the white race. There was a certain force in this reasoning. The mass of the slave-holders seem to have been fully convinced of its soundness, although it did not entirely quiet the consciences of the best men among them to the many painful incidents connected with the separation of the slaves, made subject to this traffic, from their old homes and associations.

It is easy to see, however, that the raising of negro slaves, having become a most profitable industry in the older Commonwealths, acted as a vast bribe upon the ideas of men in regard to the questions of the perpetuation and extension of slavery, and beclouded their consciences in respect thereto.

Finally, the capture and abduction of negro slaves by the British forces during the War of 1812, and the demand of the slave-holders that the United States Government should secure the restitution of their slaves, or compensation for the loss of them, from the British Government, moved the United States Government to assume its attitude toward slavery in the administration of the international affairs of the country. The cardinal political principle of the slave-holding statesmen, at that period, was that slavery was a "State" matter with which the United States Government had no concern, and in regard to which it had no powers. This appeal to the Government to voice and enforce their demands against Great Britain in respect to their slave property has seemed, therefore, to some of the later and more radical critics of American history to have been a gross inconsistency, and they have represented it as a proof of the insincerity of the slave-holders wherever their pecuniary interests were involved.

*The relation of slavery to the diplomacy of the United States.*

This criticism is rather taking, but a sound view of the Constitution will hardly support it. In making the United States Government the *exclusive* organ for dealing with foreign countries, the Constitution impliedly confers upon that Government a protectorate against foreign states over interests which are regulated, internally, only by the powers of the respective Commonwealths of the Union. It is true that this doctrine rests upon a national view of the federal system of government in the United States, a view which the slave-holding statesmen did not later share. From their later particularistic principle of the fundamental character of the Union, such a general protectorate over "State" interests by the United States Government against foreign countries could hardly be inferred from the Constitution. If this principle could be assumed by these critics as having been held at that time by the slave-holding statesmen, their charge of inconsistency, if not of insincerity, would be fairly made out. But such, as we have seen, was not the case. Many of the slave-holding statesmen of 1816 were stronger in the national view of the character of the Union than were the statesmen of New England itself.

The United States Government recognized its duty to extend the protection demanded in the case, and it secured from the British Government compensation to the masters for the loss of slave property occasioned by the acts of the British officers during the War.

Such was the status of the slavery question at the close of the War of 1812–15, at the commencement, therefore, of the period when, withdrawing themselves from foreign complications, the people of the United States began to adjust the different parts of their political system, chiefly if not solely, to the demands of their internal interests, and to solve the problems of their polity from the point of view of their domestic institutions. It is not strange, then, that from this point of time onward the powerful institution of negro slavery recognized more and more clearly its natural relations to all of these questions of internal policy and law, and sought more and more determinedly to bring the political system and the policies of the United States into accord with its own exclusive interests. For the first three or four years after the close of the War this tendency did not, as has been pointed out, appear upon the surface, but it was working in the depths. From 1820 to 1861, certainly, it furnishes the point of view for the correct elucidation of the majority of the great problems of the history of the United States.

# CHAPTER IV.

## THE CREATION OF THE COMMONWEALTH OF MISSOURI

The Growth of Slavery not Seriously Checked by the Prohibition of the Foreign Slave-trade—The General Government Powerless Against Slavery in the Existing Commonwealths—The Powers of the General Government in Respect to Slavery in the Territories—The Powers of Congress in the Admission of new "States" into the Union—Slavery in the Missouri Territory—The First Petition from Missouri Territory for the Permission to form a Commonwealth—The Second Petition, and the First Bill in Congress, for the Admission of Missouri—The Tallmadge Amendment to the Bill—Passage of the Amendment by the House of Representatives—Passage of the Original Bill by the Senate—The Missouri Bill during the Session of 1819-20—Mr. Taylor's Proposition—The Bill for the Admission of Maine Reported and Passed by the House of Representatives—The Failure of Mr. Taylor's Plan—The Missouri Bill again before the House of Representatives—Mr. Taylor's Amendment to the Bill—The Independent Missouri Bill of the Senate—The Refusal of the Senate to Disconnect the two Measures—The Conference on the Subject, and the First Missouri Compromise—President Monroe's Approval of the Compromise—Review of the Points Involved in the Contest—The Revival of the Missouri Struggle—The Missouri Constitution in Congress—Mr. Lowndes' Bill for the Admission of Missouri with the Instrument Unchanged—Defeat of the Lowndes Bill in the House—Passage of the Senate Bill with a Proviso by the Senate—The Senate Bill Tabled by the House—Mr. Clay and the Second Missouri Compromise—Passage of the Second Missouri Compromise Act—The General Effects of the Decisions Reached in the Missouri Question.

ALREADY before the year 1819, as we have seen in the preceding chapter, had it become manifest that the influences and measures relied upon by the forefathers for the ultimate extirpation of negro slavery were not effecting the desired result in the Commonwealths south of the line of Pennsylvania and of the Ohio. It was evident that the revolutionary enthusiasm for universal liberty and the rights of man was not so strongly felt by the generation which grew up after " '76 " as by the generation of " '76," that the laws against the importation of slaves were being evaded, and that the slaves were increasing by birth many times more rapidly than they were decreasing by emancipation and removal to the colonies of the American Society for Emancipation. Moreover, four new Commonwealths had been established—Kentucky, Tennessee, Louisiana, and Mississippi—in which slavery was legalized, and a fifth—Alabama—was even then in process of creation. It was manifest from all sides to the friends of universal freedom that other means than those hitherto relied upon must be found, if any progress was to be made in the advancement of liberty, yea if the evident retrogression in respect to this prime element of political civilization was to be checked.

*The growth of slavery not seriously checked by the prohibition of the foreign slave-trade.*

All had been done by the United States Government, however, against slavery within the existing Commonwealths that the Constitution allowed. Before anything more could be undertaken, the Constitution itself would have to be so amended as to authorize it. The extraordinary majorities required for the initiation and adoption of amendments made it practically impossible to effect anything by such means. Of the thirteen original Commonwealths, seven had abolished slavery and six had retained it. To these had now been added four—Vermont, Ohio, Indiana, and Illinois—in

*The general Government powerless against slavery in the existing Commonwealths.*

which slavery was forbidden, and five in which it was permitted—Kentucky, Tennessee, Louisiana, Mississippi, and Alabama—making thus the number upon each side the same. And although the population in the Commonwealths north of the line of Pennsylvania and the Ohio had outstripped, in increase, that in those south of this line by near half a million of souls in thirty years, and the representation in the national House of Representatives stood consequently in favor of the former section in the ratio of 104 to 79, still the method of representation in the Senate, and the equality in the number of the Commonwealths permitting, with those prohibiting, slavery, stood firmly in the way of any amendment of the Constitution, either favorable or unfavorable to the slavery interest.

The Constitution furnished, however, an indirect way of reaching the desired result. It gave the Congress general powers within the Territories and did not restrict these powers in behalf of slavery. Congress might thus prohibit slavery in the Territories, and the Territories would thus become settled by a free population, an anti-slavery population, which would form Commonwealths at the proper time, in which the free status would be perpetuated by Commonwealth law. *The powers of the general Government in respect to slavery in the Territories.* And when a sufficient number of free Commonwealths had been thus created to give the necessary majorities to amend the Constitution in the direction of abolition, slavery might be extinguished in the Commonwealths which had already legalized it. But the first difficulty in the way of the effectiveness of this line of action was the fact that Congress had already forfeited, in part, the opportunity, by failing to keep the southern portion of Louisiana Territory under a Territorial organization until slavery could have been eradicated in it. And it was probably, in

1819, already too late to attempt to keep the remaining parts of this vast region, so far as it had been settled at all, under Territorial organization until this result could have been effected. At least, the advocates of freedom in 1819 evidently thought so, for they searched the Constitution to find some other power in the general Government by which to deal with the question.

There was another provision which had been already several times applied to this very subject and to other subjects. It was the provision which conferred upon Congress the power to create, or co-operate in creating, new Commonwealths out of the Territories of the United States. This power is expressed in general terms, and in its employment Congress had imposed a number of limitations upon the powers of the new Commonwealths which the Constitution did not impose upon those of the original Commonwealths. Here, then, was a possible way for those seeking the advancement of liberty to effect their purpose. If their interpretation of the Constitution, in regard to the extent of this power, was correct, and they could only command the President and a simple majority in both branches of Congress, they could abolish slavery in every new Commonwealth at the time of its creation, and make the continuance of the free status the perpetual condition of its continued existence as a Commonwealth. It would then be only a question of time when sufficient majorities would be secured for so amending the Constitution of the United States as to expel slavery from the old Commonwealths through the regular forms for constitutional development. It was an attractive scheme, and appeared to provide the means for ridding the country peaceably of its great evil at no very far distant day. It was the last possible means which the Constitution afforded. It was

*The powers of Congress in the admission of new "States" into the Union.*

tried in the creation of the Commonwealth of Missouri and it failed. It is this which constitutes the significance of the great movement. The result attained made the abolition of slavery by the United States Government, through legal and peaceable means, an utter impossibility. It contributed, at least, toward making the War of 1861 an historical necessity.

As we have seen in the preceding chapter, slaveholding had become established by custom in the vast region known as the Louisiana province, wherever it was inhabited, during the periods when it belonged to Spain and France, and had been permitted to continue after its acquisition by the United States; and that in 1812 this province was divided into one slave-holding Commonwealth, Louisiana, and one slave-holding Territory, Missouri.

From 1812 to 1818 Congress did nothing toward the extinction of slavery in the Missouri Territory, or preventing the free immigration of masters with their slaves into the Territory. Neither had the legislature of the Territory done anything touching these subjects. It may, therefore, be assumed that in the year 1818, the holding of negroes as slaves was legal by custom, if not by positive law, in the whole of the Missouri Territory, so far as it had been settled, and that unless something should thereafter be done, either by the United States Government or by the Territorial government, forbidding it, slavery would be likewise legal wherever the Territory might become settled. *Slavery in the Missouri Territory.*

Before the beginning of the year 1818, the population in the Territory which looked to the town of St. Louis as its centre had begun to agitate the question of the establishment of Commonwealth government. During the Congressional session of 1817–18, petitions appeared in the House of Representatives from this population, praying for the erection of that part of Missouri Territory, bounded roughly by the thirty-sixth parallel of latitude on the south, the line of longitude passing through the point of confluence of the Kansas River and the Missouri River on the west, the Falls of the Des Moines River and the course of that river on the north, and the Mississippi on the east, into a Commonwealth of the Union. The petitions were referred and reported on, and the bill presented reached the stage for debate in the committee of the Whole House, but was not taken up during the session.

*The first petition from Missouri Territory for the permission to form a Commonwealth.*

Early in the following session, that of 1818–19, the Speaker of the House of Representatives presented a memorial from the Territorial legislature of Missouri which contained substantially the same prayer as the petitions presented at the preceding session. This memorial was immediately referred to a committee for report, but the bill which grew out of the petitions and the memorial was not brought forward for debate in the committee of the Whole House until February 13th, 1819.

*The second petition, and the first bill in Congress, for the admission of Missouri.*

It was upon this day, and during this first debate, that Mr. James Tallmadge, of New York, offered the famous amendment to the bill, which precipitated a discussion, that lasted for more than a year, upon the great subject of the distribution of powers between the United States Government and the Commonwealths, a discussion in which all the great legal lights of both Houses of Congress participated, and during the course of which the whole country hung with painful anxiety upon the outcome. It was the first great trial of the Constitution under the issue of a domestic question, a question which threatened to

*The Tallmadge amendment to the bill.*

THE COMMONWEALTH OF MISSOURI 67

divide the country upon geographic lines, a question which, therefore, threatened the dissolution of the Union.

The exact words of this amendment are essential to a correct comprehension of the question involved. It reads: "And provided that the further introduction of slavery or involuntary servitude be prohibited, except for the punishment of crimes, whereof the party shall have been duly convicted; and that all children born within the said State, after the admission thereof into the Union, shall be free at the age of twenty-five years."

The debate upon this motion is not fully reported in the annals of Congress, but it is sufficiently reported to give a correct idea of the constitutional questions involved. The discussion proceeded from the two points of view of constitutional powers and public policy. *The debate upon the Tallmadge amendment.* Of course the first point for the restrictionists, as those who favored the amendment were termed, to establish was the constitutionality of the power of Congress to impose this restriction in erecting a Territory into a Commonwealth. If Congress has, or had, no such power, the question of policy need not have been considered. They claimed the power, and based it upon that paragraph of Article IV. section three, which reads: "New States may be admitted by the Congress into this Union." It will be readily seen that this is a very loose statement concerning the powers of Congress in establishing this most fundamental relation. Taken apart from all connections, its most natural meaning is that foreign states may become politically joined with the United States by an Act of Congress, in so far as this country is concerned. On the other hand, taken with the context, it appears to mean that Congress may establish Commonwealth governments, or, in the language of the Constitution, "States," upon the territory belonging to the United States, or to some "State" or "States" already within the Union. This is, without any reasonable doubt, its only meaning. For if it had any reference to the connection of foreign states with the United States, it would confer the most important diplomatic power of the United States Government upon the Congress, while the Constitution certainly confers the whole of this class of powers upon the President and the Senate.

This was not, however, the point at issue in the Missouri question. That point was, whether, in the creation of new Commonwealths by Congress upon territory already within the Union, and subject to the exclusive jurisdiction of the general Government, Congress had the constitutional power to impose restrictions upon the new Commonwealths thus created, which the Constitution did not impose upon the original Commonwealths. The restrictionists, led by Mr. Tallmadge and Mr. Taylor, of New York, and Mr. Fuller, of Massachusetts, contended that Congress possessed this power. Their argument, reduced to a pair of propositions, was, that the Constitution did not *require* Congress to "admit new States into this Union," but only *empowered* Congress to do so at its discretion; that therefore Congress could *refuse* to admit at its discretion, and that if Congress could admit or refuse to admit at its own discretion, it could admit upon conditions, upon such conditions as it might deem wise to impose, and could make the continued existence of the new Commonwealth, as a Commonwealth, depend upon the continued observance by it of these conditions.

*[Sidenote: The exact question at issue in the first debate on the Missouri question.]*

They pointed to the precedents of Ohio, Indiana, and Illinois, upon all of which Congress had imposed, as a con-

# THE COMMONWEALTH OF MISSOURI

dition of their assumption of Commonwealth powers and government as "States of the Union," the requirement that their constitutions should not be repugnant to the "Ordinance of the Northwest Territory of 1787," the sixth article of which provided that there should be neither slavery nor involuntary servitude, except as a criminal penalty, in the Territory, from which these Commonwealths were carved out. They contended that Congress thus prohibited slavery in these new Commonwealths as the condition of its assent to their assumption of the status of Commonwealths of the Union and of their continued existence with that status. *The precedents cited in support of the Tallmadge amendment.*

They further pointed to the precedent of Louisiana, upon whose "admission into the Union as a State," Congress imposed the conditions that the new Commonwealth should use the English language as its official language, should guarantee the writ of *habeas corpus* and trial by jury in all criminal cases, and should incorporate in its organic law the fundamental principles of civil and religious liberty.

They went so far as to assert that the Constitution not only permitted Congress to lay the prohibition of slavery upon every new Commonwealth which it might "admit into the Union," but obligated Congress to do so by the constitutional provision which makes it the duty of the United States Government to guarantee a republican form of government to every Commonwealth of the Union. That is, they claimed that slavery was incompatible with the republican form of government, and that Congress was therefore bound by the Constitution to prohibit slavery whenever called upon to act in regard to it. *Argument for the amendment from the duty of the United States to guarantee a republican form of government to every Commonwealth.*

Having thus, from their point of view, vindicated the

constitutional power and duty of Congress to enact the restriction, they claimed the personal liberty of every human being to be a self-evident principle of ethics, specifically recognized in the Declaration of Independence, and therefore a principle of the political system of the United States. And, finally, they demonstrated the ruinous policy of the system of slave labor in the economy of the country.

*Argument from morals and policy.*

There is no question that Mr. Tallmadge and his friends had taken strong ground, and that it would require extraordinary efforts to dislodge them.

During the first debate upon the subject, the opponents of the restriction do not seem to have been so clear in their own minds in reference to the principles involved as they became later, and their arguments do not appear so convincing. Nevertheless, they touched the point which was the real gist of the contention, and dealt with it ably from the first. Mr. Scott, the delegate from Missouri Territory, and Mr. P. P. Barbour, of Virginia, made a vigorous attack upon the claim of a power in Congress to enact the restriction, as a condition of admitting Missouri, "as a State," into the Union. They demonstrated quite clearly that the interpretation which the restrictionists placed upon the constitutional provision empowering Congress "to admit new States into the Union" would enable Congress to establish inequalities *ad libitum* between the original Commonwealths and the new ones; would, in principle, enable Congress to make mere provinces of the new Commonwealths. They showed conclusively that the real question of the controversy was not whether slavery should exist in Missouri or not, but was whether the Commonwealth of Missouri should be allowed to determine that matter for herself or should have it determined for her by the Con-

*Replies to the arguments of the restrictionists.*

gress of the United States. They pointed to the facts that the original Commonwealths exercised, before the formation of the existing Constitution of the United States, exclusive power over this matter, each for itself; that the Constitution had not withdrawn this power from them, nor prohibited it to them; and that the Constitution declared all powers not delegated to the United States Government, nor prohibited to the "States," to be reserved to the "States" respectively or to the people. They, therefore, claimed that the determination of the question whether slavery should exist in any Commonwealth or not was a power reserved by the Constitution to each Commonwealth for itself, and that the attempt to introduce a distinction between the old Commonwealths and the new, in regard to the possession of this power, was an attack upon the first principle of federal liberty, the principle of equality in powers and duties between the members of the Union, an attack which could be justified legally only by an express warrant from the Constitution itself.

They disputed outright the constitutionality of the restrictions in regard to slavery which Congress had imposed upon the Commonwealths of Ohio, Indiana, and Illinois, and held that these Commonwealths might, at any time, so amend their organic law as to introduce slavery; and they justified the restrictions imposed upon Louisiana as having express warrant from the Constitution.

They did not deny the claims of the restrictionists that slavery was ethically wrong and economically destructive, but they contended that the evil and the impolicy of it would be mitigated by allowing the slaves to be spread over a larger extent of territory, reducing thus their numerical ratio to the white population in the older Commonwealths, and enabling their masters to emigrate with them from poor and exhausted lands to rich virgin soil, instead of being obliged to keep them in want, or sell them to new and, therefore, less considerate masters. They argued, upon this point, that all importation of slaves from foreign countries having been strictly prohibited, not one slave could be added to the number already existing by allowing their movement into new territory, but that their condition would be vastly improved by the increased products of their labor.

They contended, finally, that the treaty with France by which Louisiana was ceded to the United States contained an express provision pledging the United States Government to protect all the existing property rights of the inhabitants of the province, and to admit these inhabitants, so soon as consistent with the principles of the Constitution of the United States, to the enjoyment of Commonwealth powers on an equality with those of the other Commonwealths of the Union.

*The pledge to maintain slave property in Louisiana in the Treaty of cession.*

There is no question that hostility to slavery colored the views of the restrictionists in regard to the constitutional powers of Congress, and there is also no question that the anxiety of the slaveholders to maintain the security of their property led them to exaggerate all of the defences of the Constitution in its behalf. It must, however, be conceded that the opponents of the restriction had, from the outset, the better of the argument in the question of constitutional law, and maintained it throughout the debate. They did not express themselves as clearly and as exactly as the political scientist of this age would do, but they demonstrated quite convincingly that the questions of political ethics and public policy were, at the moment, entirely impertinent, unless it could be satisfactorily established that Congress possessed the constitutional power to act in the premises. And they showed that no federal system of government could exist, as to the new Commonwealths, if Congress had the unlimited authority to distribute powers between the general Government and these Commonwealths, which the interpretation that the restrictionists placed upon the clause of the Constitution vesting Congress with the authority to "admit new States into this Union" involved.

The ethical and economical influences and considerations weighed more heavily in the minds of the Northern members than the arguments from constitutional law, although they asserted that the Constitution also was upon their side.

They carried the first part of Mr. Tallmadge's amendment, the prohibition upon the further introduction of slavery into Missouri, by a majority of eleven votes, and the second part, the provision for the emancipation of all slaves born in Missouri, after its admission as a Commonwealth, when they should have reached the age of twenty-five years, by a majority of four votes. *Passage of the Tallmadge amendment by the House of Representatives.*

The leading men from the North who voted against the amendment were Parrot, of New Hampshire, Holmes, Mason, and Shaw, of Massachusetts, Storrs, of New York, Bloomfield, of New Jersey, Harrison, of Ohio, and McLean, of Illinois. They were strong and fearless men and no friends to slavery, but they were good constitutional lawyers, and they felt that it was better to stand by the Constitution with slavery than to expose it to the strain of exaggerated interpretations.

It was upon February 17th, 1819, that the Missouri bill was finally passed by the House and sent to the Senate. It was immediately read twice in the Senate and referred to the committee in charge of the bill for admitting Alabama. *The Missouri bill in the Senate.*

On the 22nd, Mr. Tait, of Georgia, in behalf of the committee, reported the bill to the Senate, with the recommendation that the Tallmadge amendment be stricken out.

The annals of Congress state that "a long and animated debate" took place, upon this recommendation, but the speeches are not reported. It may be safely concluded, however, that the argument against the power of Congress to pass the amendment prevailed very decidedly in the minds of the members of this more calm and judicial body. They voted, twenty-two to sixteen, against the first part of the amendment, and thirty-one to seven against the second part. Such men as Otis, of Massachusetts, and Lacock, of Pennsylvania, voted against the entire amendment, and Daggett, of Connecticut, and even Rufus King, of New York, recorded their voices against the second part of it.

The bill admitting Missouri, without the Tallmadge amendment, passed the Senate on March 2nd, and was returned to the House substantially in this form. The House immediately refused to agree to the striking out of the amendment, and the Senate resolved thereupon to adhere to its own act. The bill was thus lost for the session, and the Missouri question became the firebrand with which to light up fanatical and incendiary passions, both at the North and at the South, during the following recess of the Congress.

*Passage of the original bill by the Senate.*

At the beginning of the session of 1819–20, Mr. Scott secured the reference of the memorials concerning the admission of Missouri, presented at the preceding session, to a select committee. On the following day, December 9th, Mr. Scott reported a bill from this committee, which authorized the inhabitants of that part of Missouri Territory already described to form a constitution and Commonwealth

*The Missouri bill during the session of 1819–20.*

government. This new bill was read twice and referred to the committee of the Whole House for discussion.

Warned by the experiences of the preceding session, the restrictionists now took another tack. They developed the plan of delaying the formation of any more Commonwealths in the Missouri Territory until Congress could abolish slavery in the whole of it. *The policy of the restrictionists to delay the admission of any new Commonwealths.*

During the debate of the preceding session upon the power of Congress to impose upon new Commonwealths, at the time of their creation, limitations not prescribed by the Constitution, it had been asserted by the restrictionists, and not denied by their opponents, that Congress could control the status of the Territories, and keep slavery out of them or abolish it in them, at its own discretion, during the period before the Territories should be permitted to assume Commonwealth government. This seems to have been considered by nearly all, if not quite all, as a fair interpretation of that provision of the Constitution which vests in Congress the power to make all needful rules and regulations respecting the Territories of the United States. The friends of slavery restriction now determined to take advantage of this possibility, even at this late day, and go back to the work of clearing all the Territories west of the Mississippi of slavery by a Congressional Act; after which the formation of new Commonwealths in these Territories might be delayed until they could be settled by a population, which would, by local law, maintain the free status. Mr. John W. Taylor, of New York, seems to have formulated the plan. On the 14th of December he moved the appointment of a committee to consider the question of prohibiting the further introduction of slavery into the Territories of the United States west of the Mississippi. The proposition was voted, and Mr. Taylor himself was appointed the chairman of the committee. Mr. Taylor then moved that the consideration of the Missouri bill be postponed to the first Monday of the following February. The friends of this bill objected most strenuously to this proposition, and Mr. Taylor's party compromised with them by agreeing to shorten the period of the proposed postponement to the second Monday of January.

Mr. Taylor's plan was moderate in its character. He did not propose to emancipate slaves already held with-

*Mr. Taylor's proposition.* in these Territories or their issue born therein, but simply to prevent any further increase by immigration or importation. It is difficult to see how the slaveholders themselves could have opposed this proposition with much vigor. They had, nearly all of them, professed to regard slavery as an evil, though they had suggested that the evil would be mitigated by the spreading of the slaves over more territory  It was at any rate to be expected that those Representatives and Senators from the North, who had voted against the Tallmadge amendment from legal scruples only, would join with the restrictionists in the support of Mr. Taylor's measure, since they all regarded slavery restriction as sound policy wherever the Constitution would permit it. There certainly seemed to be a fair chance for the passage of a law which would protect the Territories from, at least, any considerable increase of the slave population which might already be within them, and give white immigration a chance to occupy and fill them, and form free Commonwealths in them. But this passing hope was dashed by a conjunction of events, the elements of which had already presented themselves.

The people resident in that part of Massachusetts known as the district of Maine had, through delegates in convention assembled, framed a Commonwealth constitution and government. The assent of Massachusetts had been regularly given to the division of the old Commonwealth. And on December 8th, 1819, Mr. Holmes, of Massachusetts, presented to the House of Representatives a petition from the constitutional convention in the district of Maine, praying for the admission of Maine, as a Commonwealth, into the Union, on an equality with the Commonwealths already existing. The people of this district had not asked the permission of Congress to form a constitution and government, for the reason afterwards alleged that they were already in the enjoyment of this status as a part of Massachusetts. The reason offered was not, however, entirely satisfactory, and the people of the district were hardly able to clear themselves from the charge of an undue assumption of powers. The petition was, however, immediately referred to a committee, with Mr. Holmes as chairman. On the 21st, Mr. Holmes reported a bill to the House providing for the admission of the district as a Commonwealth. On the 30th, the House, in committee of the Whole, took up the bill for consideration, and in the course of the debate upon it Mr. Clay suggested the connection of the Missouri bill with the Maine bill. Mr. Clay did not, however, put his suggestion into the form of a motion, and therefore the House came to no vote upon the point at this juncture. The bill for the admission of Maine was passed on January 3rd, 1820, without any connection with the Missouri bill, and without any restrictions or limitations upon the powers of the new Commonwealth beyond what the Constitution of the United States placed upon those of the original Commonwealths. Mr. Clay's suggestion was not, however, lost upon the Senate, as will be seen later.

*The petition from the convention in Maine for the admission of Maine.*

*The bill for the admission of Maine reported and passed by the House of Representatives.*

Meanwhile Mr. Taylor's committee had not been able to come to any agreement. On December 28th, 1819, before the final passage of the Maine bill, Mr. Taylor stated to the House that the committee had instructed him to ask for its discharge. The House agreed to his request, and he immediately moved that a new committee be appointed, and "instructed to report a bill" prohibiting the further admission of slaves into the Territories of the United States west of the Mississippi River. This motion evidently appeared to the House to be a prejudgment of the whole question, since it postponed the consideration of it indefinitely.

*The failure of Mr. Taylor's plan for preventing slavery extension.*

The Missouri bill was, however, also allowed to rest until January 24th, 1820, and when, upon that day, the Speaker announced the bill as the first order, Mr. Taylor moved for another week's delay, and the motion was lost by only a single vote. On the next day the House, in committee of the Whole, proceeded to consider the bill. On the 26th, Mr. Storrs, of New York, undertook to connect the prohibition of slavery in the region north of the thirty-eighth parallel of latitude and west of the Mississippi River and the proposed Missouri boundary with the grant of the permission to form a Commonwealth in Missouri. The opponents of slavery extension did not, however, regard this as sufficient compensation for their support of the bill, and Mr. Storrs' motion was lost.

*The Missouri bill again before the House of Representatives.*

Whereupon Mr. Taylor moved that the people of Missouri should be required to ordain and establish in their constitution the prohibition of slavery and involuntary servitude, except as a punishment for crime, in the proposed Commonwealth. Conceding, as the result of the discussions, and

*Mr. Taylor's amendment to the bill.*

the action of the Congress during the preceding session, that Congress had no constitutional authority to impose restrictions upon new Commonwealths, as the condition of their admission into the Union, which the Constitution did not impose upon the original Commonwealths, the new question involved in Mr. Taylor's motion, from the point of view of constitutional law, now was, whether Congress could require of a new Commonwealth, as the condition of its admission to the Union, that it should impose any limitations upon itself which the Constitution of the United States did not impose upon the original Commonwealths. Could Congress effect indirectly what it could not do directly?

Mr. Taylor's argument rested substantially upon the proposition, upheld by the restrictionists during the preceding session, that if Congress could admit, it could refuse to admit, and if it could admit or refuse to admit, it could admit upon conditions. *Mr. Taylor's argument in support of his amendment.* He, however, advanced other propositions and suggestions. He held that the admission of a new Commonwealth into the Union was a procedure in the nature of a contract between the United States Government and the people of the new Commonwealth, and, therefore, admitted of any terms accepted by both parties. He further held that the provision of the Constitution, which impliedly vested in Congress the power to prohibit, after 1808, the importation or migration of slaves, covered the case, in that the word migration meant passage from one Commonwealth into another, in distinction from importation, which meant the bringing of slaves into the United States from foreign countries. And he suggested that territory acquired by the United States subsequent to the formation of the Constitution need not be treated with the same consideration, as to the rights of its inhabitants, as that which belonged to the United States at the time of the formation of the Constitution.

Of course the members from the South resisted Mr. Taylor's conclusions. But they were not alone in their position. Some of the strongest opponents of slavery from the North stood up with them in resisting what they considered to be an attack upon the principle of federal government. Mr. Holmes, of Massachusetts, was again chief among them, and it is to his argument that one must look for the most scientific and unprejudiced view of the subject.

*Replies to Mr. Taylor's reasoning.*

After demonstrating most convincingly that the clauses of the Constitution which vested in Congress the power to prohibit the migration of persons into the United States after 1808 and to regulate commerce between the Commonwealths could not be interpreted as giving Congress the power to prevent the transportation of slaves from one Commonwealth into another, Mr. Holmes attacked the fundamental proposition upon which Mr. Taylor relied, the proposition that if Congress could admit, it could refuse to admit, and if it could admit or refuse to admit at pleasure, it could admit upon conditions. Mr. Holmes contended that the power to determine whether slavery should exist or not in any community was possessed by each Colony before the Revolution, and by each "State" after the Revolution, and that the Constitution of 1787 had not deprived the "States" of it, but had recognized it as belonging to each of them exclusively; that new "States" admitted by Congress into the Union must have all the rights, and be subject to all the duties, which the original "States" possessed, on the one side, and were obligated to discharge, on the other; that Congress could not increase the powers of the general

*Mr. Holmes' argument against the amendment.*

Government within the new Commonwealths by selling the Territories a license to the Commonwealth status, and taking the pay for it in powers to be exercised by the general Government in the new Commonwealths, which that Government could not, by the Constitution, exercise within the original Commonwealths; and that if Congress assumed to exercise such power, and the people of the Territory seeking the Commonwealth status should even accept the imposed condition, the new Commonwealth had the right and the power to free itself from the condition, and the Congress was powerless to prevent it.

Mr. McLane, of Delaware, a Commonwealth whose legislature had instructed the representatives from the Commonwealth in Congress to support all measures for preventing the spread of slavery in the Territories of the Union west of the Mississippi, presented the question with even greater clearness and conciseness. *Mr. McLane's argument against the amendment.* He simply analyzed the words of the Constitution which make up the clause conferring power on Congress "to admit new States into this Union." He said that the power to admit was not the power to create; that the very use of the word presupposed that the power to create the "State" resided elsewhere than in Congress; that Congress must admit a "*State*," not a Territory or a province or anything but a "*State;*" that a "State," in the system of federal government of the United States, was an organization whose powers and duties had been determined by the Constitution of the United States itself, and could not be altered by Congressional definitions and limitations; that Congress must admit the "State" into *this Union,* not into some other union; and that *this Union* was a system of federal government, in which the relations between the general Government and the "States" had been fixed by the Constitution of the United States, and could not be altered by a mere Congressional act. This was strong reasoning, and it had a powerful effect upon the minds of all who heard it and of all who read it.

Meanwhile events were occurring in the Senate which were to exercise a controlling influence over the fate of the bill in the House. On December 29th, 1819, a memorial from the Territorial legislature of Missouri, praying for the admission of that part of the Territory already described in the memorial to the House, had been presented in the Senate, and referred to the Judiciary committee. On January 3rd, 1820, the House bill admitting Maine was sent into the Senate. Mr. James Barbour, of Virginia, immediately gave notice of his intention to move the connection of the two subjects in the same bill, and on the same terms. As we have seen, Mr. Clay had already made this suggestion in the House, but had not formally proposed it.

*The independent Missouri bill of the Senate.*

The House bill admitting Maine was immediately referred to the Judiciary committee, which committee already had the Missouri bill in its charge, and on January 6th, Mr. Smith, of South Carolina, the chairman of this committee, reported from it to the Senate the House bill admitting Maine, with an amendment authorizing the people of Missouri, within the general geographical boundaries already described, to form a constitution and Commonwealth government. The amendment contained no restrictions or conditions with regard to slavery.

*The connection of the House bill admitting Maine with the Senate's bill admitting Missouri.*

On January 13th, the day fixed for considering the report of the committee, Mr. Roberts, of Pennsylvania, moved the recommitment of the Maine bill to the Judi-

## THE COMMONWEALTH OF MISSOURI 83

ciary committee, with the instruction that the bill should be divested of the amendment in regard to Missouri. The vote upon this motion would, therefore, reveal the attitude of the Senate upon the question of tacking the two subjects together. Such men as Mr. Roberts, Mr. Mellen, Mr. Burrill, and Mr. Otis argued that they should be disconnected, on the ground of the discordance of the two provisions. The people of Maine, they said, had already formed their constitution and government, and were simply asking for admission, while the Missouri bill was a measure for enabling the people of a part of the Missouri Territory to form a constitution and government, under which they might be admitted later, provided that constitution should prove satisfactory to Congress.

On the other hand, such men as Mr. Barbour, Mr. Smith, and Mr. Macon contended that the two subjects were entirely germane, and that any contrary appearance was caused by the unwarranted action of the people of Maine in proceeding so far as they had done without asking the consent of Congress, for which wrongful procedure presumptuous Maine should not be rewarded and respectful Missouri punished.

On the 14th, the vote was taken upon the motion to recommit, and it was lost by a majority of seven votes in forty-three. A number of the Senators from the Northern Commonwealths voted with the Southerners in refusing to separate the two subjects. *The refusal of the Senate to disconnect the two measures.*

The question then came upon the contents of the bill as reported by the Judiciary committee. Mr. Roberts immediately moved to amend the bill by a provision prohibiting the further introduction of slavery into Missouri. The arguments upon this motion were substantially a repetition of what had already been said upon the subject in the House of Representatives. The amendment was voted down, on February 1st, by a large majority.

On the 3rd, Mr. Thomas, of Illinois, offered an amendment, which was destined to play a very impor-
Mr. Thomas' amendment to the joint measure.
tant part in the further development of the subject. It was the proposition to exclude slavery from the Louisiana territory above thirty-six degrees and thirty minutes, except within the limits of the proposed Commonwealth of Missouri. The Senate was not yet prepared, however, to consider this, the question before it, at the moment, being the question of procedure, the question whether the two subjects should be united in one bill. The Senate had only voted not to recommit the bill to the Judiciary committee with instructions, and it was thought necessary to take a formal vote upon the question of the connection of the two subjects as proposed by the committee before considering any further amendments to it. Mr. Thomas, therefore, withdrew his motion for the moment.

It was at this stage of the proceedings, when apparently there was nothing before the Senate but the
Mr. Pinkney's great argument against the power of Congress to lay restrictions on new Commonwealths not imposed by the Constitution on the original Commonwealths.
question of the union of the two subjects, that Mr. Pinkney of Maryland made his brilliant and unanswerable argument upon the question of the powers of Congress in the premises. It differed logically very little from Mr. McLane's powerful analysis of the subject in the House, but it was elaborated and embellished as only Mr. Pinkney's beautiful diction could do it. The gist of the reasoning was, however, contained in a few sentences which ran as follows: "What, then, is the professed result? To admit a State into this Union. What is this Union? A confederation of States, equal

in sovereignty, capable of everything which the Constitution does not forbid, or authorize Congress to forbid. It is an equal union between parties equally sovereign. They were sovereign, independent of the Union. The object of the Union was common protection for the exercise of already existing sovereignty. The parties gave up a portion of that sovereignty to insure the remainder. As far as they gave it up by the common compact, they have ceased to be sovereign. The Union provides the means for securing the residue; and it is into *that* Union that a new State is to come. By acceding to it, the new State is placed on the same footing with the original States. It accedes for the same purpose, that is, protection for its unsurrendered sovereignty. If it comes in shorn of its beams, crippled and disparaged beyond the original States, it is not into the original Union that it comes. For it is a different sort of Union. The first was a Union *inter pares*. This is a Union *inter disparates*, between giants and a dwarf, between power and feebleness, between full proportioned sovereignties and a miserable image of power—a thing which that very Union has shrunk and shrivelled from its just size instead of preserving it in its true dimensions. It is into *this* Union, that is the Union of the Federal Constitution, that you are to admit or refuse to admit. You can admit into no other. You cannot make the Union, as to the new States, what it is not as to the old; for then it is not *this* Union that you open for the entrance of a new party. If you make it enter into a new and additional compact is it any longer the same Union ? . . . But it is a State which you are to admit. What is a *State* in the sense of the Constitution ? It is not a State in general, but a State as you find it in the Constitution. . . . Ask the Constitution. It shows you what it means by a State by reference to the parties to it. It must be such a State as Massachusetts, Virginia, and the other members of the American Confederacy— a State with full sovereignty except as the Constitution restricts it. The whole amount of the argument on the other side is, that you may refuse to admit a new State, and that, therefore, if you admit, you may prescribe the terms. The answer to that argument is, that even if you can refuse, you can prescribe no terms which are inconsistent with the act you are to do. You can prescribe no conditions which, if carried into effect, would make the new State less a sovereign State than, under the Union as it stands, it would be. You can prescribe no terms which will make the compact of Union between it and the original States essentially different from that compact among the original States. You may admit or refuse to admit, but if you admit, you must admit a State in the sense of the Constitution—a State with all such sovereignty as belongs to the original parties; and it must be into *this* Union that you are to admit it, not into a Union of your own dictating, formed out of the existing Union by qualifications and new compacts, altering its character and effect, and making it fall short of its protecting energy in reference to the new State, whilst it requires an energy of another sort—the energy of restraint and destruction."

This is the old-fashioned political and rhetorical way of saying what the modern publicist would state in such language as this: In a federal system of government, all powers are distributed by the state, the nation, the ultimate sovereignty, through the Constitution, between the central Government and the Commonwealths. The assumption by the central Government of the authority to redistribute these powers in a different manner, in any given case, is an assumption of sovereignty, the Constitution-making power, and the possession of any such power by the central Government makes a federal system of government impossible. It makes the Commonwealths only creatures and agencies of the central Government. It changes the whole system from federal government to centralized government. In the federal system of government as it existed, in 1820, in the United States, the determination of the question whether slavery should exist or not in any Commonwealth was reserved through the Constitution to each Commonwealth for itself, since this power was neither vested in the central Government nor denied to the Commonwealths. If Congress could assume this power, it could assume any and every other power and right which the Commonwealths possessed. Such authority in the central Government would destroy in principle the federal system, at once, and make the government a centralized form.

There was nobody in the Senate who did, or could, answer this argument. The amendments proposed after this to the bill as reported from the Judiciary committee contained no further restrictions upon the Commonwealth powers of Missouri, but had reference only to what remained of the Louisiana territory north and west of the boundaries of the proposed Commonwealth. *Pinkney's argument successful.*

The formal vote connecting the two subjects of Maine and Missouri was taken in the Senate on February 16th, and after this was resolved upon, Mr. Thomas immediately renewed his motion to amend the bill by the addition of a clause prohibiting slavery in the Louisiana territory above thirty-six degrees and thirty minutes, outside of the boundaries of the proposed Commonwealth of Missouri. After an attempt, on the *The adoption of Mr. Thomas' amendment by the Senate, and the passage of the Maine-Missouri bill thus amended.*

one side, to carry this line up to the fortieth parallel, and a counter attempt on the other to make the prohibition extend to all the territory west of the Mississippi, except that already under Commonwealth government, or in process of being put under Commonwealth government by the existing bill—the result of which would have been the prohibition of slavery in the just organized Territory of Arkansas—Mr. Thomas' amendment was adopted as the fair compromise. The bill, as thus amended, passed the Senate on February 18th, 1820, and was sent immediately to the House of Representatives.

The form of the bill was now the House bill in regard to Maine, with the Missouri bill and the Thomas proposition attached to it as amendments. The House voted to disagree to these amendments, and sent the bill, stripped of them, back to the Senate. The Senate voted immediately to insist upon its amendments, and the House answered with a vote insisting upon its position. Thereupon, the Senate requested a conference with the House upon the subject, and appointed Mr. Pinkney, Mr. Barbour, and Mr. Thomas as its representatives. The House acceded to the request and appointed Mr. Holmes, Mr. Taylor, Mr. Lowndes, Mr. Parker, and Mr. Kinsey as its representatives. These gentlemen met and agreed without much difficulty to the following points: That the Senate should withdraw its amendments to the House bill for the admission of Maine; that both the Senate and the House should pass the Missouri bill, without the condition in reference to the restriction of slavery in the proposed Commonwealth; and that both the Senate and the House should add a provision to the Missouri bill prohibiting slavery in the remainder of the Louisiana territory north of thirty-six degrees and thirty minutes. That is, the House should gain its point of order in the separation of the two subjects; the Senate should gain its point of constitutional law in defending the new Commonwealth against restrictions not imposed by the Constitution upon the original Commonwealths; and the two should compromise upon a fair division of the remaining parts of the Louisiana territory between the interests of the North and those of the South. The Senate accepted the recommendations of the committee without much difficulty, and voted the measures contained in them. The House also accepted the recommendations and voted the necessary provisions upon its part.

When the measures were placed before President Monroe for his approval, he called a meeting of the Cabinet to consider the subject. There was no difficulty except upon a single point, the prohibition of slavery in the remainder of the Louisiana territory above thirty-six degrees and thirty minutes north latitude. *President Monroe's approval of the Compromise.* Was this to be taken as prohibiting slavery in the Commonwealths which might be formed upon this territory in the future, or did the Congress only intend to lay this restriction upon this territory merely for the period during which it might continue subject to the exclusive jurisdiction of the general Government, the period of Territorial organization? If the former, the Missouri question would have to be fought over again whenever a new Commonwealth should be formed in this territory. The Cabinet interpreted the prohibition as applying only during the period before the Commonwealth organization should be established, and upon the basis of this interpretation advised the President that the measure was constitutional. The President signed the Maine bill on the 3rd of March and the Missouri bill on the 6th (1820).

So far as the questions of constitutional and parliamentary law were concerned, the settlement reached was in accordance with right principles. It was right that the two subjects, which the Senate united in one bill, should be separated. The only justification for this act of the Senate was the manifest determination on the part of the House to impose an unconstitutional restriction as the condition upon which the people of Missouri should be allowed to assume the status and the powers of a Commonwealth of the Union. It was the only weapon left to the more conservative Senate, by which to defend the Constitution against the rashness of the more radical House. It need astonish no impartial student of our history that the Senate used it. No such momentous question was involved in this point of parliamentary procedure as there was in the exaggerated interpretation of the powers of Congress by the House. The Senate showed its willingness to yield its position upon this point so soon as the House would return to sound constitutional principle in the Missouri question. It was fortunate for the development of the parliamentary practice of Congress that the House so changed its position in reference to the greater question of constitutional law as to enable the Senate to return to the true parliamentary principle of the separation of subjects which differ in essence or in circumstances in the slightest degree. While, therefore, the Senate should not be too strongly criticised for using its power over its own rules of procedure, as a means of retaliation, it is a matter of great satisfaction that expedients were at last found for maintaining right principle and sound parliamentary custom in the case. And it was surely right that the attempt to make Congress the distributor of powers between the general Government and the Commonwealths

*Review of the points involved in the contest.*

was abandoned. The power which *made* the Constitution can alone set up the metes and bounds between the realm of authority of the general Government and that of the Commonwealths. This is the indispensable condition of federal government. If the general Government possesses such power, the system is centralized in theory, and may become so in fact at the pleasure of the general Government. If, on the other hand, the Commonwealths possess such power, the system is the loosest form of confederation, an international league.

It is true that the Constitution may authorize the general Government to limit the powers of the Commonwealths in regard to certain specified points and the federal system be still preserved, but a general authority in the general Government to do so, such as was claimed by the restrictionists from the vague provision vesting in Congress the power to "admit new States into this Union," amounts to nothing less than a claim of sovereignty by Congress over the new Commonwealths. Such was not the system which those who framed and ratified the Constitution intended to establish. Such is not the system which comports with the vast territorial extent and the climatic differences of the United States, and with the ethnical variety of the population of the country.

It is also true that those who resisted the restriction upon Missouri used terms and propositions, in reference to the genesis of the Union and the relation of the general Government to the Commonwealths, which will hardly bear the test of correct history and exact political science, but they had the true principle in respect to the point at issue, when they held that "the State," in the sense of the Constitution, is defined in the Constitution; that its powers are the residue after what the Constitution vests exclusively in the general Government and denies to the "States" shall have been subtracted from sovereignty; and that Congress cannot vary these relations under an interpretation of a general provision. They conceded that Congress might, as the general principle, admit or not admit, as it might judge proper, with all that this involved in reference to geographical boundaries and ripeness of the population for self-government, but they held that the thing admitted was created by the Constitution, through the people inhabiting the district to be formed into a Commonwealth, and not by Congress. And they repudiated the idea that the Declaration of Independence is any part of the constitutional law of the country, or that Congress can define the republican form of government which the United States is obligated by the Constitution to guarantee to every Commonwealth, in any other sense than that concretely expressed in the original Commonwealths.

They held this ground under enormous strain and pressure brought from without. Cross-roads assemblies, town and city meetings, and Commonwealth legislatures poured petitions and memorials in upon them in behalf of slavery restriction. The excitement, throughout the Northeast especially, was intense. They had to fight their battle under an ignoble issue. But it will not be denied by any impartial constitutional lawyer that they were, for this time, the upholders of the Constitution against an unwarranted attempt to stretch Congressional power.

Finally, the compromise provision, drawing the line of thirty-six degrees and thirty minutes through the Louisiana territory, and securing all north of it, which was by far the greater part, against the introduction of slavery during the period that it might remain under the exclusive jurisdiction of the general Government, was tantamount to a surrender, forever, of this vast domain to immigration from the North almost exclusively, and to the creation therein of new Commonwealths into which slaveholders could not take their slave property. Many American historians treat the express exclusion of slavery north of this line as no concession to the North, but as a mask under which the real concession, the concession to the South, was hidden. This they claim to have been the implied concession to hold slaves south of that line. But slavery was legal by custom in the whole of the province of Louisiana, when the United States received it from France. That is, a master might have taken slaves into any part of it, into which he might have gone himself, and would not thereby have violated any law, and the United States Government had not, down to 1820, changed this state of things by any act of its own.

The compromise upon the line of thirty-six degrees and thirty minutes was, therefore, a very decided limitation upon the existing rights of slave-masters. And even if slavery had not already penetrated into this region, it can hardly be claimed that the balance of advantage created by the compromise provision lay with the South, except upon the principle that the South ought not to have had anything, and the North ought to have had everything. Ethically, perhaps, this is the correct principle from which to judge the question, but politically and legally it was not, at that moment.

The Union consisted of Commonwealths, in all of which slavery existed at the time of and during the War for Independence, in almost all of which it existed when the Constitution of 1787 was framed and adopted, and in about half of which it existed, as the most important institution, at the period of the Missouri controversy. Further, it can hardly be denied that the Constitution contained recognition and guarantees of slave property.

The vague phrases of the Declaration of Independence, even if intended to touch the relation of master and slave within the country, were not law. It is true that slavery was regarded both in the North and in the South as an evil, but men differed in opinion as to whether confining the slaves to a particular section was a better means for its mitigation than spreading them over a larger area, and reducing thus their number relative to the white population in any particular section.

Surrounded in thought with the ideas and conditions of 1820, it is difficult to see why the balance of advantage contained in the compromise provision of the Missouri bill did not lie with the North. Compromise or no compromise about the remainder of the Louisiana territory, Missouri was bound to be admitted without restriction as to slavery. The customary law of the region seeking to become a Commonwealth permitted slaveholding. The population was sufficient to warrant the assumption of Commonwealth powers. The Constitution did not authorize Congress to impose the slavery restriction, and the people of the region had protested against it. The admission of Missouri was, therefore, no legitimate element in the compromise. Neither was the agreement on the part of the Senate to separate Maine from Missouri any proper element in the compromise. The restriction placed by the House on Missouri rested on a false interpretation of constitutional law, and the connection of the two subjects in the same bill rested on a false interpretation of parliamentary law. In principle both had to be abandoned. The compromise was in reality only about the remainder of the Louisiana territory after the admission of Missouri, in no part of which had slavery, to that moment, been prohibited. How much of it should continue open to the further introduction of slavery by the immigration of

THE COMMONWEALTH OF MISSOURI 95

masters with their slaves, and how much should be given over to practically exclusive immigration from the North —these were the only proper terms of the compromise. What the South finally obtained out of it was one Commonwealth, while the vast region from which slavery was excluded has produced eight or nine Commonwealths. In the light of these considerations it certainly appears that the cause of free labor won a substantial triumph in the Missouri compromise, and that, in place of that shameful surrender of freedom to slavery, so emphasized by certain historians, a mighty step forward in the progress of liberty was taken.

It was confidently hoped and believed that the compromise had solved the slavery problem, in so far as Congress could solve it. The whole country breathed more easily and the thoughts of men were turned to other subjects.

But the peace proved to be only an armistice. In less than twelve months the battle was raging again with more than its former fury. *The revival of the Missouri struggle.*

The Missouri convention, which drew up and voted, in the middle of the year 1820, the organic law for the new Commonwealth, inserted a paragraph therein which made it the duty of the legislature, proposed to be established by that law, to enact measures for preventing mulattoes and free negroes from immigrating into and settling within the Commonwealth.

On November 14th, 1820, this instrument was presented to the Senate of the United States, and on the 16th to the House of Representatives, for the purpose of moving these bodies to pass an act admitting Missouri into the Union as a Commonwealth. *The Missouri constitution in Congress.* The instrument was immediately referred by each House to a committee; and on the 23rd, Mr. Lowndes, the chairman of the House Committee, reported a bill for effecting this result, and, on the 29th, Mr. Smith reported a bill of like tenor to the Senate.

Mr. Lowndes' bill was prefaced by a statement of views, which presented the questions of constitutional interpretation to which the provision referred to in the Missouri instrument gave rise. He alluded to the possible repugnance of the provision to that clause in the Constitution of the United States which guarantees to the citizens of each Commonwealth all the privileges and immunities of citizens in every other Commonwealth; but said that the provision in the Missouri instrument could be interpreted to mean only such mulattoes and free negroes as were not citizens in any Commonwealth. And he held that, whether this be the true interpretation or not, the judiciary of the United States, and not the Congress, should determine the question of repugnance between the Missouri instrument and the Constitution of the United States. He finally took the ground that Missouri was now already a Commonwealth by virtue of the Act of Congress giving her people permission to form Commonwealth government, and by virtue of the act of her people in forming a Commonwealth constitution, and he declared that the refusal or failure of Congress, at this time, to pass a formal act of admission could not reduce her again to the Territorial status.

*Mr. Lowndes' bill for the admission of Missouri with the instrument unchanged.*

Mr. Sergeant, the spokesman of the opposition to Mr. Lowndes' report, met these propositions with the counter-propositions, that a Territory becomes a Commonwealth of the Union only by a Congressional Act admitting it to that status; that no other kind of a Commonwealth than a Commonwealth in the Union is known to the political

*Serious opposition to the Lowndes bill.*

system of the United States; that all the acts done by Congress and by the people resident within a Territory before the Congressional Act of admission are nothing more than preliminaries, and that a Territory remains a Territory until the passage of this latter act; that the provision in the Missouri instrument in regard to the exclusion of mulattoes and free negroes was repugnant to that clause in the Constitution of the United States which guarantees to the citizens of any Commonwealth the privileges and immunities of citizens in every other Commonwealth of the Union into which they may go; and that Congress, not the Judiciary, is the body which should determine whether such repugnance exists, and, if so, correct it.

There is no doubt that, from the point of view of a correct political logic, the opponents of Mr. Lowndes' propositions in regard to the making of a Commonwealth of the Union stood upon the firmer ground, despite the fact that the precedents did not sustain fully their claims. As a fact, Congress had been guilty of such irregularities in the admission of some of the Commonwealths as to give much support to the notion that there could be a Commonwealth in the political system of the United States before its formal admission into the Union. But the argument is unanswerable, that a Commonwealth not in the Union is a foreign state; that in order that a Territory shall attain this latter position and status its constitutional right to secede from the United States must be recognized, which is absurd; and that, therefore, the Congressional Act of admission is what makes a Territory of the Union into a Commonwealth of the Union, the only kind of a Commonwealth known to the political system of the United States.

They also stood upon the firmer ground in holding

that it is the duty of Congress to scrutinize closely the measures proposed for enactment by it from the point of view of their constitutionality, and to pass no act, of the constitutionality of which it is not reasonably convinced, under the pretext that the Judiciary is the proper body to correct the usurpation. The members of Congress take the same oath to uphold the Constitution as the judges do. The revisory powers of the Judiciary over the acts of Congress were not given in order to excuse the Congress from exercising its preliminary judgment upon the constitutionality of its own acts. They were given simply to correct errors in judgment.

On the other hand, when a citizen of one Commonwealth immigrated into and settled in another, it was a question whether he did not lose the right to be treated as a citizen in the latter Commonwealth, in so far as the Constitution of the United States, as it was in 1820, was concerned, and become subject to the laws of the latter Commonwealth as to his status. If he were only passing through, or sojourning temporarily in, the latter Commonwealth, it was clear that the Constitution of the United States protected him as a citizen of another Commonwealth, but when he changed his residence and citizenship to the latter Commonwealth, the question became much more complicated. It was now whether the laws of one Commonwealth were, by virtue of the Constitution of the United States, valid in another Commonwealth for the protection of persons against the laws of the latter Commonwealth, who had become citizens and residents of the latter Commonwealth.

*The protection of the rights of citizens of one Commonwealth within the territory of another by the United States.*

It must be remembered, however, that the immediate question involved in the provision of the Missouri instrument was whether a Commonwealth could prohibit the citizens of other Commonwealths from immigrating into, and gaining residence and citizenship within, itself. How it might treat such persons after these things had been accomplished was a subsequent matter. But even limiting the question to this point, it was certainly a startling thing to the Southerners to be told that, by virtue of the Constitution of the United States, a negro citizen of Massachusetts had the right to immigrate into, and become a citizen of, South Carolina, when the laws of South Carolina did not admit negroes to citizenship.

On December 13th (1820), after a long, earnest, and, at times, acrimonious debate, the Lowndes measure for the admission of Missouri was defeated by a vote of ninety-three to seventy-nine. *Defeat of the Lowndes bill in the House.*

The bill presented by Mr. Smith in the Senate was taken up for consideration on December 4th. The arguments pro and con were about the same as those offered in the House, but the bitterness of feeling which seemed to animate the members of the opposition to the measure in the House was not manifested by those adverse to it in the Senate. Nevertheless, there was a majority in the Senate against passing a simple measure for admission without any limitations. They finally voted the bill, with the proviso attached: "That nothing herein contained shall be so construed as to give the assent of Congress to any provision in the constitution of Missouri, if any such there be, which contravenes that clause in the Constitution of the United States which declares that 'the citizens of each State shall be entitled to all the privileges and immunities of citizens in the several States.'" *Passage of the Senate bill with a proviso by the Senate.*

The House tabled this bill on the same day that it rejected the measure offered by its own committee. But what now was the status of Missouri? Her people had elected a governor and members of the legislature under the organic law formed in July, and it was considered doubtful whether there still existed any Territorial officials exercising governmental powers. The House, however, would not even inquire into this fact. They said the question before them was one of law and not of fact at all.

*The Senate bill tabled by the House.*

After some futile attempts made by Mr. Eustis, of Massachusetts, for the admission of Missouri upon a future day, provided the obnoxious clause should be expunged from her organic law before that day, Mr. Clay came forward and assumed the management of the question.

*Mr. Clay and the second Missouri Compromise.*

On January 29th, 1821, he asked the House to go into committee of the Whole to consider the Senate bill admitting Missouri. This proposition was naturally agreed to, and, after several unsuccessful attempts made by others at an immediate amendment of the Senate bill in the committee of the Whole House, Mr. Clay moved the reference of the bill to a select committee of thirteen persons. This motion was passed, and the committee was chosen, with Mr. Clay as its chairman.

On February 10th, 1821, Mr. Clay reported the recommendations of the committee. They were expressed in the proposition: That Missouri should be "admitted into this Union on an equal footing with the original States, in all respects whatever, upon the fundamental condition that the said State shall never pass any law preventing any description of persons from coming to and settling in the said State, who may now be or hereafter become citizens of any of the States of this Union; *and provided also*, that the legislature of the said State, by a solemn public act, shall declare the assent of the said State to the said fundamental condition, and shall transmit to the President of the United States, on or before the fourth

THE COMMONWEALTH OF MISSOURI 101

Monday of November next, an authentic copy of the said act : upon the reception whereof, the President, by proclamation, shall announce the fact : whereupon, and without any further proceedings on the part of Congress, the admission of the said State shall be considered as complete : *and provided* further, that nothing herein contained shall be construed to take from the said State of Missouri, when admitted into this Union, the exercise of any right or power, which can now be constitutionally exercised by any of the original States."

Mr. Tomlinson, of the committee, took the floor against the report, and showed so conclusively that the legislature of a Commonwealth could not bind the makers of the organic law of the Commonwealth, and that, therefore, any obligation which the legislature of Missouri might assume toward Congress might prove nugatory, that the Senate bill, with the amendment offered by Mr. Clay's committee, was voted down. *The failure of Mr. Clay's first attempt.*

Mr. Clay waited ten days after this in order to let the feelings of the members become mollified, and on February 22nd, one of the most significant days in American history, made his final attempt to secure a compromise. He moved that members to a conference committee be appointed by the House. The motion was carried, and on the next day the members of the House contingent of the committee, consisting of twenty-three persons, under the lead of Mr. Clay, were appointed. The Senate met the advance promptly and appointed seven members to represent it. *Mr. Clay's second attempt to secure a Compromise.*

On the 26th, Mr. Clay reported the results of the conference, in the form of a resolution of the following tenor : " Resolved, by the Senate and House of Representatives of the United States, in Congress assembled, that Missouri shall be admitted into this Union on an equal footing with the original States in all respects whatever, upon the fundamental condition, that the fourth clause of the twenty-sixth section of the third article of the constitution submitted on the part of said State to Congress shall never be construed to authorize the passage of any law, and that no law shall be passed in conformity thereto, by which any citizen of either of the States of this Union shall be excluded from the enjoyment of any of the privileges and immunities to which such citizen is entitled under the Constitution of the United States: Provided that the legislature of the said State, by a solemn public act, shall declare the assent of the said State to the said fundamental condition, and shall transmit to the President of the United States, on or before the fourth Monday in November next, an authentic copy of the said act; upon the receipt whereof the President, by proclamation, shall announce the fact; whereupon, and without any further proceeding on the part of Congress, the admission of the said State into this Union shall be considered as complete."

*The second Missouri Compromise.*

It will be seen that this recommendation contained the same objectionable feature as did that of the committee of Thirteen of the House, that is, the proposition to rely upon the Missouri legislature to enter into an obligation to Congress, which should bind all future legislatures and also the constituent power of the Commonwealth. It was, therefore, attacked upon the same ground, but the supporters urged so strongly that Congress should put a reasonable faith in the honor of Missouri to keep the pledge made by her first legislature, that the resolution was finally adopted by the House, by a very small majority, on the same day that it was reported. It was immediately sent to the

*Passage of the second Missouri Compromise Act.*

# THE COMMONWEALTH OF MISSOURI

Senate for concurrence, and, after a brief debate, was voted by that body on the 28th, by a large majority.

The great struggle was at last over, and it was sincerely hoped that the "era of good feeling," so suddenly interrupted by it, had been restored. Apparently it was so, but while the decision finally reached saved the country from one great danger, it sowed the seeds of another. A brief review of the effects of that decision upon the constitutional law, political science, and social conditions of the Republic will make this apparent.

In the first place, the decision involved the constitutional and political principle that, in the federal system of government generally, and in the system of the United States in particular, the powers of government are, and must be, distributed by the sovereignty behind, and supreme over, both the general Government and the Commonwealths, and not by either of the two governments, unless expressly empowered to do so, in specific cases, by the sovereignty through the Constitution. This is undoubtedly a sound principle, both of political science and constitutional law, but it taught the Southerners that protection of their property in slaves would depend upon strict construction of the Constitution. It caused their leaders to desert the broad national ground in the interpretation of the Constitution which they had occupied since 1812, and to seek more and more to limit and restrict the powers of Congress, in which the majority of the members of one House, at least, must always come from the North, and in the other House of which no more than an exact balance could be maintained.

*The general effects of the decisions reached in the Missouri question.*

It introduced, therefore, the principle which led necessarily to a division of the all-comprehending Republican party into two branches, the one branch holding to the latitudinarian and national views of the party from 1812 to 1819, and the other to the earlier creed of 1798 to 1812. The former finally coalesced with the remnants of the Federal party and formed the National Republican or Whig party, while the latter called itself the Democratic party.

It is necessary to keep clearly in mind the cause of the division of the Republican party into its two branches in order to understand the principles which distinguished them, for their names are somewhat misleading. For example, it is quite difficult to understand, upon general principles, why the slaveholders of the South should be called Democrats, while many of the little farmers and the artisans of the North should be called Whigs. The element of democracy which was to be found in the political creed of the Southern masters was strict construction of governmental powers, the least possible interference of government in private affairs, and the largest possible individual autonomy—in a word, individual immunity against government. The master could take care of himself, if left free to rule his slaves.

In the second place, the Missouri decision involved the principle of constitutional law that the Congress has general powers of legislation in the Territories, and may do anything therein not forbidden by the Constitution. This is also a sound and valuable principle. It was this which won the great Northwest for free labor, so far as government could affect the question, and gave the Union the strength to meet the crisis of 1861–65. The Southerners eventually saw what they had lost in conceding this interpretation of the powers of Congress, and, as will be seen further on, sought to repudiate it; but their long acquiescence in it had allowed it to gain the power of constitutional precedent, too strong to be successfully overcome.

In the third place, the Missouri decision involved the principle that there was, before the Fourteenth Amendment was adopted, an United States citizenship which carried with it immunities and privileges which no Commonwealth could lawfully deny or abridge, and which the United States Government was bound to protect and defend against any Commonwealth seeking to impair them. It demonstrated the difficulties which could arise by allowing a Commonwealth to confer United States citizenship, and thereby bind the United States Government to sustain the acts of one Commonwealth within the jurisdiction of another Commonwealth, whose laws might be directly contradictory to those of the first Commonwealth upon the subject in point. It did not undertake to solve the difficulty. It only held firmly to the principle, while it made many of the best minds aware that this most national provision of the Constitution would, sooner or later, certainly require an advance all along the line in the further development of the governmental system of the country.

In the fourth place, the Missouri decision taught the inhabitants of the older Commonwealths that the West could not be held in a provincial or quasi-provincial status; that it must be carved up and formed into Commonwealths having the same powers and privileges as the older Commonwealths; and that, therefore, the political centre of the United States was bound to move westward, and the East was ultimately to come, in large degree, under the influence of the West. It was this which has helped powerfully to carry the brain and the money of the East to the West, and is making in the West a new, and, in some respects, more enterprising, East.

Finally, the Missouri decision taught the South that there was a provision in the Constitution of the United

States which probably made it possible for the Northern Commonwealths to force, through the power of the general Government, a class of persons upon the Southern Commonwealths, in the enjoyment of the full rights of citizenship, whom these Commonwealths did not and would not recognize as citizens in any respect; and that there was a growing disposition at the North to make an advance against slavery at every possible point. The effect of this conviction was most baleful both upon the spirit of the masters and the status of the slaves. It created that resentment in the minds of the Southerners against interference in their domestic affairs, which closed their ears to all arguments against slavery, and it moved them to the enactment of measures in their several Commonwealths for the purpose of keeping the slaves under stricter discipline and in denser ignorance. It increased vastly, if it did not introduce, that utter misunderstanding of each other's feelings and motives between the people of the two sections, which made it possible for the people of the North to believe, finally, that the story of "Uncle Tom's Cabin" was the sober truth, and the general rule of conduct of master toward slave in the South, and for the people of the South to believe that jealousy of riches and comfort was the sole spirit which prompted the attacks of the North upon slavery—a misunderstanding, therefore, which proved irreconcilable so long as the subject of it remained.

The Missouri decision made thus both for good and for evil—for good, surely, in that it produced clearer ideas upon the character of federal government, and preserved the East from an illiberal political policy toward the West; and in that it secured the great Northwest for free labor;—for evil, possibly, in that it estranged the two sections of the Union, and put a stop to any movement in the South for the gradual and peaceable emancipation of the slaves, or for the substantial amelioration of their condition. It is not very likely, however, that any such movement would have proved successful, and it is, therefore, probable that what appears on the outside to have been an evil was in reality a good, in that it drove the disease in the body politic of the South onward toward the crisis, which must be passed in order that the permanent cure might be effected.

## CHAPTER V.

### THE BEGINNING OF THE PARTICULARISTIC REACTION

Slavery and the Industrial Policies of the Union—President Monroe and Protection after 1820—The Committee on Manufactures—The Tariff Bill of 1823—The General Character of the Bill, and its Failure to Pass—President Monroe's Message of 1823, and Protection—The Tariff Bill of 1824—Mr. Clay's Argument in its Support—Mr. Clay's Argument Answered—The First Expression of the Doctrine that Protection and Slavery were Hostile Interests—The Bill Amended and Passed—The Tariff of 1824 not yet Considered Sectional Legislation—South Carolina and the Tariff of 1824—The Historical Development of the Doctrine of Internal Improvements—Madison's Ideas upon Internal Improvements—The Bill of 1822 for Internal Improvements—Passage of the Bill, and Analysis of the Vote upon it—The Bill in the Interests of the West—President Monroe's Veto, and Communication of May 4th, 1822—President Monroe's Argument, and the Vote upon the Veto—Congressional Act of 1824 for Distinguishing National from Local Improvements — Foreign Relations During Monroe's Second Term—Russia and the Northwest Coast of America—The Holy Alliance—The Congress at Verona — Mr. Adams' Declaration to Baron Tuyl—Mr. Canning's Proposal to Mr. Rush—Mr. Canning's Declaration to Prince Polignac—The "Monroe Doctrine"—The Meaning of the Monroe Propositions in 1824—Failure to Commit Congress to these Propositions—The Particularistic Reaction Scarcely Discoverable before 1824.

IT was hoped and believed that the settlement of the Missouri question and the compromise in reference to the remainder of the Louisiana cession had put the problem of negro slavery out of the realm of national politics. In fact, however, the struggle over these questions had introduced it into that realm, and had first opened the eyes of the slaveholders to the bearings of the slavery interest upon all the questions of constitutional law and public policy. From the point of view of that interest their attitude toward all these questions was more and more determined as they came to understand more and more clearly the relation of these questions to that interest. While, therefore, the settlement and the compromise served to withdraw the question of slavery from the direct and immediate issue, they, at the same time, left it the secret influence over views and actions in many, if not most, directions.

*Slavery and the industrial policies of the Union.*

At the next session, beginning in December of 1821, propositions were introduced into the Senate to limit and decrease the admiralty jurisdiction of the United States courts, to make the Senate itself a court of appeal from the regular Judiciary in cases where a "State" should be a party, and to limit to two hundred the number of members in the House of Representatives.

The purpose of all these projects is apparent. Indeed, their proposers said openly and frankly that their purpose was to lessen and limit the powers of the general Government in the interests of "States'-rights."

It was natural, however, that the new spirit of particularism should attack the policies of the Government rather than the structure of the political system, or, more correctly, should undertake to control these policies before it sought to transform that system.

We have seen with what unanimity and national enthusiasm the protection of home industries was regarded, in the half decade between 1815 and 1820, as a measure indispensable to the attainment and maintenance of industrial independence. Not even Calhoun then understood the relation between this policy and the interests of slavery. The Presidents, Madison and

Monroe, were utterly oblivious to it. Even after the Missouri struggle, Mr. Monroe continued to recommend the protection of manufactures for the attainment of industrial independence as the true national policy. His annual messages of 1821 and of 1822 contain this recommendation. He either did not comprehend the relation of the slavery interests to the protective system or disregarded it. It could hardly have been the latter, for, although he was no radical supporter of slavery, he was a slaveholder and a very conservative man.

*President Monroe and protection after 1820.*

The House of Representatives, the body which had upheld even radically national views of the character of the political system during the Missouri struggle, very naturally responded to Mr. Monroe's recommendation, and referred it to its committee on Manufactures for consideration and support. Heretofore this subject had been referred to the committee on Ways and Means, the regular revenue-raising committee. Its reference now to the committee on Manufactures is good evidence that the House of Representatives regarded a protective tariff as a subject which Congress might deal with independently, and without any necessary connection with the subject of the revenue. Such a view is radically national. It rests upon the doctrine that Congress may do anything in the regulation of foreign trade and commerce which, in its own opinion, is conducive to the general welfare, regardless of the pecuniary needs of the Government.

*The committee on Manufactures.*

On January 9th, 1823, Mr. Tod, of Pennsylvania, the chairman of the committee on Manufactures, reported a tariff bill. It proposed to nearly double the existing duty upon iron, quadruple that upon coarse woollens, and to increase the custom-house valuation of dyed cotton goods by some forty per centum.

*The Tariff Bill of 1823.*

# BEGINNING OF PARTICULARISTIC REACTION 111

Moreover, the bill made no provision for the future reduction of these duties. It therefore indicated that protection was to be the permanent policy, protection so high as to amount to the prohibition of the importation of coarse cottons and woollens and bar iron. In fact, Mr. Tod conceded that the prohibition of the importation of coarse woollens was intended. He said that the tariff of 1816 on coarse cotton goods had given a monopoly of the domestic markets for such goods to the home manufacturers, while the price of the goods had been reduced through home competition by one-half, and that his committee desired to bring about the same result in regard to the manufacture of coarse woollens.

Mr. Tod was not able to get a vote upon his bill at this session of the Congress. Three significant facts, however, were elicited in the course of the debate upon it, facts which indicated the trend of political history. These facts were that the bill was a Pennsylvania measure, *The general character of the bill, and its failure to pass.* that the South would oppose it, and that Massachusetts and New York City would unite with the South in this opposition. It was, in fact, a Massachusetts man, Mr. Gorham, who denounced the bill as sectional legislation, and advised the South to resist it to the utmost. Cotton and commerce, and that meant slavery and commerce, were beginning to discover their affinity.

President Monroe, however, does not seem to have shared this view of the subject. In his message of December 2nd, 1823, he again recommended additional protection to "those articles which we are prepared to manufacture, *President Monroe's Message of 1823 and protection.* or which are more immediately connected with the defence and independence of the country."

Thus encouraged by the President, the House of Representatives again referred the question of increasing the tariff to Mr. Tod's committee.

On January 9th, 1824, Mr. Tod brought in his new bill. It was a more moderate proposition than that of the preceding session; still it provided for a substantial increase of the duties on woollens and iron.

*The Tariff Bill of 1824.*

Mr. Tod assumed the constitutionality of the bill to be a settled question, and supported the policy of it by arguments from the necessity of attaining industrial independence in the manufacture of the necessaries of life, from the necessity of creating new and more remunerative employments for labor, and from the policy of developing better home markets for agricultural products. He predicted that an ultimate reduction of the prices of manufactured goods would be the result of the increased home competition produced by higher duties. He did not, however, make out any very satisfactory prospects for commerce. This branch of the national pursuits was to make the sacrifice.

Mr. Clay made the great argument in defence of the measure. He elaborated the patriotic reason in every direction. He pointed out the utter dependence of the country upon foreign markets, both for the sale of its agricultural products and for the purchase of manufactured goods. He demonstrated that these relations had been created by the quarter of a century of war in Europe, forcing the European countries to buy the agricultural products of the United States to an unusual amount, and at high prices, and showed how the restoration of general peace in Europe had reduced the demand for, and the price of, these products, while it left the United States dependent upon Europe for manufactured articles. And he urged the accomplishment of industrial independence

*Mr. Clay's argument in its support.*

as a necessary corollary of political independence. He contended that the aid granted to the manufacturing interests would impose no sacrifice upon the agricultural and commercial interests; that by the establishment of new manufacturing centres new home markets for the products of agriculture would be created, which would not only emancipate the country from the necessity of foreign markets for these products, but would give the country steady and certain markets, under its own control; and that the growth of manufactures would speedily result in the establishment of an export trade in manufactured goods to all parts of the world, and especially to South America, which would ultimately more than compensate the commercial interests for the temporary losses they might incur by reason of the increased duties. This was a strongly tinted picture upon both sides. It represented the distress of the country too darkly, and it painted the speculative benefits of the high tariff in too vivid colors. Moreover, Mr. Clay now omitted any reference to the temporary character of protection. It now appeared to be a permanent article of his creed.

Webster for Massachusetts, Cambreleng for the city of New York, and Barbour for the South, denied Mr. Clay's statement in regard to the intense and general financial distress throughout the country, and demonstrated the destructive effects of a high tariff upon agriculture and commerce, and upon the existing manufacturing interests themselves. They contended that such a tariff would so prohibit importation of foreign products as to make it impossible for Europe to buy the agricultural products of the United States, since Europe would not be able to pay for them; that the promised increase of domestic markets would not at all compensate for the loss of

*Mr. Clay's argument answered.*

foreign markets; that commerce would thus be destroyed both ways; and that even the manufacturing industries already established would suffer from the unnatural competition which would be created by the inducements which the high tariff would hold out to capital otherwise employed. Mr. Barbour frankly declared that the slave labor of the South could not be used in the development of manufactures, and that, therefore, the high tariff must inure to the benefit of the North, by making the South tributary to the North for all manufactured goods.

*The first expression of the doctrine that protection and slavery were hostile interests.*

The theory accepted by all parties, however, at the moment, was, that the duties were paid ultimately by the consumers of the imported goods. Senator Hayne, of South Carolina, pronounced this doctrine himself. Upon this view the North must pay the duties equally, at least, with the South. So long, then, as this idea was held, and so long as the commercial interests of Massachusetts, Maine, and the city of New York made common cause with the agricultural interests of the South against the bill, it could not be strictly regarded as sectional legislation, it could not develop into a political and constitutional question between the North and the South.

While this combination of interests was not able to prevent the House from finally passing the bill by a narrow majority, it did succeed in imposing several very substantial modifications upon it in the direction of more moderate protection.

*The bill amended and passed.*

In the Senate the bill suffered still further modification in the same direction. The burden of the Senate's amendments fell, however, on the wool- and hemp-growing and liquor-distilling West. It was for this reason that the House of Representatives refused to concur in

## BEGINNING OF PARTICULARISTIC REACTION 115

them. Recourse was then had to a conference committee, which arranged a compromise that gave a little less protection than the House had voted, and a little more than the Senate had voted.

The tariff of May, 1824, was still only a moderately protective tariff. It was certainly in only one particular anything like prohibitory; it preserved the high tariff of 1816 on coarse cotton goods. In other respects it was not much more than a continuation of the reasonable duties already imposed.

So long as the tariff remained moderately protective, and was approved in Kentucky and Missouri, and disapproved in Massachusetts, New Hampshire, Maine, and the city of New York, and so long as its burdens were generally believed to fall ultimately upon the consumers of the dutiable articles, it could not take on the form of a sectional issue, dominated by the question of slavery. *The tariff of 1824 not yet considered sectional legislation.* Some of the Southerners had, indeed, discovered that slave labor could not be employed in the mills, and that, therefore, protection of manufactures would not secure the establishment of these industries in the South, and had begun to treat the tariff question in a manner to develop a party issue out of it. But this tendency had not advanced far enough in 1824 to produce a division of the all-comprehending Republican party. It needed another four years of personal differences among the leaders, another revision of the tariff in the direction of higher duties, and a more complete consolidation of the North for protection, before this result could be attained.

During the passage of the bill public meetings had been held throughout South Carolina protesting against it, and the year subsequent to its enactment the South Carolina legislature denounced it as unconstitutional, but the people *South Carolina and the tariff of 1824.*

of the Commonwealth acquiesced, though with very bad temper, in the execution of the law.

The other question of internal policy, to which certain of the historians refer as suffering under the baleful influences of the slavery interest immediately after 1820, was the question of national internal improvements.

This question became a definite issue in Congress for the first time on December 19th, 1805, when a committee of the Senate, charged with the duty of reporting to the Senate an opinion as to how the money appropriated in the Enabling Act for Ohio ought to be applied, recommended the use of it for the building of a road across the Alleghanies from Cumberland, in Maryland, to a point upon the Ohio River, near Wheeling, in Virginia.

*The historical development of the doctrine of internal improvements.*

If we may take the first Act passed by Congress, that of March 29th, 1806, in regard to the matter as expressing the views of the Government and the people upon the subject, we must conclude that the first matured ideas were that the general Government had the power to lay out and construct roads within and through the Commonwealths, by and with the consent of the Commonwealths through which they might pass. The Cumberland road was originally built by the general Government, after the consent thereto of Maryland, Pennsylvania, and Virginia had been obtained. The appropriations for subsequent repairs upon the road were, however, not considered as requiring the consent of those Commonwealths before being made or expended.

The second stage in the evolution of opinion upon the subject was attained in the year 1817, when Mr. Madison vetoed Mr. Calhoun's bill for setting aside the bonus and the dividends to be paid to the Government by the United States Bank as a fund for constructing roads and canals, and

*Madison's ideas upon internal improvements.*

improving the navigation of water-courses in the several Commonwealths. This bill proposed to authorize the general Government to expend the money, thus appropriated, only with the consent of the Commonwealth, or Commonwealths, in which the proposed improvement might lay, antecedently given, and distributed the sum to be spent among the Commonwealths according to the ratio of their representation in the national House of Representatives. As has been pointed out, Madison vetoed this bill on the ground that the power to enact it was not to be found among the enumerated powers of Congress, and could not be regarded as a necessary and proper means for carrying out any of the enumerated powers.

The President drew no distinction between the power to construct internal improvements and the power to appropriate money for their construction, nor between such powers and the power to administer them, or to exercise jurisdiction over them. He regarded all, or any of these things, as unwarranted by the Constitution. He furthermore declared that the consent of the several Commonwealths to the exercise of such powers by the general Government could not make the exercise of them constitutional, unless that consent should be given in the form of an amendment to the Constitution.

The vote upon the vetoed bill in the House of Representatives manifested the fact that a substantial majority of that body remained unconvinced by the President's argument. It is reasonably certain that Mr. Madison's views were not the views of the country at that moment. A large majority of the people felt that he had abandoned his earlier faith in regard to this subject. An analysis of the vote upon the vetoed bill shows that New England was almost unanimous in opposing the measure; that Virginia and North Carolina also opposed it, though less decidedly; that New York, Pennsylvania, Maryland, and the Northwest, together with South Carolina and Georgia, favored it; and that Kentucky and Tennessee inclined to favor it. Certainly, down to 1817, no influence of the slavery interest upon the question of internal improvements is discoverable. It was evident that the general opinion was, that the middle Atlantic section and the Northwest would receive the larger share of the benefits of a national system of internal improvements. It was also evident that New England viewed the matter purely in that light, and that Virginia was impelled wholly by her ancient principle of strict construction of the powers of the general Government. It was South Carolina and Georgia whose actions appeared at this juncture to spring from unselfish and patriotic motives.

The third stage in the development of constitutional interpretation in reference to this subject was attained in the year 1822. In May of that year Congress passed a bill appropriating money for the repair of the Cumberland road, and authorizing the President to cause the erection of toll-gates upon it, and to appoint toll-gatherers. The toll charges, and penalties for attempting to avoid paying them, and for not keeping to the left in passing, were fixed in the bill itself. That is, this bill assumed for the general Government not only the powers of appropriating and expending money for the construction of the road, but the power of operating the road and jurisdiction over it. The passage of such a bill is certainly very good evidence that President Madison's views, as expressed in his veto message of March 3rd, 1817, were not the views of the country in 1822 upon the subject of internal improvements.

*The bill of 1822 for internal improvements.*

It is interesting and instructive to analyze the vote upon this bill. In the House of Representatives the members from the New England section were nearly evenly divided, pro and con. The majority of the New Yorkers voted against it. The Pennsylvanians were nearly balanced. The Marylanders voted for it. The Virginians were against it by a decided majority. The North Carolinians were indifferent. The South Carolinians and Georgians abandoned their high national ground of 1817, and voted unanimously against it. The Representatives from the Northwest went unanimously for it; and those from Kentucky now wheeled into line with them. Lastly, while the Tennesseeans still maintained their attitude of indifference, the members from the Commonwealths south of Tennessee, and west of Georgia, all voted for the bill. *Passage of the bill, and analysis of the vote upon it.*

In the Senate the majority in favor of the measure was very large. Only the Senators from the Carolinas and Alabama, and one Senator from Missouri, voted against it.

There is somewhat more of an appearance of slavery influence in the vote upon this bill than upon the bill of 1817, in that South Carolina showed herself practically a unit against this bill. Still it is probable that this opposition rested upon other grounds. Certainly when we read in the "Annals of Congress," that so stanch a friend of free labor, so eminent a lawyer, and so honorable a man as John W. Taylor, of New York, said of this bill that it was so important in its character, and proposed such a violation of the Constitution, that he felt obliged to call for the yeas and nays upon it, we must concede that other motives may have influenced the statesmen of South Carolina than such as might have sprung from subserviency to the interests of slavery.

If we review the analysis of the vote in the House of Representatives we shall see that the entire West—taking the Appalachian range as the dividing line, for that period, between the East and the West—was for the bill, while the whole East, with the exception of Maryland, which was specially interested in the road, was either against it or indifferent to it. The Eastern Commonwealths had made their roads with Commonwealth money, and did not wish to assist the Western Commonwealths to make theirs by giving them national money with which to do it. The West, on the other hand, was new and comparatively poor, and wanted the nation to help it out of the mud. This is unquestionably the plain statement of the situation from the point of view of interests. The interests of slavery played but little part, if any at all, in the distribution of the vote.

*The bill in the interests of the West.*

President Monroe promptly vetoed the bill, on the ground that it was in excess of the powers granted to Congress by the Constitution. He also sent a communication, of the same date as the veto, to the House of Representatives, explaining his views upon the principles of the Constitution generally, and upon those provisions specially, which could be regarded as vesting powers in the general Government concerning internal improvements. The paper is prolix, confused, and confusing, but, upon the specific question at issue, the propositions advanced are definite and intelligible. He held that the power of Congress in regard to internal improvements was to be found in the Constitution only by implication, by implication from the power to appropriate money, and that, therefore, its nature and limitations were to be drawn from the character of the power to appropriate money. He contended, on the one side, that the power of Congress to appropriate money was not limited to the objects enumerated in the

*President Monroe's veto, and communication of May 4th, 1822.*

Constitution, but was, on the other side, limited by the spirit of the Constitution to national purposes. He concluded, therefore, that Congress was empowered to appropriate money to internal improvements of a national character. But he asserted that Congress could not, under the power to appropriate money, establish jurisdiction over such improvements, or authorize the executive department of the Government to administer them. The bill in question did just that, and it was for this reason that the President returned it with his objections.

The President's views were apparently convincing to many who had voted for the bill. Upon its passage, the vote in the House of Representatives was eighty-seven for, and sixty-eight against, the measure. After the veto, it stood sixty-eight yeas and seventy-two nays. *President Monroe's argument, and the vote upon the veto.*

It may be safely assumed that the view expressed by President Monroe in the paper accompanying the veto of this bill was the view which prevailed throughout the country in the year 1824. It may be also said that the power of Congress to authorize the President to expend the appropriation by causing the improvements to be planned and constructed was generally regarded, in 1824, as a necessary consequence of the power to appropriate money for the same. The acts of Congress appropriating money for the construction and repair of roads, canals, etc., after, as well as before, that date, seem to proceed upon this theory.

The great difficulty which lay in the way of the realization of President Monroe's principle of the appropriation of national money for internal improvements of a national character was the proper determination of the question as to what improvements were really of that character. The danger was that the appropriation bills would become log-rolling measures for the purpose of obtaining national money for matters of local concern. This difficulty was distinctly felt, and Congress undertook to meet it by the Act of April 30th, 1824, which authorized the President to cause "surveys, plans, and estimates to be made of the routes of such roads and canals as he might deem of national importance," and required him to lay the same before Congress.

<small>Congressional Act of 1824 for distinguishing national from local improvements.</small>

From all this it is apparent that, down to the presidential election of 1824, the development of a pro-slavery, strict-constructionist, "States' rights" party is hardly to be discovered in the attitude of the different sections of the country toward the question of internal improvements. Despite the fact that the slaveholders had become conscious during the Missouri struggle that their interests demanded the establishment of a particularistic view of the Constitution and a particularistic practice in the working of the governmental system of the country, not much progress had been made, in the period between 1820 and 1824, in the way of twisting the policies developed during the previous eight years into line with such a view. In fact the foreign relations of the United States were again, in 1822, of a somewhat threatening character, and the consideration of these relations was acting as a certain hindrance to the development of parties upon internal issues.

The menace, or perhaps it would be more correct to say the apparent menace, came from two quarters; but in neither case did it relate immediately to the territory or interests of the United States. In both cases it was consequential and more or less remote.

<small>Foreign relations during Monroe's second term.</small>

# BEGINNING OF PARTICULARISTIC REACTION 123

In the first place, the movements of Russia in the North Pacific had created grave apprehensions. At the close of the first decade of the century the Russian American Company put forward a claim to the territory of the North American continent along the Pacific coast from Behring's Strait to the mouth of the Columbia River, and even to points south of the Columbia. Really this claim came into conflict only with the rights of Great Britain and Spain, but the United States, having the presentiment of its future, if not a legal claim to any part of this territory as a part of Louisiana, regarded the Russian movement with jealous discontent. And when, on September 16th, the Russian Czar issued an edict, asserting Russia's rights to the North Pacific territory from Behring's Strait to the fifty-first parallel of north latitude, it was natural that this discontent should become hostile in its nature. The Government of the United States declared its dissent from the Russian pretensions, and the matter rested momentarily with that. *Russia and the northwest coast of America.*

At the same time the other danger was developing. The European reaction against the terrible excesses of the Revolution and the despotism of Bonaparte had assumed the form of an alliance between the Governments of the great continental states, Russia, Austria, Prussia, and France, for the purpose of maintaining each by the power of all against the reappearance of revolutionary movements anywhere. Great Britain had scented in this Holy Alliance a combination of continental powers which might prove, in some degree at least, as dangerous to her continental relations as the commercial system of Bonaparte had been. There is no doubt, too, that there was a large party in England which repudiated the fundamental *The Holy Alliance.*

political doctrine of the Holy Alliance Powers, the doctrine of the *jure divino* monarchy. England had, in fact, repudiated that doctrine at the close of the seventeenth century. For these reasons the British Government had declined to enter the Holy League, and regarded it with suspicion and ill-concealed hostility.

The United States Government paid little attention to its workings so long as they were confined to purely European relations, but when, in 1822, at the congress of these powers at Verona, which had been assembled to consider the question of aiding the Spanish Government to suppress the insurrection against its authority in Spain, the subject of aiding that Government to re-establish its authority over Spain's revolting colonies in North and South America was discussed, serious apprehensions were roused in both Great Britain and the United States. It was stated, and generally believed, in the United States, that the plan was the re-establishment of the Spanish power over all of Spain's American possessions, except Mexico and California, and the cession of Mexico to France, and of California to Russia, in consideration of the military aid to be rendered to Spain by these two great powers in the work of restoration.

*The Congress at Verona.*

To the United States the supposed intentions of Russia in respect to the Pacific coast appeared the more immediate danger, and the United States Government addressed its diplomacy to this question first. On July 17th, 1823, the Secretary of State, Mr. John Quincy Adams, declared to the Russian Minister at Washington, Baron Tuyl, that "we should contest the right of Russia to any territorial establishment on this continent, and that we should assume distinctly the principle that the American con-

*Mr. Adams' declaration to Baron Tuyl.*

## BEGINNING OF PARTICULARISTIC REACTION 125

tinents are no longer subjects for any new European colonial establishments."

The following month, the British Minister of Foreign Affairs, Mr. George Canning, proposed to the Minister of the United States at the Court of St. James, Mr. Richard Rush, a joint declaration by the British Government and the Government of the United States to Europe, that the two Governments would not remain indifferent to an intervention by the Holy Alliance Powers to restore the Spanish authority over Spain's revolting American colonies. Both commercial interests and political principles moved the British Government to make this proposition. *Mr. Canning's proposal to Mr. Rush.*

Mr. Rush had not been instructed by his Government in anticipation of the British advances, but he offered to assume the responsibility of joining for the United States in the declaration, provided the British Government would acknowledge the independence of the revolting Spanish colonies in America, as the Government of the United States had already done. The British minister was not then prepared to go so far, and the plan of the joint declaration fell through. But Mr. Canning declared for his Government to the French ambassador at St. James, Prince Polignac, that Great Britain would resist any intervention on the part of the Holy Alliance Powers in the question between Spain and her revolting American colonies, and the President of the United States, in his annual message of December 2nd, 1823, stated the position which the United States Government and the people of the United States ought, in his opinion, to assume, and would, in his opinion, assume, in regard to the whole subject. *Mr. Canning's declaration to Prince Polignac.*

Mr. Monroe dealt first with the question of Russian

colonization upon the Pacific coast. After informing Congress of the instructions which had been given to the Minister representing the United States at St. Petersburg for negotiating with the Czar's Government, he said : "In the discussions to which this interest has given rise, and in the arrangements by which they may terminate, the occasion has been judged proper for asserting, as a principle in which the rights and interests of the United States are involved, that the American continents, by the free and independent condition which they have assumed and maintained, are henceforth not to be considered as subjects for future colonization by any European powers."

*The "Monroe Doctrine."*

Toward the close of the message Mr. Monroe addressed himself to the other question, the question of intervention by the Holy Alliance Powers in the contest between Spain and her revolting American colonies in the following language: "In the wars of European powers, in matters relating to themselves, we have never taken any part, nor does it comport with our policy so to do. It is only when our rights are invaded or seriously menaced that we resent injuries or make preparations for our defence. With the movements in this hemisphere we are, of necessity, more immediately connected, and by causes which must be obvious to all enlightened and impartial observers. The political system of the allied powers is essentially different in this respect from that of America. This difference proceeds from that which exists in their respective governments, and to the defence of our own, which has been achieved by the loss of so much blood and treasure, and matured by the wisdom of our most enlightened citizens, and under which we have enjoyed unexampled felicity, this whole nation is devoted. We owe it, therefore, to candor and to the amicable relations existing between the United

## BEGINNING OF PARTICULARISTIC REACTION 127

States and those powers, to declare that we should consider any attempt on their part to extend their system to any portion of this hemisphere as dangerous to our peace and safety. With the existing colonies of any European power we have not interfered and shall not interfere, but with the Governments who have declared their independence and maintained it, and whose independence we have on great consideration and on just principles acknowledged, we could not view any interposition for the purpose of oppressing them, or controlling in any other manner their destiny, by any European power, in any other light than as a manifestation of an unfriendly disposition toward the United States. . . . It is impossible that the allied powers should extend their political system to any portion of either continent without endangering our peace and happiness; nor can anyone believe that our Southern brethren, if left to themselves, would adopt it of their own accord. It is equally impossible, therefore, that we should behold such interposition, in any form, with indifference. If we look to the comparative strength and resources of Spain and these new Governments, and their distance from each other, it must be obvious that she can never subdue them. It is still the true policy of the United States to leave the parties to themselves, in the hope that other powers will pursue the same course."

These statements by Mr. Monroe of his opinion as to what the diplomacy of the United States ought to be, and would be, upon the subjects of the establishment of new European colonies in America, the intervention of the Holy Alliance Powers in the question between Spain and her revolting American colonies, and the forcible imposition by these powers of the *jure divino* monarchy

<small>The meaning of the Monroe propositions in 1824.</small>

upon these peoples, who had established republican forms of government for themselves, have had the name fixed upon them by a later generation of "The Monroe Doctrine." There is no difficulty in understanding these statements as Mr. Monroe understood them.

Neither he nor his Secretary of State ever called them a "Doctrine." With them they were simply the opinions of the Administration in regard to the course which the United States ought to pursue, and would probably pursue, in meeting certain exigencies, the possibility of the arising of which passed entirely away before the close of the first half of this century. These opinions were simply that the United States ought to resist, and would resist, the planting of any new colonial establishments in America, or the intervention of the Holy Alliance Powers in the question between Spain and her revolting American colonies, or the forcible imposition of the *jure divino* monarchy, the political system of these powers, upon the new republican governments of South and Middle America.

The month following the publication of this message, January, 1824, Mr. Clay attempted to move Congress to indorse that part of the President's opinions which referred to the intervention of the Allied Powers in the conflict between Spain and her revolting colonies, but the resolution which he offered to that effect was laid on the table, and never called up. Mr. Poinsett, of South Carolina, made a like attempt later, but with no more success. The Congress of that day had altogether too much intelligence to make diplomatic opinions, advanced by the Administration, either laws of the land, or joint or concurrent resolutions of the legislative department of the Government.

# BEGINNING OF PARTICULARISTIC REACTION

Thus neither in the question of the tariff, nor in that of internal improvements, nor, naturally, in the diplomatic questions, is anything more than the faint beginnings of the particularistic reaction to be discovered in the period between 1820 and 1824. In fact, it may be said that the year 1820 marks roughly the date of the extinction of the old Federal party, and of the almost complete absorption of the whole voting population in the Republican party. In the presidential election of that year the candidate of the Republican party, Mr. Monroe, received two hundred and thirty-one of the two hundred and thirty-two electoral votes cast, and the one elector who did not vote for him was a Republican. The Federal party did not even undertake to present a ticket. From the point of view of the preservation of its own dominance, the Federal party had committed two grave errors, one of principle and one of policy. It had held to the principle that the mass of men are not fit to govern themselves, but should be governed by the few who are wise and good; and it had adopted the policy of too close alliance with the commercial interests of the country. The levelling, not to say debasing, influences of the French political philosophy, which rolled like a tidal wave over the country during the last decade of the eighteenth century, and was worked up into a political dogma by Jefferson and his disciples, together with the reflex influence of the practical equality which established itself among the first adventurers who settled the lands beyond the Alleghanies, destroyed the Federal party, upon the side of principle; while the great extension of the agricultural interests, produced by these same settlements, made it intolerable upon the side of policy. The earlier advantage which the Federal party, as the upholder of centralization, enjoyed

*The particularistic reaction scarcely discoverable before 1824.*

over the Republican party, as the champion of "States'-rights," had been lost by the nationalization of the Republican party through the War of 1812, and the denationalization of the Federal party through the same experiences. In 1820, therefore, there was only one party in fact and in principle. It is undoubtedly true that the struggle of the years 1819 and 1820 over the Missouri question had sowed the seeds of dissension in this all-comprehending party; but four years did not constitute a period of time sufficient for their completed growth and fructification. The presidential contest of 1824 could not, therefore, be fought under the issues of party principles. It was little more, and, under the circumstances, it could be little more, than a personal contest between the leaders of the Republican party. The result of it, however, contributed very largely to the development of political differences, and to the organization of parties upon the basis of these differences. It must, therefore, be described with some particularity.

# CHAPTER VI.

## THE PRESIDENTIAL ELECTION OF 1824

General Character of the Presidential Contest of 1824—John
Quincy Adams—DeWitt Clinton—William H. Crawford—John
C. Calhoun—Daniel Webster—Henry Clay—Andrew Jackson
—The Nomination of Presidential Candidates in 1824—Failure
of the Electors to Elect the President—Territorial Distribution
of the Electoral Vote—New York in the Election of 1824—
South Carolina in the Election of 1824—Pennsylvania in the
Election of 1824—The Election in the House of Representatives—Clay Master of the Situation—Clay's Support of Adams,
and Kremer's Charge of Bargain and Corruption—The Election of Adams by the House of Representatives—Clay and the
Secretaryship of State—Threats of the Organization of an
Anti-administration Party—The Bargain between Clay and
Adams a mere Suspicion—Clay's Nomination to the Secretaryship of State in the Senate—The Composition of the new Antiadministration Party.

As has been pointed out, from 1820 to 1824 the political arena was clear of the combats of principles, and furnished the tilting-ground for the jousts of personal ambition. The "Virginia dynasty" became extinct with the expiration of Monroe's second term, and the way was open for anyone to enter the lists who was willing to risk the shocks of the encounter.

*General character of the presidential contest of 1824.*

At no time in our history has the roll of our political nobility been more full of brilliant names and characters.

First of all, there was John Quincy Adams, the Secretary of State, the "knight without fear and without reproach," blunt, grim, almost rude, through an unconscious suspicion that politeness might encourage the approach of temptation ; now fifty-seven years old, and trained in statecraft and diplomacy almost from childhood ; the best equipped statesman and the most experienced statesman that America had up to that time produced ; ready to serve his country in any honorable capacity to which that country might freely call him, and just as ready to withdraw from that service when his country indicated the desire to dispense with him ; puritanic, austere, and to the last degree patriotic, his one qualification for the presidential office was the capacity to discharge its duties wisely, honestly, and loyally, a qualification which too rarely wins in popular elections.

Then, there was DeWitt Clinton, noble in personal appearance, dignified in manners, eloquent in debate, sagacious and far-sighted in business, a lover of science and a scientist himself ; the great promoter of the Erie Canal, which was now on the point of completion, and which was destined to revolutionize the commerce of the country ; still only fifty-five years of age, although he had been considered more than twenty years before as the most promising man of the nation, and had within that period been United States Senator, mayor of New York City, candidate for the presidency against Mr. Madison, and twice Governor of New York.

Then, there was William H. Crawford, a Virginian by birth and a Georgian by education ; a man of large wealth and of imposing bearing ; enjoying a very great reputation for statesmanship without any easily discoverable foundation therefor ; now

## THE PRESIDENTIAL ELECTION OF 1824    133

fifty-two years of age, and having already been United States Senator, Minister to France, Secretary of War, and Secretary of the Treasury, which latter office he still held; with the exception, perhaps, of Martin Van Buren, the most astute politician among the great men of his time. He had the political friendship and support of Van Buren. The two seem to have been attracted to each other by the similarity of their methods. He was the author of the law of 1820, limiting the term of the officials of the Treasury to four years, the first step in the direction of making the United States civil service a political machine, such as Van Buren and his fellows in the "Regency" had made out of the civil service of the Commonwealth of New York. It is not astonishing that he, rather than any of the other aspirants for the presidency, procured the assembling of a caucus of the members of Congress, and secured a nomination from it, thus making himself the "regular" candidate. Not a third of the members, however, appeared at the caucus, and the nomination did him more harm than good.

Then, there was Calhoun, grave, pure, and patriotic as Adams himself, and almost as puritanic; South Carolinian by birth, Scotch-Irish by blood, Presbyterian in religion, and New Englander by education; great, both in dialectics and in the administration of affairs; rather more given to introspection than to objective research; speculative, therefore, rather than inductive in his mental processes; most fascinating in conversation, kind and generous in his feelings, and a gentleman everywhere and upon all occasions; a personality to be looked up to with reverence, admiration, and confidence. He was still only forty-two years of age, and yet he had already passed fourteen years in public service, first as member of the South Carolina Legislature, then as member of Congress, and

*John C. Calhoun.*

then as Monroe's Secretary of War for both terms, which office he still held.

Then, there was Webster, of the same age with Calhoun, though as yet only five years in public service; the most majestic personality which America has ever produced, though born of the hardy yeomanry of New England; profound in thought, grandly eloquent in speech, and royally impressive in bearing; full of good cheer, in spite of the puritanism of his ancestry, enjoying his friends and adored by his friends; a splendid lawyer, a great statesman, and an incomparable orator—in a word, a demigod; by no means so austere in character as in appearance; liable, as genius too often is, to sometimes break over the restraints of customary morality, but doing it in so grand and natural a manner as to make the rule which he had broken seem narrow, insignificant, and mean.

*Daniel Webster.*

And then, there was Clay, the most genuine American of them all; rather superficial in thought, entrancing in his oratory, with a voice as winning as the siren's song, elegant and gallant in his manners, perfectly irresistible in conversation, jovial and cheery and happy, the prince of good fellows, loved and worshipped by everybody who knew him; enthusiastic in his patriotism, seeking to make his country not only independent of the world in all its policies but the leader of the world in civilization, a zealous propagandist of American republicanism, the "lion-hearted knight" of American statesmen. He was now in the prime of his manhood, forty-seven years of age. He had been a member of the Senate of the United States at thirty, but it was upon the floor of the House of Representatives, and as Speaker of the House, which office he again held, that he had won his most brilliant laurels. He was at the moment the great champion of the tar-

*Henry Clay.*

iff, of national internal improvements, and of the cause
of the South American States in their struggle for independence
against Spain and Portugal—of what he called
the American system of political and industrial independence.
Of his competitors only Crawford differed
with him in regard to these principles in anything more
than a slight degree. Crawford was considered as rather
more particularistic, especially in his views on the question
of internal improvements. But Clay, with his
genial self-confidence and irresistible self-assertion, had
assumed in the popular mind, as well as in the Congress,
the part of the leading representative of these policies.
He had the advantage or the disadvantage of that,
whichever it might prove to be.

And lastly, Jackson, the noblest Roman of them all;
ignorant and irascible indeed, but virtuous, brave, and
patriotic beyond any cavil or question; *Andrew Jackson.*
faithful and devoted in his domestic life,
absolutely unapproachable by pecuniary inducements;
the best of friends and the most implacable of enemies;
quick, hasty in forming his judgments and tenacious
beyond expression in holding to them; prone to elevate
every whim and impulse to a behest of conscience; earnest,
terrible in the inflexibility of his purposes; excited
by opposition to an ever-increasing degree of determination;
unflinching and recklessly daring in the performance
of what he felt to be his duty; restless under the
legal restraints which might appear to hinder him in
the discharge of duty and the accomplishment of any
great enterprise intrusted to him; hostile to all gradations
of power and privilege, and inclined to break through
any official net-work interposed between himself and the
rank and file subject to his command; a great soldier,
and yet a man of the people; the military hero of the
country and a martyr to the persecutions of the poli-

ticians—here were certainly qualities calculated to rouse the enthusiasm of the masses, if not of the classes. He was now fifty-seven years of age, and was not in strong health. He had shown no qualities of statesmanship, although he had been twice a member of the Senate of the United States, and was at the moment holding that most advantageous position for a display of civic talent; but he had the fortune to live at a time and in a country when and where the lower strata of society were just coming to a full participation in political power, and when and where high qualifications simply to discharge the duties of an office were beginning to be regarded by the majority of the people as disqualifications for holding the office.

These were by no means all of the great characters from among whom the nation had its choice in 1824, but they were unquestionably the first on the list. Different as they were in personal qualities, they were not yet far apart in political opinions. Crawford leaned more toward "States' rights" than the others. Clay was more pronounced in the opposite direction. While Jackson was rather more uncommitted.

Webster was not put forward by anybody, and did not offer himself as a candidate. Clay was nominated by the legislature of Kentucky. Jackson was nominated by the legislature of Tennessee, and by two Pennsylvania conventions. While Adams had the advantage of the precedent which, for nearly a quarter of a century, had pointed to the Secretary of State as the natural successor to the presidential office.

*The nomination of presidential candidates in 1824.*

As was to be expected, the electors did not choose any one of the four, since the Constitution requires a majority of the whole number of the electors for a choice. Jackson led with ninety-nine votes; Adams was next with eighty-four;

*Failure of the electors to elect the President.*

THE PRESIDENTIAL ELECTION OF 1824   137

Crawford followed with forty-one; and Clay came last with thirty-seven.

The electoral vote was distributed territorially as might have been naturally anticipated, except in two particulars. These were, the failure of Van Buren to secure the electoral vote of New York for Crawford, and the solid vote of Pennsylvania and South Carolina for Jackson. These facts had some significance in connection with subsequent developments, and require a little explanation. *Territorial distribution of the electoral vote.*

New York was one of the Commonwealths which, down to 1824, permitted the legislature to choose the presidential electors. In 1823 the legislature was still under the control of Van Buren and his colleagues in the "Regency," the Albany machine, and had the election taken place in 1823 he could doubtless have delivered the electoral vote entire to Crawford. But one of Jackson's shrewdest supporters, probably Clinton, started the scheme for transferring the choice of the electors from the legislature to the voters. This, if successful, would destroy the control of the "Regency" over the electoral vote. The opposition of the "Regency" to the bill, when it appeared in the legislature, caused its rejection by that body; but the popular indignation was roused to such a pitch against the "Regency" and its adherents in the legislature, in consequence of this act, that, in the Commonwealth elections of 1824, the "Regency" party was driven from power, and the new legislature chose electors who cast the electoral vote of the Commonwealth chiefly for Adams, as the Northern candidate. *New York in the Election of 1824.*

The fact that South Carolina cast her electoral vote for Jackson instead of for Crawford is good evidence that there was still no question of "States' rights" versus the powers of the Union at issue, or that South

Carolina was still nationally disposed; and that, either there was no tariff question at issue, or South Caro-
South Carolina in the Election of 1824. lina had not yet clearly discovered the hostility of the tariff to her interests, or she believed Jackson to be opposed to the tariff.

Jackson, or rather his manager, William B. Lewis, a most astute politician, had written a letter to a Dr. Coleman, of Warrenton, Va., upon the subject of the tariff. The letter was ostensibly a reply to one from Dr. Coleman, inquiring of Jackson his views upon this question. Very probably, however, Dr. Coleman's letter was also dictated by Mr. Lewis. Jackson's reply contained nothing definite in regard to the subject. It was a first-class political document, that is, it was a document which could be interpreted to mean anything which might be made necessary or desirable by time, place, and circumstances. In a word, Lewis had made for Jackson a sort of *tabula rasa* record on the subject of the tariff. In such a state of things it is certainly reasonable to ascribe South Carolina's preference for Jackson to the facts that he claimed to be her son by birth, and that Calhoun, rightly discerning Jackson to be the coming man, withdrew from the race for the presidency, and was regarded as running for the vice-presidency on the Jackson ticket.

It is somewhat more difficult to account for the attitude of Pennsylvania. We are now so accustomed to consider Pennsylvania the "tariff State" *par excellence*, that it is difficult to conceive of a time when she was not such. She was indeed, in 1824, for the tariff, but her interests had not then become so completely linked together with it as after 1840. In 1824 her vast beds of anthracite had not been applied to the preparation of her iron ores, in fact had hardly been discovered. Pennsylvania west of the Alleghanies was then an agricultural country, and was filled with a population intensely democratic and almost lawless. So far as they had any political science it was based upon the most radical postulates of the French philosophy. The principal " plank " of the platform of the Harrisburg convention of March 4th, 1824, which nominated Jackson, read as follows : " This artificial system of cabinet succession to the presidency is little less dangerous and anti-republican than the hereditary monarchies of Europe. If a link in this chain of successive secretary dynasties be not broken now, then may we be fettered by it forever. Andrew Jackson comes pure, untrammelled, and unpledged from the people." Adams, Crawford, and Calhoun were then members of President Monroe's cabinet, and Clay was Speaker of the House of Representatives. Jackson alone of all the candidates seemed to possess the qualifications required by the Harrisburg doctrine. While this may explain the attachment of the Pennsylvania Republicans to Jackson, we must not forget that the remnant of the Pennsylvania Federalists were also for him. In 1816 Jackson had written some letters to President Monroe advising him not to ignore the Federalists in his appointments to office, but to unite the country by showing himself superior to the distinctions of party in his Administration. These letters were now drawn forth and published by Jackson's manager, and the inference which they conveyed was that Jackson would follow this policy, in case he should be chosen to the presidency. Even Webster was inclined to him, and Mrs. Webster was entirely won by his gallantry. Jackson in the rôle of a fascinating gentleman and a popular ladies' man is hardly the usual character under which the imagination of this generation pictures him. It is, nevertheless, strictly true that the "Old Hero" knew how to make himself very acceptable to the ladies. Pennsylvania was, chiefly, by this conjunction of influences, carried for Jackson by an overwhelming majority.

The failure of the electors to give a majority to any one of the candidates threw the election into the House of Representatives, which is empowered by the Constitution to choose, in such a case, one of the three who shall have received the highest number of electoral votes.

<small>The Election in the House of Representatives.</small>

From the day when it became known that the new President must be chosen in this manner to the day of the election by the House, that is, from about the middle of December to the ninth day of February, the politicians in Washington were "laying pipe," "pulling wires," and "making deals." It soon became manifest that Clay, while he could not be chosen himself, since he could not be legally voted for, was the master of the situation. So great was his popularity with the House that, it is almost certain, he would have been chosen to the great office himself had he been among the three having the highest number of electoral votes. Everybody reasoned, therefore, that not only the Representatives from the Commonwealths which had given their electoral votes to Clay would follow his lead in voting in the House, but that many others from other Commonwealths would act under inspiration from him. After a good deal of talk among the members of the House and the politicians generally as to whether the members were bound to vote as the electors from their respective Commonwealths had voted, and as to whether the legislatures of the respective Commonwealths possessed any power to instruct the members of the House of Representatives from the several Commonwealths in regard to

<small>Clay master of the situation.</small>

the casting of their votes, the opinion finally prevailed that each Representative was entirely free to vote according to his own judgment and preference; and that meant that the popular and persuasive Speaker would be able to carry enough votes with him to elect the candidate upon whom his favor might fall.

Propositions were made to him from the friends of the different candidates, but he held them all at arm's length. It might have been easily foreseen that he would support Adams. Crawford was a man of exhausted powers, unfit physically and mentally to discharge the duties of the great office. Jackson was only a military chieftain, according to Clay's view a very dangerous character for the presidency. There remained only Adams, probably the best-fitted man in the country for the office. It was generally felt, for several days before the election, that these considerations would determine Clay's course of action. There were those, however, who were ready to ascribe Clay's supposed attitude to other, and more selfish, motives. An insignificant member from Pennsylvania, Kremer by name, gave it out in public print that there was a bargain between Adams and Clay, according to which Clay was to support Adams, and to receive in return the secretaryship of State. This happened on January 28th, 1825, just after the delegations from Ohio and Kentucky in the House had declared their intention of supporting Adams. The small mind of Kremer could not conceive of this attitude on the part of Clay save from the point of view of selfish interests. Clay immediately called for an investigation of the charge by the House, but Kremer sneaked out of it.

*Clay's support of Adams, and Kremer's charge of bargain and corruption.*

On February 9th, 1825, the two Houses of Congress met in joint assembly to count the electoral vote. It was immediately found that no candidate had a majority, and that, therefore, the choice lay with the House. The House, on the same day, and on the first ballot, elected Adams. The delegations from thirteen of the twenty-four Commonwealths voted for him. The delegations from seven voted for Jackson; and those from four for Crawford. Adams received the votes of the delegations from all of the Commonwealths which had given their electoral votes, or the majority of their electoral votes, to himself and to Clay, and from three of the Commonwealths which had given the majority of their electoral vote to Jackson.

*The election of Adams by the House of Representatives.*

The twelfth day of February, 1825, is the date in Mr. Adams' diary under which he recorded his offer of the secretaryship of State to Mr. Clay. We find in the diary, for the day before this, an account of a visit from a Mr. G. Sullivan, who told Mr. Adams "that the Calhounites said that if Mr. Clay should be appointed Secretary of State, a determined opposition to the administration would be organized from the outset; that the opposition would use the name of General Jackson as its head; and that the administration would be supported only by the New England States — New York being doubtful, the West much divided, and strongly favoring Jackson as a Western man, Virginia already in opposition, and all the South decidedly adverse."

*Clay and the Secretaryship of State.*

Exactly who the Calhounites were at that moment, as distinct from the followers of Adams and Clay, is difficult to determine, since all the electors who voted for Adams for President also voted for Calhoun for Vice-President, except eight electors from Connecticut and one from New Hampshire, and of the thirty-seven electors who voted

*Threats of the organization of an anti-administration party.*

for Clay, at least seven of them voted also for Calhoun. It was Crawford's supporters who had opposed Calhoun for the second place, not one of them having voted for him. This declaration made by Mr. Sullivan meant, therefore, that Jackson's friends were going to organize an opposition party to the Adams-Clay Administration and that the Vice-President was going to cast his lot with them.

This was certainly a threat of danger, but Adams was not the man to be frightened from the course which he had chosen as just and politic. He immediately offered the first position in the cabinet to Clay, and, after some six days of reflection and of consultation with friends, Clay accepted.

No sufficient evidence has ever been produced to convince a judicial mind that Adams and Clay had come to any understanding in regard to this matter either before Clay announced publicly that he should support Adams, or afterward. But men generally do not have judicial minds. *The bargain between Clay and Adams a mere suspicion.*
"Diffused distrust and indiscriminate suspicion" mark the attitude of the vulgar mind toward personages in high station. Politicians know only too well that this is one of the most potent forces which can be called into play, and they know only too well how to take advantage of it. Conscious as both Adams and Clay doubtless were of their own rectitude, they did not sufficiently appreciate the proneness of the masses to believe in the corruption of their superiors. Neither did they correctly appreciate the ungenerous and uncandid spirit of the leaders among their opponents in clinging to this charge, and reiterating it, after they had failed to substantiate it by any credible evidence. They certainly did not comprehend that they had given their opponents a shibboleth which would lead them to certain victory.

The opposition began at once their attack in the Senate under the issue of Clay's appointment. Fifteen of the forty-one Senators present voted against it. Among the fifteen was Jackson, who, upon his way, a few days later, from Washington to his home in Tennessee, repeated and re-enlivened the charge of "bargain and corruption." It is more than probable that Jackson believed in it himself. He was so convinced of his own honesty that he believed every one who differed with him to be dishonest. This is a trait of character frequently met with, and it is a most dangerous force with which to deal. The "Old Hero" possessed it in an extraordinary degree.

<small>Clay's nomination to the secretaryship of State in the Senate.</small>

Despite the fact that there were no material differences in political principles, and the further fact that Adams retained Monroe's cabinet so far as he could, appointing new members only to the positions made vacant therein by his own and Calhoun's promotion to the presidency and the vice-presidency, and by Crawford's refusal to accept the Treasury for another term, it was now perfectly evident that Jackson, Calhoun, and Crawford, with their followers, were determined upon an organized opposition to the Adams-Clay Administration, no matter what principles and policies that Administration should follow; that Jackson would, on account of his popularity with the masses, be put forward as the head of the new party; and that the cry of "bargain and corruption" between the President and the chief officer of his Administration, for robbing the "Old Hero" of his rights and the people of their choice, was to be their watchword in the conflict.

<small>The composition of the new Anti-administration party.</small>

## CHAPTER VII.

**THE DIVISION OF THE REPUBLICAN PARTY**

Personal Differences, and Party Division—Military Confederation of the Spanish-American States—Invitation to the United States to send Representatives to the Congress at Panama—The Acceptance of the Invitation—Opposition in the Senate to the sending of Representatives to Panama—Popular Sympathy in the United States for the South-American States—The President's Nominations Confirmed—The Haytian Question at the Congress—Cuba and Porto Rico—Real Nature of the Opposition to the Panama Mission—The Failure of the Panama Congress—Adams on Internal Improvements in his Message of December 6th, 1825—Van Buren's Resolution against Internal Improvements—The Practices of the Adams Administration in respect to Internal Improvements—The Chief Practical Difficulty in the way of a National System of Internal Improvements—The Tariff of 1824 a Failure—The Tariff Bill of 1827—Development of the Industrial Antithesis between the North and the South—Hostility to the Measure in South Carolina—The Tariff of 1828—The Character of the Bill as Reflected in the Analysis of the Vote Upon It—The Tariff of 1828 not a Complete Party Measure—The Presidential Campaign of 1828 still Dominated by Personal Considerations—Election of Jackson—Advent of the Parvenus—Foreign Affairs under Jackson's Administration—The Democratic Party and its Divisions.

IN the absence of any well defined differences in political opinions, and in the state of determined personal hostility between the leaders developed by the election of 1824, the fact that Adams and Clay took broad national views, placed a liberal construction upon the Constitution, and insisted upon the employment of all the powers vested by it in the general Government to the highest point of their usefulness in the promotion of the general welfare, had the natural effect of forcing the opposition upon the opposite grounds, and, therefore, tended to make a particularistic party, the so-called "States' rights" party, out of the Jackson-Calhoun-Crawford faction.

*Personal differences, and party division.*

One of the most patent indications of the correctness of the proposition that the opposition in principle between the National Republican party and the Democratic party, as the Administrationists and the Anti-administrationists were soon termed, took its rise largely in the personal hostility of the leaders, is to be found in the history of the chief question of the foreign relations with which the Adams Administration had to deal in the years 1825 and 1826.

The Spanish Americans had taken the cautious utterances of President Monroe, in his December message of 1823, for much more than he meant them. They thought, or professed to think, that the Government had pledged itself to meet any intervention of the Allied Powers of Europe in American affairs by any resistance necessary to defeat it. They were also acquainted with the fact that both Mr. Adams and Mr. Clay were more pronounced than President Monroe in favor of going to the support of the new republics of South and Middle America. Naturally then, when these two men came to the head of the Government, on March 4th, 1825, the Spanish Americans felt encouraged to expect some sub-

*Spanish-American interpretations of "the Monroe Doctrine."*

# THE DIVISION OF THE REPUBLICAN PARTY 147

stantial aid from the United States in the further course of their struggle with Spain and her possible allies.

Already in the summer of 1822 the Republic of Colombia had initiated the plan of a Confederation of the Spanish-American states. By a treaty with Peru, bearing date of July 12th, 1823, by another with Chili of the same date, by another with the United Provinces of Central America, of April 12th, 1825, and by another with Mexico, of September 20th, 1825, the Republic of Colombia had established a military confederation between these five states, and had pledged them to send plenipotentiaries to a "general assembly of American states . . . with the charge of cementing, in the most solid and stable manner, the intimate relations which ought to exist between all and every one of them." According to this agreement the assembly of plenipotentiaries was to serve as a council in conflicts, as a rallying-point in common dangers, as a faithful interpreter of treaties between their respective states, and as an umpire and conciliator in the disputes and differences which might arise between their respective states. *Military Confederation of the Spanish-American states.*

During the spring of the year 1825 the Ministers of Colombia and Mexico sought Mr. Clay, and communicated to him the desires of their respective governments to have the United States send representatives to this proposed congress; but before giving the formal invitation they asked to know if it would be accepted. They stated to Mr. Clay that they did not expect the United States to abandon the attitude of neutrality, or to take part in those deliberations of the congress which might relate to the prosecution of the existing war. *Invitation to the United States to send representatives to the congress at Panama.*

Clay's genial spirit was much excited by the grand prospect of a league of the American states under the hegemony of the United States. It satisfied the plan of his daring imagination. It filled the bounds of his far-reaching vision. He immediately communicated the propositions of the two ministers, Mr. Salazar and Mr. Obregon, to President Adams, and urged the President to allow him to give them the assurance that the invitation to send representatives to the congress, to be held the following October at Panama, would be accepted by the United States. The President, however, proceeded rather cautiously. He was, indeed, very friendly in his feelings toward the Spanish-American states, and was ready to aid their cause in any manner consistent with the duties of a neutral. But he had a calmer way of regarding things than his brilliant Secretary of State, and, moreover, upon him rested the ultimate responsibility. He required Mr. Clay to procure from Messrs. Salazar and Obregon some information in regard to the subjects which would be considered by the congress, the nature and form of the powers to be given to the diplomatic agents which were to compose it, and the mode of its organization and procedure. At the same time he allowed Mr. Clay to encourage them to believe that, if satisfactory answers should be returned to these inquiries, their invitation would be accepted. He also caused Mr. Clay to warn them that the United States could not become a party to the existing war with Spain, or give any counsel in regard to its further prosecution.

*The President's hesitation to accept the invitation.*

The answers to these inquiries were not received until the following November, and in Mr. Clay's letter acknowledging their receipt, they were said to be not entirely satisfactory to the President. The ministers were informed, however, that the President had resolved to send commis-

*The acceptance of the invitation.*

THE DIVISION OF THE REPUBLICAN PARTY  149

sioners to the congress at Panama, in case the Senate, which was to assemble in a few days, should assent to it; but that the commissioners would not be empowered to do or say anything which would compromise the neutrality of the United States.

As a matter of fact, the replies from the Governments of Colombia and Mexico to President Adams' questions would have been regarded as highly unsatisfactory by any judicious mind, entirely uncommitted; for, while they left the President's second and third questions entirely unanswered, *The President too hasty after all.* they suggested a joint resistance of all the American states to European interference in American affairs, and to any further European colonization upon the American continents, as the principal subjects in the discussion and determination of which the United States would be expected to take part. They referred to the fact that President Monroe in his noted message had characterized these things as being matters of common interest to both North and South America.

Here was certainly a fine opportunity for all sorts of entanglements; and it is not at all astonishing that, when the subject was brought before the Senate of the United States by the President's message of December 26th, 1825, asking the Senate to approve his nominations of *Opposition in the Senate to the sending of representatives to Panama.* Richard C. Anderson and John Sergeant as ministers from the United States to the "Assembly of American Nations at Panama," a very strong opposition to the project was developed in that body. The Senate referred the nominations to a committee, and called for the diplomatic correspondence and other papers relating to the subject, which, upon examination, revealed the facts briefly stated above.

The committee, which was the regular committee on

Foreign Relations, reported against the nominations, or rather against the policy of having representatives at the congress at all, on the ground that it might compromise the neutrality of the United States, and involve the United States in entangling connections with foreign powers. This report was made to the Senate on January 16th, 1826. The Senate debated, in secret session, the questions involved in the report during the latter half of February and the first half of March. The view held by those who favored the report was that the Panama congress was to have the character of a military confederation, and that membership in it would be inconsistent with a status of neutrality toward Spain and her revolting American colonies. The view of those who opposed the report and desired to send representatives to the congress was, that the congress was only a meeting, in one place, of the plenipotentiaries of the different states for an interchange of opinions, and would not necessarily alter the attitude of any of the powers taking part in it upon any subject, or toward any other power.

The strong sympathy of the people of the United States for the cause of independence in Middle and South America really violated the spirit of neutrality, and the influence of this sympathy upon the Senators and Representatives in Congress was very disturbing to a cool and judicial consideration of the attitude which the Government should preserve in the matter of the Panama mission.

*Popular sympathy in the United States for the South-American states.*

The friends of the mission at last won the day by a vote of twenty-four to nineteen. Fifteen Northern Senators voted to send representatives to the congress, and seven voted against doing so. Nine Southern Senators voted to send representatives, and twelve voted against doing so. This

*The President's nominations confirmed.*

## THE DIVISION OF THE REPUBLICAN PARTY  151

vote hardly sustains the claim of certain of the historians, that the slavery interest was the primal cause of the opposition to the Panama mission. One of the most eminent among these says that the historical significance of the contest over the question was that slavery threw aside its municipal character, its character as a Commonwealth institution, and demanded to prescribe both the internal and external policies of the nation. This sounds dramatic, but if it means, as it appears to mean, that when, in a federal system of government, any interest or institution regulated by Commonwealth law asks protection from the general Government against foreign influence and interference it thereby asserts command over the nation, it is a proposition which also sounds decidedly *outré* to an American lawyer. The Constitution of the United States imposed the international protection of all such interests and institutions upon the general Government when it reserved such interests and institutions to the jurisdiction of the Commonwealths and gave the general Government alone international standing. When, then, such interests and institutions claim that protection, they are only asking for a right guaranteed to them by the Constitution, and are by no means asserting an authority over the Constitution and the country.

<small>No influence of slavery perceptible in the vote upon the nominations.</small>

It is true that Mr. Salazar said in his communication something about the status of Hayti being a subject of deliberation for the congress. It was also true that Hayti had been for thirty years in a state of chronic insurrection and revolution, and that the former negro slave population had, by the assassination of their former masters and mistresses, freed themselves from bondage, taken possession of the country, and were reducing it to barbarism at a rapid

<small>The Haytian question at the congress.</small>

pace. It is furthermore true that the slaveholders in the United States did not wish their own homes to be made the scenes of any such ruin and savagery, or themselves or their families to be made subject to any such fate; and, it may be confidently hazarded, that no Northerner, at that day, viewed such possibilities with anything but aversion and horror. It required a quarter of a century of radical abolition recklessness, the blundercrime of secession, and the desperation of long-continued, and at first unsuccessful, war, to make the men of the North regard without sympathy such dangers to their Southern brethren. The North and the South simply could not have divided, at that time, upon the question of the relation to Hayti. There was only one view upon that subject, and that was that the example and influence of Hayti must be held far away from these shores. This could have been accomplished, however, as well by attending the congress as by staying away, perhaps better. At least, the Haytian question was no chief ground of opposition to the mission, and certainly no chief ground in favor of the mission.

It is more probable that one of the reasons which moved President Adams and Mr. Clay to urge attendance upon the congress was to be in a position to restrain the Spanish-American states from attempting to seize Cuba and Porto Rico. During the latter half of the year 1825, at the very moment when the Government was communicating with the Spanish-American states in regard to the congress, Mr. Clay was urging the Czar of Russia, on the one side, to exercise his influence upon the Spanish court for the cessation of hostilities on the part of Spain against the revolting American colonies, on the ground that Spain could never resubjugate them, and would by a continuance of hostilities exasperate them and excite them to attack

THE DIVISION OF THE REPUBLICAN PARTY   153

Cuba and Porto Rico with the purpose of expelling the Spanish power from these islands, and was urging the Spanish-American states, on the other side, to refrain from such an attack, on the ground that if they did attempt to seize these islands the Czar would not only cease his good offices with the Spanish King to end the war, but might bring the entire power of the Holy Alliance to the aid of the Spanish King for the resubjection of his former American colonies. The policy of President Adams' Administration was clearly opposed to the occupation of Cuba and Porto Rico, either by the Spanish Americans or by any European state other than Spain herself. In this matter, also, the Administration and the opposition held the same view.

The only natural explanations of the determined opposition to the Panama mission were, thus, either the dread of embarrassing entanglements with the Spanish-American states, and the consequent compromise of the status of neutrality toward them and their motherland, or the spirit of personal hostility to the Administration. From the merits of the question the former would seem the more likely. It was certainly, to any candid mind, a sufficient reason. On the other hand, an expression uttered by Mr. Van Buren as he left the Senate chamber, after having just made a most earnest appeal against the mission and cast his vote against it, would indicate that the opposition fought the Administration in this matter from factional motives purely. He is reported to have said: "They have beaten us by a few votes, after a hard battle; but if they had only taken the other side and refused the mission, we should have had them." *Real nature of the opposition to the Panama mission.*

The debate continued so long, however, that the congress at Panama adjourned to Tacubaya before the representatives from the United States appeared. Spain ceased to wage war against her former colonies. The Holy Alliance did not interfere. The Spanish-American states suspended their operations against Cuba and Porto Rico. Hayti remained in isolated barbarism. And the congress of the American nations never reassembled.

*The failure of the Panama congress.*

It is possible that the jingo policy of the Administration may have helped to produce all these results. It is probable that the same results would have followed had the Senate refused the mission to Panama. It is certainly most fortunate that these results were attained without the attendance of the representatives of the United States upon the congress. All possible entanglements were thus avoided, while the purposes of the Administration, in so far at least as they subserved the true interests of the country, were substantially accomplished.

It is true that the special commercial advantages which Clay had hoped for were not secured, nor his dream of an American Confederacy under the protectorate of the United States realized. Neither were the President's ideas in regard to methods for settling mooted questions of international relations, nor those in regard to the advancement of religious liberty, fulfilled. But these things were all premature, to say the least, and none of them would, probably, have been helped onward by any discussion in the congress of the American nations. With the exception of the United States, those nations were altogether too immature to deal with such problems; and the United States itself was not sufficiently consolidated and powerful to assume the duties of instructor and guardian over them. It is not probable that any opportunity for doing good or receiving good was lost by the non-attendance of representatives

THE DIVISION OF THE REPUBLICAN PARTY   155

from the United States upon the deliberations of the Panama congress. It is far more probable that both the doing and the suffering of injury were escaped.

While the question of the relation of the United States to the other states upon the American continents is by no means transitory, the question of the Panama mission was so, at least so much so as not to serve well as an issue for the division of the Republican party into two permanently hostile forces.

The question of internal improvements was a better issue, from this point of view. In his first annual message President Adams took high national ground upon this subject. He seemed to attribute to the general Government unlimited power to construct roads and canals, establish universities and observatories, and to do any and every thing conducive to the improvement of the people. Clay himself, it is said, was a little staggered by the exceeding broadness of Mr. Adams' ideas. While Mr. Van Buren, the leader of the opposition in the Senate, offered a resolution in that body, a fortnight after the message, which declared that Congress did not possess the power to make roads and canals within the respective Commonwealths, and proposed the formation of an amendment to the Constitution, which should prescribe the powers that the general Government should have over the subject of internal improvements. *Adams on internal improvements in his message of December 6th, 1825.* *Van Buren's resolution against internal improvements.*

Mr. Adams seems to have yielded before the opposition in this matter, and to have thus avoided making it a further issue. In his subsequent messages he confined himself chiefly to observations upon the work done by the engineers appointed under the Congressional Act of April 30th, 1824, for making surveys, plans, *The practices of the Adams Administration in respect to internal improvements.*

and estimates for national routes. The Administration and Congress simply put into practice the Monroe ideas upon the subject. Money was appropriated by Congress for the construction and repair of roads, and was expended under the supervision of the President, and stock was taken by the Government in private corporations, organized under Commonwealth law, and subject to Commonwealth jurisdiction, for the construction of canals; but no jurisdiction and no administrative powers were exercised or asserted by the general Government over such improvements, except, perhaps, the power of eminent domain.

The opposition, however, which had been excited at first by Mr. Adams' proposition to make a large advance upon Mr. Monroe's principles, was not satisfied with his return in practice to those principles. They professed to entertain the fear that the Administration had a settled policy of encroachment upon the reserved rights and powers of the Commonwealths, and they now began to watch and combat the movements of the Administration chiefly from this point of view. This attitude must not yet, however, be ascribed wholly or chiefly to the conscious influences of the slavery interest. Factional hostility to the Administration, and the general settling back into the "States' rights" view of the Constitution, which manifests itself all through the history of the United States as a reaction from the tension of war and the enthusiasm of strong national exertion, did more to determine it than the views of the slaveholders in regard to the interests of their peculiar institution.

The great practical difficulty in regard to the subject was in making such determinations as to the national or local character of the proposed improvements as would be satisfactory to the mass of the people. Natu-

## THE DIVISION OF THE REPUBLICAN PARTY 157

rally every Congressman considered the roads of his district as matters of national concern ; and, in spite of the law of 1824 vesting in the President and his board of engineers the laying out of such routes as the President might decide to be required by the general welfare, the scramble for national money to be expended for local purposes increased from one session to another.

*The chief practical difficulty in the way of a national system of internal improvements.*

It was the question of the tariff which showed more clearly than anything else the influence of the interests of slavery in the attitude which the slaveholders would finally take toward the industrial policies of the nation, and which would contribute more than anything else to the division of the Republican party from the point of view of principle.

The great purpose of the Tariff of 1824 was to give the American manufacturers of coarse woollens a substantial control of the home markets. In two years of trial this result had not been realized. A vast amount of capital had been transferred from other enterprises to build new woollen mills, and the markets were so glutted with their fabrics that sale for them could only be found by virtually excluding foreign goods of the same material and grade. It was claimed that the foreign goods were sold upon foreign account, and not by *bona fide* American merchants, and that the goods were thus undervalued by the fictitious parties to the importation, and the duty thus so largely avoided as to make the importation practically free. It was, therefore, contended that the agent of the foreign manufacturer or merchant was ruining the American manufacturer, on the one hand, and the American merchant, on the other. President Adams himself, in his message of December 5th, 1826, referred to the frauds thus committed on the revenue. The

*The Tariff of 1824 a failure.*

manufacturers of woollens in New England and Pennsylvania memorialized Congress, during the latter part of the year 1826, representing themselves to be in dire distress and praying for aid. These memorials were referred to the Committee on Manufactures of the House of Representatives for report. On January 10th, 1827, the chairman of this committee, Mr. Mallary, of Vermont, introduced a bill to meet the difficulties above described.

This bill proposed to introduce a system of minimal valuations at the custom-house instead of taking the foreign invoice as the basis for the levy of the duty, as was the existing practice, and it placed the valuation of coarse woollens so high as practically to prohibit their importation. The bill proposed, however, to raise the tariff on wool to such a rate as would deprive the manufacturers very largely of the benefit to be secured by the system of minimal valuations. It was questionable whether the manufacturers would get any very material aid out of this bill, which contained so high a rate of duty upon the raw material, but it was necessary to incorporate the provision in order to secure the support of the West to the measure.

*The Tariff Bill of 1827.*

The industrial antithesis between the North and the South became more exactly organized under the issue presented by this bill. Massachusetts joined the high protection ranks, and Kentucky went over to the side of the South. Missouri, however, still voted for the tariff, while New York City still preserved its attitude of opposition, and Maine's Representatives were evenly divided in the final vote on the bill. The protection phalanx from Pennsylvania was broken, too, by the defection of her two most important Representatives, Ingham and Buchanan. The attitude of

*Development of the industrial antithesis between the North and the South.*

Buchanan was a matter of especial note. He held that the constitutionality of the tariff and the policy of a moderate protection had been completely settled by the founders of the Constitution and by the uniform practice of the Government, but that so high a tariff as the one now proposed on woollens was impolitic, from the point of view of the general welfare, and unjust, from that of an equal distribution of the burdens of taxation. Mr. Buchanan owed much of his subsequent success to the moderate views which he advanced and adhered to at this juncture.

It will be seen, however, that the supporters of, and the opposition to, the tariff respectively had not yet become entirely sectional, though an advance had been made since 1824 toward that result. The bill passed the House on February 10th, 1827, but the Senate did not reach its consideration before the conclusion of the session.

<small>The bill passed by the House of Representatives.</small>

It had the effect, however, of arousing most intense excitement and bitter opposition in South Carolina. In fact, it is from this date and issue that we must trace the history of nullification in South Carolina. In the summer following the Congressional session of 1826-27 the chief personages of the Commonwealth assembled at Columbia. The Governor, Mr. Taylor, presided, and the principal orator of the occasion was the President of the College of the Commonwealth, Dr. Cooper, a man of rare powers and great learning, an Englishman by birth and education, a free-trader in his political economy, and a "States' rights" man in his political science. In his speech he suggested disunion as preferable to submission to the tariff legislation of Congress. The resolutions passed by the assembly were not so inflammatory as the Doctor's speech, but they declared that such legislation

<small>Hostility to the measure in S. C.</small>

was calculated to give rise to the inquiry whether the Union was of any benefit, under such conditions, to the Southern Commonwealths.

Copies of these resolutions were sent to the legislative bodies of the several Southern Commonwealths, but they evoked no response whatsoever. The proposed tariff had, by the inaction of the Senate, been virtually abandoned, and it was therefore unnecessary to protest against its passage as law, or make threats against its execution.

*The bill neglected by the Senate.*

At the beginning of the next session of Congress, that of 1827-28, the committee on Manufactures brought in another bill. It advanced the duty on iron by from ten to fifteen per centum; it advanced the duty on wool by from about fifty to more than one hundred per centum, imposing both a specific and an *ad valorem* duty upon it. It changed the duty upon woollen goods costing less than $2.50 a square yard from an *ad valorem* to a specific duty, and increased the duty by about twenty per centum. It retained the *ad valorem* duty on woollens costing more than $2.50 a square yard, and increased the same by about twenty per centum, and in addition thereto it imposed a minimum valuation of $4 a square yard upon all such goods costing between $2.50 and $4 a square yard, which would effect an additional increase of duty of about fifty per centum on the average. It finally increased the duty on hemp by about twenty-five per centum immediately, and by about eighty per centum in three years.

*The Tariff of 1828.*

This was a far more moderate protection upon woollen fabrics than that proposed at the previous session, on account of the fact that the duty on the raw material was so greatly increased. It was at least questionable whether the manufacturers would receive any substantial benefit out of the measure. Mr. Mallary, the chairman of the committee, felt so dubious about this that he dissented from the committee's report in regard to woollen fabrics, and offered an amendment to the bill for the purpose of curing this defect. He could not, however, bring the House to accept his proposition, but his opposition to the committee's report opened the way for some modification of the bill to the advantage of the manufacturers. It was still, however, no great boon to the manufacturers. It was about as much a wool- and hemp-grower's bill as a manufacturer's bill. Nobody could tell whether it would be more beneficial to the manufacturers than to the wool- and hemp-growers.

One thing alone was certain, and that was, that the cotton-planters and those engaged in foreign commerce would have no direct share in the benefits of the measure. And it was also very difficult to figure out any indirect benefits for them. It would not widen the domestic market for raw cotton. It would increase the price of woollen fabrics. It would increase the domestic demand for the products of Western agriculture, and thereby increase the price of these products to the Southern consumers of them. And it would discourage the importation of woollen goods. These were all the results easily discernible, and every one of them bore hard upon the planting and shipping interests. The representatives from the Southern Commonwealths pointed out these things, but they were told to establish manufactures themselves, and then they would be tributary to nobody.

Some of the Southerners, like Colonel Hayne, frankly replied that they could not establish manufactures with slave labor; while others, like Mr. McDuffie, threatened ruin to the Northern manufacturers if they succeeded in having the duties raised so high as to drive the South, with its cheap slave labor, into manufactures.

*The Southerners not yet agreed that slave labor could not be employed in manufacture.*

The vote in the House of Representatives reflects quite perfectly the character of the bill. The members from the wool- and hemp-growing sections supported the bill; those from the manufacturing section were indifferent; those from the shipping and commercial sections opposed it; and those from the planting section opposed it unanimously.

<small>The character of the bill as reflected in the analysis of the vote upon it.</small>

In the Senate, amendments were made to the bill which altered it in the direction of a slightly increased protection to the manufacturers. Still, Mr. Webster, who had become a champion of protection since his section had become a manufacturing section, claimed that the bill was of little worth to the manufacturers, while the increased duty on hemp would bear heavily on the shipping interests of New England. He voted for the bill, however, while his colleague, Mr. Silsbee, voted against it. The vote in the Senate differed only slightly, as regards sectional distribution, from that in the House. It was finally passed by both Houses as amended by the Senate, and was signed by the President on the nineteenth day of May, 1828; and opposition to it thereafter must take on the form of petition for its repeal, or that of resistance to its execution. Before it could come to the latter, however, three things must be accomplished. The first was the invention of the morale of such resistance. The second was the creation of the party of resistance. And the last was the capture of some existing governmental organization by that party.

While thus it cannot be said that the "Jackson men" voted against this bill and the Administration men for it, still there was something which looked like an approach toward this relation. Certainly the Southern wing of the Jacksonians, or of the Democratic party, as the Jacksonians now called

<small>The Tariff of 1828 not a complete party measure.</small>

## THE DIVISION OF THE REPUBLICAN PARTY 163

themselves in distinction from the National Republicans, opposed the measure with something like unanimity. Many of Jackson's Northern supporters, however, voted for the bill, and it may be said that the Democratic party of the North was then in favor of moderate protection to all the interests of the country.

The party divisions of 1828 were still largely dominated by considerations of personal partisanship, and the organization of the two parties, which had now emerged from the all-comprehending Republican party, upon the basis of different political creeds, still lacked much of completion.

The campaign of 1828 was not fought upon the issues of any well established differences in political and economic policies. Jackson and his followers simply appealed to the mass of the people, especially to the lower classes, "to turn the rascals out," on the ground that the "Old Hero," the friend of the people, had been cheated, by a corrupt bargain between the two chiefs of the Administration, out of his rights in 1824, and that the whole pack of officials serving under them had been corrupted by the venality of their superiors. The people must take possession of their Government and send the wicked aristocracy of office holders to the right about, was the chief demand of the Democracy of 1828, and it was with the empty phrases, with which they rang the changes upon this demand, that they won the battle. *The presidential campaign of 1828 still dominated by personal considerations.*

Jackson and Calhoun were elected by an electoral vote of more than two to one. Every Commonwealth west of the Alleghanies, and every one south of Mason and Dixon's line, except Delaware and Maryland, gave its electoral vote entire to Jackson and Calhoun; and in addition thereto Pennsylvania *Election of Jackson.*

gave them its entire vote, New York gave them twenty of its thirty-six votes, Maine one of its nine, and Maryland five of its eleven.

It was a tremendous *bouleversement*. The mob of malcontents had gotten together, had pulled together, and had accomplished their purpose. The old ruling class in American society was driven from place and power, and a new, untried, and inexperienced set of men seized the reins of Government. It looked something like a combination of the South and West against the East. They had, however, secured the two most important Eastern Commonwealths through Van Buren's activity in New York and Jackson's own popularity in Pennsylvania. It was not yet, however, a socialistic uprising against the wealth of the East. It was a political uprising against the monopoly of office-holding by the old official aristocracy. It was the introduction of a new class of eligibles into the official positions. Whether the subsequent effects of this change would be a modification of the structure of the Union or the policies of the Government remained to be seen.

*Advent of the parvenus.*

Jackson placed Van Buren at the head of the Department of State, and under the influence of this most astute politician started out upon his presidential career. The foreign diplomacy of the Administration was naturally successful. The disputes with Great Britain in regard to the northeast boundary of the United States, and in regard to trade between the United States and the British colonies, and the dispute with France in regard to indemnity for the spoliations committed by the French upon American commerce in the first years of the century, were successfully dealt with, by a judicious admixture of shrewdness, conciliatoriness, and firmness. These questions were not, however, of sufficient importance to

*Foreign affairs under Jackson's Administration.*

## THE DIVISION OF THE REPUBLICAN PARTY 165

turn the attention from the internal questions of constitutional interpretation and governmental policies.

The Jackson party, or the Democratic party, must make its creed, both political and economic, and it must adjust that creed both to the Constitution and to the working of the Government. The party was composed of three tolerably distinct divisions, which may be termed the Southern, the Western, and the Eastern divisions. Of these, the Western division alone was a real democracy. The Southern and Eastern divisions were rather aristocracies. The Southern division was emphatically so. And when it came to policies, the Western division favored internal improvements, and the Eastern and Southern divisions opposed them; the Western division favored a tariff on wool and hemp, the Eastern favored moderate protection of manufactures, and the Southern division wanted as nearly free trade as the revenues of the Government would allow. It was a great task for the Administration to maintain the combination, and keep a reliable majority in Congress.

*The Democratic party and its divisions.*

# CHAPTER VIII.

## DEMOCRATIC OPPOSITION TO INTERNAL IMPROVEMENTS AND PROTECTION

Jackson's Ideas Concerning Internal Improvements—The Maysville Road Bill—The Slavery Question not Involved in the Vote on the Bill or in the Veto — Railway Building Begun — The Commencement of the Struggle for the Repeal of the Tariff of 1828—Jackson on the Tariff of 1828, in his First Annual Message—George McDuffie as South Carolina's Political Economist—Dr. Thomas Cooper—Mr. McDuffie's Tariff Bill—The Tariff Bill of 1830—McDuffie's Amendment — McDuffie's Doctrine that the Producers of Exports Pay Finally the Duties on the Imports—The Acceptance of Mr. McDuffie's Doctrine at the South—Growing Belief in the Incapacity of Slave Labor for Manufacture — The Tariff Pronounced Unconstitutional — Growth of the Protection Idea—Jackson on the Tariff and the Surplus Revenue Derived therefrom, in the Message of December, 1830 — Southern Disappointment — "The South Carolina Exposition"—Calhoun's Doctrine of "States' rights"—Nullification in Theory—The Nullification and Anti-nullification Parties in South Carolina—First Attempt to try the Validity of the Tariff in the United States Courts—Nullification and Rebellion—Jackson's Message of December, 1831, on the Tariff Issue—The Bill from the Committee on Ways and Means—The Tariff Bill of 1832 from the Committee on Manufactures—Passage of the Tariff of 1832 by the House of Representatives—The "American System."

IN his first annual message President Jackson referred to the general dissatisfaction with the manner of deal-

INTERNAL IMPROVEMENTS AND PROTECTION 167

ing with the question of internal improvements which had prevailed to that time, and proposed that the general Government should abandon the subject entirely and should distribute the surplus of the revenue, above the wants of the Government, among the Commonwealths, and leave to them the expenditure of the money upon internal improvements. *Jackson's ideas concerning internal improvements.*

The Congress, however, paid no regard to the President's recommendation. In May, 1830, it sent up to the President for his approval a bill authorizing and requiring the Government to take stock in a Kentucky turnpike, running from Maysville on the Ohio River to Lexington, some sixty miles inward. *The Maysville Road Bill.*

The President vetoed the bill, May 27th. His special reason was that the road was not a national, but a local, matter. He did not attack the Monroe principle upon the general subject of internal improvements, but he referred to the recommendation contained in his annual message as still expressing his view of the manner in which the Government should rid itself of the embarrassments into which it was being farther and farther drawn by the practice of voting national money for internal improvements. He argued that the subject must be considered upon its own merits, and not brought into connection with the tariff policy. He thus saw the prospect of the expenditure of millions of national money upon internal improvements in order to relieve the protectionists of the embarrassment of a great surplus, and denounced it. He contended that the Government should adopt its policy upon each of these subjects as if the other did not exist. He urged, finally, that, if the people wanted the general Government to undertake internal improvements, they should *The veto of the Bill.*

so amend the Constitution as to give the Government sufficient jurisdiction over the roads and canals, which it might build, to protect them against wanton injury, and to collect the tolls necessary to keep them in repair. This he declared to be necessary to any satisfactory exercise of powers upon the general subject by the Government.

The veto certainly exerted some influence upon the minds of the Representatives. A majority still voted for the bill, but it was a much reduced majority. The vote upon the vetoed bill stood ninety-six to ninety. The bill was therefore lost.

The exact question at issue was not, as we have seen, the general policy of internal improvements, but it

<small>The slavery question not involved in the vote on the bill or in the veto.</small> was whether the Maysville road was a national improvement. An analysis of the vote upon the subject may not, therefore, have any significance, from the point of view of the general question. Roughly, we may say that a majority of the Representatives from the South voted against the bill, a large majority of those from the Northwest voted for it, a majority of those from Pennsylvania and New Jersey voted for it, while a majority of those from New York voted against it, and, lastly, the Representatives from New England were divided. It thus appears rather far fetched to ascribe the attitude of the opponents of the bill, in any section, to the influence of the slavery interest. Those who voted against the bill said they did so because the object for which the appropriation was sought was a local affair, managed by a private corporation, for private gain. That uncompromising enemy of slavery, Mr. John W. Taylor, of New York, was prominent among those who took this position and voted against the bill. He even pronounced it unconstitutional, and was inclined to the

INTERNAL IMPROVEMENTS AND PROTECTION 169

view, as we have seen, that internal improvements generally were left by the Constitution for the Commonwealths to construct and control.

It is usual to attribute to the veto of this bill the overthrow of the policy of internal improvements by the general Government. This proposition will hardly bear close examination. Congress continued to make appropriations for internal improvements, which the President usually vetoed, if they were in separate bills, and usually approved, if they were included in the general appropriation bills. *Too much influence in determining the national policy toward internal improvements usually ascribed to the veto.* It is calculated that while Adams signed appropriations for internal improvements to the amount of less than two millions and a half of dollars, Jackson approved disbursements for these purposes to the amount of more than ten millions of dollars.

The fact is that the building of railways was the chief force which put an end to road- and canal-making by the general Government. The construction of the Mohawk and Hudson Railroad, the parent of the New York Central system, was begun in 1825. *Railway building begun.* In 1827 the survey of the Boston and Albany line was begun. The same year the Pennsylvania system had its origin. One year later the Baltimore and Ohio system was founded. The year of the veto of the Maysville road bill forty-one miles of railroad were being operated in the United States, and at the close of the decade more than two thousand miles. As the railway system spread over the country, through private enterprise, the appropriations of national money for internal improvements became more and more confined to the specific improvements of rivers and harbors. The roads and canals of a national character were being made unnecessary by the extension of the railways. It is undoubtedly, then, far more plausible and natural to attribute the overthrow of the policy of internal improvements by the general Government to the growth of the railways, constructed and operated by private corporations under Commonwealth charters, on the one side, and, on the other, to the settled conviction that the general Government did not have the constitutional powers adequate to the successful establishment and protection of a system of works based upon that policy, and to the unsatisfactory experience which the country had had in attempting to distinguish local from national enterprises and to confine appropriations to those of the latter character.

It is difficult to see any special connection of the interests of slavery with the decline of the policy. It is true that the slaveholders were becoming strict constructionists generally. They had learned from the Missouri struggle that Congress must not be allowed to magnify its powers when forming the Territories into Commonwealths, and they had learned from the tariff struggles that Congress must not be allowed to magnify its powers in regard to the regulation of foreign commerce and the raising of revenue, but, as to internal improvements, no reliable evidence of a consciousness, on the part of the slaveholders, of any particular connection between their peculiar interest and a policy upon this subject by the general Government is discoverable.

On the contrary, in the struggle for the repeal of the Tariff of 1828 the influence of the slavery interest is easily remarked, and is clearly seen to have been controlling.

On February 10th, 1829, Mr. William Smith, the senior Senator from South Carolina, presented to the Senate the protest of the legislature of South Caro-

INTERNAL IMPROVEMENTS AND PROTECTION 171

lina against Congressional protection to domestic manufactures. This memorial pronounced all such acts to be unconstitutional, except as incidental to raising the revenue or regulating commerce, and impolitic even then, when their operation would be unequal upon the different sections of the country, and felt by any section to be oppressive. *The commencement of the struggle for the repeal of the Tariff of 1828.* The language of the paper was respectful, moderate, dignified, and forcible, and it contained no threats of disunion, or of violent or unlawful resistance. The legislature asked that the protest should be entered on the journal of the Senate. The Senate, however, only ordered it to be printed.

The South Carolinians promised themselves, nevertheless, some measure of relief from what they supposed would be the policy of the newly elected President. Being a Southern man, it was naturally supposed that he would recognize Southern interests in the policy upon this subject which he would recommend. But, while Jackson had not committed himself to protection for the sake of the manufacturers or of the producers of raw material, he was a strong Union man and an American, and the argument for the tariff from the point of view of national industrial independence exercised a prevailing influence in determining his attitude toward the subject.

In his message of December 8th, 1829, he wrote that the Tariff of 1828 had not proved itself so beneficial to the manufacturers or so injurious to commerce and agriculture as had been anticipated; that he regretted that all nations would not abolish restrictions, and refer the management of trade to individual enterprise; that since, however, they would not do so, a tariff was the necessary policy of the United States; but that in the *Jackson on the Tariff of 1828, in his first annual message.*

face of the fact that the national debt would soon be paid, and the sinking fund would not be much longer required, a modification of the existing tariff in the direction of a reduction of duties would soon be the true and necessary policy ; and that the principle to be followed in making such a modification ought to be to reduce the duties upon such articles as might come into competition with home products no further than would leave to the latter a fair chance in such competition ; and that from the general principle of a reduction to this point must be excepted the duties on the implements and prime necessities of war, all of which should enjoy a higher protection than that accorded to other articles.

Jackson's views on the Tariff as a general policy. Evidently, according to this doctrine, the chief reductions should fall upon articles not coming into competition with home products, such articles as tea, coffee, etc., at that time termed the unprotected articles. Jackson had thus anticipated Clay's American system of the tariff by nearly three years, as we shall see.

The South Carolinians were greatly disappointed by this expression of the President's views, although they claimed that the message recommended substantial tariff reduction. This part of the message was referred to the committee on Manufactures, according to the rule of procedure which had prevailed in the House of Representatives for nearly a decade, and which showed that the matter of the tariff was not regarded as something purely incidental to the raising of revenue.

The claim was now put forward, however, that the subject properly belonged to the domain of George McDuffie as South Carolina's political economist. the committee on Ways and Means. Mr. George McDuffie, of South Carolina, was at this moment the chairman of this committee. He was a man of keen intelligence, strong cour-

INTERNAL IMPROVEMENTS AND PROTECTION 173

age, and great persistence. He was the political economist of the slave-labor system, as Calhoun was its political scientist and constitutional lawyer. It is to be surmised, at least, that he learned much of his political economy from the notorious, if not famous, Dr. Thomas Cooper, the British President of South Carolina College. It is true that Mr. McDuffie's college days had passed before Dr. Cooper taught in the institution, but the Doctor wrote and published much upon economic and political subjects between 1820 and 1830. In fact, he set the direction of thought upon such subjects in South Carolina and throughout a large portion of the South during that period. As has been already mentioned, he was an Englishman by birth. He had spent a part of his earlier life in France, and had imbibed the doctrines of French republicanism. For this reason he was disliked and shunned by conservative men in England to such a degree as to make longer residence in his native country uncomfortable to him. He came to the United States in the last decade of the eighteenth century. His radical views and his violent expressions of them soon drew attention to him here. He was one of the men prosecuted under the Alien and Sedition laws of 1798. He made his way to South Carolina about the beginning of the third decade of this century, and found there a well prepared soil for his Girondist views of federal Government and his free-trade views in political economy. A true estimate of responsibilities for the events of 1832 in South Carolina would probably hold him more culpable than Calhoun himself. It was from such a thinker, and he was a keen and vigorous thinker, that Mr. McDuffie received impulse, if not actual instruction, in his reasoning.

*Dr. Thomas Cooper.*

Mr. McDuffie argued that the power to impose a tariff

was not expressly vested by the Constitution in the Government; that, therefore, if it existed at all, as a power of the Government, it must be incidental to some express provision; and that it could be incidental only to the power for raising the revenue. He, therefore, contended further that all tariff bills must originate in the House of Representatives, and in the regular revenue committee of that House, the committee of Ways and Means.

Congress had disregarded the protest of the South Carolina Legislature of the previous February. It was well known that the committee on Manufactures in the House was favorable to the maintenance of the existing duties. It seemed, therefore, to Mr. McDuffie, and those who thought with him, both natural and necessary that the committee of Ways and Means should claim their constitutional prerogative, and make an effort to get the ear of Congress to their representations. Consequently, on February 5th, 1830, Mr. McDuffie reported a tariff bill from his committee, without having had the subject specifically referred to them by the House. The bill provided for a moderate reduction of the tariff all around, but still left a duty of thirty-three and one-third per centum *ad valorem* upon woollen fabrics.

Mr. McDuffie's Tariff Bill.

The interest attaching to this proposition lies in the fact that it contains substantially the terms upon which the South Carolinians were willing to compromise the tariff question. It shows them to have been still moderate tariff men, rather than out and out free-traders. To the unprejudiced mind of the present day it certainly appears to have been an offer which merited some consideration, but, after a single reading, it was ordered to lie on the table, from which it was never taken up.

## INTERNAL IMPROVEMENTS AND PROTECTION    175

Meanwhile the committee on Manufactures were very deliberately maturing a measure. It was reported to the House early in April, and taken up for consideration on the 15th. It was nothing more than an administrative measure for the purpose of securing a stricter execution of the existing tariff.

*The Tariff Bill of 1830.*

Mr. McDuffie made another effort to move the House to consider a reduction of duties, in the form of an amendment to this bill. He offered such an amendment, which provided for a return to the duties imposed before 1824 upon woollens, cottons, iron, hemp, etc.

*McDuffie's Amendment.*

It was in support of this amendment that he made his famous argument of April 29th, 1830, in which he developed, for the first time, the doctrine in regard to the final payment of the duties which furnished the economic basis of nullification. That doctrine was that the producers of the exports, which are exchanged in the foreign markets for the imports, pay, finally, the duty upon the imports. His course of reasoning in the establishment of this doctrine was as follows: He reduced all trade ultimately to barter between producers, and then declared it to be self-evident that when a producer of exports should be obliged to pay a duty of twenty-five per centum upon the imports, which he had received in pay for his exports, before he could bring them into the country of his residence, he had received finally twenty-five per centum less for his exports than he would have received had he not been compelled to pay any duty upon his imports.

*McDuffie's doctrine that the producers of exports pay finally the duties on the imports.*

Mr. McDuffie then drew from the statistics of the foreign trade of the United States the fact that the sections cultivating cotton and rice, constituting less than one-fifth of the Union, both in territory and population, produced thirty of the fifty-eight millions' worth of annual exports ; and finally drew the conclusion from these premises that one-fifth of the people, the population of the planting sections, paid more than one-half of the duties on the imports of the country.

If this were true it was indeed a grievous burden. And if the people of the South, or that part of the South devoted to the production of these staples, believed it to be true, then would the reason for one great scruple against resistance to the execution of the tariff laws be removed, namely, the general belief theretofore prevailing, from the doctrine that the consumers of the imports ultimately pay the duties, that the burden of the duties fell nearly equally upon the different sections. So long as this belief was general the sense of oppression in any particular part or section of the country could not become very keen. Substitute for this old idea, however, the new doctrine advanced by Mr. McDuffie, and, under the existing distribution of the articles of export, there could not fail to be developed a most bitter sense of wrong and oppression on the part of the producers of the Southern staples.

*The danger in Mr. McDuffie's conclusions.*

The Southerners, especially the South Carolinians, did embrace the new doctrine, apparently, at least, with all sincerity. It was utterly futile that Mr. Gorham and Mr. Everett pointed out to them the fact that they consumed only a comparatively small portion of the imports received in exchange for their exports, and sold the rest to the people of the other sections with the duties added on, thus shifting the duties upon the other sections. They clung to the new doctrine as if it were something for which they had long been seeking, and to which their

*The acceptance of Mr. McDuffie's doctrine at the South.*

# INTERNAL IMPROVEMENTS AND PROTECTION 177

hearts were already too much attached to be drawn away by argument.

It was in this speech, furthermore, that Mr. McDuffie abandoned his former view of the capacity of slave labor for manufacturing industry, and embraced and enounced the doctrine held before this by Colonel Hayne upon that subject, which was that slave labor could only be employed successfully in agriculture. This was, of course, another necessary element in the consolidation of the interests of the South against the tariff. *Growing belief in the incapacity of slave labor for manufacture.*

It was in this speech, also, that Mr. McDuffie, for the first time, pronounced the tariff unconstitutional. He did not yet declare any and every tariff unconstitutional, but only such a tariff as sacrificed one interest to another, or the interests of one section to those of another. This he claimed the existing tariff did do. The belief in the unconstitutionality of the tariff was, of course, another necessary element in the preparation for resistance to its execution. *The Tariff pronounced unconstitutional.*

Finally, Mr. McDuffie uttered, in this speech, the threat of resistance to the execution of the tariff laws, the threat of nullification. It was ill timed, as threats generally are, and it had the effect of producing the large majority by which Mr. McDuffie's amendment was voted down. *McDuffie's threat of resistance to the execution of the Tariff laws.*

The bill suffered some modification in the course of its passage, but its principle remained the same. It reduced the duty on no article whatever, but only provided for a stricter enforcement of the existing laws.

By another bill, which received the President's approval on May 20th (1830), eight days before this administrative bill was signed, the duties on tea, coffee, and cocoa had been reduced. This meant that the protectionists were very *Growth of the protection idea.*

12

willing to free those articles from duty which did not come into competition with home productions, in order to preserve and increase the duties on those that did. This was the direction in which the tariff system was growing. It became, two years later, the pronounced principle of the "American system," as we shall see.

In the message of December 7th, 1830, President Jackson defended the constitutionality of the protective system, said that the existing tariff needed some corrections in details, and expressed the opinion that no law reducing duties could be made which would be satisfactory to the American people that would not leave a considerable surplus in the Treasury. He suggested the employment of such surplus upon internal improvements under the direction of the legislatures of the several Commonwealths.

<small>Jackson on the Tariff and the surplus revenue derived therefrom, in the message of December, 1830.</small>

This was a stunning blow to the hopes of the Southerners. The extinction of the debt and the existence of an unemployed surplus were the conditions to which they had looked forward as necessitating in all conservative minds the reduction of the duties. But here was a plan, suggested by a Southern President, for relieving the Treasury of any amount of surplus for an indefinite period, without the reduction of a single penny of duty upon a single article. Thus encouraged the protectionists in both Houses of Congress refused, during the session of 1830-31, to consider any propositions looking toward a reduction of duties.

<small>Southern disappointment.</small>

It is hardly a cause of wonder that the South Carolinians began to despair of obtaining through Congress any relief from what they regarded as dire oppression, and that some of them were reviewing the Constitution, and the political principles upon which it was founded, with the purpose of finding other means with which to meet the great emergency. It was in this part of the work that Mr. Calhoun took the lead.

As far back as 1828, just after the enactment of the tariff measure which was giving so much offence, Mr. Calhoun had started out in this direction in the paper which he furnished the South Carolina legislature, which served as the basis of the first pronunciamento from that body upon the subject, the so-called South Carolina Exposition. This document by Mr. Calhoun was comparatively temperate in its language and not very clear in its political doctrines and its constitutional interpretation. The great debate between Hayne and Webster on the floor of the Senate, over which body Mr. Calhoun, as Vice-President, presided, in regard to the fundamental principles of the Union, taught Mr. Calhoun several very important points in the evolution of his doctrine of "States' rights." Especially was he warned against the great error, made by Mr. Hayne, of representing the United States Government as one of the parties to the "constitutional pact" and the "States" as the other. Mr. Webster so completely demolished this theory that Mr. Calhoun was preserved from introducing this fallacy or any of its corollaries into his reasoning, if he had ever been inclined to do so. In his "Address on the Relations of the States and Federal Government," and in his "Address to the People of South Carolina," both published in the summer of 1831, he shows that he had maturely reflected upon all that had been said and written upon the fundamental question of the relation of the "States" to the Union and to the general Government. He had given up his hope both in the Congress and in the President. With him the question of the tariff had now, therefore, been removed from the domain of governmental policy into that of constitutional powers and political principle. This was the point of view which he took in the documents just mentioned.

He began, as innovators generally do, with the assertion that his interpretation of the Constitution was no new invention of his own, but was the ancient principle of the Constitution. That principle was, he contended, that the Constitution was made by the "States," as sovereign bodies, and that through it the "States" created only a governmental agent for their general affairs. The term or phrase United States was only the name of the general governmental agent of the "States." Sovereignty was in the "States" only. Consequently, when the United States assumed powers not conferred by the "States" in the Constitution, the "States," by virtue of the sovereign attribute, might and should interpose, interpose individually, not collectively as they, of course, might do constitutionally through the regular form of procedure for amending the Constitution.

Calhoun, like every other real statesman of his day, held that there is a domain of liberty secured not only to the minority, but to the individual, by the Constitution, upon which the majority shall not encroach. The practical question was how to prevent the majority, in possession of the powers and machinery of the Government, from doing so. The answer to this question developed by precedent, and formulated clearly by Webster at that very moment, was that it could be done only by invoking the aid of the judicial power of the United States. But Calhoun said in reply to this, that the United States courts were a part of the Government, substantially under the control of Congress and the President, through the power of Congress to constitute judgeships at pleasure, and of the President and the

Senate to fill them, and that they were interested, therefore, in the usurpations of power by the Government. He further held that these courts could not decide political questions, although these questions might incidentally involve the most sacred rights of individuals, and that, anyhow, they were as much subject to the "States," acting in their sovereign capacities, as any other part of the Government. He could see no way for preserving the rights of the minority and of individuals, in last resort, against governmental usurpation, save through the power of "*each of the parties* to the compact" to prevent the execution within the territory subject to its jurisdiction of such governmental measures as it might deem usurpations. Nullification in theory.

Down to the time of these utterances of Calhoun the party in South Carolina opposed to any resistance, by force, to the execution of the tariff laws, had been able to prevent the outbreak of nullification. The leaders of this party were among the most distinguished and influential men of the Commonwealth. They were Mr. Drayton, the member of Congress from the Charleston district, Judge Johnson of the United States Supreme Court, Mr. Petigru, Mr. Grimke, the Lowndes, and others of scarcely less note. In the first half of the year 1831 they still held control of the municipal government of Charleston, and of the legislature of the Commonwealth, although the "States' rights" men had obtained the governorship. Nearly all of the opponents of nullification denounced the tariff laws as unjust and oppressive to the South, but they also denounced the doctrine that the execution of any law of the United States could be constitutionally resisted, except by means of the judicial processes provided for the case by the Constitution itself. Resistance in any other manner, they declared, would be rebellion at the outset, revolution if successful. They said that they were not willing to assume any such responsibilities in opposing the tariff laws, and that they regarded the blessings of the Union as too great and manifold to hazard disunion, even if it could be successfully and peaceably accomplished.

Their views were so candid and reasonable that, in spite of the intense excitement which prevailed during the legislative session following the failure of the attempt to modify the tariff, they prevented the nullifiers from securing a sufficient majority in the legislature to order the call of a convention. The nullifiers had committed themselves to the doctrine that the nullifying power was a power of sovereignty, not of government, and that it resided, therefore, in the convention, not in the legislature. So long, then, as the assembly of the convention could be prevented, nullification could be certainly thwarted.

But the publication of Calhoun's new doctrine in the summer of 1831 gave great strength to the nullifiers, and in the municipal election of the latter part of the year they captured the mayorship of Charleston.

*Capture of the municipal government of Charleston by the nullifiers.*

One of the strongest moral forces in the hands of the opponents of nullification against which the nullifiers had to contend was the generally received doctrine that the constitutional means for meeting Congressional usurpation in any given case was a process in the United States courts. Unless they could say that they had tried this means in vain, they would still have to suffer the imputation of too hasty action, if nothing more. In order to escape this, two Charleston lawyers imported a package of dutiable goods, gave bonds for the payment of the duty,

*First attempt to try the validity of the Tariff in the United States courts.*

refused payment, and were sued upon their bonds in the United States District Court. The plan was to have the question of the constitutionality of the tariff submitted to the jury, but the court refused to allow the jury to decide any question except that which pertained to the due execution of the bond.

The nullifiers could now declare that every means suggested by their opponents as regular and lawful had been tried and had failed, and that there now remained only submission to oppression, or nullification, or rebellion. They said that no true South Carolinian could accept the first, and that, therefore, the choice lay between nullification and rebellion. *Nullification and rebellion.* Calhoun taught that there was a vast difference between the two ; that the former was a constitutional, as well as a sovereign, method of resistance. He asserted that it was the great conservative principle of the Constitution, and defined it to be that reserved right whereby a "State," in convention assembled, might suspend the operation of a Congressional act upon its citizens which it considered unconstitutional, until conventions in three-fourths of the "States" should pronounce the Congressional act to be constitutional. He did not claim that this right was reserved specifically, but by implication from the general language of the Tenth Amendment. He was doubtless sincere, or at least thought he was. Many of his followers certainly were, and the masses, who could not understand the doctrine, but took it on faith, were so certain of its truth that they were ready to risk anything for its vindication.

The Unionists, however, branded the doctrine as a deception. An editorial in one of their principal newspapers contained this sentence : "But this everlasting cant of devotion to the Union, accompanied by a recommendation to do those acts that must necessarily destroy it, is beyond patient endurance from a people not absolutely confined in their own mad-houses." It was clear to them, at the outset, that nullification was piecemeal secession and rebellion.

This was the state of things in South Carolina when Congress assembled on the first Monday of December, 1831. On the 6th the President's annual message was laid before the two Houses. It contained a much more distinct and decided recommendation for the reduction of duties than he had ever before expressed. He called attention to the prospect of the early extinguishment of the public debt, when the annual instalment to the sinking fund would be no longer needed, and recommended that Congress should at once deal with the question of the reduction of the duties to a point where they would produce no more revenue than would be necessary for an economical administration of the Government. He farther recommended the readjustment of the duties with a view to equal justice to all national interests, and said that the interests of both merchant and manufacturer required that the change should be prospective.

*Jackson's message of December, 1831, on the Tariff issue.*

There was no suggestion in the message of increasing the expenditures of the Government for internal improvements, or for any other purpose. The plain inference from the message was that by March 4th, 1833, the debt would all be paid, and the revenue could then be reduced by ten or twelve millions a year, and should be.

This was all that the South Carolinians had asked, and it would have been the height of folly for them to have pursued extraordinary means to relieve themselves when regular methods promised at last a prospect of success. This part of the message was referred to the committee on Manufactures, of which ex-President John Quincy Adams was then chairman. Mr. Adams had far more moderate views in regard to the tariff than the majority of his protectionist brethren, and it could be reasonably hoped that he would report a bill from his committee which would be conciliatory in character. The Southerners were not quite willing, however, to rest entirely on his own good will, and raised the contention that the subject of the tariff ought to be referred either to the committee on Ways and Means, or to the committee on Commerce, since the power to impose duties was incident either to the raising of revenue or to the regulation of commerce. The result of the contention was that a resolution was introduced, and taken up, requesting the committee on Commerce to make a report on the working of the tariff, and the committee on Ways and Means was allowed to report a tariff bill, which was read twice and referred to the committee of the Whole House. *(The question of the proper committee to frame Tariff Bills.)*

The bill from the committee on Ways and Means provided for the reduction of the duty to twelve and one-half per centum *ad valorem* on all articles; on some, immediately and totally, but on the more important articles gradually, and in a period of a little more than three years. *(The bill from the Committee on Ways and Means.)*

This was undoubtedly an ill digested measure. It was not only a radical reduction of duties, but it was an indiscriminate reduction. Mr. McDuffie's own committee were not unanimous in recommending it.

On May 23rd Mr. Adams reported the bill from the committee on Manufactures. Mr. Adams based his bill on the report of the Secretary of the Treasury, of December 7th, 1831, and proposed the repeal of the existing system of minimal valuations and the duty on coarse wool altogether, and a slight reduction of the duties on fine wool and woollen fabrics. *(The Tariff Bill of 1832 from the Committee on Manufactures.)*

It was calculated that Mr. Adams' bill would reduce the receipts from the customs by about five or six millions of dollars, leaving thus still an annual surplus of some five or six millions after the extinguishment of the debt.

Mr. McDuffie's bill was taken up first in the committee of the Whole House. Mr. McDuffie defended it with his argument, already stated, that the producers of the exports pay finally the duties on the imports for which the exports are exchanged in the foreign markets, and cited recent utterances of Professor Senior, the noted political economist of Oxford University, in support of his position. He could not, however, convince the House, and his bill was finally disposed of in less than a week. Mr. Adams' bill was then taken up. It was understood as proposing a slight reduction all around. It was intended to do so. But Mr. McDuffie made an argument against it, in which he undertook to prove, and declared that he did prove, that it discriminated still further against the South, and imposed a heavier burden upon that section than it was even then bearing, grievous as that was. He declared, finally, that he would not submit to it.

The House, however, was neither convinced by his argument nor intimidated by his threat. It passed the bill on June 28th, by a large majority, a majority of more than two to one.

*Passage of the Tariff of 1832 by the House of Representatives.*

Meanwhile the Senate had been occupying itself with an exhaustive discussion of the principle of the tariff. On January 9th, 1832, Mr. Clay introduced the famous resolution for making the tariff upon articles coming into competition with home manufactures a system of permanent high duties, and for abolishing, or greatly reducing, the duties upon all other articles.

# INTERNAL IMPROVEMENTS AND PROTECTION 187

Senator Hayne immediately grasped the import of this proposition. He declared that it marked a new era in the tariff system. He demonstrated that down to that time the protection of manufactures had been regarded by all persons and parties as a temporary policy and had been justified as such, while this proposition looked to its establishment as a permanent principle of the policy of the country, which neither revenue surplus nor manufacturing experience should affect.

Mr. Clay, who had himself spoken of protection before this as only a temporary policy, acknowledged the truth of Colonel Hayne's criticism, and proceeded, in his famous three days' speech, to develop "The American System." the arguments for the permanent protective system, the "American System," as he termed it, which made up the text-book for the later supporters of that system. His idea was simply to collect the duties from those foreign products which come into competition in the home markets with domestic products, and prevent the accumulation of a Treasury surplus by fixing the duties so high in rate as to make them largely prohibitory. As we have seen, this idea had been already foreshadowed in one of President Jackson's earlier messages. It now received its complete formulation and its economic justification.

But it was a sad prospect for the South. The South had looked forward to the extinguishment of the debt as necessarily bringing in its train the decrease of duties to the gross amount of at least ten millions of dollars per annum, and now it was called upon to consider the plan for a decrease of revenue by an increase of duties. It is hardly astonishing that the disappointment should have been bitter, and that passionate men should have thought of resistance to what appeared to them so grievously unjust.

The Senate referred Mr. Clay's resolution, together with an amendment to it, proposed by Colonel Hayne, for a general reduction of duties, to its committee on Manufactures. The committee reported a bill based on Mr. Clay's principle. The Constitution does not, however, allow the Senate to originate a bill for raising revenue, and the majority of the Senators voted to lay the bill on the table, and await the movements in the House.

On June 29th the House bill appeared in the Senate, and was referred by that body to its committee on Manufactures. On July 2nd Mr. Dickerson reported from this committee the House bill, with a series of amendments to it, proposed by the committee. These amendments were all in the direction of Mr. Clay's idea, and were adopted by the Senate. The bill as thus amended passed the Senate on July 9th, the Senators from every Northern Commonwealth voting for it, and those from every Southern Commonwealth, except Kentucky, Missouri, and Louisiana, voting against it. Missouri was hardly to be then classed as a Southern Commonwealth. Louisiana was won by an increase of the duty on sugar. And only one of the Senators from Kentucky voted against the measure.

*The bill in the Senate.*

The House of Representatives refused to concur in some of the amendments, and the measure was sent to a Conference committee. This committee patched up a compromise, and the bill became a law on July 14th.

*The bill as finally passed.*

On the whole, it was doubtful if the bill, with the changes imposed upon it by the Senate, would prove to be any relief to the South. Many of the Southerners claimed that it would increase the burden upon that section, while none of them appeared to think it would lighten it.

## INTERNAL IMPROVEMENTS AND PROTECTION

What now were the planters to do? They had waited for the extinguishment of the debt, and for the period when the Treasury would no longer require the sixteen millions of dollars per annum applied to its cancellation, hoping for a general reduction of duties by something like this sum as the necessary result; but instead of this they were now offered, as a final solution of the tariff question, a slight reduction of duties on articles coming into competition with home products, a practical abolition of the duties on those which did not come into competition with home products, and an increase in the expenses of the Government to the amount of the receipts whatever they might be. This was to be the permanent policy of the country, the "American System."

They were indeed wofully disappointed, not to say deceived. There seemed now no further hope of aid to them, from either Congress, the President, or the courts. They must yield unconditionally and hopelessly, or resist the execution of the law. The former course was too much to expect from the proud barons of South Carolina. The only question was whether some legal basis for the resistance could be found, or whether it must take on the form of rebellion. We have already considered Calhoun's doctrine of nullification, and his claim that it was a constitutional remedy; it now remains for us to trace briefly the history of the attempt to apply it. Before, however, we can do this intelligently, we must consider the other political developments of the year 1832, occasioned chiefly by the presidential election of that year, but affecting directly or indirectly the attitude of the Administration toward events in South Carolina, and the attitude of Congress toward the President in dealing with nullification.

# CHAPTER IX.

## THE UNITED STATES BANK AND THE PRESIDENTIAL CONTEST OF 1832

Jackson and the Bank in his First Annual Message—Jackson's Relations to the Portsmouth Branch of the Bank—Jackson's Opposition in Principle to the Bank—The Political Science of the Constitution of 1787—Western Democracy—The West and the "Money Power" of the East—"States' rights" and the Bank — The Case of Brown and Maryland — Democracy and Socialism—Benton's Attack on the Bank—Benton Repulsed—Jackson and Benton—The Bank and the People—The Existence of the Bank made a Political Issue—Jackson's Second Attack on the Bank—Jackson's Plan for a Bank—Benton's Resolution against the Re-charter of the Bank— Jackson's Challenge to make the Continued Existence of the Bank the Issue in the Campaign of 1832—The Challenge Accepted—The Bank's Petition for Re-charter—Benton's Charge of Illegal Practices—Passage of the Bill for Re-charter—The Veto of the Bank Bill—The Bank and Foreign Powers—The Bank and the West—The Bank and the Rich—Structure and Powers of the Bank — Jackson on Executive Independence—Von Holst's Criticism of the Veto Message—The President's Real Meaning.

IN his first annual message, that of December 8th, 1829, President Jackson began his war upon the United States Bank. He declared in it that the constitutionality and expediency of the law creating the Bank were well questioned by a large portion of the people, and that its failure to establish a sound and uniform currency, the great end of its existence, must be admitted by all.

*Jackson and the Bank in his first annual message.*

# THE UNITED STATES BANK 191

Basing themselves chiefly upon an individual report made by Mr. John Quincy Adams on May 14th, 1832, in regard to the condition of the Bank, and upon documents referred to in that report, recent historians attribute President Jackson's first attack upon the United States Bank to a personal feud between his friends in New Hampshire and Mr. Webster's friends there.

*Jackson's relations to the Portsmouth branch of the Bank.*

Senator Levi Woodbury, of New Hampshire, the leader of the Jackson party in New Hampshire, endeavored, in the summer of 1829, to have Jeremiah Mason, Mr. Webster's great friend, removed from the presidency of the branch of the United States Bank at Portsmouth, N. H., and Isaac Hill, another New Hampshire friend of the President, attempted at the same time to have the United States pension agency, connected with the Portsmouth branch of the United States Bank, removed to Concord, and connected with a little bank there of which Hill had been president, and in which he was still interested. Jackson's Secretary of the Treasury, Mr. Ingham, asked Mr. Biddle, the president of the United States Bank, to have Mason removed, and his Secretary of War, Mr. Eaton, ordered Mason to transfer the pension agency to Hill's bank in Concord. Mr. Biddle looked into the matter, and being convinced that the whole thing was a political scheme, refused to have Mason removed from office, and prevented the execution of Eaton's order in regard to the transfer of the pension agency.

These are, very briefly stated, the facts upon which some of the American historians found the theory that Jackson, entertaining no opposition in principle to the Bank at the beginning of his Administration, became so enraged at its managers, because of their success in these petty bouts with his Cabinet officers, that he resolved upon its destruction. The treatment which Adams and Clay had received at the hands of Jackson and his friends from 1824 onward had led them to feel that Jackson's whole nature was full of personal rancor, and that he could see nothing except from a personal point of view. There is little doubt that this feeling largely determined Adams' ideas of Jackson's attitude in the Bank question, and that the historians have written the account of the Bank controversy under the influence of Adams' representations.

There is undoubtedly some truth in this view of the matter, but it is far from being the whole truth. It is Jackson's opposition in principle to the Bank. not even that part of the truth which is most valuable to the student of American history. There was an opposition in principle to the United States Bank, as well as a personal conflict between leaders in regard to it. That opposition in principle was the opposition of "States' rights" democracy to centralized privilege.

In all political systems there is a political science as well as a public, or constitutional, law. The political science of a state is based chiefly upon the actual social conditions and relations of its population, and its public or constitutional law ought to be based upon its political science. In fact, however, we seldom see social conditions, political theory, and public law in a state of perfect harmony. It is the prime problem of political and legal progress to work out this great result.

The political science or theory upon which the Constitution of 1787 was founded was thoroughly English. The political science of the Constitution of 1787. It recognized social distinctions, and its most fundamental principle was compromise between conflicting interests. It was substantially in harmony with social conditions, on the one side,

## THE UNITED STATES BANK 193

and was fairly expressed through the Constitution of 1787, on the other. Without the interposition of other forces it would have made out of the United States a new England. But French political science had already gained a foothold in the country. It was contained in the Declaration of Independence, and its prime postulate was "the equality of all men." It did not then comport with the social condition of the country, and the Constitution did not make its principle into positive law. It was, therefore, at the beginning, abstract, and theoretical. The man who taught it, however, became President, and the party which embraced it became the governing party. But their practice was not made consistent with their theory, and could not be, so long as the social conditions of the country contradicted their theory. It was the settlement of the country west of the Alleghanies which first created social conditions in harmony with their theory. The distinction between master and slave was not permitted to enter the larger portion of it ; the distinction between the rich and the poor could not at first exist, or be, for many years, developed ; and the distinction between the cultivated and the ignorant was likewise obliged to remain long in abeyance ; while the dangers and the hardships of frontier life developed, speedily, a strong sense of self-reliance and self-esteem. General equality and practical self-help were the first social results of the levelling experiences of the camp, the wilderness, and the prairie. With such influences operating upon such characters as undertook the making of the West, the most adventurous part of the population of the East, that bold and boastful Democracy was produced, which began after 1820 to make itself powerfully felt in modifying the original con- *Western Democracy.* servative principles of the institutions of the country. Connect with these new social conditions, and the political principles evolved out of them, the fact that the West, like all new countries, had little money or capital, and was a constant borrower from the East, in order to furnish itself with roads, implements, means of transportation, and manufactured articles, and we have the forces and the interests which were bound, under the first general financial pressure, to make an onslaught upon the "money power and privilege" of the East, as embodied in the United States Bank.

<small>The West and the "money power" of the East.</small>

The "States' rights" opposition to the Bank had been aroused more than a decade before Jackson's message of 1829. The Bank and its branches were the sole depositories of the funds of the Government. By refusing to accept on deposit the bills of Commonwealth banks which did not redeem their bills in specie on demand, the Bank could prevent the officers of the Government from accepting such bills for dues to the Government. The Bank used this power to force the Commonwealth banks to specie payment. It was one of the purposes for which Congress created the Bank. It made the Bank, however, very unpopular with the officers and stockholders of the banks chartered by the Commonwealths. These persons were, as a rule, men of influence in their respective communities, and they succeeded in persuading many of the people that the United States Bank was a centralized monopoly, and was using its powers and privileges to oppress the institutions of the Commonwealths.

<small>"States' rights" and the Bank.</small>

In 1818 the legislatures of Ohio and Maryland imposed a heavy tax on the branches of the Bank located within their respective jurisdictions. The purpose was to drive them out. The Bank resisted payment, and was sustained by the United States courts.

# THE UNITED STATES BANK

In the February term of 1819 the Supreme Court of the United States decided the famous case of McCulloch and Maryland, declaring the act of Congress creating the Bank constitutional, and the act of the Maryland legislature undertaking to tax it unconstitutional. *The case of Brown and Maryland.* Maryland submitted at once, but the officers of the government of Ohio forced their way into the branch of the Bank in that State, at Chillicothe, and took one hundred thousand dollars out of the vault, and that too in the face of an injunction issued by the United States Circuit Court. The directors sued the officers of the Commonwealth for trespass, and the Commonwealth refused the use of its jails to confine the persons arrested. At the same time the Commonwealth reduced the tax to ten thousand dollars, and refunded ninety thousand, and finally receded entirely from its unlawful demand.

This defeat of the "States' rights" attack, and the excellent management of the Bank by Langdon Cheves, and then by Nicholas Biddle, seem to have silenced the complaints against the Bank from 1823 to 1828.

It was during this period, however, that the "State socialistic" characteristic of radical democracy received a strong development in the Commonwealth of Kentucky, through the relief measures for debtors; which measures threatened to *Democracy and Socialism.* destroy the constitutional guarantees of private property. The "relief party" secured the legislature and the executive of the Commonwealth. The judiciary, however, stood out against them, and they did not have the necessary two-thirds majority in the legislature to remove the judges. The legislature, however, passed a new judiciary act, and created another supreme court of the Commonwealth. This scandal of judicial anarchy existed for nearly two years, when, at last, in 1826, the "anti-relief" party elected a majority of the legislative members, and the new legislature repealed the act establishing the new court.

Jackson's friends in Kentucky belonged almost exclusively to the "relief party," and it is hardly fanciful to attribute to this movement in Kentucky some influence in the formation of Jackson's ideas in regard to the United States Bank, and in regard to his plan for a Government bank, responsible to the people and managed for the benefit of the people.

On March 3rd, 1828, Senator Benton began his warfare upon the Bank. He attacked its privilege of being the depository of Government money. He claimed that there were two or three millions of dollars of Government money used in loans by the Bank, which earned about one hundred and fifty thousand dollars a year of interest, all of which went to the stockholders of the Bank and none of it to the Government, while the Government was all the time paying interest on the public debt and taxing the people for the purpose. He wanted to take the surplus deposits out of the Bank and pay a part of the public debt with them. This was the first charge of the Western Democracy upon privilege, as being opposed to the principle of universal equality.

*Benton's attack on the Bank.*

There were, however, enough practical men in the Senate who considered this privilege as only a fair compensation for the service rendered by the Bank to the Government in transporting the Government funds without any specific return therefor, and who knew that it is not good banking to pay interest on deposits, to reject Mr. Benton's resolution. Benton repeated his motion on January 1st, 1829, but with no greater success.

*Benton repulsed.*

After March 4th, 1829, the leadership of the party was

# THE UNITED STATES BANK

in the hands of the President, and Benton became Jackson's lieutenant in the Senate. There had been personal feuds between the two men, but they now harmonized politically, and in no point did that harmony become more complete than in the war against the Bank.

*Jackson and Benton.*

It is probable that at the moment of his accession to power Jackson had not thought out the relation of the democratic principle to the Bank, but he undoubtedly felt it, and the feeling guided him to the position which he assumed, first toward the questions of detail in the Bank's policy and management, and then toward the general question of its existence. The controversy between his Secretaries and the Bank's officers, upon which Mr. Adams laid so much stress, probably precipitated matters, but the crisis would have developed under other circumstances had not these existed. The social and political forces at play were bound to bring it about under one issue or another. It may have astonished the politicians and statesmen of the East then, and it may astonish the casual reader of American history now, that Jackson attacked the question of the future existence of the Bank in his first annual message, but there is nothing surprising in it to the careful student of American history, who comprehends the development of the democratic spirit of the West during the third decade of the century.

It is doubtful whether the President was correct in saying, as he did in his message of 1829, that a large portion of the people questioned the constitutionality and expediency of the law creating the Bank, and it is certain that the Bank was not considered by all to have failed in the establishment of a sound and uniform currency. It is far more probable that the people generally acquiesced in

*The Bank and the people.*

the decision of the Court pronouncing th Bank law constitutional, and that the majority of the people, at that moment, regarded it as good policy, and believed that the Bank had fairly fulfilled the purpose of its creation. The President was simply assuming that the people thought as he did, as democratic leaders usually do. Taken in that sense there was nothing extraordinary in what he said. He had a right to disagree in opinion with the Court, and to say so, and to make any recommendation to Congress which seemed wise to him, in regard to the re-charter of the Bank. That an expiring law is constitutional is not always a convincing argument for its re-enactment.

The President's criticism occasioned an investigation into the principle and status of the Bank, and brought the Bank question into the politics of the day.

*The existence of the Bank made a political issue.*

The committee on Finance of the Senate, and the committee on Ways and Means of the House, made reports, in March and April of 1830, vigorously defending the constitutionality, the expediency, and the management of the Bank, and demonstrating the great political and financial dangers of such a Government bank as the President suggested. The chairman of the committee on Ways and Means was, it will be remembered, Mr. McDuffie, the political economist of the slavery interest. To his mind the Bank question had evidently little connection with the slavery question.

The President, however, returned to the attack in his message of December 10th, 1830. He also presented, in this message, an elaboration of his idea of a Government bank. His proposition was for a bank as a branch of the Treasury Department, based on the deposits of the funds of the Government and also on those made by individuals, but

*Jackson's second attack on the Bank.*

## THE UNITED STATES BANK

having no power to issue notes or make loans or purchase property. Its chief purpose would be to do the business of the Government, and its expenses might be met by selling exchange to private persons at a small rate.

The President thought that this scheme avoided all the objections to the existing Bank, and yet preserved all of the latter's advantages. It would require no charter of incorporation, would have neither stockholders, nor debtors, nor property, would require few officers, and would leave to the Commonwealths the creation of their own local paper currency through their own banks, while the new Government bank would be able to check the issues of the Commonwealth banks through its power to refuse to take their bills on deposit or for exchange, unless they redeemed them with specie. In a sentence, his doctrine now was that banking must be left as far as possible to Commonwealth law, and that such powers as the general Government had received from the Constitution over the subject should be exercised by the Government, if at all, through its own officials, for the benefit of the people, and not be conferred as privileges upon a corporation of private persons, to be exercised for their private gain. This will be at once recognized as a democratic, "States' rights," socialistic scheme in the essential elements of its composition. *Jackson's plan for a bank.*

Before the report of the Finance committee of the Senate upon this part of the message was presented Senator Benton offered a resolution, on February 2nd, 1831, which provided that the charter of the Bank ought not to be renewed. In his speech supporting the resolution the senator developed the whole "States' rights," socialistic, democratic argument against the Bank with great elaboration, both in principle and in detail. *Benton's resolution against the recharter of the Bank.*

It is true that Benton did not go so far as Jackson in the socialistic direction. He said that he was willing to vote for the President's Government bank scheme, since it would substitute for the existing Bank an institution which would be divested of the essential features of a bank, the power to make loans and discounts, but that he would prefer to see the charter of the Bank expire without any substitute being created for it.

The Senate was not, however, convinced by Mr. Benton's argument, and refused to allow him to introduce his resolution.

In his message of December 6th, 1831, President Jackson referred to what he had said in former messages concerning the Bank, and closed his allusion with the following significant words: "Having thus conscientiously discharged a constitutional duty, I deem it proper, on this occasion, without a more particular reference to the views of the subject then expressed, to leave it for the present to the investigation of an enlightened people and their representatives."

*Jackson's challenge to make the continued existence of the Bank the issue in the campaign of 1832.*

This language certainly seemed to imply that the President would, so far as he was able, make the question of the re-charter of the Bank one of the issues of the election campaign of 1832. His opponents so interpreted him, and they gladly accepted the challenge, for they believed the Bank to be popular with the voters. They thought that the Senators and Representatives in Congress, a majority of whom favored the Bank, truly represented the views of their constituencies, and they calculated to be able to split the Democratic party itself on the issue.

*The challenge accepted.*

The president and directors of the Bank, however, were most reluctant to have the existence of the Bank made a party question. The leaders of the National

## THE UNITED STATES BANK

Republicans, on the other hand, insisted upon it. Clay, who, six days after the appearance of the President's message, had been nominated by a national convention at Baltimore as the candidate of the National Republicans for the presidency, was certain that under the issue of the renewal of the Bank's charter Jackson would be signally defeated. The Bank's officers yielded to his advice, enforced by that of Mr. Webster, and on January 9th, 1832, sent in the memorial for a re-charter.

Senator Dallas presented the memorial, but said that he personally had discouraged its presentation at that juncture out of apprehension that the question of the re-charter of the Bank might, at the moment, be drawn into real or imagined conflict with "some higher, some more favorite, some more immediate wish or purpose of the American people." Senator Dallas was a Bank Democrat. The more favorite wish to which he referred was the re-election of Jackson, and the inference to be drawn from his words was that the Bank Democrats did not want to be obliged to choose between the Bank and Jackson at the next election. *(The Bank's petition for re-charter.)*

The Senate referred the petition for re-charter to a committee composed of Mr. Dallas, Mr. Webster, Mr. Ewing, Mr. Hayne, and Mr. Johnston.

Before the committee made its report Mr. Benton made another attack upon the Bank. This time he charged it with illegal practices in issuing drafts which passed as currency. The Senate, however, repelled the attack and refused to allow Mr. Benton to introduce his resolution declaring such drafts illegal. *(Benton's charge of illegal practices.)*

On March 13th Mr. Dallas brought in the bill from his committee for the re-charter of the Bank for fifteen years from the expiration of its existing charter in 1836. *(Passage of the bill for re-charter.)*

While the bill was passing through the Senate a demonstration against the Bank was in progress in the House. Mr. Clayton, of Georgia, an enemy of the Bank, secured the appointment of a committee by the Speaker of the House, Mr. Stevenson, another enemy of the Bank, to inquire into the affairs of the Bank, and make report thereof to the House. A majority report was offered by Mr. Clayton severely criticising the Bank, and a minority report by Mr. McDuffie defending the Bank most ably and vigorously, and, if we may judge from the vote of the House upon the Senate bill for re-charter, which had passed the Senate, and appeared at this moment in the House for concurrence, most successfully. The House passed the Senate bill, with a few immaterial changes, by a vote of one hundred and seven to eighty-five.

The National Republicans felt sure that they had driven Jackson into a blind alley. But the "Old Hero" stood his ground and hurled a veto at the bill, which both killed it and conquered the National Republican party in the election of 1832 with its own chosen weapon.

The veto message was a curious *pot-pourri* of strength and weakness, of sound statesmanship and cheap demagogism, of shrewd politics and silly commonplaces. We may arrange its score of points under five principal heads, or rather ends in view. The first was the attempt to rouse the national spirit against the Bank, on account of the fact that some eight millions of dollars' worth of the stock was in the hands of foreigners. The President made out that this was a great danger to the United States, both in war and peace. In war, he said, the Bank would be an internal enemy, more terrible than the army and navy of the external foe. Just how the possession of the certificates of stock by foreigners, whose money, which had been paid for

*The veto of the Bank Bill.*

# THE UNITED STATES BANK 203

them, was in the United States, and therefore under the control of the United States Government, could endanger the United States in case of a war between the United States and the country or countries to which these foreign stockholders belonged, the President failed to explain. It would seem to the ordinary mind that this would be an advantage to the United States, in that the Government of the United States would have within its grasp a part of the money power of the enemy. Moreover, the Bank law prevented the foreign stockholders from voting in the election of the directors of the Bank. How these stockholders could possibly exercise any hostile influence then, except by selling their stock to citizens of the United States, and taking the money which they might receive for it out of the country, was not only not explained but is inexplicable.

*The Bank and foreign powers.*

The second object was apparently the excitement of the West against the East. The President declared that the West was being made financially tributary to the East by the Bank. He presented the statistics of stockholding and interest-paying throughout the different sections of the country in proof of this statement. He affirmed that thirteen millions five hundred and twenty-two thousand dollars' worth of the stock was owned in the Northeastern and Middle Commonwealths, that five millions six hundred and twenty-three thousand dollars' worth of it was held in Virginia, the Carolinas, and Georgia, and that only one hundred and forty thousand and two hundred dollars' worth of it was held in the nine Western Commonwealths; while one million six hundred and forty thousand and forty-eight dollars of the profits of the Bank came from these Western Commonwealths, one million four hundred and sixty-three thousand and forty-one dollars of them

*The Bank and the West.*

from the Northeastern and Middle Commonwealths, and three hundred and fifty-two thousand and five hundred and seven dollars of them from the Southern Commonwealths. This seems to ordinary intelligence to prove that the Bank was accommodating Western borrowers with Eastern money; and as the Bank was limited by its charter to a maximum of six per centum interest on its loans, it seems that the accommodation was being rendered upon quite moderate consideration. But the President said it proved that the "Eastern money power" was oppressing the West, and the West was quite willing to believe anything against the persons or institutions to whom or to which it owed money.

The third object to which the President addressed himself in the message was to call the attention of the poor to the proposition that the Government was favoring the rich through the Bank. The President called the Bank a monopoly, which means privilege conferred by Government on a few at the expense of the many. He calculated that the privilege to be granted to the existing stockholders by the re-charter of the Bank was worth seventeen millions of dollars, while the bonus which they would be required to pay was but three millions. Fourteen millions of dollars would thus be presented by the Government to the Bank, which sum the Government must take by taxation from the people. He arrived at these statistics and results by assuming that the Bank stock, after the re-charter and in consequence of it, would be worth about one hundred and fifty dollars for one hundred par, that some other body of stockholders could be found who would pay seventeen millions for the charter, and that the money thus acquired from the supposed stockholders by the Government would effect the remission of just so much taxation upon the people. The President saw also, with Senator Benton, that the use of the Government deposits by the Bank was a source of income to the stockholders at the popular expense. And he denounced the feature in the new bill, which allowed the Commonwealth banks to pay their indebtedness to any branch of the United States Bank with the notes of any other branch, but did not accord the same privilege to individuals, as favoring the rich and powerful against the poor and weak.

The entire argumentation in this part of the message seems extravagant and exaggerated, to say the least, but it sounded convincing and sympathetic to the masses. It was something which brought the question home to each one of them, and made it appear related to each one's personal interest. The statement was a powerful vote-catcher. It took wonderfully.

The fourth proposition, as we have arranged them, was the criticism on the structure and powers of the Bank provided in the new bill. The President objected to the unnecessarily large amount of the capital stock, to the right to be given the Bank to locate its own branches, to the power of the Government, as a stockholder, to own real estate for general purposes, and to the power of the Bank to coin money, as he called the power to issue its notes. *Structure and powers of the Bank.*

The final division of the message, according to our arrangement, contains the disquisition upon the relation of the departments of the Government to each other in operating the Constitution, and the relation of the general Government to the Commonwealths in regard to jurisdiction over the business of banking. The President held, upon the first of these points, that "if the opinion of the Supreme Court," in the case of McCulloch and Maryland, "covered the whole ground of this act, it ought not to control the co- *Jackson on executive independence.*

ordinate authorities of the Government. "The Congress, the Executive, and the Court," he said, "must each for itself be guided by its own opinion of the Constitution. Each public officer who takes an oath to support the Constitution swears that he will support it as he understands it, and not as it is understood by others. It is as much the duty of the House of Representatives, of the Senate, and of the President, to decide upon the constitutionality of any bill or resolution which may be presented to them for passage or approval, as it is of the Supreme Judges when it may be brought before them for decision. The opinion of the Judges has no more authority over Congress than the opinion of Congress has over the Judges ; and, on that point, the President is independent of both. The authority of the Supreme Court must not, therefore, be permitted to control the Congress or the Executive when acting in their legislative capacities, but to have only such influence as the force of their reasoning may deserve."

The President also said that he could have furnished a plan for a bank, had it been requested of him, which would have been equal to all the duties required by the Government, a plan which might have been enacted by Congress without straining or overstepping its powers, and without infringing the powers of the Commonwealths ; and he complained that the Bank, as an agent of the Executive Department, should be thrust upon the Department without the Department being consulted as to whether it needed or wanted any such agent.

One of the most celebrated historians of American politics has indulged in a very severe criticism upon this part of the message, claiming that President Jackson virtually asserted therein the power to initiate legislation, full co-ordination with the Houses of Congress in legislation, and an indepen-

<small>Von Holst's criticism of the veto message.</small>

# THE UNITED STATES BANK

dence of Congress, and especially of the Judiciary, which, in practice, would render constitutional law an impossibility. An impartial examination of the text of the message in all its parts will hardly warrant any such conclusions. It is quite clear, from such an examination, that the President meant that in the formation of administrative measures by the Congressional committees in charge of the same, the views of the Administration ought to be obtained; that the President is not limited by the Constitution to any class of subjects in the use of his veto power upon proposed legislation; and that when the Congress and the President are legislating they are not obliged to re-enact a law simply because the Judiciary have declared it constitutional, nor even prevented from repealing a law, simply because the Judiciary have declared it constitutional, and certainly not prohibited from differing in opinion with the Judiciary in regard to the constitutionality of any law already on the statute book, or any proposed measure. Conservative American lawyers, jurists, and publicists approve all of this as not only the letter but also the spirit of the Constitution. *The President's real meaning.*

Instead of destroying the Constitution in theory by the doctrine of this veto, it looks more as if the President did something to rescue the "check and balance" system of government, provided in the Constitution, from the threatened domination of a single department over the others in it. The fact is, Congress had succeeded, during the régime of the old Republican party in American politics, in winning a power over the President which the Constitution did not authorize. The members of Congress had selected all of the Presidents, from Jefferson to Jackson, either by nomination or by actual election. *Jackson's vindication of executive independence.*

The machinery constructed by the Constitution for the election of the President was wanting in its most necessary part. It contained no means of connection between the electoral colleges in the several Commonwealths in voting for the President and Vice-President, at the same time that it required a majority of all the electoral votes to elect. The members of Congress being the only national assembly of persons in the country, and being the chosen political leaders from the different Commonwealths, naturally glided into the habit of constituting themselves, in caucus, the connecting link between the electoral colleges in the several Commonwealths, and thus the Congressional caucus, or caucuses, as the case might be, became the nominating body or bodies to the electoral colleges. If the caucus nominated anybody, it left to the electors the alternative of ratifying the nomination, or of so scattering their votes as to give no person a majority, in which latter case the election of the President passed into the hands of the members of the House of Representatives. If, on the other hand, the caucus did not nominate anybody, the electors were nearly sure to fail to unite a majority of their votes upon the same person, in which case again the House of Representatives obtained possession of the election. With such an increasing control over the tenure of the President, it is not astonishing that the Congress, and even the individual members of Congress, exercised an ever increasing control over his acts and his policy. The encroaching legislature was fast developing the principle of parliamentary government as the principle of the American system, while the Constitution provides the principle of executive independence and presidential administration.

Again, the judicial department had appeared to assume the position that it possessed the supreme inter

## THE UNITED STATES BANK

preting power of the Constitution upon every point. It had not then, as it has now, clearly confined itself to questions immediately involving questions of private rights. It appeared to be claiming jurisdiction in regard to questions primarily of political science, public law, and even public policy.

The President's Bank veto called a halt in these tendencies, and exerted an influence for the restoration of executive independence, and of the "check and balance" system, provided in the Constitution ; and it called the people into a closer and more immediate relation to the President than they had before occupied, in that the President now appealed to them to decide the question between him and the Congress, in the election which was then about to take place.

These were the political principles contained in the Bank veto, and whether they, or the more democratic principle of anti-monopoly, or the more socialistic principle of government banking, moved the masses, certainly they were profoundly moved. Had the popular vote been taken, the day before the appearance of the veto, upon the question of the Bank's re-charter, it is altogether probable that an overwhelming majority would have been found in its favor. Against the veto, however, no sufficient majority could be united in Congress, and when the results of the presidential election became known, it was found that Jackson had carried the country with him in the unequal contest, and that the people had made the principles of the Jacksonian democracy the ruling spirit of the Constitution.

# CHAPTER X.

## NULLIFICATION

The Indian Question in Georgia—The Indian Springs Convention—The Repudiation of the Agreement—The Controversy between the Administration and Georgia—The Creek Convention of 1826—The Governor of Georgia Repudiates the Convention of 1826—The President Submits the Matter to Congress—Georgia and the Cherokees—Jackson and the Indian Question—Indian Policy before Jackson—The Case of the Cherokee Nation—The Case of Worcester against Georgia—The Failure of the President to Execute the Decision in the Worcester Case—Jackson and Calhoun—The Call of the Convention of 1832 in South Carolina—The Nullification Ordinance—The Addresses Issued by the Convention—The Acts of the Legislature of South Carolina for the Execution of the Ordinance—The Meaning of Nullification as Understood by the Nullifiers—Jackson's View of Nullification—The President's Proclamation of December 10th—The President's Military Preparations—The President's Instructions to the Customs Officers in South Carolina—The Popular Approval of the President's Course—The Verplanck Tariff Bill—Governor Hayne's Counter-Proclamation—The President's Message of January 16th, 1833—Calhoun's Explanations in the Senate—The "Force Bill"—The Postponement of the Execution of Nullification—The Compromise Tariff—Mr. Calhoun's Support of Mr. Clay's Bill—The Opposition to the Bill—Passage of the "Force Bill" by the Senate—Passage of the Compromise Tariff Bill and the "Force Bill" by Congress—The Nullification Ordinance Withdrawn.

BEFORE nullification was resolved upon in South Carolina, something like it had been applied in Georgia.

In the year 1802 Georgia formally ceded the lands claimed by the Commonwealth west of the Chattahoochee River to the United States for the sum of one million two hundred and fifty thousand dollars, and upon the condition that the United States Government would, at its own expense, extinguish the Indian claims to any lands in Georgia so soon as this could be done peacefully and upon reasonable terms.

*The Indian question in Georgia.*

Between 1802 and 1820 the Government made some advance in the discharge of this obligation. By this latter date, however, designing white men had joined with the Indian tribes located within the Commonwealth, and were seeking to organize an Indian State for the purposes of their own political ambition, and many well disposed white persons were aiding them from humanitarian motives. The Georgians even accused the Government of doing things that would contribute to the same result. The Georgians were forced to face a very serious question, the question of an Indian State, controlled chiefly by white adventurers and sentimentalists, within the legal limits of the Commonwealth.

Under this pressure the Georgians reviewed the whole question of Indian organization, and rights to territory. They advanced the propositions, that the Indian tribal organizations were not States and could not, therefore, exercise dominion, and give title to real property; that the Indians living within the legal limits of the Commonwealth were subject to its jurisdiction in the same manner as other persons, and to the same extent; that the original title to all land within the limits of Georgia was in the Commonwealth, and every valid title must be derived from the Commonwealth; that the claim of the Indians to the lands on which the tribes lived was simply an incumbrance upon Georgia's title, an incumbrance which the general Government was obligated to remove; and that, after the Government should discharge this duty, Georgia's title would be perfect, without any formal transfer of these lands to Georgia by the Government.

In 1819 the legislature of Georgia memorialized President Monroe to hasten the work of the Government in
*The demand of Georgia for the extinguishment of the Indian claims.* extinguishing the Indian claims. In the year 1824 the Creek chiefs in council resolved that not a foot of the lands claimed by the Creeks should be relinquished. Nevertheless, President Monroe's administration succeeded, in February of 1825, in negotiating an agreement with certain of the Creek chieftains ac-
*The Indian Springs Convention.* cording to which they relinquished to the United States the Creek claims to all lands lying within the limits of Georgia, and also to lands lying to the northwest and to the west of the Commonwealth. This agreement was ratified by the Senate of the United States in March of the same year.

The Governor of Georgia, Mr. Troup, immediately despatched the public surveyors to lay out the relinquished
*The repudiation of the agreement.* territory. They were resisted by the Indians, who declared their repudiation of the agreement of February 12th with the general Government.

At the same moment a number of the chiefs were representing to the new President, Mr. Adams, that that agreement was a fraud upon the Indians, and that the chiefs who signed were not properly authorized to do so. The agent of the Government to the Creeks supported their protest, despite the fact that he was present at the execution of the agreement. Under these circumstances the Secretary of War, Mr. James Barbour, wrote to Governor Troup that the President

## NULLIFICATION 213

expected him to abandon the survey until it could be made in accordance with the provisions of the agreement which allowed the Indians until September 1st, 1826, for their removal, and guaranteed them against all encroachments before that date.

The communication from Secretary Barbour gave rise to a spirited controversy between the Governor of Georgia and himself, in which the Governor assumed an extreme "States' rights" attitude in defence of his position. He claimed that Georgia's jurisdiction over, and title to, the lands formally relinquished by the Creeks to the United States were not originated by this act, but were only relieved by it of an incumbrance, and that, therefore, no additional act was necessary on the part of the Government to authorize Georgia to take possession and exercise jurisdiction. He declared that he would not postpone the survey, and advised the legislature of the Commonwealth to defend Georgia's rights by armed resistance, which recommendation the legislature seemed about to approve.

*The Controversy between the Administration and Georgia.*

The President sent General Gaines to the scene of action, and authorized him to place the militia of the Commonwealths adjoining Georgia in readiness for service. The Governor was highly excited by the approach of the military power of the United States, and wrote to Secretary Barbour virtually accusing the Government of inciting the Indians to violence against Georgia and her people, and demanding to be informed of the purposes of the Administration. Mr. Barbour replied that the President had decided that the survey should not proceed, and had sent General Gaines with orders to prevent it, with military power if necessary. The Governor now turned to the President himself, with both protest and threat, but the President remained firm, and the Governor was obliged to yield for the moment.

The Administration was apparently convinced that the agreement of 1825 was not fairly obtained, and, in January of 1826, entered into another agreement with the Creeks, which, while recognizing the nullity of the agreement of 1825, secured the extinguishment of their claims to all lands in Georgia lying east of the Chattahoochee, and to a considerable tract north and west of this river. The Administration asserted that all the Creek lands lying within the limits of Georgia were secured. Senator Berrien of Georgia, who represented the interests of his Commonwealth when the agreement came before the Senate for ratification, said, on the contrary, that it failed by a million of acres of having done so.

*The Creek Convention of 1826.*

Governor Troup declared that the general Government could not by an agreement with the Creeks rob Georgia of vested rights, which had been, once for all, perfected by the agreement of 1825. He ordered the public surveyors to include in their surveys the lands claimed by Georgia west of the line designated in the agreement of 1826. The Indians resisted them, and appealed to the President to protect their rights as recognized by the latter agreement. The President ordered the United States District Attorney and Marshal for Georgia to arrest any one caught in the act of surveying the lands west of the line fixed by the agreement of 1826. The Governor was informed of this order, and was given to understand that the President would uphold the agreement of 1826 by any and all power necessary. The Governor, however, defied the Administration, ordered the law officers of the Commonwealth to effect, by any means necessary, the release of the arrested surveyors, and to

*The Governor of Georgia repudiates the Convention of 1826.*

secure the arrest and trial of those persons who had taken or held them in custody, ordered the commanders of the militia of the Commonwealth to hold their forces in readiness to resist the threatened invasion by the military power of the United States, and sent a message to the legislature informing that body of what he had done in the premises. In this message he took the ground that questions of jurisdiction—he called them questions of sovereignty — between the general Government and the Commonwealths could not be determined by the judicial power of that Government, but must be settled by agreement between the two parties.

President Adams was deeply impressed with the seriousness of the situation. He felt that he must uphold the dignity and authority of the Government at all hazards and by all the means intrusted to him by the Constitution and the laws; and yet he was unwilling to provoke civil war, if it could be avoided, or to enter upon the work of coercion without the practically unanimous support of the country. He resolved, therefore, to lay the matter before Congress, and await its action. Congress did practically nothing, and the President was convinced that the nation was not prepared to have the Indian problem fought out under the issue of "States' rights" versus the Union. *The President submits the matter to Congress.*

Encouraged by this success the Georgians now resolved to subject the Cherokees living within the limits of the Commonwealth to the laws thereof or force them to emigrate. In December of 1827, the legislature passed a law extending the criminal jurisdiction of the Commonwealth over a part of the lands occupied by the Cherokees. The Indians appealed to the President. The appeal came before the President during the last month of his official term, and he dis- *Georgia and the Cherokees.*

creetly and courteously resolved not to embarrass the new Administration by committing the Government to any position in the question.

President Jackson was even less inclined than his predecessor to allow the Indian question to resolve itself into the question of the constitutional spheres of authority between the Union and the Commonwealths. Moreover, he believed that Georgia was in the right in the Indian question. He replied to the Cherokee memorial that he knew of no alternative to submission to the jurisdiction of Georgia except emigration beyond the limits of the Commonwealth. His view was that the general Government could not hinder a Commonwealth from exercising jurisdiction over every person within its limits, except in such cases as were reserved from that jurisdiction by the Constitution of the United States, and could not lend its countenance to the creation of a new political organization within these limits against the will of the Commonwealth. This was the latter part of April, 1829. The Cherokees, influenced largely by the whites among them, resented the President's advice, and the council of chiefs resolved that no lands claimed by the Cherokees should be relinquished, except by consent of the tribe or tribes, under penalty of death for violation of their resolve, and rejected the overtures of the Government for the relinquishment of their claims.

*Jackson and the Indian question.*

In his message of December 8th, 1829, President Jackson devoted much space to the Indian problem in general, and to it, as it affected Georgia and Alabama, in particular. He repeated to Congress the views which he had expressed to the Cherokees themselves, which were, as we have seen, that the general Government could not lend its countenance to the creation of an

NULLIFICATION 217

Indian State within the confines of any Commonwealth of the Union against the will of that Commonwealth, and that the only alternative to subjection to the laws of the Commonwealth on the part of the Indians was emigration beyond the limits of the same. He also suggested the setting apart of a district in the far West for the permanent home of such Indian tribes as should prefer to continue in tribal organization, independent of the jurisdiction of any Commonwealth of the Union, where they might work out their own customs unmolested.

This was the democratic, "States' rights" view of the subject. It denied all exemptions from the supremacy of the laws, and it also denied to the general Government any power to restrain a Commonwealth from the assertion of its jurisdiction over all persons within its legal limits, except in cases specially reserved by the Constitution.

The Administration of Mr. Adams, and the Administrations of all of his predecessors, had apparently inclined to the view that the Indian tribes were already states, having dominion over, and property in, the territory of the continent when the Europeans arrived upon it; that the titles of the European states to it were only valid as against each other, and meant, in relation to the aborigines, only a right of pre-emption; and that after the Constitution was established no government except the general Government of the United States could have anything to do with them. *Indian policy before Jackson.*

This was a crude and an impracticable view of the relation. It contained more of sentiment and humanitarianism than of common sense and inductive wisdom. The theory broke down completely in the Georgia case, and could not be re-enlivened for practical purposes even by judicial decisions. The necessities of civilization have forced the country to follow the course outlined by President Jackson, and that is certainly good evidence of its correctness.

The Georgians must have been encouraged by his message, for the legislature of Georgia immediately passed an act connecting the Cherokee lands with the counties which they adjoined, and imposing the full jurisdiction of the Commonwealth upon all persons living or being within the same.

The Indians then caused an original bill to be filed in the Supreme Court of the United States against Georgia, together with a supplemental bill praying for a temporary injunction to restrain the Commonwealth from enforcing its jurisdiction, and for the issuing of a subpœna to Georgia to appear before the Court. The Court issued its summons, but the Commonwealth made no answer, and the Court decided, in its January term of 1831, that the Cherokee nation was not a "State" in the sense of that provision of the Constitution which designates the parties qualified to sue in the United States Courts. This decision was pronounced immediately after the execution of the Cherokee Tassells by the Georgia authorities, in defiance of a writ of error addressed to the Commonwealth by a United States court, requiring the Commonwealth to show cause why he should not be discharged from custody. It is probable that the Supreme Court was impressed by this demonstration of the impotence of the judiciary to interfere successfully with the political policy of a Commonwealth, even in behalf of personal liberty.

*The case of the Cherokee Nation.*

A year later the Court took a more national view and stand. A Presbyterian missionary to the Cherokees, the Rev. Samuel A. Worcester, of Vermont, had vio-

# NULLIFICATION

lated the Georgia statute, which made it a criminal offence to reside among the Cherokees after March 1st, 1831, without a license from the Governor, and without having taken an oath to support and defend the laws of the Commonwealth.

*The case of Worcester against Georgia.*

He was indicted and tried by a Georgia court, found guilty, and condemned to imprisonment in the penitentiary of the Commonwealth. A writ of error was issued by one of the Justices of the Supreme Court of the United States, requiring the Commonwealth of Georgia to show cause why the prisoner should not be discharged. The writ was served on the Governor and the Attorney-General of the Commonwealth. The only answer which the Commonwealth gave to the summons was the sending up of the record of the case, signed by the clerk of the court which pronounced the judgment, and authenticated by the seal of the court. The judge of the Georgia court did not sign the record. Nevertheless the Supreme Court of the United States decided that the record of the Georgia court was properly before it, and the Chief Justice proceeded to make, in the Court's opinion of the case, an exhaustive review of the Indian relations of the United States, in accord with the principles of the Adams Administration, and to pronounce the statute of Georgia, asserting the jurisdiction of the Commonwealth over the Cherokee lands and over all persons residing or being on them, unconstitutional, null, and void, and the arrest, trial, and sentence of Mr. Worcester under the same to have been, therefore, without warrant of law.

But the Georgia authorities paid no attention to the decision. They did not liberate the prisoner or accord him a new trial. Later on, the Governor of the Commonwealth pardoned him as his own act of grace.

It was certainly the duty of the President of the

United States to have executed this decision of the Court with all the power necessary for the purpose which the Constitution conferred upon him. He did not do it. It is said on very good authority that he intimated, at least, that he would not do it. The Commonwealth simply defied the Court successfully, and the President and Congress acquiesced in the result. The President agreed in opinion with the Georgians upon the subject, and the doctrine which here triumphed was one more plank in the platform of the Jacksonian democracy, a real "States' rights" principle.

*The failure of the President to execute the decision in the Worcester case.*

There is no doubt that the South Carolinians were encouraged by the course of events in Georgia to believe that they would have something like the same experiences and results in their contest with the Government. In this they do not seem to have fully realized the fact that President Jackson did not agree with them in their view of the unconstitutionality of the tariff, as he agreed with the Georgians in their view of the Indian question. Moreover, there was a personal element in the controversy which they do not seem to have appreciated at all. Jackson had, down to 1830, supposed that Mr. Crawford was the member of the Cabinet of Mr. Monroe, in 1819, who wanted to have him arrested and tried by a court-martial for disobeying orders, or acting in excess of orders, during the Seminole War, and that Mr. Calhoun was his defender. Jackson's hatred of Crawford had been intense during these years for this reason. In 1830 Governor Forsyth, of Georgia, revealed to Jackson the truth in regard to this matter, which was that Calhoun was for arraigning him and Adams was his defender. Jackson immediately demanded an explanation of Calhoun, but the reply did not at all satisfy him, and the hostility which he had

*Jackson and Calhoun.*

felt for Crawford was now turned with redoubled force against Calhoun. Calhoun was now regarded by Jackson as a traitor to Jackson, and that meant, in Jackson's mind, that he was a traitor to his country. Any movement against the Government or the laws of the United States headed by Calhoun would be considered by Jackson as rebellion, most surely so while Jackson was President.

Following the principles developed in Mr. Calhoun's letter of August 28th, 1832, Governor Hamilton issued a call for a special session of the legislature of South Carolina, in the autumn of 1832, for the purpose of effecting through it the assembly of the convention of the Commonwealth. *The call of the Convention of 1832 in South Carolina.* The party in favor of nullification had at last secured both branches of the legislature, and on October 24th, 1832, the assembled legislature voted to issue the call for the convention, and appointed November 19th as the day upon which it should meet.

The convention assembled at the time designated, elected Governor Hamilton as its chairman, and appointed a committee of twenty-one members to consider the situation and report a proposition to meet it. In due time this *The work of the Nullification Convention.* committee made its report to the convention, in which was contained, first, a review of the development of the tariff from a revenue measure to a measure for the protection of manufactures, of the ten years of fruitless struggle in Congress by the South against the oppression inflicted by the protective system upon that section, and of the theories advanced by the fathers of the Republic for meeting, in last instance, such a condition of affairs ; and, second, the famous Ordinance of Nullification as the remedy of last resort. The convention voted to receive the report and to adopt its recommendations.

On November 24th the convention passed, in solemn form, the Ordinance of Nullification of the existing tariff laws of the United States.

The convention declared and ordained in this instrument, that "the several acts and parts of acts of the Congress of the United States, purporting to be laws for the imposing of duties and imposts on the importation of foreign commodities, and now having actual operation and effect within the United States, and, more especially," the Act of May 19th, 1828, and that of July 14th, 1832, "are unauthorized by the Constitution of the United States and violate the true meaning and intent thereof, and are null and void and no law, nor binding upon this State, its officers or citizens; and all promises, contracts, and obligations made or entered into, or to be made or entered into, with purpose to secure the duties imposed by the said acts, and all judicial proceedings which shall be hereafter had in affirmance thereof, are and shall be held utterly null and void."

*The Nullification Ordinance.*

It further ordained that no appeal should be allowed from the decisions of the courts of the Commonwealth to the Supreme Court of the United States in questions involving the validity of the aforesaid Acts of Congress, or of the Ordinance of the convention annulling them, or of the acts of the legislature giving effect to the Ordinance, and that no copy of the proceedings in the courts of the Commonwealth should be allowed for any such purpose, but that the courts of the Commonwealth should proceed to execute their decisions upon such issues without regard to any attempts to appeal therefrom, and should deal with any person making such attempt as being guilty of contempt of court. It then commanded that all the officers of the Commonwealth, civil and military, and the jurors empanelled in the courts should take the

# NULLIFICATION

oath to obey, execute, and enforce the Ordinance, under penalty of dismissal and disqualification; and finally, it declared that South Carolina would regard her connection with the Union as absolved, in case Congress should pass any act authorizing the employment of military force to reduce her to obedience to the nullified acts, or any act abolishing or closing the ports, or obstructing the free ingress and egress of vessels, or in case the United States should undertake to coerce the Commonwealth, or enforce the nullified acts otherwise than through the civil tribunals of the country.

For the execution of the provisions of the Ordinance the convention commanded the legislature to pass such measures as would prevent the enforcement of the nullified acts, and give full effect to the nullifying Ordinance, from and after February 1st, 1833, and commanded the obedience of all persons within the limits of the Commonwealth to the Ordinance and the legislative acts passed for its execution.

With the Ordinance the convention issued two addresses, one to the people of South Carolina, and the other to the peoples of the other Commonwealths, naming each separately. The one to the people of South Carolina contained the theory of nullification, as elaborated by Calhoun, and the justification of its employment in the existing situation. It closed with an appeal to their love of liberty and a demand of obedience. The address to the peoples of the several Commonwealths contained an announcement of the passage of the nullifying Ordinance, the theory upon which it was based, an assertion of the unconstitutionality of the protective tariff, and its oppression upon the people of South Carolina, and a declaration of the spirit and feeling of the convention, and of the people it represented, toward the Union, the Con-

*The Addresses issued by the Convention.*

stitution and the people of the manufacturing Commonwealths. The latter part of this address contained the only new point to be noticed. It was the offer of a plan for a compromise tariff which would satisfy the South Carolinians. The plan was the imposition of the same rate of duty upon all articles, those not coming into competition with the products of the country and those coming into such competition, and the raising of no more revenue than should be necessary to meet the demands of the Government for constitutional purposes.

In a message of November 27th, Governor Hamilton communicated to the legislature of the Commonwealth the Ordinance of Nullification and recommended the enactment of measures by that body for the execution of the Ordinance.

*The Ordinance communicated to the Legislature of South Carolina.*

On December 13th, the new Governor, Colonel Hayne, who had resigned his seat in the Senate in order that Mr. Calhoun, who had himself resigned the vice-presidency, might be made South Carolina's representative in the Senate, or, as the South Carolinians now considered it, South Carolina's ambassador to the Government of the United States, pronounced his inaugural address before the legislature, dedicating himself to the service of the Commonwealth in the execution of her Ordinance of Nullification.

The legislature immediately passed the acts required by the convention and recommended by the Governor.

*The Acts of the Legislature for the execution of the Ordinance.*

The first act, termed the Replevin Act, authorized any consignee of merchandise, or any person lawfully entitled to the possession of merchandise, held or detained for the payment of the duties imposed upon the same by the nullified Acts of Congress, to recover possession of the same, with damages for its detention, by a writ of replevin, that is, by a summary procedure executed by an officer of the Commonwealth; and the Act authorized this officer, on initiation of the plaintiff in replevin, to seize the private property of the person detaining the merchandise to double the value of the latter, in case this person should refuse to deliver the detained merchandise to the sheriff, or should put it out of the sheriff's way, and to hold the property so seized until the merchandise in question should be produced and delivered to the sheriff.

This Act also authorized any person paying the nullified duties to recover the money paid, with interest on the same, by an action, in a court of the Commonwealth, for money had and received; and it authorized any person suffering arrest or imprisonment by order of any United States court, in execution of the nullified Acts, to demand the privilege of the writ of habeas corpus, and to maintain an action for unlawful arrest and imprisonment.

It declared the sale of any property seized by a United States court, in execution of the nullified Acts, to be illegal, and ordained that such sale should convey no title to the purchaser. It forbade any officer of a court of the Commonwealth to furnish the record, or a copy of the record, or allow a copy of the record to be taken, of any case in which the validity of the nullified Acts or the nullifying Acts should be drawn in question, under penalty of both fine and imprisonment, and it forbade any person to attempt to recapture the goods delivered by the sheriff to the plaintiff in replevin, under threat of the same punishment.

It further forbade the keepers of the jails to receive and detain any person arrested or committed by virtue of any proceeding for enforcing the nullified Acts, under penalty of both fine and imprisonment; and it imposed a similar penalty upon the offence of hiring, letting, or procuring any place to be used as a place of confinement for such person.

Finally, it forbade any person to disobey, obstruct, prevent, or resist any process allowed by this Act, under penalty of both fine and imprisonment; and it threatened every plaintiff, who should bring suit against any officer or person executing or aiding in the execution of the provisions of this Act, with adverse judgment and double costs.

The second Act of the legislature was a measure to provide for the event of the employment of military power by the general Government to enforce the nullified Acts in South Carolina. It authorized the Governor of the Commonwealth to resist the same; and for this purpose to order into service the whole military power of the Commonwealth at his discretion, to purchase arms, accoutrements, and ammunitions, and to appoint his military staff; and it authorized and obligated the Governor to use military power in suppressing opposition to the laws of the Commonwealth by combinations too powerful to be controlled by the civil officers.

The third Act was the test oath, the oath to obey, execute, and enforce the Ordinance of Nullification, and all the acts of the legislature for its enforcement, which every officer of the Commonwealth must take before dealing with any question touching the nullified Acts or the nullifying Acts, and which the Governor might require of any officer whatever.

These were the details and the forms of the issue which South Carolina now offered to the United States. Was it rebellion, or was it constitutional and legal opposition?

As we have seen, Calhoun and the members of the

nullifying convention held it to be the latter. They argued that the reserved powers of the Commonwealths are recognized by the Constitution; that every conceivable power is reserved to the Commonwealths, except such as are vested by the Constitution in the general Government exclusively, or are denied by the Constitution to the Commonwealths; that the power to pronounce an act of the general Government null and void had been neither so vested nor so denied; that this was, therefore, a reserved power of the Commonwealths, and was, like all other reserved powers, a constitutional power; that South Carolina proposed to use this power through judicial means only, which means were legally and constitutionally at her disposal through the principle of the governmental system of the United States that general criminal jurisdiction belongs exclusively to the Commonwealths; and that the employment of military power by the Commonwealth, indicated in the Ordinance and the legislative acts for its enforcement, was to be resorted to only in self-defence, only to repel the possible attack of the military power of the general Government upon South Carolina.

*The meaning of Nullification as understood by the Nullifiers.*

It is entirely evident that the South Carolina statesmen and lawyers thought they had so fashioned the laws of the Commonwealth as to force the general Government to the first violation of legal order in attempting to execute the nullified Acts of Congress—that is, they thought they had made it impossible for the general Government to execute these Acts by regular legal methods; and that they had done so without themselves violating any rule or principle of American jurisprudence. They repeated the assertion, again and again, that they did not rest their case on moral, or on revolutionary, principles, but on strict constitutional right; and it is impossible to prove that they were insincere.

The great question now was, what attitude the general Government would take toward the attempt of a Commonwealth to defeat the supremacy of its laws. Naturally the Executive Department must act first, since nullification was directed against the execution of existing laws.

In his message of December 4th (1832), President Jackson referred briefly to the events of the preceding month in South Carolina, but did not seem to have fully appreciated their purport. He said he hoped the United States courts would be able to cope successfully with the difficulties in South Carolina, and that, if they were not, he thought that the existing laws gave the President sufficient power to suppress any attempts which might be immediately made against the supremacy of the Government.

<small>Jackson's view of Nullification.</small>

He devoted a much larger portion of the message to a consideration of the tariff, and declared that the time had arrived for the United States to enter upon the realization of the policy of a tariff for revenue only, and of the ultimate limitation of protection to those articles of domestic manufacture indispensable to the country in time of war.

<small>The Tariff in the Annual Message of 1832.</small>

It is possible that the President did, after all, understand the serious nature of the situation from the outset, and hoped, by his pronounced recommendations in regard to the tariff, and his very mild utterances concerning nullification, to influence the South Carolinians to a reconsideration of their hasty acts, and give them a loophole of escape from their very dubious and embarrassing position.

He waited for six days, and then issued the noted proclamation of December 10th, which presented the

President's idea of the relation of the United States, as a nation, and of the general Government, to the Commonwealths, asserted the supremacy of United States law over Commonwealth law, demonstrated the true character of nullification as rebellion, and declared the President's intention to execute the laws of the United States against any and all opposition.

*The President's Proclamation of December 10th.*

The President assumed as his cardinal principle that the Union preceded independence, and that by a joint act the people of the united colonies declared themselves a nation; that, as a nation, the people of the United States established the Constitution of 1787, and placed in that instrument the provision that the Constitution, and the laws and treaties made in accordance therewith, are "the supreme law" of the land, and that "the judges in every State shall be bound thereby, anything in the constitution or laws of any State to the contrary notwithstanding." From these principles the President derived the conclusions that no legal processes, which South Carolina could contrive, could prevent the execution of the laws of the United States in South Carolina; that to accomplish this South Carolina would be obliged to have recourse to violence; and that this necessity stamped nullification as rebellion.

The President stopped the loop-hole of escape from this reasoning, made by the claim of the nullifiers that the nullified Acts were not laws made in accordance with the Constitution, by the declaration that the Judicial Department of the general Government was the body designated by the Constitution to determine that question, and not a Commonwealth convention.

After warning the nullifiers to desist from their unlawful enterprise, the President closed his message with an eloquent appeal to the people of South Carolina to withdraw from their unjustifiable and dangerous position, and an equally eloquent appeal to the people of the United States for aid and support in preserving the Union and maintaining the supremacy of the Government and the laws.

Already before the passage of the Ordinance of Nullification, the President had caused the United States military officers stationed in and about Charleston to be informed of their danger, had ordered two artillery companies from Fort Monroe to Fort Moultrie, had commanded General Scott to go to Charleston and do what might be necessary for a successful defence of the forts and places held by the Army of the United States, and had directed all the officers in command to defend their possession of these forts and places to the last extremity.

*The President's military preparations.*

The President had also caused the collectors of the customs at Charleston, Georgetown, and Beaufort to be reminded of their powers under the laws of the United States, and had authorized them to make use of all the revenue cutters in the harbors, and of such other vessels as they could secure, and to call to their assistance the officers of the cutters, and to appoint a number of inspectors sufficient to execute successfully the laws of the United States for the collection of the duties. The collector at Charleston was specially authorized to remove the custom-house to Castle Pinckney, at his discretion; and the United States District Attorney at Charleston was ordered to aid the collector with counsel and advice.

*The President's instructions to the customs officers in South Carolina.*

After the passage of the Ordinance, the President ordered five more companies of artillery from Fort Monroe to Fort Moultrie, commanded the removal of the custom-house from Charleston to Castle Pinckney, and sent General Scott to Charleston Harbor to take command, on the spot, of all the forts and garrisons there, instructing him to avoid collision with the forces of the Commonwealth so long as possible, but, in case the exigency should arise requiring the exercise of military power, to act with firmness and decision, and to hold possession of the forts by all means and at every hazard.

The brave, loyal, and patriotic, yet wise and considerate, stand taken by the President was supported with great unanimity and enthusiasm throughout the North; and though the people of the Southern Commonwealths felt more sympathy with their South Carolina brethren, yet the dissent from the President's views and attitude in that section was rare and feeble. The nation was with the President, and the President had done his duty nobly and fearlessly. *The popular approval of the President's course.*

The turn now came upon Congress. Would Congress sustain the President, and give him all the means necessary to conquer nullification and secession in fact, and destroy them in principle? Unfortunately, so far as finite reason can judge, the first movements made in Congress were in the opposite direction. That part of the President's message which dealt with the question of the tariff was referred by the House of Representatives to its committee on Ways and Means, and on December 27th, 1832, the chairman of that committee, Mr. Verplanck, of New York, reported a bill from the committee which proposed to reduce and equalize duties largely, and in the direction of the South Carolina principle. If this bill should pass, the nullifiers could well assume that their Ordinance had accomplished its purpose without being applied, and could with triumphant dignity desist from the application of it; and they could defer with almost equal dignity the application of the Ordinance, *The Verplanck Tariff Bill.*

so long as there was any probability of the passage of this bill.

Seven days before the introduction of this bill, Governor Hayne had issued a counter-proclamation to the President's proclamation of December 10th, in which he went over again the ground of nullification and secession, warned the citizens of South Carolina against the President's "pernicious" doctrines, and accused the President of indulging in unwarrantable imputations upon South Carolina. He gave notice, on the same day, that he would accept the service of volunteers. The legislature supported the Governor in defiant resolutions, which it sent to Congress, and caused to be read in that body.

*Governor Hayne's Counter-proclamation.*

The President was much ruffled by the arrogant language of the Governor and legislature, and when the Verplanck bill appeared, it must have looked to him too much like surrendering the entire field, which he was not now in any mood to do. He felt that something more must be done to vindicate the authority and the dignity of the Government. On January 16th, 1833, he sent another message to Congress, demonstrating and denouncing again the pernicious character of the nullification doctrine, informing Congress that he had removed the custom-house from Charleston to Castle Pinckney, and asking Congress for the power to change the customs districts and ports of entry, to exact the payment of duties in cash, and to use the land and naval forces when necessary for the execution of the revenue laws.

*The President's Message of January 16th, 1833.*

The message was referred by the Houses of Congress to their respective committees on the Judiciary; but immediately upon the reading of the message, and before the Senate had passed the motion to refer, Mr. Calhoun said, in that body, that there was no foundation whatever for the statement in the message that the movements made by South Carolina were intended as hostile to the Union, or were so. He called the attention of the Senate to the fact that before the Ordinance of Nullification was passed, before the con- *Calhoun's explanations in the Senate.* vention had assembled, United States troops had been sent to Charleston Harbor; and he declared that, previous to this circumstance, South Carolina had looked to nothing beyond a civil process, and had intended to give effect to her opposition merely in the form of a suit at law, and that it was only when a military force had been displayed on her borders, and in her limits, and when a menace was thrown out against the lives of her citizens, that they found themselves driven to an attitude of resistance.

On the 21st of the month (January), Mr. Wilkins, the chairman of the Judiciary committee of the Senate, reported from his committee the bill for the collection of the revenue. This bill *The "Force Bill."* provided for extending the jurisdiction of the Circuit Courts of the United States over all cases in law or equity arising under the revenue laws of the United States; for making all property taken or detained by any officer or person under authority of any law of the United States irrepleviable by any order or process of the tribunals of a Commonwealth; for effecting the removal of suits commenced in a Commonwealth court against any officer or person for any act done under the laws of the United States, or on account of any right, authority, or title claimed under those laws, to the Circuit Courts of the United States, by means of proof laid before the Circuit Court that the defendant had petitioned the Commonwealth court for the removal of the cause. The bill provided, further, for substituting for a copy of the record of the proceedings in the Commonwealth court, in case of the failure of that court to furnish a copy, an affidavit, or other evidence, as the circumstances of the case might require ; for giving to the United States judges the power to grant writs of habeas corpus in all cases where persons were in confinement for acts done in pursuance of a law of the United States, or of an order, process, or decree of any United States court or judge ; for empowering the United States marshals, under direction of the United States judges, to provide places of confinement for persons arrested or committed under the laws of the United States, where any Commonwealth should refuse the use of its jails for the confinement of such persons ; for allowing the President to change the custom-house from one place in a collection district to another, and to require the duties to be paid in cash ; and for empowering the President to use the land and naval forces for suppressing any resistance to the execution of the revenue laws too powerful to be overcome by the civil officers of the general Government.

It was a good, stiff measure, but it was constitutional at every point, and it was demanded by the exigencies of the situation. It was a complete answer to the Replevin Act of South Carolina, and it would inevitably throw the responsibility for committing the first act of violence upon the Commonwealth in any resistance to the collection of the duties. It pricked the bubble completely of South Carolina's proposed legal resistance to the execution of the laws of the United States.

Of course the bill was denounced at once by the South Carolinians as a "Force Bill." Calhoun attacked it as a measure for coercing a sovereign "State," and offered a series of "States' rights" propositions, which he declared to be indisputable, and which must, therefore, prevent the passage of the bill. The discussion upon these resolutions, and upon the bill which they were meant to destroy, dragged on from day to day in the Senate, while that upon the Verplanck bill in the House proceeded even more slowly.

The chiefs of the nullifiers, professing to feel that the Government was yielding, reassembled in convention in the last days of January, and postponed the execution of their Ordinance until the end of the existing Congressional session. *The postponement of the execution of nullification.*

On February 8th, Mr. Bell, the chairman of the Judiciary committee of the House of Representatives, reported to that body that his committee did not recommend vesting the President with any further powers for the execution of the revenue laws than those already possessed by him, and that they could not approve of the employment of military force for the purpose.

Such was the situation when, on February 12th, Mr. Clay astonished the Senate with the noted proposition for compromise. This was his bill for the gradual reduction of the duties to a revenue basis. The revenue basis was fixed in the *The Compromise Tariff.* bill at twenty per centum *ad valorem* on all articles then paying a higher duty, and the excess was to be remitted in biennial instalments, and entirely abolished from and after June 30th, 1842. The free list was slightly extended, and cash payments, from and after June 30th, 1842, were provided.

Mr. Clay said, in introducing this bill, that he had two purposes in view: one to save what could be saved of the protective tariff, and the other to allow South Carolina to withdraw with dignity *Mr. Clay on the situation.* from the position which she had rashly assumed. He claimed that his feeling toward the action of South Carolina had changed since her Representatives and Senators in Congress had disavowed rebellion and had asserted that they were only trying to invent legal methods for protecting themselves against the oppression of the tariff Acts. He demonstrated very clearly the error of supposing that they could do any such thing, and then urged his brother Senators to join him in the proposed measure of conciliation.

Mr. Calhoun immediately indicated that the bill would have his support, and would solve the difficulties between South Carolina and the general Government. He professed to see in it the concession of about all that South Carolina had asked.

*Mr. Calhoun's support of Mr. Clay's bill.*

The opposition to the bill came from three quarters—from the protectionists, who clung to the existing law, from the strong nationalists, who were against any show of compromise with nullification, and from the strict parliamentarians, who held that any bill touching the tariff must originate in the House of Representatives.

*The opposition to the bill.*

The protectionists were answered, and many of them won over, by the argument that the Verplanck bill would pass if they did not accept Mr. Clay's bill. The strong nationalists were told that if Congress should pass the Wilkins bill before the Clay bill a sufficient vindication of their position would be attained. They were inclined to accept that view, but the South Carolinians set themselves against this order of procedure with all their strength. Mr. Calhoun came forward again with his "States' sovereignty" exposition of the Constitution, and denounced the Wilkins bill in the most vehement language as "utterly unconstitutional, as an attempt to enforce robbery by murder, an attempt to decree the massacre of the citizens of South Carolina," and declared that the citizens of South Carolina would, should it become law, resist its execution "at every hazard, even that of death itself."

On the following day Mr. Webster answered Mr. Calhoun's argument, and demonstrated so clearly the nationality of the Constitution, the supremacy of the laws of the United States, and the rebellious character of nullification, that the Senate was convinced of the necessity of passing the Wilkins bill before voting upon Mr. Clay's bill. On the 20th of the month (February), the Senate passed the Wilkins bill by a vote of thirty-two to one. The objections of the strong nationalists to Mr. Clay's bill were now substantially satisfied; but the high protectionists still held out in considerable number for some modification of the bill in their favor, and on the day after the passage of the Wilkins bill by the Senate, Mr. Clay moved to amend his own bill by the proposition to base the duties on home valuation instead of on the foreign invoice. The protectionists were satisfied by this, but Mr. Calhoun immediately declared that South Carolina would not accept the bill with this change. The protectionists, in sufficient number to defeat the bill, declared that they would not accept it without the change. Mr. Calhoun had at last come to see the peril which lay in South Carolina's course, and to understand the feeling of the nation toward her. He wisely concluded to abandon his opposition to the amendment, and to vote for the bill.

*Passage of the "Force Bill" by the Senate.*

The opposition of the strict parliamentarians, on the ground that the Senate could not originate a revenue bill, was overcome by the action of the House of Representatives in substituting the Clay bill for the Verplanck bill, and passing it on the 26th, and sending it to the Senate for concurrence. The Senate now passed the House bill on March 1st, and the House immediately passed the Wilkins bill, against the protest of

*Passage of the Compromise Tariff bill and the "Force Bill" by Congress.*

the South Carolinians that it could now have no purpose since every member of Congress from South Carolina had voted for the new Tariff Act.

The President signed both bills at the same time, March 2nd, and South Carolina rescinded the Nullification Ordinance.

*The nullification ordinance withdrawn.*

It is not easy to see what principles or what party finally triumphed in this contest, or to comprehend all the motives of the chief actors in it. It has been said, or hinted, that Mr. Calhoun, chagrined and disappointed at not gaining the presidency in 1832, was induced to take the course which he followed in reference to nullification by the hope of breaking up the Union and winning, thus, the presidency of a Southern confederacy; that President Jackson was largely influenced, in the decided attitude which he assumed, by the desire to take revenge on Mr. Calhoun and South Carolina for Mr. Calhoun's attempt to court-martial him more than a dozen years before, and for South Carolina's slight upon him in the election of 1832; and that Mr. Clay was moved far more by his jealousy of President Jackson, and his fear of trusting him with extraordinary powers, than by any dread of the destruction of the Union.

*Motives and general results.*

There is probably some truth in certain, if not in all, of these speculations, but such things are not the matters of chief value in the search for the line of development of the constitutional history of this country. They do indeed help us to appreciate the motives for the particular form of adjustment put upon that development at any stage of its course; but our chief concern must be with the advance or retrogression in principle of that development, our question must be whether the Union and the Constitution were strengthened or weakened by the events of 1832 and 1833, whether the political nationality of the country was cemented or suffered disintegration, and whether strength was gathered, or the seeds of weakness were sown, in the results attained.

From the point of view of the present, a point so much more national than any reached before 1860, the settlement of 1833 is usually regarded as a great misfortune, as a fateful error, which led the country finally into civil war. It is now usually said that the national cause lost everything in principle, and that nullification was virtually acknowledged by the Act of Congress in repealing the nullified laws, at the same moment that it enacted the measure for upholding the supremacy of the laws of the United States.

From a purely historical view of the development of the constitutional law of the country, this proposition does not seem to be true, at least not without great modification. From such a point of view it seems more correct to say, that the doctrine formulated by Mr. Calhoun and his colleagues in South Carolina was only the exact logical statement of the principles advanced by Mr. Jefferson in 1798, principles through the advocacy of which Mr. Jefferson and the Republicans turned the Federalists out of power and captured the Government; that under the pressure of foreign war and through its results, the Republican practice in administering the Government had been driven into lines almost, if not quite, contradictory to the Republican doctrine; that in the gradual relapse, after 1815, into the humdrum of peace and business, the conditions were being revived for the reassertion of the principles of 1800; and that, under such conditions and in such a period, the doctrines advanced by President Jackson, doctrines of a far more completely national system of sovereignty, government, and liberty than were ever expressed by any preceding President, certainly mark a great advance in the development of the national theory of the Constitution.

The South Carolinians said that John Quincy Adams invented these doctrines, and that Jackson first essayed their application. Even Clay declared that they were an advance upon his own views. And some of Jackson's friends undertook, it was said with authority from Jackson himself, to explain them away, so startled were they by their strong nationalism.

But the spoken word cannot be recalled. It had gone forth, and the nation had approved it. The politicians might split hairs in its interpretation, but the people had heard from the highest authority which they recognized that the United States was a sovereign nation, and that the attempt of any combination of persons, whether calling themselves a "State" or not, to resist by violence the execution of the laws of the United States, or to withdraw themselves from their operation, was rebellion, which the President was empowered and required by the Constitution to suppress with the whole physical power of the nation.

And besides the Proclamation there was the "Force Bill," which rested upon the same theory of the political system of the country as the Proclamation. The Congress as well as the President was now inculcating the national doctrine. Calhoun and his friends knew what an influence this would exert. He said that he and they would never rest content until this measure was expunged from among the Acts of Congress.

It is true that the passage of the new Tariff Act appeared to take the virtue out of the Proclamation and the "Force Bill;" but it is not at all probable that the nullifiers would have retreated from their ground so promptly, to say the least, except for the determined words of the President and the Congress, and the popular approval with which they were received; and it is almost certain that, when it came to the great crisis, twenty-eight years later, the people would not have understood and supported the great principle that the general Government has the right of self-preservation, in the exercise of all its powers, throughout the whole territory of the Union, against everything and everybody but the sovereign nation itself, except for the great education in national principles which they received from the Proclamation, and through the enactment of the law which gave the sanction of Congress to the enforcement of its principles.

# CHAPTER XI.

## ABOLITION

The Philosophy of Abolition—William Lloyd Garrison—The Civil Status under the Constitution of 1787—Points at which Slavery Could be Legally Attacked—Garrison's Methods—The Southampton Massacre—The Attempt to Suppress the Abolition Movement at the North—Growth of the Abolition Movement—The Methods of the Moderate Abolitionists—The Abolition Petitions—The Earlier Method of Dealing with the Petitions—Beginning of the Conflict over the Abolition Petitions—The New Method for Dealing with Petitions in the House of Representatives—True View of the Right of Petition—Mr. Polk's Fatal Error in Regard to the Right of Petition—The Pinckney Resolutions—The New Rule of the House of Representatives in Regard to the Abolition Petitions—The Increase of Petitions, and the Denunciation of the Pinckney Rule—The Final Denial of the Right of Petition on the Subject of Slavery by the House of Representatives—The Abolition Petitions in the Senate—Mr. Rives and Mr. Calhoun in Regard to the Morality of Slavery—Mr. Calhoun's Resolutions in Regard to the Political Relations of Slavery—The Anti-Slavery Petition from the Vermont Legislature—The Abolition Documents and the United States Mails—The Postmaster-General's Ruling in Regard to the Abolition Documents in the Mails—Jackson on the Use of the Mails by the Abolitionists—Mr. Calhoun's Report and Bill on the Subject—Clay's Criticism of Calhoun's Proposition—The Act of Congress Protecting the Abolition Documents in the Mails—General Results of the Struggle over the Right of Petition and the Freedom of the Mails.

WHEN a state has fairly accomplished the primal end of establishing its governmental system, its public policy will be found to be pursuing, in ultimate generalization, two great all-comprehending purposes, namely, national development and universal human progress. Rarely, if ever, will any state be found to have succeeded in so bal- *The ends of the state.* ancing these two principal objects of its public policy as to make the resultant of its two main lines of progress follow an unchanging angle. At one period, the principle of national development will prevail, even to the point of national exclusiveness; at another, an enthusiastic humanism will almost threaten the existence of national distinctions. But in all the convulsions of political history, described as advance and reaction, the scientific student of history is able to discover that the zigzags of progress are ever bearing in the general direction which the combined impulses toward nationalism and humanism compel.

After the humanitarian outburst of the revolutionary period in the latter part of the eighteenth century had expended its force, the states of the world veered in their policies toward the line of national development. The United States, which had been excessively humanitarian during that period, both in its doctrine of *The purposes of the state, as seen in the history of the United States.* rights and in its policy, became, in the succeeding period, the first three decades of the nineteenth century, more and more national in disposition and in practice, until industrial exclusiveness and race domination appeared, at the close of the period, to be the sole principles of the policy of the country.

Had the two elements of this policy been equally, or almost equally, sustained throughout the whole country, there is little question that the human purpose, the world-purpose, as Hegel calls it, of state existence, would have been ignored to a higher degree, and for a longer period, than it was. But curiously and fortunately, the race domination in the South produced economic conditions which demanded trade and commerce with the world, and which finally forced upon the North the conviction that the cause of those conditions—race domination, slavery—must be removed, in order to secure the industrial interests of the North against the competition of the world's markets. The destruction of that domination must proceed, however, upon a humanitarian principle, namely, the right of man to personal liberty. Thus it clearly appears that the two elements of the national exclusiveness of the United States in 1830 were, in the peculiar relation which finally obtained between them, preparing the nation for a new advance in the direction of world intercourse and human rights.

In the summer of 1830 the wave of revolution rolled again over Europe. The rights of man, the brotherhood of man, and the sovereignty of the people, were the principles which pressed again to the front. While no actual connection can be established between the Revolution of 1830 in Europe and the rise of Abolition in the United States, yet they belong to the same period of time, and harmonize in principle. The impulses which move the human race, or those parts of the human race which stand upon the same plane of civilization, are not broken by mountain heights or broad seas. Their manifestations appear spontaneously and coetaneously in widely separated places.

*The Revolution of 1830.*

Before 1830, indeed, as we have so often seen, slavery in the United States had been regarded as a grievous evil by most of the great spirits of the age and country, and schemes for gradual emancipation had been invented, and, in some slight degree, had been put into operation. It was, however, the humanitarian outburst of 1830, and the succeeding years, which represented slavery as a sin and a crime against the universal principle of human liberty and the rights of man, a sin which called for immediate expiation by instantaneous, unqualified, and uncompensated abolition.

There is nothing strange about the philosophy of Abolition. It is simply the idealistic view of the beginning and the progress of human history. It assumes liberty as the original state of man, condemns every species of modification of liberty suffered by any human being, or any class of human beings, as resulting from the unrighteous act of some other human being, or class or race of human beings, and demands the immediate discontinuance of the tyranny as the only approximately adequate satisfaction which can be made to those who have suffered that tyranny. It is the orthodox, paradisaical view of the origin, unity, and primal perfection of the human race. It is the literal interpretation of the Declaration of Independence. It is thorough-going, radical humanitarianism. Its political principle, in the language of its chief exponent, was: "The world our country, and all mankind our countrymen."

*The philosophy of Abolition.*

Over against it stands the pessimistic view of man and of civilization, which divides the human race into the few intelligent and good, and the great mass of the ignorant and vicious, and considers the permanent subjection of the latter to the former as the divinely constituted, and therefore the permanent, order of the world.

And between the two lies the true historical view, which regards liberty, equality, and brotherhood as the products of civilization, as the final, not the primal, status of the human race, and determines the character of every stage of development from barbarism to civilization, not by its distance from the perfect condition, but by the fact of its advance upon, or its retrogression from, the stage immediately antecedent.

The latter is, unquestionably, the true philosophy of history, but the former has its uses as well as its abuses. It contains those forces of mystical enthusiasm, self-sacrifice, and reckless disregard of consequences so necessary, at times, to drag the world out of the ruts of materialism and the love of peace. Such was its mission in the fourth decade of the nineteenth century in American history.

If we must give a name, a date, and a place to the first open appearance of a movement which was a product of the age, that name is Garrison; the date, the beginning of the year 1831; and the place, Boston. The character of William Lloyd Garrison, whether noble or vulgar; his purposes, whether generous or selfish; and the motives which impelled him, whether narrow and personal or grandly humane, are not subjects for treatment in a work upon constitutional history. Constitutional history has to do only with the doctrines of political ethics and public jurisprudence which he formulated, and with the means proposed by him, and those who thought and acted with him, for their realization; and the historian does neither him nor them any injustice in saying that, while those doctrines are to be justified from the point of view of an extreme idealism, the means for their realization, at first only indicated, but later boldly and rudely expressed, were revolutionary, almost anarchic.

*William Lloyd Garrison.*

There is now certainly little question that the determination of the civil status of all persons is, from an ethical point of view, a matter of national concern, and that that status must be fixed, in general principle, by a national act. There is just as little question that the denial of personal liberty to any human being of adult years does not comport with the civilization of the nineteenth century. In espousing these principles the Abolitionists were only prophets ahead of their time, and must be accorded the honor which belongs to such. *The civil status under the Constitution of 1787.* On the other hand, it is entirely unquestionable that the Constitution of the United States recognized to the Commonwealths, respectively, the exclusive control of the civil status of persons belonging within their several jurisdictions, and it is entirely improbable that the Constitution of 1787 could ever have been established without the guarantees, expressed and implied in it, of such power to the Commonwealths. There is no question at all that the slavery or freedom of the negro race within the several Commonwealths was, under the Constitution of 1787, not only left, as it had been before, a matter for each Commonwealth to determine for itself, but that the exclusive power of determination in regard to it was guaranteed by the Constitution to the several Commonwealths. The Commonwealths in which slaveholding generally and extensively prevailed regarded the guarantee as the principal consideration for their assent to the "compact." The attempt to violate, or weaken, or even to cast doubt upon, these guarantees appeared to them to be an attack upon the fundamental covenants of the Union. The Constitution might, indeed, be so amended as to withdraw these powers and guarantees from the Commonwealths, by the regular procedure provided in the Constitution itself; and the general Government was vested by the Constitution with the general powers of exclusive government in the Territories, the District of Columbia, and the places owned by the United States within Commonwealths and used by the general Government for governmental purposes. But so long as the Constitution remained what it was, there was no constitutional power in the general Government to attack slavery in the Commonwealths; and the slaveholders could certainly claim that, in the exercise of its powers in the Territories, the District, and other places where those powers were exclusive, the general Government should act fairly toward all the members of the Union.

Nevertheless, here were legal points of attack for the Abolitionists. They might memorialize Congress for the abolition of slavery in the Territories and in the District, and for the initiation of an amendment which would abolish slavery in the Commonwealths or would give Congress the power to do so, and they might appeal to the legislatures of the Commonwealths to demand of Congress the calling of a constitutional convention of the United States to initiate such an amendment. But Garrison would have nothing to do with the Constitution, or with existing legal methods. He denounced the Constitution, "as a covenant with death and an agreement with hell," and declared that he wanted "no union with slaveholders." His violent language, his repudiation of vested rights and constitutional agreements, and his fanatical disregard of other men's opinions and feelings, led the people both of the North and the South to believe that his methods were incendiary and his morals loose; that he and his co-workers were planning and plotting slave insurrection, and thereby the wholesale massacre of slaveholders; and that he and they were endeavoring to attain, through violence and anarchy, a leadership which they could not otherwise reach.

*Points at which slavery could be legally attacked.*

*Garrison's methods.*

In August of 1831, a slave insurrection broke out in Southampton County, Va., under the leadership of a negro named Nat Turner, and more than sixty white persons, most of them women and children, were massacred in cold blood. The Southerners said, and no doubt believed, that the insurrection was incited by the Abolitionists in the North. Governor Floyd, of Virginia, declared, in his message to the legislature upon the subject, that there was ample proof of it in the documents accompanying the message. The great mass of the people at the North believed the same thing. The Abolitionist historians assert, on the contrary, that there was no connection between the work of the Abolitionists and this event. We shall probably never know whether there was or not. This much we can say, that the radical character of the Abolition doctrines and the violence of the language in which they were expressed—not so much before as after this event, indeed—produced the universal feeling, both in the North and in the South, that these doctrines and this event were in perfect harmony, and that the latter might very naturally be the outcome of the former. The moral sentiment of the North was not prepared for the destruction of slavery by any such means. It considered these methods as containing ten times more evil and barbarism than slavery itself. It is just to say that what appeared to be the methods of the Abolitionists were revolting to the moral feelings of all the decent people of the North, and to ninety-nine one-hundredths of all the people of the North, while the Southerners saw in them nothing but the destruction of all law and order, the plunder of their property, the burning of their firesides, and the massacre of their families. The pronounced and determined manner in which the people of the North went about the work of suppressing the agitation occasioned by the Abolitionists is ample evidence to any sane mind that the indignation of a

*The Southampton massacre.*

righteous conscience was fully aroused, and not the fury of a guilty conscience.

The details of the breaking up of the Abolition meetings and of the destruction of the Abolition printing-presses by the citizens of the Northern Commonwealths, as well as those of the Southampton massacre, may be passed over, in a work like this, with the single remark that only one person, the Rev. Mr. Lovejoy, was murdered in these collisions; that this happened under circumstances of some aggravation; and that, if the excitement at the South over the massacre of sixty-one innocent persons was out of proportion with the event, then not too much should be made out of the killing of a single person, who was not entirely guiltless on his part of giving provocation.

*The attempt to suppress the Abolition movement at the North.*

The things of importance to the student of constitutional history in connection with these events are the increase of the Abolitionists in number, their organization into societies, the dissatisfaction of the Southerners with the unofficial, merely popular, way of dealing with the agitation at the North, and their demands upon the governments of the Northern Commonwealths to deal with the Abolitionists through the processes of their criminal law.

So long as men only talk and write, it is the impulse of our Anglo-Saxon character to place no further restraint upon them than the law of slander and libel of private character imposes, no matter what may be, or may be thought to be, the ultimate consequences of acting according to what they may say or write. To deny this privilege to anybody appears like a deprivation of the liberty of speech and of the press, appears like persecution. There is no country in the world in which the making of martyrs is an easier procedure than in the United States.  Persecution is the soil in which new movements grow best, no matter what may be the character of the movement.

In a single year from the date of the first number of Garrison's newspaper, *The Liberator,* that is, in January of 1832, the New England Anti-slavery Society was formed, and in December of 1833 the American Anti-slavery Society was organized, which soon established branches in many quarters. The exaggerated demands of the Southerners, that the Northern Commonwealths should forbid Abolition agitation by law, thus identifying the interests of slavery with the denial of the freedom of speaking and writing in the Northern Commonwealths, helped greatly to swell the ranks of the Abolitionists, and to mollify public opinion in the North against them.  *Growth of the Abolition movement.*

The new Abolitionists were naturally of a more moderate type than Garrison, and most of them would listen only to regular legal methods for the accomplishment of their purposes. The quickening of the public opinion in the North, the conviction of the slaveholders themselves of the error, if not the sin, of slavery, and the appeal to the Government to do all within its constitutional powers against slavery, were the only means which many of them were willing to employ. Their petitions to Congress, and the transmission of their literature of Abolition to the Southerners through the United States mails, brought the whole question of their rights and purposes before the Government, and before the nation, for which that Government was bound to act with impartial justice to all its parts.  *The methods of the moderate Abolitionists.*

Petitions for the abolition of slavery in the District of Columbia had been sent to Congress, generally from

Quaker sources, almost from the day that the capital of the country was established there, but they were not numerous and were not pushed by any anti-slavery organization. In the session of 1826-27, a petition from citizens of Baltimore, probably instigated by Benjamin Lundy, was presented, which contained the same prayer; and in the session of 1827-28, one of like tenor from citizens of the District itself was presented. Such petitions were usually read and referred to the committee on the District. They were irritating to the slaveholders from the first, but it was not until after the excitement of the Southampton massacre that they were angrily resented as an interference with the domestic institutions of the slaveholding Commonwealths.

*The Abolition petitions.*

It was in the session of 1831-32, that the first mutterings of the petition storm were heard. On December 12th, 1831, Mr. John Quincy Adams presented, in the House of Representatives, fifteen petitions from sundry inhabitants of Pennsylvania, the chief prayer of all of which was for the abolition of slavery in the District of Columbia. Mr. Adams said that he would give no countenance to that prayer, but that there was a prayer in the petitions for the abolition of the slave-trade in the District, which, he thought, might properly be considered, and he moved the reference of the petitions, for this purpose, to the regular committee of the House for the District.

There was in this little to indicate the terrible earnestness which Mr. Adams later displayed in behalf of the Abolition petitions. He seemed at this time to be annoyed at being asked to present them, and to feel that there were superior moral reasons why a slavery agitation should not be excited within the halls of Congress. But all this was soon to change. Mr. Adams's advance toward radical Abolitionism is as marked a feature of the struggle over the right of petition as Mr. Calhoun's declaration of the righteousness of slavery.

The committee on the District reported, on December 19th, that as the District was composed of cessions of territory from Maryland and Virginia, it would, in the opinion of the members of the committee, be unwise, if not unjust, for Congress to interfere in the question of the relation of slave to master in the District, until Virginia and Maryland should take steps to eradicate the evil from their respective territories. This report seemed to settle the question for the session, and no more petitions appeared in either House. *The earlier method of dealing with the petitions.*

In the middle of the next session, Mr. Hiester, of Pennsylvania, presented a petition to the House of Representatives from sundry citizens of Pennsylvania praying for the abolition of slavery in the District of Columbia. This was again a Quaker petition, as were the petitions presented by Mr. Adams. Mr. Hiester moved to refer the petition to the committee on the District, and Mr. Mason, of Virginia, rashly called for the yeas and nays, which opened the question to debate. Mr. Adams immediately pointed out this fact to Mr. Mason, and advised him to withdraw his motion, which advice Mr. Mason wisely adopted. The petition went to the Committee, and nothing further was heard of it.

It was first in the session of 1833–34, that petitions for the abolition of slavery in the District from others than Quakers, presumably from the members of the new anti-slavery societies, appeared in both Houses of Congress. Those presented in the Senate were referred to the committee of the Senate for the District, and nothing more was heard of them. Those presented in the House of Representatives were dealt with in the same manner.

It was not until the session of 1834–35, that the first real note of the conflict was sounded. On January 26th, 1835, Mr. Dickson, of New York, presented several petitions praying for the abolition of the slave-trade and of slavery in the District. They were laid over until February 2nd, when Mr. Dickson called them up, made a rather irritating speech, in which he said that the committee on the District had smothered all such petitions referred to it, and moved the reference of those offered by him to a select committee.

Mr. Chinn, of Virginia, the chairman of the regular committee on the District, resented Mr. Dickson's rude assault, and moved to lay the petitions and Mr. Dickson's motion on the table. The House voted Mr. Chinn's motion by a large majority.

At length, in the session of 1835–36, the storm broke in all its fury, in both the Senate and the House. It began in the House, December 16th, 1835, upon the presentation of a petition, containing the usual prayer in regard to slavery in the District, by Mr. Fairfield, of Maine.

Beginning of the conflict over the Abolition petitions.

Mr. Cramer, of New York, moved to lay the petition on the table, and the motion was voted. Mr. Fairfield immediately presented another petition of like purport, and himself moved that it be laid upon the table. Mr. Boon, of Indiana, asked that the petition be read, which was done. Thereupon Mr. Slade, of Vermont, moved that it be printed. This meant, of course, that Mr. Slade was determined to have the slavery question agitated in Congress, if he could. Upon him rather than upon Mr. Adams rests the honor, or the blame, whichever it may be, of provoking the excitement over the Abolition petitions, and of upholding the right of petition in the most extreme degree.

The House first voted to lay the petition on the table.

ABOLITION 255

The Speaker, Mr. James K. Polk, then put Mr. Slade's motion to print. Whereupon Mr. Slade attempted to debate the whole question of slavery in the District under the motion. The Speaker ruled that the contents of the petition could not be debated under the motion to print. Mr. Vanderpoel, of New York, then moved to lay Mr. Slade's motion on the table, and the House voted to do so by a large majority.

Two days later the play was on again. Mr. Jackson, of Massachusetts, presented a petition from sundry citizens of Massachusetts, containing the usual prayer, and moved its reference to a select committee. Whereupon Mr. Hammond, of South Carolina, moved that the petition should not be received. *Mr. Hammond's motion involving the denial of the right of petition.* This was the ultra-Southern position in regard to the anti-slavery petitions, and Mr. Hammond's enunciation of it in the House antedates Mr. Calhoun's in the Senate by more than a fortnight.

The Constitution guarantees the right of the people to assemble peaceably and petition the Government for redress of grievances. The right to petition certainly includes the right to have the petitions heard by the body petitioned. If the body refuses to receive the petition, it prevents its being heard, and by preventing its being heard it makes the right itself a mockery. On the other hand, the Constitution vests in each House of Congress the power to make its own rules of procedure. This power must, of course, be so used as not to violate any other clause of the Constitution. Under this power, however, each House may and should protect itself against all obstacles thrown by outsiders in the way of the discharge of its duties in legislating for the country. If any number of people undertake, by an abuse of the right of petition, to obstruct the legitimate work of the Congress for the whole people, each House certainly has the right to meet this attempt in any way which will not deny the right of petition, the right of any one or any number of the people to be heard in asking for a redress of grievances.

Down to 1834, the custom of procedure in Congress had been to receive, hear, and refer all petitions. That was going one step farther than was required by the constitutional right of petition; still it was the regular course, and such men as Mr. Adams thought it unwise to depart from the custom in the case of the Abolition petitions. At any rate, Mr. Hammond's motion was a new proposition. The Speaker said that he was "not aware that such a motion had ever been sustained by the former practice of the House," and appeared to rule Mr. Hammond's motion out of order. A confused wrangle ensued over the attitude assumed by the Speaker, during which Mr. Hammond made a motion to reject the petition, and the Speaker, becoming confused by the two motions, the one not to receive, and the other to reject, and knowing that the House could of course reject the prayer of a petition, yielded to the representations of Mr. Hammond, and put Mr. Hammond's motion not to *receive* the petition to the House. The House voted not to refuse to receive the petition, but the ruling of the Speaker in putting the motion implied that the House possessed the power to refuse to receive, that is, to refuse to hear, a petition. Another confused wrangle ensued over the question whether the House had voted merely not to refuse to receive the petition, or had voted to consider its contents at once. After a day of heated debate and three days of adjournment, during which excited feelings were somewhat calmed, the House reversed all former action, and voted to lay the petition and all the motions relating to it on the table.

<small>The new method for dealing with petitions in the House of Representatives.</small>

Another petition, which, during this wrangle had been inadvertently referred to the committee on the District, was now recalled by a motion to reconsider the vote of reference. It was upon this motion that Mr. Adams made his first great appeal for the right of petition. As we have seen, his view before this was that petitions must be received, heard, and referred. In this speech, however, he indicated that there should be a report from the committee, and a vote upon the report. Mr. Jones, of Virginia, met Mr. Adams' assertions quite successfully, and showed conclusively that, if the right of petition should be interpreted to reach any farther than the right to have the petition received and heard, it would so modify the constitutional right of the House to establish its own rules of procedure as to put it in the power of a few determined obstructionists outside the House, acting with a single member of the House, to prevent the House from doing anything but consider petitions upon a single subject, sacrificing thus the interests of the whole people to the obstinacy of a small number of the people.

*True view of the right of petition.*

Mr. Jones' argument was so sound and rational that it would probably have settled the minds of almost all of the members in regard to the complicated questions of the right of petition, and the powers of the House over its rules of procedure, had not Mr. Granger, of New York, and Mr. Ingersoll, of Pennsylvania, thrown another firebrand into the House during this debate, in the form of an intimation that Congress had the constitutional power to abolish slavery in the District of Columbia. The Southerners now advanced to the position of denying that power to Congress, and Mr. Wise, of Virginia, in a long and violent speech, demanded that Congress

*The power of Congress over slavery in the District of Columbia.*

should pass a resolution disclaiming the possession of any such power. Mr. Slade immediately accepted the challenge of Mr. Wise, and delivered an anti-slavery speech in reply, such as had never before been heard upon the floors of Congress. He not only vindicated the power of Congress over the question of slavery in the District, but he discussed the whole question of slavery upon its merits. His words were simply a declaration of relentless war upon slavery in the halls of Congress. They created indescribable consternation in all parts of the House, and roused the resentment and anger of the slaveholders to a veritable fury. In the midst of the confusion, Mr. Garland, of Virginia, gained the Speaker's recognition, and made a good argument against some of Mr. Slade's more radical statements. So soon as he had finished, Mr. Mann, of New York, moved to stop the debate with the previous question. This was voted, and the Speaker then put the motion for the reconsideration of the reference of the petition, under which motion this debate had proceeded. This was voted, and immediately the motion was made to lay the recalled petition, with the reconsidered motion to refer it, on the table. This was voted by a majority of more than two to one.

Evidently the House thought that, in receiving and hearing the petitions and then laying them on the table, it had found the solution of the question, which neither violated the right of petition in the people, nor encroached upon the power of the House over its rules of procedure, nor opened the way for anti-slavery agitation in Congress.

It would have been wise for the slaveholders to have left this solution of the question undisturbed, but they did not see it so. On January 4th, 1836, Mr. Adams presented a petition from sundry citizens of Massa-

## ABOLITION 259

chusetts containing the usual prayer, and said that "in conformity with the course heretofore adopted, he should move that the petition, without reading, be laid on the table." Mr. Patton interrupted Mr. Adams with an inquiry addressed to the Speaker as to whether the petition had been received by the House, and the Speaker replied that it had not. He said that, upon looking up the authorities, he "had formed the opinion that the first question to be decided, upon the motion of a member, was whether the petition be received or not." The Speaker, Mr. Polk, had now come out of his uncertainty about the right of petition including the reception of the petition by the House, as a constitutional obligation, and now definitely denied that the right of petition included the right to have the petition received by the House. This was a fatal move, a fatal mistake upon his part. The object professedly sought by all parties, except such Abolitionists as Mr. Slade, was the prevention of agitation upon the slavery question in the halls of Congress. Whether all were sincere in this profession is questionable. It had been insinuated that there were agitators upon this question from both sections of the country, who were disingenuously claiming to be classed with the maintainers of peace. It does really seem that the innuendo was justified as to certain of the Southerners by the position now assumed by Mr. Patton and Mr. Polk, and then by Mr. Glascock, who, immediately after the ruling of the Speaker, moved that this petition be not received. While Mr. Adams, who sincerely believed that reference as well as reception was a necessary consequence of the right of petition, had accommodated himself to the decision which the House had made a fortnight before, these Southern gentlemen were now proposing to drive the House from

*Mr. Polk's fatal error in regard to the right of petition.*

the solid middle ground, then occupied, toward a position which the majority considered to be an encroachment upon the constitutional right of petition, a movement upon their part which was certain, and known by all to be certain, to provoke an excited debate upon the question of slavery. It may be that they thought the refusal to receive one of these anti-slavery petitions would prevent any more from being presented, and that it was better to have it out once for all than to be continually receiving, and listening to the reading of, these petitions. If so, they were wofully mistaken.

Mr. Adams now made one more effort to preserve the Southerners against the consequences of their own folly.

Mr. Adams' futile attempt to prevent slavery agitation in Congress. He undertook to arrest the debate by calling for the application of the forty-fifth rule of the House, which required that no petition should be debated or decided on the day of its presentation. But the Speaker now decided that this rule could not apply to a petition until it had been received. The gates of Janus were flung wide open, and the House went into an agitation upon the subject, to which all that had gone before was only a prelude. The struggle lasted for more than four months, during which period petitions for the abolition of slavery in the District, signed by over thirty thousand persons, were poured into the House. The slavery question was at last brought before the people of the United States in a way most highly satisfactory to the most radical Abolitionist, and no matter what the immediate compromise upon the subject might be, it was evident to all farseeing minds then that a death-blow had been struck at slavery.

There is not space in this work to recount the scenes enacted on the floor of the House during these four exciting months, or even to give a résumé of the debate.

The conflict was ended for the moment by the adoption, on May 25th (1836), of a series of resolutions reported by a committee appointed for the purpose, of which Mr. Pinckney, of South Carolina, was the chairman. These resolutions provided: "That Congress possesses no constitutional authority to interfere in any way with the institution of slavery in any of the States of this Confederacy; that Congress ought not to interfere with slavery in the District of Columbia; and whereas it is extremely important and desirable that the agitation of this subject should be finally arrested, for the purpose of restoring tranquillity to the public mind, . . . that all petitions, memorials, propositions, or papers, relating in any way, or to any extent whatsoever, to the subject of slavery, or the abolition of slavery, shall, without being printed or referred, be laid upon the table, and that no further action whatever shall be had thereon."

*The Pinckney resolutions.*

The solution thus reached by the House of the question of the power of the House to control its procedure, over against the right of a number of individuals to excite interminable discussions and paralyze the business of the House by flooding it with petitions upon one and the same subject, was the laying of all such petitions on the table *as a rule of the House.*

*The new rule of the House of Representatives in regard to the Abolition petitions.*

Of course this rule must be readopted at the beginning of each session, and a debate upon the readoption might be thus precipitated, but, so long as a majority supported the rule, the previous question could be voted after giving a reasonable opportunity to discuss the question of readoption, and such discussion was then not likely to be renewed during the session. It was possible also for petitions to be presented, at the beginning of the session, before the re-adoption of the rule, and these could be disposed of only by a special vote in each case to lay upon the table. There were thus still opportunities for the Abolitionists to cause the House to resolve itself into something more like a bear-garden than an assembly of Witan, as was evident from the scenes which were enacted on February 6th, 1837, when Mr. Adams came into the House with a petition in regard to slavery signed by some twenty slaves, and asked the Speaker if it came under the rule for laying such petitions on the table. Everybody supposed that the petition contained the usual prayer for the abolition of slavery, and that the Abolitionists had incited the slaves to the act. Mr. Adams allowed the excitement produced by this supposition to rage for a time, and then coolly and derisively informed the House that the prayer of the petition was not for abolition but against it. The members now felt that Mr. Adams was playing with the peace, order, and dignity of the House in a scandalous way, and for several days the question of censuring him was considered, but the matter was finally disposed of by a resolution declaring : "That slaves do not possess the right of petition secured to the people of the United States by the Constitution."

At the beginning of the next session, that of 1837-38, Mr. Slade seized the opportunity to present an abolition petition before the re-enactment of the Pinckney rule, and to provoke a debate on the subject of slavery. He was substantially foiled, however, by a vote to adjourn, and, upon reassembly, by a suspension of the rules and a re-enactment of the resolution to lay everything in reference to slavery on the table. This rule covered all matters relating to slavery in the Territories as well as in the Commonwealths and the District.

The more the House did to discourage the petitions the more they increased. In two years from the adoption of the Pinckney resolutions the number of petitioners was tenfold greater than it was before their enactment. At the same time the legislatures of the New England Commonwealths were passing resolutions declaring the rule of the House of Representatives in regard to the abolition petitions to be a violation of the people's constitutional right, and also declaring that Congress possessed the power to abolish slavery in the District of Columbia.

*The increase of petitions, and the denunciation of the Pinckney rule.*

To meet these demonstrations of increasing strength and increasing determination on the part of the Abolitionists, the House not only repeated its rule, but made it more stringent, until, at last, irritated beyond measure at the persistence of the petitioners, it took the fatal step, and, on January 8th, 1840, enacted as a standing rule of the House: "That no petition, memorial, resolution, or other paper, praying the abolition of slavery in the District of Columbia, or any State or Territory, or the slave-trade between the States or Territories of the United States in which it now exists, *shall be received by this House, or entertained in any way whatever.*"

*The final denial of the right of petition on the subject of Slavery by the House of Representatives.*

At last the House had encroached upon the most essential part of the right of petition, the right to have the petition heard. The moderate men of the South and twenty-eight members from the North had given way before the radical men of the South, and had fallen into the ranks under their lead. The Southern radicals thought that they had won a great victory, but it was not so. They had only identified the denial of the right of petition with the interests of slavery. They had only demonstrated that slavery was a matter of national concern, since its interests required that limitations should be placed upon the well understood rights of the people in the non-slaveholding Commonwealths. They only made it manifest that, sooner or later, the nation must deal with the question. Their most violent enemies could not have wished them a more disastrous result.

The proceedings in the Senate in regard to the Abolition petitions must be even more concisely stated. The course pursued and the result reached were similar to what has been described in the account of the experiences of the House. The Senate first received and heard the petitions, and voted immediately to deny their prayer. Then, when it became evident that this would not prevent anti-slavery agitation on the floor of the Senate, the body adopted the custom of hearing a motion not to receive a petition, and voting immediately to lay the motion not to receive, and along with it the petition itself, on the table. This practice was modified a little later, by a ruling of the presiding officer, to the effect that an objection to the petition by any member would raise the question of the reception of the petition without a formal motion. Mr. Calhoun had contended for this method of raising the question in regard to the reception of the petitions from the beginning of the struggle over the subject, in January of 1836. He seemed, however, to desire to dispose of them by simply voting not to receive them. In fact, he made a motion to this effect, at the very outset of the contest, but without success. While thus the Senate did not formally adopt the practice finally reached in the House of refusing to receive the petitions, it arrived at about the same result in practice. It is true that the presiding officer of the Senate allowed the petitions to be read before putting the motion upon their reception, which seems to have been an illogical practice indeed, and that any member might move to call up the motion not to receive, and with it the petition or petitions to which that motion referred ; but the reading before the motion not to receive, or before the objection to receiving, was perfunctory, and there was no member of the Senate who desired to call up the tabled petitions or persisted in so doing. As a matter of fact, the public opinion which the Abolitionists succeeded in creating in the North concerning the attitude of the Senate toward the Abolition petitions was that the Senate had done the same violence to the people's constitutional right of petition that the House had done. It was held and believed throughout the North, in 1840, that the Congress of the United States, in both of its branches, had set the interests of slavery above the liberties of the people of the North.

There were two incidents which happened during the course of the proceedings in the Senate upon the subject to which brief reference should be made. One was the noted passage of words between Mr. Calhoun and Mr. Rives, of Virginia, in regard to the morality of slavery, and the other was the petition from the legislature of Vermont for the abolition of slavery in the District of Columbia.

The Abolitionists had assumed to have the ethical principle entirely upon their side, and this had not, down to 1836, been clearly disputed by the slave- *Mr. Rives* holders. The slaveholders had, themselves, *and Mr. Calhoun in regard to the morality of slavery.* as we have so often seen, acknowledged slavery to be an evil, and had, therefore, defended it chiefly from the point of view of positive law. Of course so profound a thinker as Mr. Calhoun knew that positive law cannot permanently withstand the assaults of ethical principle. He knew that the moral arguments against slavery must be met upon moral grounds, as well as upon legal grounds. The discussion was carried over upon ethical premises by the remark of Mr. Rives that he, though a slaveholder, was not in favor of slavery in the abstract, and differed on that point with the gentleman from South Carolina. Mr. Calhoun immediately denied that he had expressed any opinion in regard to the question of slavery in the abstract, and said he had spoken of slavery only "as existing where two races of men, of different color, and striking dissimilarity in conformation, habits, and a thousand other particulars, were placed in immediate juxtaposition." Mr. Calhoun elaborated his argument in many directions, but the gist of it was that where a civilized race and a barbarous race, nearly equal numerically, must live together, the civilized race must, in the interests of the civilization of both races, control the barbarous race, through the relation of the slavery of the latter to the former, and that the only alternative to this would be the barbarizing of the whole society by the uncontrolled deeds and passions of the barbarous race, if the two races are left to themselves, or the establishment of a barbaric despotism over the civilized race, if the barbaric race be aided by successful interference from without. In contrast with either of these conditions, Mr. Calhoun contended that the slavery of the barbarous race to the civilized race was a moral good.

From a metaphysical point of view the only question between Mr. Rives and Mr. Calhoun was whether every departure from the perfect good must be considered an evil, or whether a nearer approximation to the perfect good may be called a good in contrast with a lower approximation. Mr. Rives was looking at the subject from an abstract, transcendental point of view, while Mr. Calhoun was regarding it from the historical point of view. Mr. Rives was with the Abolitionists upon the abstract principle, but against them as to the time and means of applying it. Mr. Calhoun was not against the Abolitionists upon the abstract principle, but the time of its possible application appeared to him so far distant, and the impropriety and unfairness of interference by outsiders in the matter and the disastrous consequences which must flow from such interference seemed to him so plain and so certain, that he almost lost sight of the abstract height upon which the Abolitionists stood behind the many intervening elevations, which must be first attained and traversed in order to reach their position.

There was a possible moral ground upon which Mr. Calhoun and the Abolitionists might have met. Could the Abolitionists have conceived that the existence of certain conditions would justify domestic slavery as a relation which could *temporarily* produce a better state of morals in a particularly constituted society than any other relation, that is, could they have taken the historical view of ethics, the evolutionary view of morals, and could Mr. Calhoun have seen that the time had come for a modification of the existing form of negro slavery in the South, for a step toward a greater degree of personal liberty for the slave, an approach between him and them might have been, at least, begun; but their implacable dogmatism, and his stern resentment at their persistent interference in what he thought no concern of theirs, widened the gulf between him and them from day to day. They regarded him as a sinner and a criminal because he held persons to service and labor who had not freely agreed to the same, and he

*The moral ground upon which Calhoun and the Abolitionists could have met.*

considered them to be greater sinners and criminals because they would overturn the existing order of society in communities where they had no personal interests to be affected, and would introduce into these communities the reign of plunder, rapine, and murder.

When Mr. Calhoun saw that he could not bring the Senate to refuse formally to receive the Abolition petitions, he undertook to bring the Senate over to his views of the "States' sovereignty" character of the Union, of the obligation of the general Government to protect slavery in the slaveholding Commonwealths, of the ethical obligation of the people of the non-slaveholding Commonwealths not to attack the institution of slavery, and of the practical impotence of Congress to deal with slavery in the District of Columbia and in the Territories. He did not, however, succeed. The Senate did not repudiate his "States' sovereignty" view of the Union, but, while it was willing to say that neither the Northern Commonwealths nor the Northern people had any legal right to attack slavery under moral or religious pretexts, it would not say that they were under moral or religious obligations to abstain from the attack. Neither would the Senate say that the general Government must so exercise its powers as to give increased security to slavery, nor that the general Government had no power over the subject of slavery in the District and the Territories. It modified these demands of Mr. Calhoun so as to make them read, that the general Government should not so exercise its powers as to interfere with the security of the domestic institutions of the Commonwealths, and that the general Government ought not in good faith to undertake to abolish slavery in the District or in the Territories, except under certain conditions.

# ABOLITION

The immediate occasion of the presentation of these resolutions of December 27th, 1837, by Mr. Calhoun, was probably the other incident to which reference has been made, the introduction, by Senator Swift, of Vermont, of a petition from the legislature of Vermont praying for the abolition of slavery in the District of Columbia.

*The anti-slavery petition from the Vermont legislature.*

This shaft had struck Mr. Calhoun in his most vulnerable part. Here was, according to his own doctrine, a "sovereign State" instructing its governmental agent for general affairs. Could that agent refuse to receive the instructions of one of his principals? There certainly was no precedent for any such procedure as that in any system of jurisprudence known to the world. Mr. Calhoun recognized fully the embarrassment of his position. He begged that the communication from the Vermont legislature might lay upon the table until he could prepare his mind for action upon the subject, and pledged himself to call it up very shortly, if no one else should do so. Mr. Swift helped the Senate, and Mr. Calhoun especially, out of the dilemma by withdrawing the petition for the time being. This incident occurred on December 19th.

Mr. Swift assumed that Mr. Calhoun's resolutions of the 27th contained the results of his preparation of mind to meet the Vermont memorial, and after the consideration of them by the Senate, Mr. Swift reintroduced the memorial on January 16th (1838). The Southerners had been thrown into such confusion by the *coup de surprise* sprung upon them by the Vermonters that they had not been able to agree upon any plan for meeting the exigency. Some of them denounced the action of the Vermont legislature as incendiary, outrageous, and degrading. Mr. King gave his "States' sovereignty" creed entirely away in saying: "We defend the legitimate rights of the States, but we do not defend a sovereign State when she asserts calumny and falsehood."

Mr. Calhoun was measured in his language, but evidently greatly disturbed in mind. He said that as a "States' rights" man, in the strongest sense, he believed that the "State" of Vermont had a right to come there and be heard; that, on the best reflection he could give to the matter, he could not vote against receiving the petition; but that, on the other hand, he considered the language of the memorial so objectionable that he could not vote to receive it.

It does seem as if this incident should have taught Mr. Calhoun the fallacy of his logic in insisting upon the power of the Senate to refuse to receive a petition. Here was a case in which his doctrine of parliamentary procedure had absolutely broken down, according to his own acknowledgment. Mr. Strange, of North Carolina, committed the folly of objecting to the reception of the petition, and moving that the question of reception, and with it the petition, be laid on the table. The motion was defeated by a vote of twenty-six to twelve. The memorial was received and the debate upon it was in order. The Southerners were helpless, and had not Mr. Swift himself come to their rescue, no man can say what would have happened. Mr. Swift moved that the papers from the Vermont legislature be laid upon the table, without being printed. They had accomplished their immediate purpose, and it was wise as well as patriotic to let them rest in dignity and honor.

The Abolitionists were more successful in their attempt to use the United States mails for the distribution of their literature throughout the South. During the course of the year 1835, it became known that their opinions and doctrines were being disseminated by this means. The Southerners considered these opinions to be incendiary and dangerous to the peace and safety of their communities and their firesides. They thought that they had the legal right to prevent the delivery of such mail matter in their respective communities. They did not wait, however, to deal with the subject through legal forms. On the night of July 29th, 1835, a mob of respectables broke into the post-office at Charleston, S. C., in search of Abolition documents. They found a sack full of them, took it away with them, and publicly burned its contents. On August 4th following, a meeting of the citizens took place, at which a committee of public safety was elected, which should, in understanding with the postmaster, determine what mail matter should not be delivered by him to the addressees. The postmaster apparently acquiesced in this arrangement, but he wrote, upon his own responsibility, a letter to the postmaster of New York City, whence the Abolition pamphlets had come, requesting him not to forward any more such documents. The postmaster at New York endeavored to induce the Abolitionists not to put any more of their literature into the mails until he could receive instructions from the Postmaster-General at Washington in regard to the question; and when the Abolitionists repelled his request, he refused to forward their documents, pending his conference with the Postmaster-General.

*The Abolition documents and the United States mails.*

The Postmaster-General, Mr. Amos Kendall, one of the shrewdest of politicians, though no great constitutional lawyer, answered the appeal from the postmaster at New York immediately. He instructed his subordinate that the executive power of the Government had no legal authority to exclude mail matter, as defined by

Congress, from the mails on account of the character of its contents, real or supposed. If Mr. Kendall had stopped with this he would have been entirely correct; but he went on to say that he would not direct the postmaster at New York to forward the Abolition documents or the postmaster at Charleston to deliver them, commended their assumption of the responsibility of withholding them from the addressees, and declared that the United States officials owed an obligation to the laws of the United States, but a higher one to the communities in which they lived. Mr. Kendall probably meant this part of his communication as the advice of one private citizen to another. Looked at in the most charitable light possible, however, it was unjustifiable and pernicious. It was nothing less than an encouragement to his subordinates to suspend the execution of the laws which they were appointed to execute and sworn to execute, when in their several opinions the welfare of the communities in which they might live should require it. This was nullification, not by a "State" convention, but by an individual United States officer. How the President, who had always so sternly denounced any attempt to prevent the execution of the laws, could approve this is difficult to understand. His indignation at the Abolitionists in persisting in what he considered an abuse of the freedom of the mails probably blinded him to the real significance of the matter.

*The Postmaster-General's ruling in regard to the Abolition documents in the mails.*

In his message of the following December, the President denounced the methods of the Abolitionists in sending their incendiary literature into the South as calculated and intended to excite a servile war with all its horrors, and recommended Congress to pass a law prohibiting, "under severe penalties, the circulation in the Southern States,

*Jackson on the use of the mails by the Abolitionists.*

## ABOLITION

through the mail, of incendiary publications intended to instigate the slaves to insurrection."

Mr. Calhoun himself moved the reference of this part of the President's message to a select committee in the Senate. Mr. Calhoun was appointed the chairman of the committee, and on February 4th, 1836, he brought in a report and a bill.

In the report Mr. Calhoun took the ground that the freedom of the mails was a necessary part of the freedom of the press, and argued that, as Congress was prohibited by the first amendment to the Constitution from passing any law abridging the freedom of the press, so Congress possessed no power to pass any law excluding mail matter from the mails on account of the character of its contents or authorizing such matter to be withheld from the addressees. Mr. Calhoun's conclusion was that only the "States" could make such laws as would effect these things. He proposed in his bill, therefore, that no deputy postmaster in any "State," Territory, or district of the Union should knowingly receive and put into the mail any printed or written paper or pictorial representation touching the subject of slavery, addressed to a person or a post-office within any "State," Territory, or district in which the circulation of such papers and representations was forbidden by the local laws; that the officers and agents of the Post-Office Department should co-operate with the local officials in preventing the circulation of such papers and representations where their circulation was prohibited by the local laws; that the matter so detained from transmission by a post-office official should be burned, after one month's notice, if the person depositing the same should not claim it within that period; and that the post-office officials who should violate these duties should not be

*Mr. Calhoun's report and bill on the subject.*

protected by the laws of the United States against the jurisdiction of the local law and government.

Mr. Clay immediately pointed out the fatal weaknesses of this proposition. He argued that it attributed *Clay's criticism of Calhoun's proposition.* to Congress either the power to adopt the laws of the "States" upon subjects in regard to which Congress itself had not the power to legislate, or the power to pass laws in execution of laws which it had no power to make. The argument was unanswerable, and the conclusion was unavoidable that if Congress could not itself pass a law excluding the Abolition papers and documents from the mail, or forbidding their delivery to the addressees, it could not enact Mr. Calhoun's proposition. After four months of deliberation the Senate rejected the proposed bill by a vote of twenty-five to nineteen. Mr. Calhoun thus lost the aid of the general Government in his contest with the Abolitionists over the use of the mails chiefly through his exaggerated "States' rights" doctrine.

Encouraged by this victory, the friends of free mails succeeded in having a provision incorporated into the *The act of Congress protecting the Abolition documents in the mails.* Act of July 2nd, 1836, for changing the organization of the Post-Office Department, which ordains that any postmaster intentionally detaining any mail matter from the addressees shall be fined and imprisoned, and incapacitated to hold thereafter the office of a postmaster in the United States.

It would not be extravagant to say that the whole course of the internal history of the United *General results of the struggle over the right of petition and the freedom of the mails.* States from 1836 to 1861 was more largely determined by the struggle in Congress over the Abolition petitions and the use of the mails for the distribution of the Abolition literature than by anything else.

## ABOLITION

In the first place, it did more than anything else to make a political party out of the Abolitionists, through the conviction which it produced throughout the North that the demands of the slavery system in the South would ultimately destroy civil and political liberty in the North, and it increased the strength of the Abolitionists an hundredfold in less than four years. The development and ultimate triumph of this party in the North became inevitable from the moment that it was clearly recognized that the preservation of slavery at the South required and demanded the denial of the freedom of speech and of the press, and of the right of petition, to the people of the North.

In the second place, it taught the South that there was a growing party in the North which was determined to attack slavery at every possible legal point, and prosecute its warfare at every hazard, and that the only safety for the South, with its slavery system, in the Union, was to hold at least equal power in the Congress with the representation from the North. In self-defence the South must secure, therefore, the formation of new slaveholding Commonwealths. At the moment the representation in the Senate was evenly balanced, but in the House it stood against the South, one hundred and forty-one to ninety-nine. One more non-slaveholding Commonwealth, without an offset on the other side, would destroy the balance in the Senate and enable the North to undertake legislation hostile to slavery. The extension of slavery to new Commonwealths was thus manifestly a necessity to its permanent security, and even continuance, in the Commonwealths where it already existed. The policy of the slaveholders must be to allow no new non-slaveholding Commonwealth to be formed without another slaveholding Commonwealth to match it, and to secure the extension of the territory of the United States toward the South.

In the third place, it aroused the apprehension of slave insurrection, by Abolition incitement, throughout the South, and caused thereby two marked movements in the South, the one legal and the other social. The first was the legislation sharpening and increasing the police power of the public authorities over the slaves, for the purpose of preventing the access of the Abolition doctrines to their minds, and of preventing communication and intercourse between strangers and slaves, and between the slaves themselves. The control of the slave by the master was thus more and more interfered with by the public authorities, for the purpose indeed of aiding the master, which, however, did not alter the fact that from being primarily for the most part a household affair, slavery was becoming more and more an affair of the community. This meant no improvement to the condition of the slave; quite the contrary. The intervention of the whites in the South who owned no slaves in the control of the slaves marks an increase of rigor in the treatment of the slaves. In fact much of the cruelty inflicted upon the slaves during the twenty years between 1840 and 1860 was executed by non-slaveholders, by virtue of the increased control assumed by the public authorities over the relation between master and slave, through the local legislation of that period. The other movement was toward the development of a military caste in the society. The slaveholders, and especially the sons of the slaveholders, now began to understand that they must unite in military organization and make themselves the exclusive military class. The spirit of chivalry and the practices of knighthood were largely developed during this period, with both their good and their bad consequences. On the one side they produced a high-toned society of proud, noble women, and courtly, haughty men, among the slaveholders. On the other, they degraded all other classes, both white and black. In fact they degraded the poor whites more than they did the blacks. The blacks felt, and were proud of, the increased importance of their masters. And, naturally, this spirit and life among the slaveholding class made the generation which grew up under them eager for adventure and war, intensely tenacious of rights, sensitive to every only apparent discourtesy, and resentful of every semblance of interference from without. The War with Mexico, the filibustering expeditions, and the Civil War itself, were all national consequences of the social development in the South after 1836.

## CHAPTER XII.

### THE BANK, THE SUB-TREASURY, AND PARTY DEVELOPMENT BETWEEN 1832 AND 1842

Jackson and the Bank after the Election of 1832—The Power of the Secretary of the Treasury over the Government Deposits—Removal of McLane and Duane—Taney's Report to Congress of December 3rd, 1835—Abuses of Power by Jackson and Taney—The Senate's Censure of the President and Secretary of the Treasury—National Republicans Take the Name of Whigs—The Cardinal Doctrine of the Whigs—The Change of the Deposits and the Specie Order of 1836—Van Buren's Election and the Panic of "'37"—The Sub-Treasury Idea—The Establishment of the Sub-Treasury System—The Election of 1840—Whig Legislative Projects in Regard to the Bank and the Tariff—The Party Treason of Tyler and the Whig War upon the President's Veto Power—The Whigs Unable to Encounter the Questions of Territorial Extension and Slavery Extension.

WHEN the violent agitation of the slavery question, in the middle of the fourth decade, came so suddenly upon the nation, it found the great political parties divided upon issues which partook more of the character of economic policies than that of rights, or of governmental forms and powers. It is true that the protective tariff, the Bank, and internal improvements had been denounced by some persons as unconstitutional, but neither party held this view of these subjects at the beginning of the fourth decade of the century. They were regarded by the two great parties from the point

# THE BANK AND THE SUB-TREASURY

of view of economic policy, and were supported or opposed by them on the ground of conduciveness or lack of conduciveness to the public welfare. More exactly, the Bank was the chief political issue between 1832 and 1840. It was in the conflict between Congress and the President in regard to the Bank that the national Republicans took the title of Whigs, anti-prerogative men.

After the election of 1832 upon the Bank issue, President Jackson, naturally for him, regarded himself as the only representative of the present will of the people in the Government. The Congress, at the time of the election, was, as we know, favorable to the Bank. The newly elected members of the House of Representatives would not assemble for a year probably, and the Senate would probably sustain the Bank after that. The President, therefore, resolved to do by edict what Congress would not do by statute— destroy the Bank. *[Jackson and the Bank after the election of 1832.]*

The sixteenth section of the Bank Act provided that the funds of the United States should be deposited in the Bank or its branches, unless the Secretary of the Treasury should at any time otherwise order and direct. The Secretary of the Treasury was thus impliedly authorized by Congress to cease depositing these funds in the Bank or its branches at his own discretion, and was made directly responsible to Congress in the exercise of this authority, by the provision that he must report, so soon as possible, to Congress his reasons for making use of the power. The President thus had no direct authority in the matter. He could exercise only an indirect control through his power over the tenure of the Secretary. At this period in the history of the tenure of office in the United States, the power of removal was regarded as a prerogative of the President alone. *[The power of the Secretary of the Treasury over the Government deposits.]*

President Jackson was within the letter of his prerogative when, in the spring of 1833, he removed Mr. McLane, and later, Mr. Duane, from the secretaryship of the Treasury. That he did this because of their refusal to be controlled by him in regard to the deposit of the funds of the United States in the Bank and its branches was, legally, no concern of anybody else.

*Removal of McLane and Duane.*

The new Secretary, Mr. Taney, appointed to succeed Mr. Duane, was also acting within the letter of his authority when he ceased to make deposit of the Government funds in the Bank and its branches, and reported his action to Congress at the commencement of the session following the recess of Congress during which he made this change.

*Taney's report to Congress of December 3rd, 1835.*

On the other hand, it was very questionable whether the President was not abusing his power of dismissal from office, in spirit, by requiring the obedience of the Secretary of the Treasury to himself in regard to a subject concerning which Congress had vested discretionary power in the Secretary, and in the use of which power Congress had made the Secretary directly and exclusively responsible to itself. And it was likewise very questionable whether the Secretary was not abusing his authority, in spirit, in ceasing, during a recess of Congress, to deposit the funds of the United States in the Bank and its branches, when, less than a year before this, Congress had made a full investigation of the condition of the Bank and had disapproved, by large majorities in both Houses, of the President's recommendation that the deposits be made elsewhere than in the Bank and its branches.

*Abuses of power by Jackson and Taney.*

Secretary Taney, afterward Chief Justice, to whose legal opinions, therefore, great respect must be paid,

# THE BANK AND THE SUB-TREASURY 281

contended that Congress itself could not have caused the removal of the deposits without violating the contract with the Bank, as expressed in the Bank's charter, and that the Secretary of the Treasury alone was exempted from this obligation by the provisions of the contract. The Secretary alone, he said, could, therefore, act for the welfare of the people in the matter, and by the oath which he had sworn upon the Constitution he must so act. He declared it to be his conviction that the public welfare would suffer by his continuing to deposit the funds of the Government in the Bank and its branches, and that he felt, therefore, in duty bound to make the order discontinuing the same.

The Senate, however, took a different view of the subject. It considered the act of the Secretary to have been done under the order of the President, and in condemnatory resolutions held the President responsible therefor. These resolutions of censure connected the Secretary with the President, however, by declaring the reasons offered by the Secretary for the change in regard to the deposits to be "unsatisfactory and insufficient." The President made a vigorous protest against the Senate's resolution charging him with usurpation, and flung the accusation back at the body. He certainly showed that the Senate had no constitutional power to make any such charge against the President; and Senator Benton immediately gave notice that he should move the expunging of the resolutions from the journal at every session of Congress until it should be accomplished. *[The Senate's censure of the President and Secretary of the Treasury.]*

It was in the midst of this conflict, and in consequence of it, a conflict in principle between the legislative and executive departments of the Government, in regard to the extent of their respective powers, that Mr. James Watson *[National Republicans take the name of Whigs.]*

Webb, the editor of the *New York Courier and Enquirer*, began, about February, 1834, to denominate, in his newspaper articles, the opposition party to the President, led by Mr. Clay, Whigs. This title signified opposition to high executive prerogative, and approval of strong Congressional control over the President. The name was gradually substituted for that of National Republicans, as the different members and factions of the party came together upon the principle involved in the name.

It seemed, for the moment, as if the parties had returned to the condition of bands of retainers under the lead of Clay and Jackson respectively, but this was more apparent than real. There was a real and comprehensive question at issue, one of the most fundamental questions of political science, the question of parliamentary government or presidential government in the United States. The triumph of President Jackson in this conflict—for the Bank was not rechartered, the deposits were not restored, and the President was not impeached, but the Senate's resolutions of censure were expunged—settled that question, and preserved the American system of government from further following the tendency which, from the accession of Jefferson to that of Jackson, had been slowly asserting itself, the tendency toward Congressional control over the Administration.

*The cardinal doctrine of the Whigs.*

The original character of the Whig party explains many important things in its composition and subsequent history. In the first place, it explains why the party was composed, as to its leading element, of hightoned, courteous gentlemen—the larger part of the aristocracy of the land—since it is the instinct of the aristocracy to control the executive through the legislature. It explains further why the Whig party was unable to cope with the problem of slavery, since its fundamental principle was not a doctrine of rights, but of governmental form. It explains, lastly, why, in the development of the country's history, the defeat of the Whig party was necessary to the very existence of the country, when the great struggle should come, since its principle of Congressional control of the Administration would, if realized, have greatly weakened that executive independence, power, and unity, without which victory could hardly have been won.

The failure of the Whigs in the campaign of 1836, and their momentary triumph in that of 1840, were experienced under the true issue of the Whig principle. The modification of the tariff by the Act of 1833, and the change of the place of deposit of the funds of the Government, after October 1st, 1833, from the United States Bank and its branches to certain Commonwealth banks, designated by the Secretary of the Treasury, had brought about much business embarrassment, since the one depressed the manufacturing interests, and the other forced the United States Bank and its branches to call in the loans made upon the strength of the Government's deposits. This embarrassment was greatly increased by the issue of the executive order of July 11th, 1836, directing that only specie should be taken at the land offices for public lands. At the moment there was a general speculation in Western lands, and only those banks which held Government deposits could furnish their customers with specie; the others, when called upon for gold and silver in exchange for their notes, were compelled to suspend.

*The change of the deposits, and the specie order of 1836.*

The Congress, disapproving the favoritism shown by the Secretary of the Treasury, and, probably foreseeing that a financial crisis of some sort was impending, had, on June 23rd preceding, passed an Act ordering a more general distribution of the deposits than the Secretary of the Treasury had made. After the specie order, and a little experience with its effect, the demand was raised from every quarter for an immediate execution of the Act of Congress of June 23rd. The Secretary hastened to carry out the provision, with the result of driving those banks into insolvency which had been able to stand, the existing deposit banks, since they had loaned the money of the Government deposited in them, and were compelled to call in these loans in the proportion that they were called upon to give up these deposits, and were left also without the gold and silver of the Government to redeem their own notes. The sudden calling in of the loans also forced a great number of the borrowers into insolvency.

Had the full force of the financial distress come in 1836, instead of a year later, it might have turned the election against Jackson's heir, Mr. Van Buren; but as things were, the Van Buren Administration was established, and had had an opportunity to get a little foothold, when the financial panic spread over the land. Mr. Van Buren and his advisers decided very properly not to involve the Government, but to let the people work themselves through the disaster by the natural course of business. This, as is usual in such cases, turned hosts of supporters into opponents.

<small>Van Buren's election and the panic of "'37."</small>

The Administration, however, pursued the even tenor of its way, and endeavored to draw the lesson of the experiences with banks as places of deposit for the funds of the Government. In his message of September 4th, 1837, President Van Buren recommended that the Government should cut loose entirely from banks, and should keep its funds in the Unit-

<small>The Sub-Treasury idea.</small>

## THE BANK AND THE SUB-TREASURY 285

ed States Treasury, and in branches of the Treasury, under the control of the officers of the Treasury. The idea was not original with Mr. Van Buren. Mr. Gordon, of Virginia, had suggested it in the House of Representatives, during the session of 1834–35, and had offered a plan for its realization, in the form of an amendment to the bill, then before the House, for regulating the deposits. Mr. Gordon's amendment was rejected on February 11th, 1835. The significant thing about it was that the plan was then supported by Whigs almost exclusively, only one Democrat voting in favor of it. It is true that only about one-half of the Whigs in the House supported it, and that it could hardly, therefore, be called a Whig party measure in 1835. On the other hand, it was certainly then opposed by the Democratic party.

Under these circumstances, it was a courageous thing in Mr. Van Buren to take up the idea anew and recommend it to Congress. Not until the session of 1839–40, however, was Congress brought to approve the plan and pass the law of July 4th, 1840, establishing the Sub-Treasury system for the keeping of the funds of the Government. *The establishment of the Sub-Treasury system.* During the discussion of the bill in Congress, its principle developed into a strict party question, the Democrats supporting it and the Whigs opposing it. The Whigs represented the scheme as an attempt to break down all the banks in the country, to keep the people's money locked up in the vaults of the Treasury, instead of maintaining it in circulation for their benefit, and to make the President the arbiter of the business of the country, and thus develop still further his autocratic power. The Whig protest was a capital piece of demagogism, and it proved immediately and immensely attractive to the people. Before the summer of 1840 wore away it was entirely clear that the people had made up their minds to try a Whig administration, and had arrived at this resolution under the issue of the financial questions.

The Whig National Convention had met in December, 1839, and had adopted no platform of principles. It had conciliated the factional differences in the Whig ranks by dropping Clay and nominating General Harrison, the military hero of the party, and the Whigs were now, therefore, free to strike any note in the campaign which would please the popular ear. The victory was a clean sweep, and the Whigs immediately set about the financial legislation, which was, as they thought, to redeem the country.

*The election of 1840.*

They had attributed the distress in the country chiefly to the failure to re-charter the Bank and to the reduction of the tariff. Consequently, they immediately passed a bill for the incorporation of a bank, when, to their dismay and confusion, Mr. Tyler, elected Vice-President, and, upon the sudden death of Mr. Harrison, successor to the presidential office, vetoed the bill. The leaders of the party in Congress consulted with the President in regard to a bank bill which would be acceptable to him, and drafted one which followed his suggestions in all essential principles, and contained only a few divergent details, put in probably for the purpose of preserving a show of legislative independence, but the President considered these differences essential and vetoed the second bill. The bills for suspending the reductions of the duties met with the same fate, two of them being successively vetoed.

*Whig legislative projects in regard to the Bank and the tariff.*

After the Bank vetoes all the members of the Cabinet, except the Secretary of State, Mr. Webster, resigned, and after the tariff vetoes Mr. Webster retired, so soon

# THE BANK AND THE SUB-TREASURY 287

as the diplomatic negotiations with Great Britain, then in progress, permitted.

The Whigs regarded Mr. Tyler as a traitor to the party and began a war upon the veto power of the President. They had come back again to their original principle of government— the supremacy of the legislature over the executive.

*The party treason of Tyler and the Whig war upon the President's veto power.*

From this account, it is clearly manifest that the Whig party did not stand upon any fundamental principle which would enable it to meet successfully those questions which, after the final settlement given to the bank and tariff issues by the vetoes of President Tyler, came to the front—the questions of territorial extension and of slavery extension.

It might be thought, at first view, that the Democratic party of that day was no better prepared than the Whig party to encounter these questions, since it, too, had reached its distinctive position through its attitude in economic issues. But the strength of the Democratic party lay in the South, and the South had a strong interest in territorial extension for the purpose of slavery extension, which, so long as the Southern wing of the Democratic party ruled the party, would furnish a clear and definite aim to the policy of the party, and would, thereby, give it great advantage over the Whigs, whose Northern and Southern contingents were much more evenly balanced, and, therefore, as to these questions, less able, or, rather, entirely unable, to gain a position upon which they might make a common stand. In a word, as to the Whig party, there was, after 1842, nothing to take the place of their overthrown economic policies, while, as to the Democratic party, there was territorial extension for the sake of slavery extension. When

*The Whigs unable to encounter the questions of territorial extension and slavery extension.*

these latter questions came to the front, therefore, they were destined, sooner or later, to disrupt the Whig party and destroy it altogether. The whole South would be for territorial extension, chiefly for the sake of slavery extension, and a large party at the North would be for territorial extension *per se*. The opposition to territorial extension must, therefore, become sectional, and as that opposition came chiefly from the Whig party it was the Whig party which would be degraded from its national character by this question, and then destroyed by it and its attendant question of slavery extension.

# CHAPTER XIII.

### TEXAS

Arkansas and Michigan—Florida and Iowa—Texas—The Austin Grant—Local Government in Texas—The Attempts by the United States to Purchase Texas—The Texan Revolution—General Sam Houston—San Jacinto and Independence—The Recognition of the Independence of Texas—Calhoun's frank Declaration in Regard to the Annexation of Texas—The Mission of Mr. Morfit to Texas, His Report and Advice—Jackson's Recommendation to Delay the Recognition of Texan Independence—Jackson's Request of Congress for Authority to Issue an Ultimatum to Mexico in the Claims Question—Texan Independence Recognized by the United States—The Question of Annexation—Texan Proposition for Annexation—The Mexican Claims Commission and Its Work—Tyler as an Advocate of Annexation—Mr. Webster in the Way of Annexation—The Adams Address on Annexation—The Retirement of Webster—The Promotion of Upshur, and His Negotiations with the Texans—The Threat of the Mexican Government to Consider the Annexation of Texas a Cause of War—The Administration Proposes Annexation to the Texan Agent—The Difficulty in the Way of Acceptance of the Proposition—The Demand of the Texans for Protection in the Interim—Mr. Calhoun in the State Department—The Treaty of Annexation Signed—The Treaty in the Senate and its Rejection—Mr. Archer's Opposition to the Treaty—The New Plan for Annexation.

AFTER the admission of Missouri there remained as territory, upon which, according to existing law, it was probable that slaveholding Commonwealths would be established, only Arkansas and Florida.

In 1836, Arkansas was admitted as a slaveholding Commonwealth, and Michigan as a non-slaveholding Commonwealth, thus keeping the exact balance in the Senate. By a compact of the year 1832, the Seminoles in Florida had agreed to emigrate within three years to the west bank of the Mississippi. At the end of this period, one of their chiefs, Osceola, repudiated the agreement, and with a large following began hostilities. By a long and expensive war the Indians were at last expelled ; and the white inhabitants immediately chose delegates to a convention, who met, in December of 1838, formed a Commonwealth constitution, one of the provisions of which legalized slavery, and demanded of Congress admission into the Union. Congress kept Florida waiting, however, for six years, until Iowa was ready, and then admitted the two at the same time and by the same Act.

*Arkansas and Michigan.*

*Florida and Iowa.*

Meanwhile the events in the Southwest had been so shaping themselves as to open up prospects for the long desired territorial extension in that quarter. The long dispute between Spain and France, and then after 1803, between Spain and the United States, in regard to the territory between the Rio Grande del Norte and the Sabine Rivers, called Texas, was first definitely settled in 1819, or rather in the Treaty of that year, between the United States and Spain, which Treaty was not executed, as we have seen, until a little later. In it this territory was recognized by the United States as belonging to Spain. It seems that a few persons from the United States had settled upon this territory, while it was disputed ground, and raised some complaint at having been left unprotected by the Government in the Treaty with Spain.

*Texas.*

The successful rebellion of Mexico against Spain made
this territory a part of the new Mexican state, and before Mexico had had time to consolidate its powers or
estimate the value of its northern possessions, a shrewd
Yankee from Connecticut, who had removed to Missouri,
and had become well skilled in the arts and *The Austin*
practices of border life, Moses Austin, went *grant.*
to Mexico, and representing himself, it is said, as the
leader of a company of Roman Catholics, who had suffered persecution in the United States, for their religion's sake, solicited a grant of land from the Catholic
government of Mexico, and permission to make a settlement upon it. The Mexicans gave ready ear to his
complaints and petition, and made him a large grant of
land in the central part of Texas on the Colorado River.
Mr. Austin died before effecting the settlement, and left
the work to his son, S. F. Austin, who, in 1822, colonized the grant, and received a ratification of the same
from the Mexican Government, the following year.

At that moment, Texas and Coahuila formed a single
Mexican province, and, after the establishment of the
federal system of government in Mexico, the
province became, in 1827, a Commonwealth. *Local government in Texas.*
In the Coahuila part the population was
Mexican, and as it was much larger than the Anglo-American population in the Texas part, the government
of the Commonwealth was practically in the hands of
Mexican officials. The rule of these officials was arbitrary and uncertain, and the race prejudice between
Spaniard and Anglo-Saxon was immediately excited by
it. It was pretty evident that the expulsion of the
Americans from Texas was intended. In 1830, came
at last the decree from the Mexican President, Bustamente, prohibiting further immigration into Texas from
the United States.

The Texan colonists now numbered some twenty thousand, mostly bold and hardy men, and it was not to be expected that they would either give up their lands, or assist in preventing further immigration, or submit much longer to the foreign rule, as they felt it to be, of Mexico or Coahuila.

Both in 1827 and in 1829, the United States Government attempted to purchase Texas, and in the latter year the proposition was actually made to the Mexican Government to sell to the United States the territory lying to the northwest of the watershed of the River Nueces. It was, however, promptly rejected by that Government.

*The attempts by the United States to purchase Texas.*

Naturally these attempts encouraged the colonists in Texas to feel that the United States sympathized with them in their desire for emancipation from Mexican rule, and to hope that this sympathy might, at some future time, lead to positive assistance.

The Texans were, however, for the moment, left to their own devices. They first tried to have Texas separated from Coahuila and made a separate Commonwealth of the Mexican Union, but the Mexican central government refused to assent to this. This was in 1833. Two years later Santa Anna, the Mexican President, forcibly displaced the federal system of government established in Mexico by the constitution of 1824, and instituted the centralized system, virtually by a presidential edict.

*Overthrow of the federal system in Mexico.*

Some of the Commonwealths of the Mexican Union resisted this usurpation of the President, and among them, naturally, was Coahuila-Texas. Moreover, some of the Coahuila members of the legislature of the Commonwealth, partisans of Santa Anna, withdrew from that body, and the Texan members found themselves, for the first time, in a majority in it. Of course the feeling of resistance to the overthrow of the right of local self-government became now a settled and resolute purpose with them, and Santa Anna, upon learning their attitude, resolved to reduce them to obedience by military power.

In September of 1835, a Mexican war-ship appeared upon the Texan coast, and its commander declared the Texan ports in a state of blockade. About the same time, the Mexican General Cos appeared, with a force of some fifteen hundred soldiers, at the Texan village of Gonzales. *The Texan revolution.* The resistance of the inhabitants of the town to Cos' order to surrender their arms precipitated the struggle. The Texans immediately organized a temporary government, drove the Mexicans out of the country before the close of the year, and, on March 2nd, 1836, declared their independence of Mexico.

While the Texan convention, which had declared independence and was framing the constitution for the state of Texas, was still in session, the Mexican soldiery, under the command of Santa Anna himself, returned to Texas and committed the atrocities of the Alamo and of Goliad. After these barbarous deeds there could no longer be any hope of an accommodation between the Mexicans and the Texans. It was independence or extermination.

Happily for the Texans they had now found their proper leader, General Sam Houston. Many of the descriptions of this hero are caricatures. Of those which approach the truth, that given by Senator Benton is perhaps most nearly correct. *General Sam Houston.* Benton was the lieutenant-colonel of the regiment in which Houston served during the war with the Creeks; and said later of his old comrade, "I then marked in him the same soldierly and gentlemanly qualities which have since distinguished his eventful career; frank, generous, and brave, ready to do, or to suffer, whatever the obligations of civil or military duty imposed; and always prompt to answer the call of honor, patriotism, and friendship." He was a Virginian by birth, but an early resident of Tennessee, and had been Governor of Tennessee before attaining his thirty-fifth year. He appeared in Texas in 1833, and in 1835 was made commander of the Texan army. It was chiefly his skill and bravery, which effected the expulsion of Cos and his army in the winter of 1835–36. After the disasters at the Alamo and at Goliad, he, in command of the remnants of the Texan army, retreated slowly before Santa Anna's comparatively large force, until Santa Anna made the blunder of dividing his army by the swollen waters of the San Jacinto, when he turned suddenly upon the Mexicans, and inflicted upon them the crushing defeat known as the battle of San Jacinto, in which the Mexican loss was double the number of Houston's army, some sixteen hundred men, including Santa Anna himself among the captives. The part of the Mexican army which had not crossed the river retreated precipitately from Texan soil, and the new state had won its independence.

*San Jacinto and independence.*

The battle of San Jacinto was fought on April 21st, 1836. The convention had finished the constitution more than a month before. In September following, General Houston was elected President of the new republic, and the constitution was almost immediately put into operation. This constitution legalized the existence of slavery in Texas, as a constitutional right of the masters, prohibited the residence of free negroes within the State without special official permission, and interdicted the importation of negro slaves, except from the United States.

*Texas as a constitutional Republic.*

A little more than a month after the battle of San Jacinto, the legislature of Connecticut set the ball in motion for the recognition of the independence of Texas by the Government of the United States. On May 27th, 1836, the two Houses of that body passed a resolution instructing the Senators, and requesting the Representatives, in Congress from Connecticut "to use their best endeavors to procure the acknowledgment, on the part of the United States, of the independence of Texas." Evidently the Yankee Commonwealth considered itself, in an especial degree, the motherland of the new state. The founder of the colony, which had now become an independent state, was one of its children, and it hastened to anticipate Virginia, the birthplace of Houston, in owning its offspring. A careful perusal of the whole of this Connecticut document will certainly leave the impression upon the mind of the impartial reader, at this day, that the people of the North then considered the Texan revolution to have been provoked by Mexican misrule and barbarism, and to have been fully justified in political ethics as well as by practical success.

*The recognition of the independence of Texas.*

On June 13th, Senator Niles, of Connecticut, presented the Connecticut memorial to the Senate, and it was immediately referred to the committee on Foreign Relations. On the 18th, Mr. Clay, the chairman of the committee, reported a resolution : "That the independence of Texas ought to be acknowledged by the United States whenever satisfactory information shall be received that it has, in successful operation, a civil government capable of performing the duties and fulfilling the obligations of an independent Power." The resolution was adopted by the Senate, on July 1st, without a dissenting voice.

During the course of the debate upon it, Mr. Calhoun

frankly told the Senate that he regarded the great importance of the recognition of the independence of Texas to consist in the fact that it prepared the way for the speedy admission of Texas into the Union, which would be a necessity to the proper balance of power in the Union between the slaveholding and the non-slaveholding Commonwealths, upon which the preservation of the Union and the perpetuation of its institutions rested. After such a statement it is difficult to see how anybody could speak of the annexation of Texas being a slaveholders' secret intrigue. Mr. Calhoun, the great leader of the slaveholders, the director of their policy, here at the very outset openly proclaimed their purpose. The fact is that, at the time of the Texan declaration of independence, almost everybody would have favored the annexation of Texas to the United States, out of race sympathy with the Texans and desire for territorial extension, except for the international complications with Mexico, which must inevitably result. It was the struggle over the Abolition petitions in 1836, 1837, and 1838 which turned the thoughts of men upon the internal questions involved in the movement, and caused the North generally to reconsider its attitude upon the question.

<small>Calhoun's frank declaration in regard to the annexation of Texas.</small>

On July 4th, 1836, the House of Representatives passed a resolution of the same tenor, and expressed in nearly the same words, as the Senate resolution of July 1st. It seems to have been called forth by memorials from citizens of Ohio and Pennsylvania.

Assured thus of the feeling of Congress, the President sent an agent, Mr. Henry M. Morfit, to Texas during the summer of 1836, in order to procure exact information of the state of affairs there. Mr. Morfit wrote to the Secretary of State, Mr. Forsyth, that the constitu-

TEXAS,
at the Time of Annexation.
Longitude West from Greenwich
SCALE OF MILES.
TERRITORY CEDED BY FRANCE TO UNITED STATES 1803
TEXAS ANNEXED TO UNITED STATES 1845
CLAIMED BY TEXAS, CLAIM QUIETED BY THE UNITED STATES 1850
10,000,000 DOLLARS
CLAIMED BY MEXICO 1846. FINALLY CONCEDED TO TEXAS 1850
Boundary of the United States Previous to the Annexation of Texas.
Present Texas Boundary.
Boundary Adopted by the Texan Constitution, 1836.
Rio Grande del Norte
APACHES
OSAGES
TEXANOS
Santa Fe
Las Vegas
Albuquerque
Bracito
El Paso del Norte
Austin
Houston
San Jacinto
Galveston
Ft. Alamo
San Antonio
Nacogdoches
Alamo
Corpus Christi
Palo Alto
Brownsville
Resaca de la Palma
Matamoras
Monterey
Buena Vista
MEXICO
GULF OF MEXICO
THE M.-N. CO, BUFFALO, N. Y.

tion of March 17th was soon to be put into operation; that General Houston had been elected President; that the constitution was fashioned after that of the United States; that the desire for annexation to the United States was universal; that the boundaries asserted by the new state were the Rio Grande del Norte on the south and southwest, the longitude from the source of the Rio Grande to the boundary of the United States on the west, the southern boundary of the United States on the north and northeast, and the Gulf of Mexico on the east; that the population amounted to about sixty-five thousand souls, of whom about fifty thousand were Anglo-Americans; that the standing army numbered about twenty-two hundred men, and could be increased to seven or eight thousand in an emergency; that the navy consisted of four vessels, carrying twenty-nine guns; that the funds of the State consisted of from fifty to one hundred millions of acres of public lands, worth, at least, ten millions of dollars, and that contributions were flowing in from private individuals in the United States; that the debt was about twelve hundred and fifty thousand dollars; that the supplies for the winter campaign were already provided; and that there was not a Mexican soldier north of the Rio Grande, although there were rumors that the Mexican government was making preparations for a new invasion in the winter, which were not, however, credited by the Texans.

*The mission of Mr. Morfit to Texas, his report and advice.*

This was certainly a good showing for Texas. If with an army of seven hundred men, under a provisory government, the Texans drove the Mexicans out of Texas, they could, under well established government, and with an army ten times as large, most surely keep them out. It must also be remembered that Santa Anna was still a prisoner in their hands. Mr. Morfit, however, expressed the belief that most of the men and money for the army came from the United States, and, therefore, advised delay in assuming a definite attitude toward the new state.

President Jackson transmitted this information to Congress, in his message of December 21st, 1836, and recommended delay in recognizing the independence of Texas. On January 11th, 1837, however, Senator Walker, of Mississippi, offered a resolution in the Senate to the effect that it would be expedient and proper to recognize the independence of Texas, and stated that he had information that the projected invasion of Texas by a new Mexican army, the rumors of which were reported by Mr. Morfit, had most probably been abandoned.

*Jackson's recommendation to delay the recognition of Texan independence.*

Before the resolution offered by Mr. Walker was taken up for discussion, a message from the President was communicated to Congress recommending the passage of an act, authorizing the President to make reprisals upon Mexico, in case Mexico should refuse another demand made upon her for an amicable adjustment of the matters in controversy between her and the United States. The citizens and the Government of the United States had many claims against Mexico and the Mexicans for depredating the commerce, seizing the seamen, and insulting the flag of the United States, and the demands for the satisfaction of these claims had been almost uniformly disregarded. The relations between the two Governments were already greatly strained on this account, and when, in the autumn of 1836, President Jackson authorized General Gaines to advance his troops into northwestern Texas, if he should deem it necessary for the protection of the frontiers of the United States against the Indians in Texas, who, on account of the

*The question of Mexico's obligations to the United States.*

War between Mexico and Texas, had been thrown into a great state of excitement and unrest, the Mexican Minister, Señor Gorastiza, demanded his passports, issued a sort of manifesto to the people of the United States, and left Washington.

It was hardly to be expected that President Jackson would quietly brook such defiance from a half civilized state and its agents. He immediately caused Mr. Ellis, the Chargé d'Affaires of the Government at the Mexican capital, to make a final demand on the Mexican government. Mr. Ellis made his demand in writing, on September 26th. After much delay the Mexican Minister of Foreign Affairs replied, admitting the justice of some of the claims, and requiring more information about others, but offering no reparation at all for insults to the flag and to the consular officers of the United States. The President's patience was exhausted, and he sent the message of February 6th, 1837, to Congress, asking for authority to make a final demand from the decks of a war-ship.

*Jackson's request of Congress for authority to issue an ultimatum to Mexico in the claims question.*

Congress was not, however, willing to invest the President with the contingent power to make offensive war. The recommendation of the President in the case had, nevertheless, considerable influence in determining the minds of the Senators in regard to the question of recognizing the independence of Texas. On March 1st, 1837, the Senate adopted Mr. Walker's resolution. On the previous day the House of Representatives had voted to insert in the civil and diplomatic appropriation bill an item for the expenses of a diplomatic agent to Texas, whenever the President should receive satisfactory evidence that Texas was an independent Power and should consider it expedient to appoint such a minister. President Jackson had invited this expression of the

300        THE MIDDLE PERIOD

views of Congress in his message of the previous December, in which he expressed the view that Congress ought to determine the expediency of recognizing the independence of Texas, and, although the resolutions of the two Houses of February 28th and March 1st, 1837, did not formally assume to recognize that independence, the President evidently attributed to them some virtue, since he soon opened diplomatic intercourse with the Texan agent at Washington. The resolutions of the two Houses of Congress and this act of the President, taken together, were regarded by the people of the United States and by foreign Powers as a recognition of Texan independence.

*Texan independence recognized by the United States.*

It was clear to all thinking minds that the next step after independence would be annexation to the United States. There is little question that Texas was big enough and strong enough to stand alone against Mexico, certainly with the aid which she was sure to receive from without and with the growth which she was destined to enjoy; but there was no natural boundary between the United States and Texas, and the inhabitants of Texas were chiefly Anglo-Americans. The natural boundary of the United States on the southwest is the desert between the Nueces and the Rio Grande, and the territorial extension of the United States to that limit was simply the fulfilment of the moral order of the world, which tends to make the lines of states correspond with the lines of physical geography and of ethnical differences. Except for the connection of the question of slavery extension with that of territorial extension after 1836, the question of the annexation of Texas would have been generally viewed in this natural and national light. That connection, however, made the North generally assume the attitude

*The question of annexation.*

# TEXAS 301

of opposition to annexation, while it greatly excited the desires of the South in favor of it.

On his way homeward from the Congress which voted in favor of annexation, Mr. Webster made a great speech in New York, in which he declared himself opposed to annexation on the ground that it would extend slavery. Mr. Calhoun had, nearly a year before, as we have seen, declared himself in favor of it for the same reason. After these two declarations, from such leaders, the eyes of the people were open to every feature of the question, and it could not have been any longer a matter of intrigue. *Webster on annexation.*

In August, 1837, the Texan agent at Washington, General Hunt, proposed to President Van Buren the annexation of Texas to the United States. The President promptly and firmly declined, and the matter rested during the remainder of his Administration. *Texan proposition for annexation.*

The sudden and unexpected accession of Vice-President Tyler to the presidency, in 1841, was the event which opened the way for the commencement of negotiations for annexation. The new President was known to be favorable to the project.

Meanwhile the diplomatic relations between the United States and Mexico, so suddenly broken off in the latter part of President Jackson's Administration, had been renewed in the early part of President Van Buren's Administration, and, after considerable negotiation in regard to the claims against Mexico, a convention between the two Powers had been arranged, and, on April 8th, 1840, proclaimed by the President as definitely concluded. The convention provided that the claims of the citizens of the United States against Mexico should be submitted to, and decided by, a commission, which should be *The Mexican Claims Commission and its work.*

composed of two members appointed by the President of the United States, and of two other members appointed by the President of Mexico; that the commissioners should meet in Washington within three months from the date of the exchange of ratifications of the convention; that the commission should terminate its duties within eighteen months from the time of its first meeting; and that when the commissioners could not come to any decision, the question upon which they might disagree should be referred to an arbiter appointed by the King of Prussia, etc. With this the question of the private claims against Mexico, already submitted, was, momentarily, put at rest. The claim of satisfaction for public injuries and affronts remained unsettled, and no provision was made for the consideration of private claims which had not been submitted before the ratification of the convention, or of those which might arise after the same date. Plenty of opportunities were thus left for the rise of difficulties in the claims question which might lead to hostile relations between the two Powers.

As early as the winter of 1841–42, it was suspected that President Tyler's Administration was preparing to move in the matter of annexation. In fact, Mr. Wise, of Virginia, the President's bosom friend, and his organ in the House of Representatives, reiterated upon the floor of the House, on January 26th, 1842, Mr. Calhoun's doctrine about annexation, pronounced in 1836, that the annexation of Texas was essential to slavery extension, that slavery extension was necessary to preserve the balance of power between the North and the South in the Union, and that the preservation of this balance of power was the necessary condition of the perpetuity of the Union.

*Tyler as an advocate of annexation.*

Mr. Wise expressed this opinion in the midst of an acrimonious debate, and whether he, in an unguarded moment, betrayed the policy of the President, or simply gave vent to his own excited feelings, is still one of the speculations of American history.

So long, however, as Mr. Webster remained at the head of the State Department it was impossible for the President to make any progress with a definite plan for annexation, even if he entertained one. Nevertheless, thirteen anti-slavery Whig members of Congress, led by Mr. John Quincy Adams, issued, on March 3rd, 1843, an address to the people of the non-slaveholding Commonwealths, declaring that there was a definite plan of annexation already settled upon, and about to be consummated, and denouncing the execution of it as being tantamount to a dissolution of the Union. *Mr. Webster in the way of annexation.* *The Adams address on annexation.*

On May 8th, 1843, Mr. Webster resigned the secretaryship of State. It was said by some that the President drove him out, in order to appoint a Secretary who would carry out his plans for the annexation of Texas; but Mr. Webster himself indicated by his acts and words that he had determined to resign more than a year before, and had remained in office only for the purpose of concluding the negotiations with Great Britain which culminated in the Ashburton Treaty, an agreement in which Mr. Webster's section had an especial interest. *The retirement of Webster.*

There is little question, however, that President Tyler was glad to have him go, for the President placed the annexation of Texas before every other policy of his Administration.

Soon after Mr. Webster's resignation the President transferred Mr. Upshur from the secretaryship of the

Navy to that of State. Mr. Upshur was the man whom suspicion had already marked as the confidant of the
<small>The promotion of Upshur, and his negotiations with the Texans.</small> President in the annexation scheme. This suspicion was speedily confirmed by his entering, almost immediately, upon negotiations with the Texan agent at Washington, Mr. Van Zandt, for annexation.

Soon after the recognition of the independence of Texas by the United States, Great Britain, France, and Belgium took the same step, presumably for the purpose of establishing commercial relations with the new state. But, in the summer of 1843, the British Government appeared in the character of the most favored mediator between Mexico and Texas for the recognition of the independence of Texas by Mexico; and a friend of President Tyler's Administration wrote, from London, that a representative of the anti-slavery men in Texas was in London, negotiating a loan of money from an English company, with which to pay for the liberation of all the slaves in Texas, and that the interest upon the loan was to be guaranteed by the British Government, on the condition that the Texan Government would abolish slavery.

The Administration professed to credit this story, and Mr. Upshur wrote to General Murphy, the diplomatic agent of the United States in Texas, informing him of this communication from London, and arguing the double danger to the United States of British interference in Texas, and of the abolition of slavery there. This letter bears date of August 8th, 1843, and is considered as marking the beginning of the actual negotiations for annexation. It was certainly intended to prompt General Murphy to sound the Texan Government upon the question of annexation.

The Mexican Government evidently discovered the

movement immediately, for, on August 23rd, the Mexican Secretary of State declared to Mr. Thompson, the Minister of the United States to Mexico, that the Mexican Government would consider any act of the United States to annex Texas as a declaration of war on Mexico. For seven years Mexico had made no war on Texas, though professing to regard the new state as only a rebellious province. In September of 1842, several marauding expeditions had crossed the Rio Grande, raided around for a few days, and then returned to Mexico. The Mexican Government called this a continuance of the war, and demanded that the states of the world should observe the attitude of neutrals toward a friendly Power engaged in suppressing a rebellion on the part of certain of its lawful subjects. This was absurd. From the point of view of international law Texas had won her independence, and might make what agreements she pleased with any other Power. The President paid no attention to the Mexican threat. On October 16th, 1843, Mr. Upshur formally proposed annexation to Mr. Van Zandt, and in his message to Congress, at the beginning of the session of 1843–44, the President indicated to Congress that the negotiations for annexation were in progress, and referred to the fact that Mexico threatened war in case the United States should resolve to annex Texas.

*The threat of the Mexican Government to consider the annexation of Texas a cause of war.*

*The Administration proposes annexation to the Texan agent.*

The great difficulty in the way of the negotiations was the fear on the part of the Texans that, upon the signature of the Treaty by the Presidents of the two countries, and before its ratification by the respective Senates, as required by the respective Constitutions, the Mexicans would collect all their forces and make one supreme effort to reconquer Texas. The Texans wanted the pro-

*The difficulty in the way of acceptance of the proposition.*

tection of the United States in this interim, and the embarrassing question for Mr. Tyler's Administration was whether the President of the United States had the constitutional power to extend it. Would not war, undertaken in defence of one foreign Power against another, be offensive war, in the sense of the Constitution of the United States, such war as Congress alone can authorize? Or, could Texas be considered a part of the United States from the moment that the two Presidents signed the Treaty of annexation, and before its ratification by the respective Senates, thus making war in her defence defensive war, such war as the President of the United States may, of his own power, undertake?

About the middle of January, 1844, Mr. Van Zandt demanded of Mr. Upshur whether, in case the President of Texas should agree to the proposition of the President of the United States for annexation, the President of the United States would protect Texas, from the moment of this agreement between the two Presidents, against all foreign attack. Mr. Upshur seems to have been greatly perplexed by the question, for he made no reply.

*The demand of the Texans for protection in the interim.*

About the middle of February, the President of Texas caused the same question to be put to the United States agent in Texas, General Murphy. Murphy was a blunt, brave man, full of chivalry, but quite empty of constitutional and international law. He immediately returned an affirmative answer, whereupon President Houston sent a special envoy to Washington, armed with plenary power to conclude a treaty of annexation.

Whether Secretary Upshur, and, of course, the President, knew of the promise which Murphy had made for his Government to Texas, before the sudden death of Mr. Upshur, on February 28th, has never been determined.

During the second week of March, Mr. John Nelson, the Secretary of the Navy, was temporarily transferred to the State Department, and one of his first acts was to officially disavow Murphy's promise to President Houston. He very nearly informed Murphy, however, that President Tyler was personally pleased with what he had done. The Texan agents at Washington refused, however, to proceed with the negotiations until President Tyler would ratify Murphy's promise. Mr. Nelson would not risk his reputation as a constitutional lawyer by inventing an interpretation of the Constitution which would warrant this. At the end of the month Mr. Calhoun was put in his place, and he was remanded to the Department of the Navy.

About a fortnight after taking possession of his office, Mr. Calhoun officially informed the Texan agents at Washington that the President had ordered the concentration of a strong squadron of war-vessels in the Gulf of Mexico, and had commanded the movement of land forces to the southwestern boundary of the United States to meet all eventualities, and that the President would use "all the means placed within his power by the Constitution" to protect Texas against foreign invasion during the pendency of the Treaty of annexation. On the day following this communication, the Treaty of annexation was signed by the President of the United States and by the Texas plenipotentiary for the President of Texas. *Mr. Calhoun in the State Department.* *The Treaty of annexation signed.*

Ten days after this, the Treaty was sent to the Senate of the United States for ratification. In the message accompanying the Treaty the President informed the Senate of the disposition he had made of the troops and naval vessels, and justified the same by the claim that the President *makes* the treaties, that the Senate only ratifies them, that the validity of the treaties, therefore, dates from the President's agreement, and that, therefore, in this case, Texas was, from and after April 12th, 1844, a part of the territory of the United States, all of which the President was bound to defend against foreign attack. Whether this was President Tyler's constitutional law or Mr. Calhoun's we do not know. If this doctrine is to be ascribed to Mr. Calhoun it certainly marks a great departure from the general principles taught by him after 1830. One would think that his "States' sovereignty" theory of the Union would have led him to attribute as little power as possible to the general Government, and as much of that little as possible to the Senate, but here were both nationalism and Cæsarism combined.

The Treaty was before the Senate, in secret session, from April 22nd until June 8th, when it was rejected by a vote of thirty-five to sixteen. It is not necessary to examine the reasons which moved the Northern Senators to vote against it, but it is important to understand some of the grounds upon which Senators from the slaveholding Commonwealths opposed it. Senator Benton declared that the Treaty annexed not only Texas but parts of four other Mexican provinces, which would be an international outrage upon Mexico. Most of the Southern Senators, however, were influenced by the fear of war with Mexico. But the most significant objection to it, from the point of view of subsequent events, was that urged by Mr. Archer, of Virginia, the chairman of the Senate committee for Foreign Affairs. He claimed that a foreign state could not be annexed to the United States by means of a treaty, and that, if a foreign state could become connected with the Union at all, it must be by means of an act of Congress. A large number of the Senators approved of this doctrine. It was a pregnant idea to the President and Mr. Calhoun. It indicated that there was another way to accomplish annexation.

While the Treaty was under consideration in the Senate, the national conventions for the nomination of presidential candidates had assembled. The Whigs had nominated Mr. Clay, who was regarded as opposed to annexation. The friends to annexation in the Democratic party had been able to put Mr. Van Buren aside, and had nominated James K. Polk, of Tennessee, an outspoken advocate of immediate annexation, and had made the "re-occupation of Oregon and the re-annexation of Texas" the chief plank in the party platform.

Here now were all the elements of a new plan for annexation, which promised more success. They were, the doctrine unwittingly advanced by Mr. Archer, and as unwittingly approved by many of the Senators, that Texas could be connected with the United States only by means of an act of Congress admitting her as a Commonwealth into the Union, the plank of the platform making annexation the chief issue of the campaign for the election of a new President and a new House of Representatives, and the connection of the Oregon question with that of annexation, in order to get votes in the North for both projects at once. *The new plan for annexation.*

On June 11th, President Tyler took the first step in the combination of these elements. He sent a copy of the rejected Treaty, and all the papers connected with it, to the House of Representatives, together with a message, in which he reviewed the subject and justified his position in regard to it, and declared, finally, that while he had regarded a treaty as the most suitable means for accomplishing annexation, he would co-operate with Congress in the use of any other means compatible with the Constitution and likely to accomplish the result.

Before, however, following the history of the annexation of Texas further, we must present briefly the main points in the development of the Oregon question.

# CHAPTER XIV.

## OREGON

Extent of Oregon and Claims to it—The Nootka Convention—Louisiana and Oregon—Astoria—The Joint Occupation Agreement of 1818—Spain's Claims on Oregon Ceded to the United States—Renewal of the Convention of 1818—The British Policy in Reference to Oregon—The Ignorance of Oregon in the United States—Dr. Marcus Whitman—Dr. Whitman's Mission to the United States Government—Dr. Whitman's Colony—The Democratic Party on the Oregon Question.

AT the close of the eighteenth century, Oregon was universally recognized as the territory lying along the North Pacific Ocean from the forty-second parallel of latitude to that of fifty-four degrees and forty minutes, and reaching inward to the Rocky Mountains. At that time it was claimed by Spain both by discovery and first settlement. *Extent of Oregon and claims to it.*

In the year 1790, Great Britain advanced claims upon it. A diplomatic discussion arose between the two Powers, which ended temporarily in an agreement called the Nootka Convention, by which no territorial or sovereign rights or powers were recognized by Spain to Great Britain, but only certain easements, so to speak, in and upon this territory, such as the right to navigate the waters and to fish in them, to trade with the natives, and to make such temporary *The Nootka Convention.*

settlements as might be necessary for the reasonable enjoyment of these rights.

In the year 1796, war was waged between Spain and Great Britain, and, according to the British principles of that day, every agreement between the two Powers was abrogated in consequence thereof; so that Spain, while retaining her sovereignty over Oregon, was now relieved of the encumbrance of the British rights.

This was the status of Oregon when Spain ceded Louisiana to France in 1800, and when France ceded the same territory to the United States in 1803; and the matter of first concern to the United States was the question whether Louisiana contained Oregon or any part of it. It is probable that President Jefferson thought it did, since the Lewis and Clark expedition, sent out by him to examine the new purchase, crossed the Rockies, discovered the sources of the Columbia River, followed this stream to the Pacific, and made report thereof to the President. But if he did, he was certainly mistaken. It is true that Louisiana had no western boundary positively fixed by any agreement between the Powers, but the general principles of international law, to which recourse must always be had in the absence of specific agreements, made the water shed of the Mississippi the western boundary, and the Treaty of Utrecht, of 1713, to which France and Great Britain were parties, made the forty-ninth parallel of latitude the northern boundary, westward from the Lake of the Woods.

*Louisiana and Oregon.*

The founding of Astoria, in 1811, on the south bank of the Columbia River, about nine miles from its mouth, is also evidence that the Government of the United States thought it had a claim upon Oregon as a part of Louisiana, since the undertaking

*Astoria.*

OREGON,
as Determined by the Treaty of 1846.
0 20 40 60 80 100 200
SCALE OF MILES.
125° 123° 121° 119° 117° Longitude 115° West from 113° Greenwich 111° 109° 107°
49° 47° 45° 43°
Agreed on as Boundary 1846
PACIFIC OCEAN
Discovered by U.S. Ship Columbia 1792
Victoria
Puget Sound
NOOTKA
SALISH
WASHINGTON
OREGON TERRITORY
Astoria
Columbia River
Walla Walla
Portland
Dalles
Salem
CHINOOK
Willamette R.
Deschutes R.
John Days R.
SAHAPTIN
IDAHO
Salmon R.
Lewis or Snake R.
Clarks Fork
Lewis & Clarke Expedition, 1805-6
CLAIMED BY SPAIN, ENGLAND AND THE UNITED STATES.
DISCOVERED BY U.S. 1792. EXPLORED, 1805-6.
JOINTLY OCCUPIED BY GREAT BRITAIN AND THE UNITED STATES, 1818-46.
Ft. Boise
Ft. Hall
Owyhee R.
OREGON
MONTANA
WYOMING
Yellowstone
Boundary of the United States Previous to the Annexation of Oregon.
TERRITORY CEDED BY FRANCE TO UNITED STATES, 1803
Boundary of 1813, by Treaty with Spain.
THE M.-N. CO., BUFFALO, N. Y.

proceeded upon an understanding between Mr. John Jacob Astor and the Government.

The British Government now did a thing which seemed to acknowledge a claim of some sort by the United States upon Oregon, so far as Great Britain could do so. Having taken forcible possession of Astoria in the War of 1812, it restored the place, at the close of the War, to the possession of the United States; and in a convention, concluded on October 18th, 1818, the two Powers agreed upon the forty-ninth parallel of north latitude as the boundary between their territories, from the Lake of the Woods to the Rocky Mountains, and upon joint occupation, as it was termed, in all territories and waters claimed by either party in North America west of the Rocky Mountains, without prejudice to any claims which either party might have to any part of the said territory, or to any claims which any other Power might have to it, or to any part of it. This agreement was to run for ten years. *The joint occupation agreement of 1818.*

An event happened the following year which made the Washington Government doubt the wisdom of basing its claims upon the Louisiana cession. It was the Treaty with Spain ceding the Floridas. As we have seen in one of the earlier chapters of this work, this Treaty contained a provision ceding to the United States all the rights and sovereignty of Spain in and over the territory lying west of the Rocky Mountains and north of the forty-second parallel of north latitude. Here was a much better claim, both as to quantity of territory and quality of right, than could be founded on the Louisiana cession. If the United States had possessed this claim in 1803, it is doubtful if we should ever have heard of the notion that Oregon was a part of Louisiana. *Spain's claims on Oregon ceded to the United States.*

In 1828, the agreement of 1818 was indefinitely continued, but might be terminated by a twelvemonth's notice by either party, at any time. The United States, was, however, in a better position than before, on account of having now the Spanish claims to all territory above the forty-second parallel on the Pacific.

*Continuation of the convention of 1818.*

The element of greatest importance in the settlement of the question was, of course, colonization within the territory, and neither party had really undertaken that. The hunters and trappers and agents of the Hudson's Bay Company had temporary abodes within the territory, especially north of the Columbia, and there was one settlement on the south bank under the protection of the United States, and that was all.

For some fourteen years longer, now, this indefinite status continued. In the negotiations between Mr. Webster and Lord Ashburton, in 1841 and 1842, Mr. Webster sounded Lord Ashburton on the Oregon question, and found that the Queen's agent had received no power to deal with the matter, but drew the conclusion that the British policy in regard to Oregon was to prolong the existing *modus vivendi*, give the Hudson's Bay Company time to settle the country north of the Columbia, and then agree to a division on the line of that river.

*The British policy in reference to Oregon.*

It was well for the United States that the Oregon question did not enter into those negotiations, for down to that moment the Government at Washington knew almost nothing about the character of Oregon north of the Columbia. The officers of the Hudson's Bay Company had continually represented it as a worthless waste, fit only for hunting and trapping ground, and almost worn out even for those purposes. It is more than probable that the Gov-

*The ignorance of Oregon in the United States.*

ernment at Washington credited these statements, and it is quite possible that, in 1842, it would have compromised with England on the line of the Columbia. The delay in the settlement of the question now gave the Government the opportunity to learn something more about Oregon from one who knew the region better than any other living man, and whose interests did not lie with those of the Hudson's Bay Company and Great Britain.

The actor who now came upon the scene was Dr. Marcus Whitman, a man of great intelligence, courage, energy, and high purpose. He had been sent out by the American Board of Missions, in the year 1835, as one of the exploring delegates among the Indians in Oregon. Dr. Whitman soon made up his mind in regard to his life work. He returned to the East in the summer of 1836, married, and went back to Oregon, accompanied by his bride and by the Rev. H. H. Spaulding and wife. This was the beginning of the settlement of Northern Oregon.  *Dr. Marcus Whitman.*

In some way, we know not exactly how, Dr. Whitman learned that the United States Government might be induced to sacrifice Northern Oregon in ignorance of its true value; and, in the latter part of the year 1842, he set out from the mission on the Walla Walla to go to Washington and inform the Government of the real character of the country which he had explored. He arrived in Washington in March of 1843, and gave President Tyler such full and truthful information concerning the great value of Oregon north of the Columbia as settled the fate of that region.  *Dr. Whitman's mission to the United States Government.*

Dr. Whitman had come also for another purpose. He saw clearly that the way to get Oregon was to colonize it. President Tyler's Administration supported him in this view and purpose. The Administration caused Dr. Whitman's descriptions of Oregon to be printed and distributed throughout the United States, and also his offer to lead a colony to take possession of the country. The place of rendezvous appointed by him was Westport, near the site of the present Kansas City, and the time was June of 1843. Nearly a thousand people, with two hundred wagons, met him there, and were successfully led by him back to the Walla Walla. He arrived there with this large colony in October of 1843; and news of his safe arrival reached Washington in January of 1844.

*Dr. Whitman's colony.*

The decisive movement for the possession of Oregon was thus made. Claims based upon discovery, or treaty, or privileges for hunting, trapping, or trading, must all give way before actual colonization. British diplomacy was confused by the success of the movement, while the people of the United States were filled with pride and enthusiasm at the achievement.

The moment had come, at last, when the United States could deal with Great Britain from the basis of actual conditions, instead of from the point of view of international theory. The connection of the Oregon question with the question of the annexation of Texas in the Democratic platform of 1844, was, therefore, by no means far fetched or artificial. It was, indeed, a clever stroke of practical politics, but it was suggested by existing conditions.

The Democrats had struck a high note in the international questions, one which was bound to catch the ear of the younger men throughout the country. Moreover, the policy in both cases rested upon sound national principles. Texas, at least to the Nueces, and Oregon, at least to the northern water shed of the Columbia, belonged geo-

*The Democratic party on the Oregon question.*

graphically to the United States, and they were settled, so far as they were settled at all, by Anglo-Americans. On the other hand, the slaveholders of the South were not particularly pleased with the connection of the two questions. Some of them had already come to doubt whether the annexation of Texas alone would subserve their interests, since the slave population might be thereby drawn away from the border slaveholding Commonwealths, and these Commonwealths might then abolish slavery by their own several acts; and now that it must be paid for by the addition of a region to the Northern side, large enough to hold a dozen such Commonwealths as New York, the price appeared to them too great. Mr. Waddy Thompson, of South Carolina, the Minister to the Mexican Government, was decidedly of this opinion; and from an original friend of annexation he became a determined opponent. To the far-seeing mind, it was certainly very questionable whether the annexation of Texas would prove any advantage to the slavery interest, and it was certain that the possession of Oregon would not.

But they would subserve, they have subserved, the interests of a true national development. The Democrats of 1844 builded better than they knew, when they made the "re-annexation of Texas and the re-occupation of Oregon" the issues of the campaign of that year. In the platform the Oregon question was given the precedence. The country, however, understood the stratagem, and the question of annexation assumed the foremost place in the great contest.

## CHAPTER XV.

### THE "RE-ANNEXATION OF TEXAS AND THE RE-OCCUPATION OF OREGON"

The Popularity of the Democratic Position, and Mr. Clay's Letter of August 16th—The Abolitionists Declare against Mr. Clay—The Triumph of Polk—Tyler's Recommendation to Annex Texas by a Joint Resolution or an Act—The Resolution for Annexation in the House of Representatives—Passage of an Enabling Act for Texas by the House of Representatives—The Resolution in the Senate and Mr. Archer's Inconsistencies—The Senate's Amendment to the Resolution of the House—The Concurrence of the House in the Senate's Amendment, and the Passage of the Act for Admission—The British Proposition in Regard to Oregon—The American Proposition—Polk's recommendation in Regard to the Matter — The Debate upon the President's Recommendation — The Conclusion Reached by Congress—The President's Retort upon Congress—The Oregon Treaty.

THE language of the Democratic platform signified that Texas had been once annexed to the United States, as a part of Louisiana, by the Treaty of 1803 with France, and had been sacrificed by the Treaty of 1819 with Spain, and that Oregon had been once occupied by the United States, either under the Treaty of 1803, or under that of 1819, or by the right of the prior discovery of the Columbia River and the establishment of a settlement upon its banks. It is thus that mortal men always seek to purge any movement which they undertake of the taint of innovation, no matter how justifiable in reason that movement may be.

In the beginning of June, the election of Mr. Clay seemed a certainty. As the campaign wore on it became manifest that annexation was rapidly growing in the popular favor, and that Mr. Clay would lose some of his Southern support, unless the opinion which prevailed in that section concerning his opposition to annexation should be modified. With this in view, and under the belief that the state of feeling upon the subject at the North had become less hostile, Mr. Clay caused to be published in an Alabama newspaper, on August 16th, a letter defining again his attitude toward annexation. *The popularity of the Democratic position and Mr. Clay's letter of August 16th.*

No sane and impartial mind can, at this day, see any material difference between the opinion expressed by Mr. Clay in his letter of April 17th, and that in his letter of August 16th. In the former, he took the ground that the United States ought not to annex Texas without the consent of Mexico, or against the decided opposition of a considerable and respectable portion of the Union. In the latter, he said he should be glad to see Texas annexed, if it could be done "without dishonor, without war, with the common consent of the Union, and upon just and fair terms." He added that he did not think the slavery question ought to enter into the consideration at all, that slavery was destined to become extinct in the United States, and that its duration would neither be lengthened nor shortened by the acquisition of Texas.

The Abolitionists, however, could see the question only from a single point of view. They wanted Mr. Clay to say that the annexation of Texas meant permanent slavery extension, and that he opposed it upon that ground. They were not satisfied by Mr. Clay's causing another letter to be published, in the *National Intelligencer*, declaring that *The Abolitionists declare against Mr. Clay.*

his two former letters were entirely consistent with each other, and that he held inflexibly to the principles of the first one. They even went so far in their extravagant fanaticism as to represent to the people that Mr. Clay's election would be more favorable to annexation than that of Mr. Polk.

It is usually said that Mr. Clay's Alabama letter turned a sufficient number of votes to the Abolitionist candidate, Mr. Birney, to cause Mr. Clay to lose the electoral votes of New York and Michigan, and thus insured the election of Mr. Polk, and consequently the annexation of Texas and the War with Mexico. It is probably true that it did cause the loss of New York and Michigan, but it is possible that it held North Carolina, Kentucky, and Tennessee in line. The failure of Mr. Clay is, therefore, more probably to be ascribed to Abolitionist fanaticism than to his own blundering. At any rate, this was the view held by Mr. Greeley, a very competent observer. He said that "the triumph of annexation was secured by the indirect aid of the more intense partisans of abolition."

*The triumph of Polk.*

The result of the election was regarded as the plebiscite upon the question of annexation, and also upon the Oregon question, but more especially upon the former. In his message to Congress at the opening of the session of 1844-45, President Tyler informed Congress that, since the rejection of the Treaty for annexation by the Senate, Mexico had threatened to renew war against Texas, and prosecute the same by barbarous means and methods, and that he had caused the Minister of the United States to Mexico to inform the Mexican Government that the question of annexation was still before the American people, and that, until their decision had been pronounced, any serious invasion of Texas could not be

*Tyler's recommendation to annex Texas by a joint resolution or an act.*

regarded by them with indifference. He declared that, in the late general election, the people had pronounced for immediate annexation; and he recommended that Congress should incorporate the terms of the late agreement for annexation into the form of an act or a joint resolution, which should be binding upon both parties when adopted in like manner by the Texan Congress. He also informed Congress that negotiations had been opened with Great Britain relative to the respective rights of the two Powers in, and over, the Oregon territory.

That part of the message relating to the question of annexation was referred, in the House of Representatives, to the committee on Foreign Affairs, and, on December 12th, Mr. Ingersoll, of Pennsylvania, reported from that committee the draft of a joint resolution for the annexation of Texas. *The resolution for annexation in the House of Representatives.* It was simply the articles of the agreement of April 12th preceding put into that form. The principal points of it were, the cession of the territory of Texas to the United States, the transfer of the public lands of Texas to the Government of the United States, the pledge of the United States to assume the debt of Texas up to ten millions of dollars, the guarantee of liberty and property to the citizens of Texas, now to be citizens of the United States, and the accordance of Commonwealth local government to Texas as soon as consistent with the Constitution of the United States.

As we have seen, the President and Mr. Calhoun had thought that the proper way to annex a foreign state to the United States was by means of a treaty, in which the foreign state should cede its territory to the United States; and that the matter of local government for the ceded territory and its population would then be a question of legislation. We have also seen that the opponents of the proposed Treaty in the Senate took the ground, among other things, that Texas was already a state, seeking admission into the Union as a "State" (Commonwealth), and that this could be effected only by an act of Congress. But now the opposition in the House of Representatives to the joint resolution, expressed in the very words of the proposed Treaty, declared that the resolution provided for a cession of territory by a foreign state to the United States, which cession could be made and accepted only through the form of a treaty. The House had never, however, committed itself to the view of the Senate, and the friends of the resolution wasted no time in demonstrating the inconsistency, but sought to so amend the resolution as to make it an act for the formation of a new Commonwealth, or, as it is usually phrased, an act for the admission of a new "State" into this Union.

On January 25th, 1845, the House passed a substitute for the committee's resolution, which substitute was a *Passage of an enabling act for Texas by the House of Representatives.* resolution for enabling the people of Texas to form a Commonwealth constitution and government, preparatory to admission into this Union, and prescribing certain conditions for the assent of Congress to the same.

When this resolution reached the Senate, it was referred to the committee of that body for Foreign Affairs, *The resolution in the Senate, and Mr. Archer's inconsistencies.* and on February 4th, Mr. Archer, the chairman of the committee, presented a report from his committee, and a recommendation that the proposition from the House be rejected. The ground for this recommendation, as contained in the report, was that the House had undertaken to do by an act of Congress what could be done only by means of a treaty. And this was from that same Mr. Archer, who, on June 8th preceding, had opposed the ratification of the Treaty, on the ground that what was proposed to be effected by a treaty could be done only by means of an act of Congress.

It was not to be expected that the Senate or the country would put up with any such inconsistent trifling. The Senators were, however, much concerned in preserving the treaty-making power of the Senate, and hesitated long, attempting to find the way out of the embarrassment, which they had prepared for themselves, by their attitude, during the preceding session, toward the proposed Treaty. At last, on February 27th, Mr. Walker, of Mississippi, offered an apparent method of escape. He moved to amend the resolution sent from the House by the provision that, if the President should deem it more advisable to negotiate with Texas for her admission into the Union than to submit the joint resolution as an overture to her, he might do so, and then might submit the agreements, which might thus be made, either to the Senate to be approved of as a treaty, or to both Houses to be approved of as an act. Everybody knew, of course, that this was a mere subterfuge to save appearances, and that the President would immediately communicate the joint resolution to the Texan authorities. *The Senate's amendment to the resolution of the House.*

The House of Representatives concurred in the Senate's amendment, and the President signed the measure on March 1st, 1845. He immediately submitted the resolution to the Texan authorities, and on December 29th, 1845, Texas was formally admitted as a "State" into this Union. *The concurrence of the House in the Senate's amendment, and the passage of the measure for Admission.*

There is little question that the President and Mr. Calhoun were correct as regards the manner in which a foreign state should be annexed to the United States, but they can hardly be justly blamed or criticised for following the method insisted upon by Congress as the constitutional form and prescript.

In his first annual message President Polk informed Congress that when he came into office he found that Great Britain had proposed to settle the Oregon question by making the divisional line between the possessions of the two Powers, west of the Rocky Mountains, the forty-ninth parallel of latitude to the northeasternmost branch of the Columbia River, and, from this point, the course of the river to the Pacific; that his predecessor had refused this; that he himself had, upon invitation from the British plenipotentiary to make a proposition, offered the forty-ninth parallel from the Rocky Mountains to the Pacific, although he believed the claim of the United States to the territory up to the parallel of fifty-four degrees and forty minutes to be good; and that this proposition had been rejected by the British minister.

*The British proposition in regard to Oregon.*

*The American proposition.*

The President further declared that all attempts to compromise with Great Britain had failed, and he recommended that Congress should give the notice, required by the convention of joint occupancy, for the termination of that agreement, as the first step toward asserting the power of the Government over the whole of Oregon. He also recommended the establishment of a line of posts along the Oregon route for the protection of emigrants to Oregon, and the immediate extension of the jurisdiction of the United States Government over the citizens of the United States in Oregon.

*Polk's recommendation in regard to the matter.*

This was distinct enough and belligerent enough. The Abolitionists and anti-slavery Whigs, who had been twitting the Administration with indifference about Oregon, now that Texas had been secured, could certainly find no fault with the President's attitude toward the question. At any rate, it was a challenge to them which could not be ignored.

Both Houses entered immediately upon the discussion of the question of giving the notice. As the debate progressed the war fever became allayed, and the conviction grew that the claim to the line of fifty-four forty was extravagant. The majority, at least, saw that the claim by occupation and settlement was the right basis for the determination of the dispute, and that this claim would give the United States the territory only to the line of the northern watershed of the Columbia.

*The debate upon the President's recommendation.*

This line does, indeed, reach at points above the forty-ninth parallel, but the fact that this parallel was already the divisional line between the possessions of the two Powers from the Great Lakes to the Rockies, and that the United States had already proposed to Great Britain the continuation of this line to the Pacific, produced the general feeling that the United States should be satisfied with the forty-ninth parallel as the northern boundary of Oregon, rather than risk war for the more northern line. Still, the opponents of the Administration had been so quick to charge the President with indifference to the acquisition of territory, upon which non-slaveholding Commonwealths would be established, that they were now fairly ashamed to lag behind him.

Owing to the course taken by the Senate, Congress did not, however, come to any conclusion upon the recommendation of the President until April 23rd, 1846, and then, in the resolution finally passed, it almost emasculated the President's proposition. It empowered the President to give the notice, but explained that the purpose of the same was

*The conclusion reached by Congress.*

to direct the attention of the two Governments toward the adoption of more earnest measures for the amicable settlement of the question, and it threw upon the President the responsibility as to the time of giving the notice, by placing that matter entirely within his discretion.

The President had already reopened negotiations with Great Britain upon the subject, and, on June 10th, he laid before the Senate a proposal, from the British Envoy, of the forty-ninth parallel for the boundary, and asked the Senate to advise him as to whether he should close with the offer. It was not customary to consult the Senate at this point of the negotiations, but there was precedent for it, and the letter of the Constitution appears to warrant it, and the President was determined to retort upon the Senate, for its action in the matter of the notice, by throwing the responsibility upon that body of sacrificing the claims of the United States to territory above the forty-ninth parallel. He plainly informed the Senate that he would reject the offer unless advised by it to accept.

*The President's retort upon Congress.*

The Senate was fairly caught in its own net, and had the good sense to refrain from a resistance which would have been only an undignified floundering in meshes prepared by itself. On the 12th, the Senate advised the President to accept the British overture. On the 15th, the President signed the treaty, and, on the 18th, the Senate ratified it by a large majority.

*The Oregon Treaty.*

Not many realized, at the moment, that the extension of the sovereignty of the United States to the Pacific above the forty-second parallel of north latitude would require the like extension to the south of it. Once across the Rockies it was inevitable that the natural boundary in the southwest, as well as in the northwest, should be ultimately attained. It came sooner than anybody expected.

## CHAPTER XVI.

### THE WAR WITH MEXICO

Slidell's Mission to Mexico—The Failure of the Mission—The Concentration of the Mexican Forces at Matamoras—The United States Forces Ordered to the Rio Grande—Hostilities Opened — The Battles of Palo Alto and Resaca de la Palma — The Attitude of Congress toward the War — Congressional Approval of the War — The Occupation of New Mexico and Upper California, and the Advance into Mexico—California's Importance — The Battle of Buena Vista — Vera Cruz and Cerro Gordo — Contreras, San Antonio, and Cherubusco — The Plan for a Cession of Territory from Mexico—The Wilmot Proviso—The Fate of the Wilmot Proviso in the Senate—The Proviso Again Voted by the House of Representatives—The Upham Amendment in the Senate—The Amendment Defeated by the Efforts of Mr. Cass—The Wilmot Proviso Dropped in the House—The Mission of Mr. Trist—Rejection of Mr. Trist's Propositions by the Mexicans — Negotiations Broken off — Molino del Rey, Chapultepec, Mexico—The Recall of Mr. Trist, and the Treaty of Guadalupe Hidalgo—Ratification of the Treaty.

As we have seen, the Mexican Government had announced to the Government of the United States that the annexation of Texas would be regarded by Mexico as a *casus belli*. Consequently, as soon as the matter was concluded, the Mexican Envoy left Washington, and all diplomatic relations between the two Powers were suspended. Some six months later, President Polk made overtures for the resumption of these relations, and, upon meeting a somewhat friendly response, commissioned Mr. John Slidell, of Louisiana, to go to Mexico and negotiate a treaty, which should settle all the differences between the two Powers.

*Slidell's mission to Mexico.*

Mr. Slidell arrived at Vera Cruz on November 30th, 1845, and found that President Herrera's Administration was afraid to receive him, because the military or war party in Mexico, led by General Paredes, was greatly excited by the attitude of the Administration toward the United States, and threatened revolution. The Mexican Government actually refused audience to Mr. Slidell, on December 21st.

Before the end of the year, President Herrera gave way to General Paredes, who assumed the presidency of the Republic, and, under direction from President Polk, Mr. Slidell announced himself to the new Administration. This was March 1st, 1846. On the 12th, he received the refusal of the Paredes Government to give him audience, and immediately left Mexico.

*The failure of the mission.*

During the summer of 1845, the Mexican Government had begun to collect troops and munitions of war at Matamoras, on the south bank of the Rio Grande near its mouth. The purpose of all this was without question an expedition across the Rio Grande, and into the region north of it.

*The concentration of the Mexican forces at Matamoras.*

By an act of the Texan Congress, of December 19th, 1836, the Rio Grande was designated as the southwestern boundary of Texas. The United States took Texas with this boundary, reserving in the resolution of annexation the right of adjusting the Texan boundaries with foreign states. This meant, of course, that the United States might change the boundary which Texas had given herself, as the result of her successful rebellion, her revolution, against Mexico, by an agreement with Mexico, in so far as Texas was concerned. It further meant that any such change must be made either by an act of the Congress of the United States or by a treaty between the United States and Mexico. Until,

## THE WAR WITH MEXICO 329

however, this adjustment should take place, it was the duty of the President of the United States to defend the boundary with which Texas came into the Union. Moreover, Congress had passed an act, on December 31st, 1845, in which Corpus Christi, a town situated on the south side of the river Nueces, was made an United States port of delivery. The town was, also, the headquarters of the United States army in Texas, and had been so from the period of annexation.

When now the Mexican Government refused to receive Mr. Slidell, and continued to increase the forces at Matamoras, President Polk felt it to be his duty to defend the line of the Rio Grande. On January 13th, he ordered General Taylor, then in command at Corpus Christi, to advance to the northern bank of the Rio Grande. The General, with his little army of about 2,000 men, arrived upon the Rio Grande, at a point opposite Matamoras, on March 28th, and began fortifying his position. *The United States forces ordered to the Rio Grande.*

On April 12th, the Mexican commander, General Ampudia, demanded the withdrawal of Taylor's forces within twenty-four hours, and their retirement across the Nueces, under threat of the appeal to arms. Taylor paid no attention to the demand, and, on the 24th, he received notice from General Arista, the successor of Ampudia, that hostilities were opened. *Hostilities opened.*

On the same day, a reconnoitring party of United States dragoons encountered a large detachment of Mexican soldiers, who had just crossed the river farther up, and were all killed or captured. General Taylor moved out from Fort Brown, opposite Matamoras, in order to cover his base of supplies at Point Isabel, and, having accomplished this, faced about again to relieve Fort Brown against assault from Matamoras.

While executing this movement he found himself, on May 8th, face to face with a Mexican army numbering three times as many men as his own. Nevertheless, he inflicted a crushing defeat upon the Mexicans in this battle of Palo Alto, and struck them again the next day at Resaca de la Palma, routing them completely, and driving the remnants of this once apparently formidable force across the Rio Grande.

<small>The battles of Palo Alto and Resaca de la Palma.</small>

As soon as the news of these events reached Washington, the President informed Congress of them, claimed that war existed by the act of Mexican invasion, and asked for the means for its successful prosecution.

From the reception of this message to the end of the War, the Whigs in both Houses condemned the War, but only a few of them voted against furnishing the means for its prosecution. Strangely enough, they were aided by Mr. Calhoun, who opposed the whole war policy from the beginning to the end. He even opposed recognizing the existence of war. He was getting old and more peaceable in disposition, and also had probably seen, with Mr. Thompson, that any further slavery extension toward the Southwest meant the extinction of slavery in the border Commonwealths, and the greater exposure of the planting section to the influences of Abolition. Some of the Whigs claimed that if war existed at all, it was offensive war, and that the President had exceeded his constitutional powers in bringing it on, and should be impeached for so doing.

<small>The attitude of Congress toward the War.</small>

The truth of this proposition depended, of course, upon the recognition by the United States of Mexico's title to the territory between the Rio Grande and the Nueces, or, at least, upon the recognition of it as a free zone, a proposition difficult to reconcile with the Acts

# THE WAR WITH MEXICO

of Congress annexing Texas, and extending the revenue laws of the United States over this very district. The fact is, it was a defensive war at the outset, and if the Mexicans were excited to their move across the Rio Grande by the appearance of United States troops on the northern bank, they had only to thank themselves for bringing them there by previously massing their own troops on the south bank.

Of course the Abolitionists could see nothing in the matter but a wicked scheme for the extension of slavery. Their attitude was, however, too narrow and bigoted to win much attention. And, as the debate on the President's message progressed, it became manifest that all the elements of the opposition were getting deeper and deeper into the quicksands. The bill for recognizing the existence of war, and authorizing the President to call for 50,000 volunteers, and for appropriating $10,000,000 to defray the expenses of the compaign, was passed by an overwhelming majority, in both Houses, on May 11th and 12th, and approved by the President on the 13th. *Congressional approval of the war.*

The President was now, certainly, authorized to carry the War into Mexico, if, indeed, he needed Congressional authority, at all, after the war had been once begun as defensive war. At any rate, General Taylor's occupation of Matamoras did not occur until May 18th, six days after Congress had recognized war.

The President now ordered General Kearny to occupy New Mexico, Commodores Sloat and Stockton to make sure of Upper California, and General Taylor to prosecute the war upon Mexican soil. Kearny, Sloat, and Stockton quickly accomplished the work assigned them, and without much difficulty, and Taylor advanced, in September, from Matamoras upon Monterey. After a *The occupation of New Mexico and Upper California, and the advance into Mexico.*

three days siege, he captured the place, on the 24th, and established winter-quarters within its walls.

At the same time, General Kearny sent Colonel Doniphan with a detachment of his army to Monterey, by way of Chihuahua, and marched himself with another detachment to San Diego in California. Doniphan's capture of Chihuahua brought the entire southern valley of the upper Rio Grande under the military control of the United States, and Kearny's successful march into California secured that territory against all eventualities.

The occupation of California was the matter of most vital importance to the United States. It is the way to Asia. Its government by Mexico was a farce. It would have been purchased or seized by Great Britain, or some other commercial Power, if the United States had not taken possession of it. Nothing was known of its vast mineral wealth at the time. Mere greed, therefore, did not prompt the movement. It was a great and correct stroke of public policy, supported by geographical, commercial, and political reasons.

*California's importance.*

Still Mexico would not yield, and the Administration at Washington now determined to carry the war into the very vitals of the Mexican state. The campaign against the Mexican capital, by way of Vera Cruz, was now resolved on, and General Scott was directed to execute it.

Santa Anna, who had now arrived in Mexico again from Cuba, and had again taken up the reins of government, thought that the army of General Scott would be unable to capture Vera Cruz without a long and painful siege, and planned to advance rapidly from the capital with the main body of his army to the north, crush Taylor, and return to the capital before Scott could pass Vera Cruz.

On February 20th, 1847, General Taylor, whose advance was now some hundred miles to the southwest of

Monterey, suddenly discovered a large Mexican force in front of him. It was Santa Anna, with about twenty thousand of his best troops. Taylor ordered his little army of about five thousand men to retire for a few miles, and take position on the rising ground at Buena Vista. *The battle of Buena Vista.* The Mexicans soon caught up, and on the 23rd, Santa Anna demanded unconditional surrender. Taylor promptly declined, and the battle immediately opened. Both sides knew the serious character of the wager. California, New Mexico, and, perhaps, a large part of Texas were staked upon the issue. Before the day closed, Taylor and his little army had won a complete victory, and the Mexicans were in full retreat, after the loss of some two thousand men. Taylor lost about eight hundred men. With this the campaign in the north was closed, and attention turned almost exclusively to the operations of General Scott.

On March 9th, General Scott effected a landing near Vera Cruz, and on the 29th captured that city. He immediately took up his line of march for the city of Mexico. *Vera Cruz and Cerro Gordo.*

The first great difficulty which he was compelled to encounter was, naturally, the forcing of the mountain pass of Cerro Gordo, through which the national road from Vera Cruz to the city of Mexico led. Santa Anna had gathered here an army of some fifteen thousand men, and had thrown up strong earthworks commanding the defile. On the morning of April 18th, General Scott stormed the heights of Cerro Gordo, and in a sanguinary battle routed the Mexicans completely. Some three thousand Mexicans were captured, with five thousand muskets and forty-three pieces of artillery. Scott's loss was not over four hundred men. Jalapa, Perote, and Puebla fell into his hands as the immediate consequences of this victory.

General Scott rested his army for two months at Puebla, and in the beginning of August resumed his march upon the capital, with an army of about eleven thousand men. On the 18th, he arrived within ten miles of the city, and found himself confronted by an army of nearly thirty thousand men, commanded by President Santa Anna himself.

On the morning of the 19th, the struggle began, and lasted through the 20th. Three distinct battles were fought—Contreras, San Antonio, and Cherubusco. The Mexicans outnumbered Scott's army three to one, and fought desperately to save their capital, but all to no avail. After killing, wounding, and capturing between seven and eight thousand Mexicans, General Scott dispersed the remainder of their army and opened his way into the city. The General was willing, however, to save the proud Mexicans from the humiliation of seeing their capital in the hands of the invader, and agreed to an armistice for the purpose of negotiating a peace.

On August 8th, 1846, President Polk had asked of Congress that two millions of dollars be placed at his disposal for use in negotiating a treaty of peace with Mexico. It was quite evident from this that the President was going to demand a large cession of territory from Mexico. Mexico had not yet paid any of the claims awarded by the Claims Commission of 1840 to the citizens of the United States. There were also millions of dollars of claims unadjudged. And then there was the war indemnity, which would undoubtedly be required. Two millions of dollars, in addition to all this, to be paid by the victorious party for peace, could mean nothing less, or other, than a vast territorial cession from the vanquished. It was evident to all that California and New Mexico, already in the possession of the United States, must constitute the sacrifice which Mexico must make.

Mr. McKay, of North Carolina, immediately introduced into the House of Representatives a bill making the appropriation asked by the President. Discussion upon the bill was scarcely under way, when a Northern Democrat, a supporter of the War and of the policy of territorial extension, Mr. David Wilmot, of Pennsylvania, moved to amend the bill by inserting in it the condition that neither slavery nor involuntary servitude should exist in any territory acquired by treaty from Mexico. The House passed the bill, with the Wilmot proviso, as it was termed, on the day of its introduction, August 8th. Territorial extension, but not slavery extension, was its principle, and therefore the South voted almost solidly against it. The bill appeared in the Senate on the 10th, which was the last day of the session, and was still under discussion when the hour for the adjournment of the body *sine die* arrived. It was thought by some competent judges that the Senate would have passed the bill, if it had then come to a vote, and would have thus settled, at the outset, the question of slavery extension; but this is at least doubtful. At the moment, the South had four more votes in the Senate than the North, and it is probable that the Whig Senators from the South would have united with their Democratic brethren upon this question.

*The Wilmot Proviso.*

*The fate of the Wilmot Proviso in the Senate.*

At the beginning of the session of 1846–47, the President again preferred his request for an appropriation for the same purpose, and during the month of January, 1847, bills were introduced into the two Houses, providing an appropriation of three millions of dollars for the President's use in his negotiations with Mexico.

*The Proviso again voted by the House of Representatives.*

When the House took up its bill for consideration, on February 1st, Mr. Wilmot immediately asked permission to move the attachment of his proviso to the appropriation, and made a strong argument in favor of the same. On the 15th, the proviso was again voted, but by a reduced majority. The members from the South voted, this time, solidly against it. A few Northern Democrats voted with them; among these was Stephen A. Douglas.

On March 1st, Senator Upham, of Vermont, introduced an amendment to the Senate bill, of the same tenor as the Wilmot proviso in the House, and urged its adoption in a strong and convincing argument. It really seemed as if the victory for Free-soil in the new acquisitions, whatever they might be, was about to be won, when, to the surprise of at least a considerable number of the Senators, General Cass, of Michigan, who was thought to have indicated his favor to the Wilmot proviso at the last session, made a determined effort against Mr. Upham's motion. Mr. Cass declared the measure premature, and contended that its only effect, if passed, at the moment would be to weaken the Government by internal dissensions upon the slavery question, and consequently encourage the Mexicans to continue the War. He urged the Senators to stand solidly together for the vigorous prosecution of the War to its successful close, and then, after the peace, take up the internal questions arising out of the settlement. The Senate rejected Mr. Upham's amendment, passed the bill without it, and, on the last day of the session, the House accepted the bill as it passed the Senate. Mr. Cass's idea that the anti-slavery proviso would embarrass the President in his negotiations with Mexico, and would

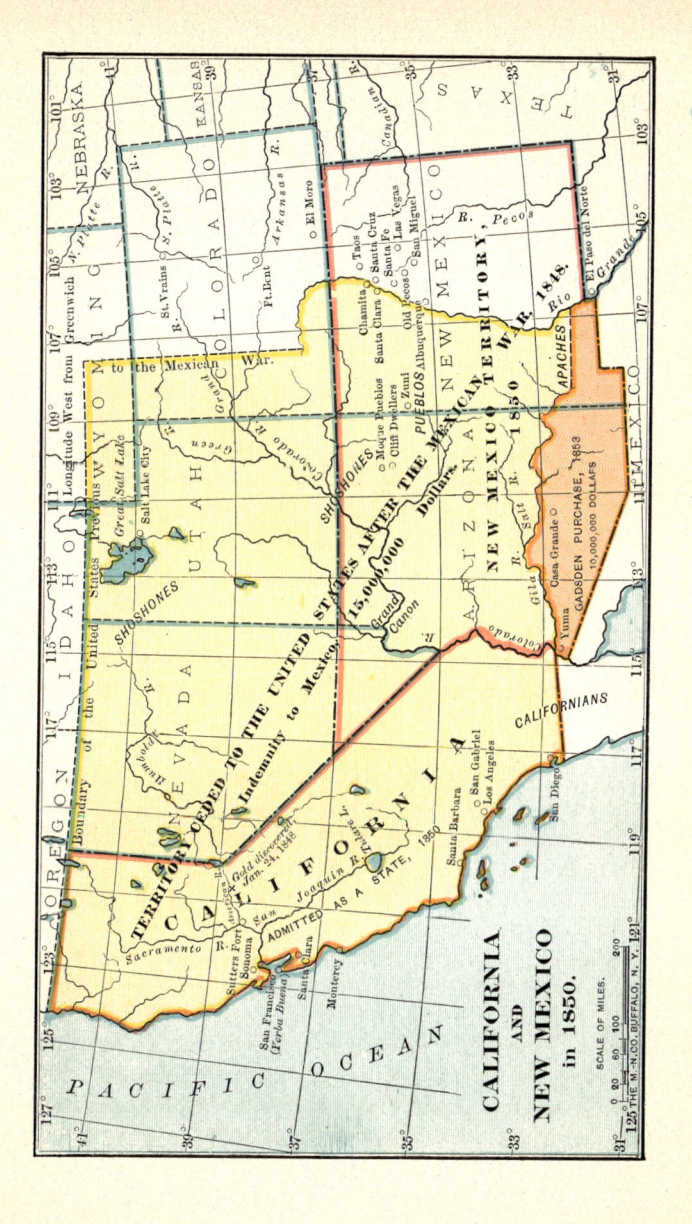

CALIFORNIA AND NEW MEXICO in 1850.

encourage the Mexicans to continue the War seems to have convinced the House as well as the Senate.

The President had now the tacit consent of Congress to the acquisition of California and New Mexico, and the means to pay for them in hand. And the greater military successes of General Scott from Vera Cruz to the Mexican capital prepared the way for the President to make use of his power.

The President sent Mr. N. P. Trist, of Virginia, to the head-quarters of General Scott with the draft of a treaty to be offered the Mexican Government. It designated the Rio Grande from the Gulf to the point where the River touched the line of New Mexico as the boundary between Mexico and the United States from the Gulf to that point, and provided for the cession of New Mexico and the Californias to the United States, and the privilege of the right of way across the Isthmus of Tehuantepec. Mr. Trist was instructed, however, that he might withdraw the demands for Lower California and for the right of way across the Isthmus, and might also offer a payment of money, if he should find these things necessary. *The mission of Mr. Trist.*

After the armistice of August 24th, the Mexican Government sent commissioners to meet Mr. Trist. They promptly rejected Mr. Trist's propositions, and offered, as their ultimatum, the Nueces boundary, the cession of Upper California above the thirty-seventh parallel of latitude for a pecuniary consideration, the payment by the United States of an indemnity for private injuries inflicted by the United States troops during the invasion, etc. Nothing, moreover, was said in their offer concerning the claims of the citizens of the United States against Mexico. *Rejection of Mr. Trist's propositions by the Mexicans.*

The proposals were so far apart, and the Mexicans

bore themselves with so much arrogance, that the negotiations were broken off, the armistice was terminated, and General Scott resumed military operations. On September 8th, he inflicted a crushing defeat upon the Mexicans at Molino del Rey. On the 13th, he stormed successfully the heights of Chapultepec and two gates of the city. And on the 14th, he captured the city.

*Negotiations broken off. Molino del Rey, Chapultepec, Mexico.*

President Polk now recalled Mr. Trist, and informed Congress of the failure of the negotiations, at the same time intimating that the policy of the Administration would be war *à outrance*. The opposition to the Administration in Congress declared that the total dismemberment of the Mexican Republic was intended, and raised their voices against it. The outcry helped the Administration, in that it called the attention of the Mexicans to the great danger they were incurring in not accepting the terms of peace which had been offered them.

Mr. Trist did not, however, return to the United States, but waited in and around the City of Mexico for something to turn up. It seems that he did not even acquaint the Mexican Government with the fact of his recall. In the latter part of January, 1848, the Mexican commissioners approached him, and, on February 2nd, they signed with him, at Guadalupe Hidalgo, a treaty of peace, which provided for the Rio Grande boundary between the two Powers, the cession of New Mexico and Upper California to the United States, the payment of $15,000,000 by the United States to Mexico, and the assumption by the United States of all the obligations of Mexico to citizens of the United States incurred before the conclusion of the Treaty.

*The recall of Mr. Trist, and the Treaty of Guadalupe Hidalgo.*

Mr. Trist immediately took the proposed Treaty to

Washington, and President Polk immediately laid it before the Senate for ratification.  After three weeks of determined opposition by Senators from both parties and both sections, ratification was voted by the requisite two-thirds majority, on March 16th, 1848.  With this the whole political energy of the nation was turned away from the international question to the internal questions involved in the organization of the vast territorial empire upon the Pacific, which had now been added to the United States by the Treaties with Great Britain and Mexico.

*Ratification of the Treaty.*

# CHAPTER XVII

## THE ORGANIZATION OF OREGON TERRITORY AND THE COMPROMISE OF 1850

Bills for Oregon Territory—Thirty-six Degrees and Thirty Minutes to the Pacific—Mr. Rhett on the Rights of the South in the Territories—The Third Oregon Bill—The Party Platforms of 1848—The President Urges the Organization of California and New Mexico—Mr. Clayton's Attempt at Compromise—Passage of the Oregon Bill by Congress—The Free-soil Party in 1848—The President's Approval of the Oregon Bill—Gold and Silver in California—The Election of Taylor, and the Disaffection of the Northern Democrats—Plans for the Organization of California and New Mexico—The House Bill for the Territorial Organization of Upper California—Mr. Walker's Scheme in the House—Mr. Webster and Mr. Berrien on the Status of Slavery in the Territory Acquired from Mexico—Emigration to California—President Taylor's Scheme—The Convention at Monterey—The Policy of the Administration—The Policy of the Slavery Extensionists—The Elements of the Slavery Question in Congress—Mr. Clay's Plan of Compromise—Objections to Mr. Clay's Plan—California's Application for Admission—Mr. Calhoun's Last Speech—Mr. Webster's March 7th Speech—Mr. Bell's Proposition—The Death of Mr. Calhoun—Mr. Foote's Motion and the Committee of Thirteen—The Report and Recommendations of the Committee—The Debate Upon the Bills Proposed by the Committee, and the Failure to Pass Them—The Temper of the Country—The Succession of Fillmore and His Message of August 6th—The Passage of Bills, Separately, Covering All Questions Contained in Mr. Clay's Compromise Measures.

On August 6th, 1846, Mr. Douglas, of Illinois, chairman of the committee on Territories, asked the House

## THE ORGANIZATION OF OREGON TERRITORY

of Representatives to consider a bill prepared by that committee for the organization of Oregon as a Territory. The House consented, and immediately upon the second reading of the bill, Mr. Thompson, of Pennsylvania, a Democrat and friend of the Administration, moved to amend the bill by the provision "that neither slavery nor involuntary servitude shall ever exist in said Territory, except for crimes, whereof the party shall have been duly convicted." The amendment was adopted by a very large majority, and the bill, as thus amended, was passed. On the following day, the bill was presented in the Senate, and referred by that body to its Judiciary committee, which committee did not report the bill during the session.

*First bill for Oregon Territory.*

At the beginning of the next session, Mr. Douglas introduced a new bill for the same purpose. This bill virtually contained the Thompson amendment in the proviso that all the restrictions in the Ordinance of 1787, in regard to the Northwest Territory, should apply to Oregon.

*The second bill.*

On January 12th, 1847, Mr. Burt, of South Carolina, moved to insert before this proviso the words, "inasmuch as the whole of the said Territory lies north of thirty-six degrees and thirty minutes north latitude, known as the line of the Missouri Compromise." The purpose of this was, of course, to commit Congress and the North to that line to the Pacific. This was so evident that the Northern members voted the amendment down. We can, however, hardly charge the invention of this idea to the South Carolinian. On August 8th preceding, Mr. Wick, of Indiana, had moved to amend the Wilmot proviso, so as to make it read, that neither slavery nor involuntary servitude should exist, in any territory ac-

*Thirty-six degrees and thirty minutes to the Pacific.*

quired from Mexico *north of thirty-six degrees and thirty minutes.*

It was during the debate on this bill, just after Mr. Burt's amendment had been rejected, that Mr. Rhett, of South Carolina, made his noted speech, in which the new view, which the South was now beginning to take upon the rights of the two sections in the Territories, was first pronounced. That view was, briefly expressed, that the "States" were joint owners of the Territories, and "co-Sovereigns" in them; that the general Government was only the agent of the "States" therein, and had only the power "to dispose of, and make all needful rules and regulations respecting the territory, or other property of the United States," from which power, the power to determine in what property should consist within the Territories could not be derived; and that the "ingress of the citizen" of any "State" into any Territory, "is the ingress of his Sovereign," his "State," who is bound to protect him in his settlement.

Mr. Rhett on the rights of the South in the Territories.

Mr. Rhett qualified this conclusion by saying that it did not mean that each "State" should set up government in the Territories over its citizens immigrating into them, but that it meant that the citizens of each "State" should have equal right to enter the Territories and settle and occupy them with their property, with whatever was recognized as property by their respective "States." Stated more clearly, it meant that the general Government must execute the laws of each "State," defining and protecting property, in each Territory of the Union—of each "State" from which citizens had emigrated into the Territory concerned—and must execute these several "State" laws over the immigrants from the several "States" separately.

## THE ORGANIZATION OF OREGON TERRITORY 343

In plain, blunt Anglo-Saxon, it meant that the general Government must recognize and protect, as property, in any Territory, anything which was so recognized and protected by any "State" of the Union. It meant the establishment of slavery in every Territory of the Union.

This was a new doctrine in 1847, and it could not immediately prevail, but its appearance is a mark of the progress which the political system of the United States was making toward confederatism and dissolution.

The bill passed the House on January 16th, 1847, by a vote of nearly four to one, and was immediately sent to the Senate. The Senate referred it to its Judiciary committee. The committee reported on it, and the bill was laid on the table, the last day of the session. *The failure of the bill in the Senate.*

During the next session, bills were introduced into both Houses for organizing Oregon as a Territory. On January 10th, 1848, Mr. Douglas, who had been transferred from the House to the Senate, presented in the Senate a bill for the organization of a Territorial government for Oregon, which provided, among other things, that the laws which the Oregon settlers had constructed for themselves should, in so far as they were compatible with the Constitution and laws of the United States, remain in force until the Territorial legislature should change them. These laws excluded slavery. Here was the germ of "squatter-sovereignty," afterward developed by Mr. Douglas in his Kansas-Nebraska bill. *The third Oregon bill.*

The House bill, containing substantially the same provision as the bill of the preceding session, was introduced on February 9th, 1848, but this time it met with much more opposition, and the discussion on it revealed the fact that Mr. Rhett's doctrine had, within the year, made many converts.

344    THE MIDDLE PERIOD

The bills were dragging along slowly in both Houses, when, on May 29th, the President sent a special mes-
<small>The President urging action on the bill.</small> sage to Congress urging immediate action on the subject. This gave some impetus to the proceedings in both Houses.

On May 21st, Mr. Hale, of New Hampshire, moved to amend the Senate bill by a provision excluding slavery,
<small>Mr. Hale's amendment.</small> and insisted upon the power and the duty of Congress to settle the question of slavery in the Territories, and to settle it in the interest of freedom. The debate in the Senate upon Mr. Hale's motion was long and acrimonious, during which the Southerners advanced to more and more radical ground, until Mr. Calhoun and his disciple, Mr. Jefferson Davis, expressed the same constitutional doctrine upon the subject of the extension of slavery to the Territories as Mr. Rhett had done, which was, in brief, that neither Congress nor the inhabitants of a Territory had any constitutional power to abolish slavery in, or exclude it from, a Territory. On June 23rd, Mr. Davis moved to amend the Oregon
<small>Mr. Davis' amendment.</small> bill by the provision that nothing in the bill should be so construed as to authorize the prohibition of domestic slavery in said Territory while it remained in the condition of a Territory. The direct contradiction between the two amendments expressed, at last, the difference of attitude now assumed between the North and the South upon the question of the extension of slavery.

It cannot be said, however, that it represented the difference of attitude of the two great parties upon the
<small>The party platforms of 1848.</small> subject. The National conventions of these parties for the nominations of candidates for the presidency had just been held. The convention of the Democratic party had refused to insert the declaration in its platform that Congress had no

## THE ORGANIZATION OF OREGON TERRITORY 345

power to interfere with slavery in the Territories, in spite of the fact that the candidate nominated by it, General Cass, had acknowledged a leaning to something akin to that view, some five months previous, in a letter to Mr. Nicholson, of Tennessee, which was probably intended for circulation in the South. The exact wording of Mr. Cass' letter does not warrant us in representing him as holding to anything more, at that time, than that it was sound policy for Congress to leave the matter of the admission of slavery to, or its exclusion from, the Territories to the people of the Territories themselves. It was hardly time for Northern men to take the view of Congressional impotence in the matter held by Messrs. Rhett, Calhoun, and Davis.

On the other hand, the convention of the Whig party had refused to make the principle of the Wilmot proviso a plank in its platform, in fact had dodged the whole question of principles by adopting no platform at all, and by nominating a military man, with no political record at all, for its candidate, the old hero of Buena Vista, General Taylor.

The contradiction of view upon the question of the extension of slavery to the Territories was, thus, not one between the parties, but one between the sections. The parties were yet to be transformed by the differences between the sections. That this was to be the outcome no far-seeing eye ought then to have failed to perceive.

For a fortnight more the confusion produced by the contradictory propositions of Mr. Hale and Mr. Davis paralyzed the efforts of the Senate to pass the Oregon bill, when, on July 6th, 1848, the President sent a special message to Congress urging the immediate organization of Territorial governments for California and New Mexico, *The President urges the organization of California and New Mexico.*

which were still under the military régime established at the time of their occupation.

It appeared to some of the Senators that here was now offered the opportunity for settling the whole question of the extension of slavery to the Territories, by compromise; and, on July 12th, Mr. Bright, of Indiana, moved to refer the whole matter of the organization of Territorial governments in Oregon, California, and New Mexico, to a select committee, composed of four Whigs and four Democrats, two of each party from the North and the South, respectively. Mr. Bright's motion was in the form of an amendment or suggestion to a motion made by Mr. Clayton, that the Oregon bill be referred to such a committee. Mr. Clayton accepted Mr. Bright's modification of his motion, and the Senate immediately voted the resolution, and appointed the committee, with Mr. Clayton as chairman.

*Mr. Clayton's attempt at compromise.*

On the 18th, Mr. Clayton reported the bill from his committee, which provided for the organization of Oregon, with its existing anti-slavery laws, and with the recognition of the power to the Territorial legislature to change them; and for the organization of California and New Mexico, referring the question of the legality of slavery in them to the Territorial courts, with appeal to the Supreme Court of the United States, as a constitutional question. That is, the proposition with reference to slavery in California and New Mexico was, that slaveholders might take their slaves into these Territories upon their own responsibility, and that if any slaveholder should be disturbed in the possession of his slave, he might bring an action in the Territorial courts against the party disturbing him, with the right of appeal to the Supreme Court of the United States, which final tribunal should determine the question as a matter

## THE ORGANIZATION OF OREGON TERRITORY 347

of constitutional law, and, therefore, upon its own independent interpretation of the Constitution.

The Senate debated this bill for a week, during which time the flimsy character of the makeshifts became painfully apparent. The Senate passed the bill, however, on the 26th, and sent it to the House. *Passage of Mr. Clayton's bill in the Senate, and rejection of it in the House.*

The House rejected it, and proceeded with its own bill, and, on August 2nd, passed the latter by a strict sectional vote, and sent it to the Senate for concurrence.

On the 10th, the Senate passed this bill, with an amendment, proposed by Mr. Douglas, extending the Missouri Compromise line of thirty-six degrees and thirty minutes to the Pacific. The House immediately rejected the amendment, and the Senate was compelled to recede, or let Oregon go without Territorial government. *The House bill in the Senate, and Mr. Douglas' amendment.*

It wisely voted, on the 12th, to recede from its amendment, and passed the bill, with the Congressional prohibition of slavery, and without compromise as to the settlement of the slavery question in California and New Mexico. Among the *Passage of the Oregon bill by Congress.*

Senators who changed their votes upon the amendment were Douglas from the North, and Benton and Houston from the South.

The feeling aroused outside of Congress by the contest within the body was most intense, and had, for its permanent result the organization of the Anti-slavery-extension party. It called itself then the "Free-soil" party. It held a National convention at Buffalo, New York, on August *The Free-soil party in 1848.*
9th, and nominated Mr. Van Buren for the presidency, on a platform which distinctly affirmed the power of Congress to exclude slavery from the Territories, and its duty to exercise the power. Here was, at last, the

principle and the party of the future. Those who composed it held to the Union and the Government, vindicated the national character of both, and while they denied none of the constitutional rights of the Southern Commonwealths, and none of the compromises of the Constitution with the slaveholders, yet they refused to allow the great evil under which the country suffered to spread into regions uncontaminated by it.

The President signed the Oregon bill, on August 14th, for the reason, he said, among other reasons, that it preserved the principle of the Missouri Compromise, making the territory north of thirty-six degrees and thirty minutes free soil. And in his message of December 5th, following, he urged the speedy organization of California and New Mexico, either upon that principle, or upon the principle of non-interference by Congress with the question of slaveholding in them, or upon the basis of an appeal of the question to the Supreme Court of the United States, which body should interpret the Constitution upon the subject. He said he believed the first way contained the true principle, and was the fair thing, but that he was willing to proceed in either of the other two ways.

*The President's approval of the Oregon bill.*

At the same time, the President gave official verification to the rumors of the discovery of great quantities of gold and silver in California, which quickened the emigration of the bold and adventurous spirits from all parts of the country to the new El Dorado.

*Gold and silver in California.*

The temper of Congress against slavery extension was even stronger in the session of 1848–49, than in the preceding session. The Whig majority in the House of Representatives remained, and now came a support to the anti-slavery-extension principle of the Northern

# THE ORGANIZATION OF OREGON TERRITORY 349

Whigs from Northern Democrats, which had not been before accorded. The elections of 1848 had greatly surprised the Northern Democrats. The Whig candidate, General Taylor, carried a majority of the Southern Commonwealths, and was chosen President. The Democrats of the North considered that they had been left in the lurch by the Democrats of the South, and came to the session of 1848-49 with revenge in their hearts. They were disposed to join hands with the Northern Whigs against the extension of slavery into any more of the Territories of the Union. This spirit was, however, far more manifest in the House of Representatives than in the Senate. On December 11th, 1848, Mr. Douglas brought into the Senate a plan for avoiding the question in respect to slavery in California and New Mexico, by immediately erecting the whole of the territory acquired from Mexico into a single Commonwealth, and reserving the right to Congress to create new Commonwealths in that part of this territory lying east of the Sierra Nevada Mountains. This proposition was referred to the Judiciary committee for report; but before the report was presented Mr. Smith, of Indiana, chairman of the committee on Territories, brought in bills for the organization of Upper California and New Mexico, with the slavery restriction of the Ordinance of 1787 in them. On January 9th, 1849, Mr. Berrien, chairman of the Judiciary committee, reported adversely upon Mr. Douglas' proposition, on the grounds, alleged by him, that Congress could not create a Commonwealth, but could only admit a Commonwealth into the Union after it had been created by the sovereign act of the people residing in it, for the performance of which act the status of Territorial organization was necessary, and that Congress could never

*The election of Taylor, and the disaffection of the Northern Democrats.*

*Plans for the organization of California and New Mexico.*

constitutionally disconnect from any Commonwealth any portion of its territory for the purpose of forming it into another Commonwealth, without the consent of the Commonwealth itself.

Mr. Douglas immediately modified his bill so as to meet the latter objection; and on January 24th, offered a substitute for his former proposition, which provided for a Commonwealth of California that would not quite cover the territory which the Mexicans included under the title of the Province of Upper California. On Mr. Douglas' own motion, this proposition was referred to a select committee, of which he was appointed chairman; and, on the 29th, he reported a bill from the committee for forming the territory acquired from Mexico into two Commonwealths, to be called California and New Mexico; but the Senate showed so much opposition to the project that it was dropped. More than half the session had now passed, and the Senate appeared to be farther than ever from any consensus in regard to what should be done for California and New Mexico. It was a serious condition of things. The inhabitants of these Territories were importunately demanding the establishment of civil government over them for the protection of life, liberty, and property, and Congress was apparently to do nothing for them during the current session.

*Mr. Douglas' plan.*

On February 19th, Mr. Walker, of Wisconsin, came forward in the Senate with an expedient. He moved to attach to the Civil and Diplomatic Appropriation Bill a provision for extending the Constitution, and the laws of the United States naturally applicable, over all the territory acquired from Mexico, and for authorizing the President to make all needful rules and regulations, and to appoint civil officials, for their execution. The Senate passed this amendment,

*Mr. Walker's expedient.*

and sent the Appropriation Bill thus modified back to the House for concurrence.

Meanwhile the bill in the House for the Territorial organization of Upper California, with the slavery prohibition clause in it, was proceeding through a most exciting debate, but with increasing prospect of final passage. On February 27th, it was passed, by an almost sectional vote, and sent to the Senate. *The House bill for the Territorial organization of Upper California.* The Senate referred it to its committee on Territories, and there it slept as in "the tomb of all the Capulets."

On March 1st, the House took up the Senate's amendment to the Civil and Diplomatic Appropriation Bill, and referred it to the committee on Ways and Means. This committee reported, on March 2nd, an amendment to the Senate's amendment, *Mr. Walker's scheme in the House.* which provided for the continuance of the status of military possession and of the Mexican laws in all the territory acquired from Mexico, until six months after the close of the next session of Congress. The purpose of this amendment was the continuance of the Mexican law excluding slavery. The House did not, however, adopt this proposition, but sent the Appropriation Bill back to the Senate stripped of the Senate's amendment. The Senate asked a conference upon the subject, which was granted by the House, but the Conference committee could come to no agreement.

The House now passed the proposition of the Ways and Means committee, slightly modified in form, and sent it to the Senate. Mr. Webster moved concurrence with the House in this proposition, and said that it meant no more than the existing status, which would continue if nothing were done. Mr. Berrien contended, on the contrary, that only the private law of the ceding country, *Mr. Webster and Mr. Berrien on the status of slavery in the territory acquired from Mexico.*

the law regulating the relations between individuals, remains in force in the territory ceded, until changed by the positive acts of the country receiving the cession; that the public law of the receiving country is extended at once, by virtue of the occupation, over the cession; and that slavery was a part of the public law of the United States, since both the system of taxation and that of representation rested in part upon it. Mr. Berrien concluded from these postulates of international and constitutional law that, if Congress did nothing in the premises, the President would continue to administer, by means of his military officials, the private law of Mexico, and the public law of the United States, in the territory acquired from Mexico, and that this would allow slaveholders to take their slaves into this territory, and hold them in slavery; but that if Congress, by a positive enactment, should adopt the Mexican laws, *en bloc*, for this territory, slavery would be thereby excluded from it. In a word, he demonstrated, or thought he did, that the proposition of the House of Representatives contained the principle of the Wilmot proviso. The Senate was so deeply impressed by Mr. Berrien's argument, and so much opposition to the proposition of the House was manifested, that Mr. Webster offered to withdraw his motion, if the Southerners would agree to recede from the Senate's amendment. The bargain was struck, and the Thirtieth Congress expired without having done anything for the governmental organization of California and New Mexico, and without having advanced, in the slightest measure, toward the solution of the fateful question of slavery extension in the vast empire conquered from Mexico.

The official announcement made by President Polk of the mineral wealth of California had increased the excitement for emigration thither to a fever, and by the

## THE ORGANIZATION OF OREGON TERRITORY 353

close of the spring of 1849, California had a population within her provincial limits numerous enough, according to prevailing conceptions, to make a Commonwealth. *Emigration to California.*

The new President, Taylor, thought that all further controversy about the Territorial organization of California might now be avoided, by skipping the Territorial period and status altogether, and organizing California immediately as a Commonwealth. *President Taylor's scheme.* He sent a commissioner to examine the situation on the ground and make report. Whether the commissioner imparted the President's scheme to General Riley, the military Governor, or not, we are not informed. We have good reason, however, to suspect it, since Riley immediately issued a call for a convention of the people of California to frame a Commonwealth.

The people quickly responded by choosing delegates, and the delegates met at Monterey on September 1st, 1849. By October 13th, their work was completed, and the organic law which they drafted was ratified by the people, on November 13th. *The convention at Monterey.* One of its provisions was the prohibition of slavery. The filling up of California by immigration had been too sudden for the holders of slaves to take part in the movement. It was accomplished, it could be accomplished, only by bold, alert, shrewd adventurers, untrammelled by families or stupid African retainers. It was reported that every delegate in the convention voted for the prohibition of slavery, and the people ratified the instrument containing it by a vote of fifteen to one.

The President informed Congress, in his message of December 4th, 1849, of the proceedings in California, and manifested his desire to admit California into the Union at once. He also predicted that the people of

New Mexico would soon follow the example of the Californians. The policy of the Administration in reference to this question was thus clearly defined, and was, whether intentional or not, a policy favorable to the prohibition of slavery in both California and New Mexico. The slaveholders, or rather the slavery extensionists, regarded the President's position as treachery to his section.

*The policy of the Administration.*

The policy of the slavery extensionists was to organize California and New Mexico as Territories, without the prohibition of slavery in them, giving thus time and opportunity for slaveholders to settle in them, with their slaves, and, when the time should come for the formation of Commonwealth governments in them, to vote an organic law perpetuating slavery. This policy was manifested anew in the bill introduced into the Senate, on the last day of December, 1849, by Mr. Foote, of Mississippi, for the organization of the entire Mexican cession into three Territories—California, Deseret or Utah, and New Mexico.

*The policy of the slavery extensionists.*

The slavery question in Congress had now come, however, to include more than the matter of the governmental organization of the territory acquired from Mexico. There was, in the first place, the question of the Texan boundary, in that, by the Joint Resolution annexing Texas, the adjustment of that boundary, as regarded foreign states, at least, was reserved to Congress. Texas, as we know, claimed the Rio Grande from mouth to source, and thence the longitude to the forty-second parallel of latitude as her southwestern and western boundary. She came into the Union with a law on her statute book asserting this boundary. The Treaty with Mexico, recognizing the line of the Rio Grande to the

*The elements of the slavery question in Congress.*

limits of New Mexico, and ceding New Mexico, made the question of the Texan boundary a purely internal question for the United States, if it was any longer a question. The Abolitionists and anti-slavery-extensionists wanted to reduce Texas in area, since slavery was established by the law of the Commonwealth throughout its entire extent. They therefore interpreted the Resolution of annexation as reserving that power to Congress, even after the question had become purely internal. The slavery extensionists, on the contrary, contended that the power reserved to Congress in reference to the Texan boundary was now obsolete, since it expressly related only to the adjustment of the same with Mexico, and that had been accomplished by the Treaty. Then, there was the war debt of Texas, which was justly a charge upon the United States—although the Resolution of annexation repudiated it—since it was hypothecated upon revenue, the proceeds from which were being covered into the United States Treasury, the customs collected in the Texan ports. And, then, there was the question of the rendition of fugitive slaves, since the execution of the existing law, that of 1793, in regard to this matter, had been rendered so difficult by the movements of the Abolitionists, after 1835, as to make a more strenuous measure necessary, unless the slaveholders would abandon their constitutional rights to the rendition of their escaped slaves. And, lastly, there was the ever-recurring question of slavery and the slave-trade in the District of Columbia, which was still clamoring for a hearing.

Already, before the closing week of January, 1850, had bills been brought forward, both in the Senate and in the House, touching all of these subjects, except, perhaps, the last, when, on the 29th, Mr. Clay came forward with his famous proposition for the adjustment of them all in one grand scheme.

This proposition provided, in the first place, for the immediate admission of California as a Commonwealth, with suitable boundaries, and without any restrictions as to slavery; in the second place, for the establishment of Territorial governments in all of the remainder of the Mexican cession, without any restrictions as to slavery; in the third place, for fixing the western boundary of Texas, so as to exclude any portion of New Mexico; in the fourth place, for the assumption of the Texan debt contracted before annexation and hypothecated upon the Texan customs, on condition of the relinquishment by Texas of all claims on New Mexico; in the fifth place, for the abolition of the slave-trade in the District of Columbia, in slaves brought into the District from the outside for the purpose of sale; and in the sixth place, for a more effective law for the rendition of fugitive slaves. The resolutions also contained declarations that slavery did not then exist in any of the territory acquired from Mexico, and that Congress had no power to prohibit or obstruct trade in slaves between the slaveholding Commonwealths.

*Mr. Clay's plan of compromise.*

In spite of the fact that Mr. Clay asked the Senators to consider his propositions carefully before committing themselves, and suggested that they should lay over for a week, the Southern Senators immediately proceeded to attack the plan at several points. They objected to California being allowed to jump the Territorial period of probation and preparation for Commonwealth government. They declared Mr. Clay's dictum about the existing illegality of slavery in the territory acquired from Mexico to be an assumption, and asserted that slavery was legal everywhere in the United States, unless a positive law forbade it. They vindicated the claims of Texas to the boundaries designated by the Act of the Texan Con-

*Slaveholders' objections to Mr. Clay's plan.*

## THE ORGANIZATION OF OREGON TERRITORY 357

gress in 1836. And while some of them were not decidedly opposed to the abolition of the slave-trade in the District of Columbia, most of them deprecated meddling with the subject at all, and wanted to substitute for Mr. Clay's proposition on the subject a declaration of the lack of any power in Congress to deal with slavery in the District. The improvement of the fugitive slave-law was about the only thing in the entire plan which met with their approval. Mr. Jefferson Davis said outright that he wanted a positive recognition from Congress of the legality of slavery in the new territory south of the parallel of thirty-six degrees and thirty minutes.

On the other hand, the Abolitionists and the anti-slavery-extensionists insisted upon the immediate admission of California, with its anti-slavery constitution; upon the insertion of the principle of the Wilmot proviso in the Territorial organization of the remainder of the acquisition from Mexico; upon the contraction of the Texan limits, without any compensation to Texas; upon the abolition of the slave-trade in the District of Columbia, and a declaration of the power of Congress to deal with slavery in the District; and upon a jury trial, at the place of apprehension, for every claimed fugitive from labor. *Anti-slavery objections to Mr. Clay's plan.*

The contradiction between these views appeared irreconcilable. We may say, however, that a start toward an approach was caused by the transmission of California's application to Congress for admission, as a Commonwealth, into the Union. *California's application for admission.*

This happened on February 13th. On the following day, Mr. Douglas moved to take up the President's message accompanying the application, and thus to consider the California question separately from the others. Mr. Clay agreed to this. Mr. Foote, of Mississippi, scolded Mr. Clay for thus betraying the South, but the

Southerners were made to feel that they must modify their opposition to Mr. Clay's plan, if they desired to avoid something like this.

On March 4th, Mr. Calhoun made his last great speech upon the whole political situation, its threatening character, and its possible rectification. He was too feeble to pronounce it himself, and it was read for him by Senator Mason. Mr. Calhoun's propositions were, that the Union was endangered; that the immediate cause of the danger was the universal discontent prevailing in the South from the feeling that the South could no longer remain with safety and honor in the Union; and that the cause of this feeling was the fact that the balance of power between the two sections of the country in the Government was gone, and the stronger section was endeavoring to make the Government an unlimited centralized democracy, and use it for interfering in the internal affairs of the weaker, and for absorbing the substance, as well as destroying the rights, of the weaker.

*Mr. Calhoun's last speech.*

He suggested as remedies for the evils, which he thought existed and impended, an equal division of the territory to the Pacific between the North and the South, an amendment to the Constitution restoring the balance of power between the two sections, proper laws for the rendition of fugitives from labor, and cessation of the agitation of the slavery question.

What should be the provisions of the amendment, restoring the balance of power in the Government, and how the cessation of the agitation could be compelled, were not explained. It was not easy to see how these points could be advanced beyond the position of general propositions. It was, however, a great and solemn presentation of the whole question, and it made a great impression.

## THE ORGANIZATION OF OREGON TERRITORY 359

On March 7th, Mr. Webster made his famous speech, giving his great influence to pacification and compromise, and to the preservation of the Constitution. He told the Northerners that they were bound by the agreement with Texas to admit four new Commonwealths from Texan territory, under the usual conditions; that they were bound by the Constitution to deliver up fugitive slaves; and that since nature had made slavery impossible in California and New Mexico, they ought not to irritate the Southerners by demanding a Congressional prohibition of slavery therein. He told the Southerners, on the other hand, that they should desist from denying to citizens from Northern Commonwealths, temporarily within the jurisdiction of Southern Commonwealths, the rights of citizens. And he told the Abolitionists that they should measure their ideas of right, in some degree at least, by the standard of the common consciousness of the country, and modify them, in some degree, thereby. His words were received with great satisfaction by all moderate and prudent men. Of course, they did not satisfy the extremists, either in the North or the South, but they settled the minds of many who were wavering, and moved the work of temporary pacification, at least, several stages onward.

*Mr. Webster's March 7th speech.*

During the course of the debate upon Mr. Clay's resolutions, and before the great efforts either of Mr. Calhoun or Mr. Webster, Mr. Bell, of Tennessee, had offered some propositions, looking to the admission of California as a Commonwealth, and to the formation of Territorial government for New Mexico. On the day after Mr. Webster's great speech, Mr. Foote moved the reference of Mr. Bell's resolutions to a select committee of thirteen members. No vote, however, was immediately taken, but the debate upon

*Mr. Bell's proposition.*

both sets of resolutions dragged on from day to day, and was made more complicated by the introduction of a bill from the committee on Territories, providing for the immediate admission of California, and the formation of Territorial governments for New Mexico and Utah.

On March 31st, Mr. Calhoun passed away. The announcement of his death, the eulogies pronounced upon his memory, and the funeral rites, were most solemn and impressive occasions. The influence of the sad event seemed, for the moment, to soften the hearts of those who had associated with him toward one another. It seemed as if political foes would be willing to join hands across his bier.

*The death of Mr. Calhoun.*

On April 11th, Mr. Mangum, of North Carolina, moved to refer the resolutions of Mr. Clay, along with those of Mr. Bell, to the committee suggested by Mr. Foote. Mr. Foote accepted Mr. Mangum's motion as an amendment to his own. After a most determined opposition by Senator Benton to Mr. Foote's motion, during which temper rose so high that Mr. Benton threatened to cudgel Mr. Foote, and Mr. Foote actually drew a pistol upon Mr. Benton, both in the course of the debate in the Senate chamber, Mr. Foote's motion was passed. On the next day, April 19th, the members of the committee were chosen by ballot. They were Mr. Clay, Mr. Bell, Mr. Berrien, Mr. Bright, Mr. Cass, Mr. Cooper, Mr. Dickinson, Mr. Downs, Mr. King, Mr. Mason, Mr. Mangum, Mr. Phelps, and Mr. Webster. Seven members, including the chairman, Mr. Clay, were from the South and six from the North.

*Mr. Foote's motion and the Committee of Thirteen.*

On May 8th, Mr. Clay made the report, and offered the bills, from the grand committee, covering all the subjects referred. The first bill provided for the admission of California, with the Commonwealth organization formed by her people the preceding autumn ; for the Territorial organization of Utah and New Mexico, without any slavery restriction, and with restrictions upon the Territorial legislatures against passing any acts in regard to slavery ; for fixing the northern boundary of Texas upon a line drawn from a point on the Rio Grande twenty miles above El Paso to the point on the Red River where the line of the one hundredth degree of longitude intersects this river ; for quit-claiming, so to speak, to Texas the claims of the United States to the country between the Nueces and the Rio Grande ; and for paying Texas a sum of money, in consideration of the discharge of the United States from all obligations to pay the Texan debt, and of the surrender of all claims by Texas to country north of the northern boundary as fixed in the bill.

*The report and recommendations of the committee.*

The second bill provided that a fugitive from labor must be delivered up on the order of any judge or commissioner of the United States authorized by the laws of the United States so to act, and that such judge or commissioner was authorized to issue such order on presentation to him, by the claimant of the fugitive, of a copy of the record of a competent court in the Commonwealth, Territory, or District from which the fugitive was said to have escaped, before which the facts of ownership, identity, and escape had been satisfactorily proven. The judge or commissioner issuing such order was required, in case the fugitive declared himself to be a free man, to demand of the claimant of the fugitive a bond, with surety, for $1,000, pledging the claimant to accord the fugitive a trial by jury of the question of his freedom, in a competent court of the Commonwealth,

Territory, or District from which he was said to have escaped.

The third bill provided for the abolition of the slave-trade in the District of Columbia, and for the liberation of any slave brought into the District for the purposes of sale or dépôt.

The debate began immediately upon the first bill, and the opposition to it from both sections advanced about the same arguments as were employed against these same subjects when presented in the form of Mr. Clay's resolutions. The discussion continued through May, June, and July, until, at the end of July, nothing remained of the bill but that part of it which provided for the Territorial organization of Utah. The general plan of the compromise was lost.

*The debate upon the bills proposed by the committee, and the failure to pass them.*

The whole country was amazed, disappointed, and angry. The Senators were quickly and decidedly made to feel that they dare not separate without doing something to heal the distractions of the land.

*The temper of the country.*

The death of President Taylor, on July 9th, and the accession of Mr. Fillmore, made the Administration more favorable to the measures included in the compromise plan. On August 6th, he communicated to Congress the fact that the Governor of Texas, P. H. Bell, in execution of an act of the Texas legislature, was extending the jurisdiction of Texas over the disputed territory on the eastern border of New Mexico, and that the President, as military Governor, in highest instance, of New Mexico, felt obliged to resist the movement, and that he had informed the Governor of Texas of his purpose. He besought Congress to avert the calamity which now threatened, by attending at once

*The succession of Fillmore and his message of August 6th.*

# THE ORGANIZATION OF OREGON TERRITORY  363

to the matter of the boundary between Texas and New Mexico.

Under this pressure, the Senate took up the Texan boundary bill, introduced by Mr. Pierce, of Maryland, which provided that the northern boundary of Texas should be the parallel of thirty-six degrees and thirty minutes from the one hundredth degree of longitude to the one hundred and third degree; that the western and southwestern boundary should be the one hundred and third parallel of longitude from the northern line to latitude thirty-two degrees, thence along this parallel westward to the Rio Grande, thence the Rio Grande to the Gulf; and that ten millions of dollars should be paid Texas for agreeing to this boundary, and for relinquishing all claims on the United States in regard to the payment of her public debt. On August 9th, the bill passed the Senate.

*The passage of bills, separately, covering all the questions contained in Mr. Clay's compromise measures.*

On the 13th, the Senate took up the bill for the immediate admission of California, reported from the committee on Territories, and passed it by a large majority.

On August 15th, the Senate passed the bill from the committee on Territories for the Territorial organization of New Mexico, without any provision as to slavery. The bill for the organization of Utah had passed, it will be remembered, on August 1st, as the remnant of the compromise plan.

The Senate then took up the Fugitive Slave Bill reported in March from the Judiciary committee. Inasmuch as the United States Supreme Court had given its opinion, in the case of Prigg versus Pennsylvania, that Commonwealth officers were not required by the Constitution of the United States to render any assistance in the rendition of fugitive slaves, the Judiciary committee had so constructed its bill as to make use of the machinery of the central Government alone in the execution of the proposed law. The bill was a somewhat more stringent measure than that proposed by Mr. Clay's committee. It did away with the right of a fugitive claiming to be a freeman to a trial by jury of the question of his freedom in a competent court of the Commonwealth, Territory, or District from which he was said to have escaped. It made it the duty of the marshals and deputy marshals of the United States courts to obey and execute all of the warrants and precepts issued under the provisions of the Act. It imposed a penalty of fine and imprisonment upon any person knowingly hindering the arrest of a fugitive, or attempting to rescue one from custody, or harboring one, or aiding one to escape. And it made the fee of the commissioner $10 in case he should issue the certificate of arrest to the claimant of the fugitive, and only $5 in case he should not. Otherwise it was substantially the same as the bill proposed by the Clay committee. The Senate passed this bill, on August 26th.

At last, on September 16th, the Senate passed the bill recommended by Mr. Clay's committee, for the abolition of the slave-trade in the District of Columbia.

One after another, all these bills passed the House of Representatives, against great opposition, but with no material alteration, except the connection of the bill for the organization of Territorial government in New Mexico with that for the adjustment of the Texan boundary, in which change the Senate acquiesced, and were all signed by the President; and before the first session of the Thirty-first Congress expired, on September 30th, 1850, the great work of pacification, as it was hoped and believed to be, had been accomplished.

# CHAPTER XVIII.

## THE EXECUTION OF THE FUGITIVE SLAVE LAW, AND THE ELECTION OF 1852

Change of Attitude of the Slaveholders by the Fugitive Slave Law
of 1850—The First Cases Under the New Law—The Opposition
to the Execution of the Law—Establishment of the "Underground"—The Support of the Law by the Political Leaders—
The President's Support of the Law—Joshua R. Giddings—
Petitions for the Repeal of the Law—The Shadrach Case—The
Investigation of the Case by Congress—The Question of Increasing the Power of the President to Execute the Law—The
Sims Case—Excitement in Boston Over the Rendition of Sims
—The "Jerry Rescue"—The President's Rebuke—Mr. Foote's
Finality Resolutions—The Failure of the Resolutions to Pass
the Senate, but Their Success in the House—The National
Conventions of 1852 and the Finality of the Compromise
Measures—The Deaths of Clay and of Webster, and the Appearance of a Free-soil Candidate—The Overwhelming Democratic Victory of 1852—The True Policy of the Slaveholders,
and Their Failure to Discern It.

DOWN to the time of the enactment of the Fugitive Slave Law of 1850, it may be said that the slaveholders *Change of attitude of the slaveholders by the Fugitive Slave Law of 1850.* were acting, in a certain sense, on the defensive. Before 1787, slavery had been regarded as a temporary relation, demanded by the moral and intellectual degradation of the Africans, and by the necessities of the social structure in which Anglo-Saxon and negro were brought together. It had been considered that the rise of the negro in civilization, by his contact with the white race, would gradually change this relation in the direction of freedom. In fact it had done so, in a considerable degree. But the formation of the Constitution of 1787, the invention and use of the cotton-gin, the acquisition of Louisiana, and the general subsidence of the revolutionary spirit of the eighteenth century, were all unfavorable to further progress in this only proper and correct direction. Between 1830 and 1840, a strong retrogressive movement set in, as we have seen, provoked indeed, in a considerable degree, by the Abolition propaganda; and in consequence of it, the slaveholders abandoned the only moral principle upon which slavery could be justified, and began to adopt the idea of the permanency of the relation, and to undertake the adjustment of the laws, customs, institutions, and policies of the country to this idea. And, at last, by the Fugitive Slave Law of 1850, they committed the whole country to this course. In a word, they made slavery by this law a national matter, and they did it from the property point of view of slavery, the point of view which exhibits it in its most hateful light, and from which no moral justification whatsoever for its existence can be found.

It is true that the Constitution commanded the return of fugitive slaves, and that the Supreme Court of the United States had interpreted the provision as vesting the power of executing this command in, and imposing the duty of its execution exclusively upon, the general Government, but it was a fatal policy for the slaveholders to insist upon the realization of this right through the general Government. In fact, it was a fatal policy to insist upon its realization at all. There was no way to effect it without requiring the aid of the North in the perpetuation of slavery. The attempt to effect it was, therefore, the assumption of an offensive attitude on the part of the slaveholders, an attitude which was bound to pro-

EXECUTION OF THE FUGITIVE SLAVE LAW 367

voke a general hostility to slavery throughout the North, instead of the indifference which had prevailed under the idea that slavery was an institution of the Southern Commonwealths, with which the North and the general Government had no concern. Calhoun and Rhett and Davis had seen this danger, and they were not supporters of a national fugitive slave law. They preferred to consider the matter of the rendition of fugitive slaves as a special compact between the "States," and treat its non-fulfilment as a rupture of the Union. Possibly, protected as their "States" were by the border slaveholding Commonwealths, they did not feel the necessity of such a law. At any rate, it was the border slaveholding Commonwealths which wanted the law.

The first apprehension of an escaped slave, under the new Act, was made in the city of New York. One James Hamlet, who had three years before left his mistress, Mary Brown, of Baltimore, was the victim. He had a wife and children in New York. He was surprised at his work, hastily tried, and delivered to Mrs. Brown's agent, who conducted him back to Baltimore. When the news of the event spread abroad it created great excitement among the negro population throughout the North, and great indignation on the part of the white citizens in many quarters. *The first cases under the new law.*

It was calculated that there were from fifteen to twenty thousand escaped slaves living at that time in the non-slaveholding Commonwealths who were liable to apprehension under the law; and every person having any negro blood, whether escaped from slavery or not, felt the insecurity created by the law. Meetings of persons belonging to these classes were immediately held in Boston and New York, and resolutions were passed at them, praying the white people to move for the repeal of the law. *The opposition to the execution of the law.*

In answer, so to speak, to these appeals, mass-meetings of white people were held in Lowell, Syracuse, and Boston, at which the law was denounced, its repeal demanded, and aid pledged to the negroes in the North in resisting the execution of the law. Ministers of the Gospel, such as Beecher, Storrs, Furness, Spear, and Cheever, rained down denunciations upon the law from their pulpits, declared it to be in direct contravention of the law of God, and counselled resistance to its execution.

In the midst of this excitement two Georgia slaves, named William and Ellen Crafts, had succeeded in reaching Boston, and were concealed by some of the most high-toned people of that city, the Hillards, Lorings, and Parkers, from their pursuers, and aided in a successful escape to England. The first branch of the "Underground," established after the passage of the law, ran through very respectable quarters.

*Establishment of the "Underground."*

The lawyers, politicians, and statesmen now felt that it was high time for them to call the people back to the proper comprehension and observance of their constitutional duties. Clay, Webster, Cass, Douglas, Buchanan, Shields, Curtis, Choate, and many others, instructed the people, both in speeches and written articles, in regard to the constitutionality of the law, and their duty to obey its requirements. With this the tide of public opinion began to change, and the idea that it was the constitutional duty of the North to the South to secure the execution of the law began to prevail. Such was the state of feeling when the Congressional session of 1850–51 opened, on December 2nd.

*The support of the law by the political leaders.*

In his message to Congress President Fillmore proclaimed his adherence to the Compromise Measures, as a

EXECUTION OF THE FUGITIVE SLAVE LAW 369

final settlement of the subjects to which they related, said that he believed the great mass of the American people sympathized with him, indicated that he would veto any measure for the repeal of the Fugitive Slave Law, and declared that he would execute the laws to the utmost of his ability and to the extent of the power vested in him. *The President's support of the law.*

This bold and determined language on the part of the President, who had been considered in the North as personally hostile to the Fugitive Slave Law, took the North somewhat by surprise, painfully so in some quarters, while it was highly approved at the South. It undoubtedly contributed, ultimately and in large degree, to the suppression of the resistance in the North to the execution of the law. At the moment, however, it drew out some of the bitterest denunciations of the law which were ever pronounced.

Mr. Joshua R. Giddings, of Ohio, moved the reference of this part of the message to the Judiciary committee in the House of Representatives, and made a speech in support of his motion, which was an anti-slavery harangue of the most radical and violent character, and in the course of which he denounced the President and Mr. Webster in unmeasured language as apostates from principle and suitors for Southern favor. The reckless outburst of radical extravagance, although somewhat balanced by many points of sound sense, disgusted the House, and it voted down Mr. Giddings' motion by a large majority. *Joshua R. Giddings.*

Petitions began now to flow into Congress for the repeal of the law. Generally they were laid upon the table, but more than once a fierce debate was opened, which threatened to precipitate another contest over the right of petition. It was about the time that the Senate was considering what *Petitions for the repeal of the law.*

24

to do with one of these petitions, offered by Mr. Hamlin, of Maine, in February of 1851, that the news of the failure of the law in the Shadrach case reached Washington. Shadrach, claimed slave of John DeBree, of Norfolk, Va., was rescued by a negro mob, while held in custody in the court-house in Boston under a warrant from the United States Commissioner, Mr. George T. Curtis, and was spirited away to Canada. The mob seems to have had no difficulty in accomplishing its purpose.

*The Shadrach case.*

The Senate, on motion of Mr. Clay, passed a resolution, on February 18th, 1851, calling upon the President for information concerning the failure of the law in the Shadrach case, and the means he had adopted to meet the occurrence, and asking the President if, in his opinion, further means should be placed at his disposal by Congress for enabling him to execute the laws with more success.

*The investigation of the case by Congress.*

On the 21st, the reply of the President was received. It contained an account of the occurrence in Boston; a summary of the laws of the United States and of Massachusetts on the subject of confining United States prisoners in the jails of the Commonwealth, which demonstrated the fact that Massachusetts had forbidden the use of her jails and the aid of her officials in fugitive slave cases; a declaration of opinion that the President was authorized by the Constitution to use the regular army and navy, when, in his judgment, it was necessary for the suppression of violence and the execution of the laws, and without giving warning of his intention by any proclamation; and a suggestion to Congress to confirm this opinion by a positive act, which would include the militia as well as the regular army and navy, and would authorize a marshal or commissioner of the

# EXECUTION OF THE FUGITIVE SLAVE LAW 371

United States to summon an organized militia force as a part of the posse comitatus.

Mr. Clay immediately moved the reference of the communication to the Judiciary committee. This motion called out a three days debate in the Senate, during which it became manifest that the extremists, from both the North and the South, had little faith in the power of the Government to execute the law, and were unfavorable to the policy of using the military power in its execution. Mr. Chase and Mr. Hale, on the one side, and Mr. Butler, Mr. Davis, and Mr. Rhett, on the other, contended that the provision of the Constitution guaranteeing the rendition of fugitive slaves did not require a Congressional act, even if it authorized one. Mr. Davis said that he would see Massachusetts quit the Union rather than execute the law by military power within her limits. It was evident that these men were not anxious to have the law executed at all. Their motives for the same must have been very different, but it would hardly be an unfair speculation if one should imagine that the slaveholders were not averse to having the failure of the law for another count in their indictment against the Union.

*The question of increasing the power of the President to execute the law.*

The moderate men, however, of both the North and the South, claimed that the law was constitutional, that it was politic and necessary, that it had been successfully executed in a number of cases, that it could be executed in practically all cases, that it must be, even though it should require the whole military power of the country, and that the great mass of the people would sustain it as carrying out the pledges of the Constitution.

Mr. Clay's motion was finally unanimously voted, and, on March 3rd, two reports were presented to the

Senate, one signed by all the members of the Judiciary committee except Mr. Butler, of South Carolina, and the other by Mr. Butler alone. The former expressed the opinion that the President already possessed full and adequate powers to execute the laws, and that no further legislation upon the subject was necessary. It also held that the organized military could be summoned and used by a civil officer as a part of the posse comitatus. Mr. Butler, while agreeing with the other members in recommending no further legislation for the execution of the law, denied that the President had the power from the Constitution to use the regular army and navy at his own discretion in suppressing insurrections and executing the laws, and held that the President could employ these forces for such purposes in the same manner only that he could employ the militia, that is, under the Congressional Acts of 1795 and 1807, which required, among other things, that a proclamation should precede the actual employment of military power in such cases.

Congress closed its session, on the next day, without having changed or modified the law, and without having given the President any additional means for its execution. The thoughts of men were turned again upon the incidents of its execution.

During the spring of 1851, several cases of slave apprehension occurred, the most exciting of which was *The Sims case.* that of Thomas Sims, claimed in Boston by Mr. James Potter, of Georgia. He was arrested by the City Marshal on the charge of having committed a larceny, and put under guard in the Court House. Charles G. Loring, Robert Rantoul, Jr., and Samuel E. Sewall, lawyers of much ability and men of high social standing, offered their services in defence of the negro. After applying to several judges of the su-

EXECUTION OF THE FUGITIVE SLAVE LAW  373

preme court of the Commonwealth, without success, for a writ of habeas corpus, they finally obtained one from Judge Woodbury, and argued the case before him. The Judge finally refused to interfere with the possession of the negro by the United States Marshal. The United States Commissioner, Mr. George T. Curtis, then heard the case, and issued the certificate for the rendition of the fugitive to his master. In the early morning of the next day, the negro was conducted by three hundred armed policemen to the wharf and placed on board a vessel bound for Savannah. The vessel sailed safely out of port, and the Fugitive Slave Law was, at last, executed in Boston.

During the trial, and for a week afterward, the city was in a fever of excitement. Meetings of the citizens were held in Tremont Temple and Washington Hall, and on the Common, at which the eloquence of Phillips, Channing, Edmund Quincy, and Horace Mann, and the violent words of Garrison and Parker, stirred the indignation of their hearers and lashed it into an almost rebellious fury. A very large part of the inhabitants felt that a stain had been put upon the city, which must be wiped out by any means necessary to accomplish it. *Excitement in Boston over the rendition of Sims.*

The summer months of 1851 now passed without any notable instances of resistance to the law, and conservative men, of both the North and the South, began to hope that the worst was over, and that the North would acquiesce without further opposition in the execution of the odious Act.

In the early autumn, however, violence again appeared. The minor outbreaks were soon overshadowed by an event which occurred at Syracuse, N. Y., in October, 1851. A negro, named Jerry McHenry, who had lived for several years in Syracuse, was suddenly *The "Jerry rescue."*

seized and carried before the United States Commissioner. In the course of the hearing he eluded the officer having him in charge, and bounded out of the court-room. He was, however, overtaken and, after a fierce struggle, recaptured and brought back. A little later, a party of highly respectable men, led by Gerrit Smith and the Rev. S. J. May, broke into the court-room, rescued the negro, and smuggled him safely across the Canadian boundary. Eighteen of these gentlemen were indicted and ordered to appear for trial. But the whole community manifested so much active sympathy with them that the matter was quietly dropped.

In his message to Congress, of December 2nd, 1851, President Fillmore referred to these cases of resistance to the execution of the law; declared the law to be required by the Constitution; denounced the opposition to its execution as directed against the Constitution and the Union itself; repeated his dictum that the Compromise Measures were a final settlement of the subjects embraced in them; and congratulated the country upon the general acquiescence in these Measures manifested throughout the Union.

*The President's rebuke.*

Two days later, Mr. Foote introduced into the Senate a resolution declaring these Measures to be a definite settlement of the questions embraced in them, and recommending acquiescence in them by all good citizens.

*Mr. Foote's finality resolutions.*

The debate upon this proposition, which began December 8th, and lasted, off and on, until February 28th, was, in the main, a discussion between four Southern members—Mr. Foote, Mr. Butler, Mr. Rhett, and Mr. Clemens—during which the history of the movements of the Southern leaders in 1850 and 1851 were brought to light, beginning with the Southern Address, issued

# EXECUTION OF THE FUGITIVE SLAVE LAW 375

from Washington before the passage of the Compromise Measures, for the purpose of producing a united action on the part of the South in behalf of Southern rights, and the call of the Nashville convention by the Mississippi legislature, and ending with the demand of the convention for the line of thirty-six degrees and thirty minutes to the Pacific Ocean, and the declaration by the convention and by conventions in Mississippi, Georgia, and South Carolina, of the abstract right of secession as a principle of the political system of the Union. It was evident that these movements had approached dangerously near to an attempt at something like practical secession, and that the Southern leaders were now anxious to underrate their significance. The Northern Senators allowed these Southern brethren to proceed with criminations and recriminations against each other, until they themselves were convinced that they would lose more by the continuance of the debate than they could gain by the passage of the resolution. After a fiery speech by Mr. Clemens, on February 28th, 1852, the attempt to pass the resolution was abandoned in the Senate.

*The failure of the resolutions to pass the Senate, but their success in the House.*

The House of Representatives, on the other hand, incited by memorials sent into it by the legislatures of New Jersey and Iowa, actually passed resolutions, on April 5th, 1852, by a large majority, declaring the finality of the Measures.

Petitions began again to pour into the Senate for the repeal of the law. Mr. Seward, Mr. Hale, and Mr. Sumner presented such petitions and tried to get a hearing upon them, but the Senate voted to lay them all on the table.

Such was the situation when the two great parties assembled in their National conventions for the nomina-

376                THE MIDDLE PERIOD

tion of their respective candidates for the presidency and vice-presidency. It was indicated from the first day of the Congressional session of 1851–52, that the finality of the Compromise Acts would be a plank in the platforms of both parties, although it was soon revealed that the Whig party leaders were divided upon the subject.

*The National conventions of 1852 and the finality of the compromise measures.*

The Democratic convention met June 1st, at Baltimore, and, on account of the three-cornered fight between Buchanan, Cass, and Douglas, was obliged to produce a "dark horse." This proved to be General Franklin Pierce, of New Hampshire, a good lawyer, a brave soldier, a fine orator, and a courtly gentleman. He was known to be a true friend to the Compromise Acts, and was entirely acceptable to the South. The platform contained the finality plank.

The Whig convention met fifteen days later, at the same place. The Northern Whigs, under the lead of Seward, were determined to defeat both Fillmore and Webster, chiefly on account of their fidelity in the execution of the Fugitive Slave Law. The Southerners were for Fillmore first, and then Webster, for the same reason. A sufficient number of the Northern delegates voted with the Southerners to put the finality plank into the platform, and then offered the Southerners one of their own fellow-citizens, General Scott, the military hero of the country. The Southerners finally accepted the offer.

If Seward desired the defeat and destruction of the Whig party, he could not have acted more adroitly. It was to be foreseen that the Northern Whigs would not be wholly faithful to their own choice upon that platform, and that many of the Southern Whigs would arrive at the conclusion that the Democratic platform and the Democratic candidate furnished stronger guarantees for

EXECUTION OF THE FUGITIVE SLAVE LAW 377

the finality of the Compromise Measures than the Whig platform and candidate did.

Clay died at the beginning of the campaign, and Webster at the end of it; and, in the midst of it, Sumner succeeded in getting in his ferocious attack on the Fugitive Slave Law, in a four hours speech before the Senate, and the Free-soilers set up a candidate, Mr. Hale, for the suffrages of the Abolitionists and the anti-slavery-extensionists. {The deaths of Clay and of Webster, and the appearance of a Free-soil candidate.} All of these events were unfavorable to the Whigs; still, they did not probably determine the result. The people were determined to have peace in regard to the slavery question, and they felt that the Democratic party was more likely to give them the peace they desired than the Whig party.

The Democratic victory was overwhelming. Twenty-seven Commonwealths gave their electoral vote for General Pierce, and only four gave theirs for General Scott; while the popular vote cast for Mr. Hale was only about one-half as large as that cast for Mr. Van Buren in 1848. {The overwhelming Democratic victory of 1852.} The Democrats themselves were surprised. Since the "era of good feeling," no presidential candidate had received such a vote, either popular or electoral, as that now given to General Pierce. The country accepted the decision, and settled down into universal acquiescence in the Compromise Measures, and in the execution of the Fugitive Slave Law, in most sections cheerfully, but in some sullenly and with bitterness of heart.

Had the slaveholders made a wise use of this, to them, most favorable turn in affairs, there is little question that they might have preserved indefinitely their peculiar institution where it existed. {The true policy of the slaveholders, and their failure to discern it.} But wisdom in the case meant that the slaveholders should themselves give no further occasion for slavery agitation. It meant that they should cease to claim the rendition of their fugitive slaves by the general Government; that they should turn their attention to perfecting the police administration in the slaveholding Commonwealths for preventing the escape of their slaves, and let the few slaves who might have cleverness enough to elude the police of these Commonwealths go; and that they should, above all things, abstain from any attempt to extend slavery beyond the limits placed upon it by existing law. The status of every inch of the territory of the United States, in reference to the legality or illegality of slavery, was now fixed, and the public opinion of the country, of the world, and of the age, would never permit that status to be altered to the advantage of slavery.

It is an interesting, though by no means an inexplicable, fact that the slaveholders in the Commonwealths south of Virginia, Kentucky, and Missouri, showed more tendency to follow this view of their best policy than those within these border Commonwealths. These latter were an efficient protection to the former in preventing the escape of slaves, while they were themselves exposed in much higher degree to loss. Still, it would have been the true policy for the slaveholders in these also to have looked to their own police administration for the recapture of their runaways before the latter had reached free soil, and to have considered that a slave having sufficient intelligence to elude this had already attained the point of mental activity and of courage which required in good morals his liberation, and made his further retention in slavery both a wrong to himself and a danger to the peace of the slaveholding community in which he might be held in bondage.

We may fairly say that the slaveholders in the more southern Commonwealths sustained the Fugitive Slave

Law more out of consideration for their brothers in the border Commonwealths than for the sake of their own immediate interests, or from their own convictions of its policy, while they would have greatly preferred the restriction of slavery to the territory south of the line of thirty-six degrees and thirty minutes to the Pacific, with some sort of a guarantee of its existence there during the Territorial period, to any chance of extending slavery north of that line by the repeal of the prohibitions already existing. It is not at all surprising, in view of this state of feeling in 1852, that, ten years later, the Confederates considered themselves left in the lurch by the border Commonwealths, in the support of whose views and interests they had done so much to provoke the North to the contest.

# CHAPTER XIX.

## THE REPEAL OF THE MISSOURI COMPROMISE

The Connection of California with the Mississippi Valley—Nebraska—Mr. Douglas' Nebraska Bill and Report—The Surprising Assumptions in the Report—Mr. Douglas' Purpose—The Report and Bill Together in Conflict with the Act of 1820—The New Section—Mr. Dixon's Proposed Amendment—Mr. Blair's Letter in Reference to Mr. Seward's Connection with Dixon's Proposition—Douglas and Dixon—Mr. Douglas' New Bill—The Free-soil Protest Against the Bill—Mr. Douglas' Reply to the Address—Mr. Chase's First Amendment to the Bill—The Southern Whigs Aroused by Mr. Wade's Accusations — Mr. Chase's Amendment Lost—Mr. Douglas' Last Change in the Wording of the Clause—Mr. Everett's Views—Mr. Houston's Opposition to the Bill—Mr. Bell's Attitude Toward the Bill—Mr. Douglas' Amendment Passed by the Senate—Mr. Chase's Amendments — Mr. Bell's Argument Against the Bill — Mr. Douglas's Final Argument—The Passage of the Kansas-Nebraska Bill by the Senate — Analysis of the Vote Upon the Bill—Development of Popular Opposition to the Bill—The Kansas-Nebraska Bill in the House—The Relation of the Administration to the Bill—President Pierce and Mr. Davis—The Bill Taken up in the Committee of the Whole of the House of Representatives—Mr. A. H. Stephens' Management of the Bill—The Bill Passed and Signed by the President—Analysis of the Vote on the Bill in the House — What the Figures Taught — The Kansas-Nebraska Act a Stupendous Fallacy.

WHEN President Fillmore's last annual message to Congress was sent in, on December 6th, 1852, the quiet of the country in regard to the slavery question was more

# REPEAL OF THE MISSOURI COMPROMISE

complete than it had been since 1830. The President did not even mention the subject. Evidently the people believed that the Measures of 1850, and their cordial endorsement in the elections just passed, had finally solved the great question, in so far as the Congress could solve it at all. But never was there a more deceptive peace. It was merely the dead calm before the dread cyclone.

This time the storm came from the Northwest. After the acquisitions of the territory upon the Pacific coast, it was immediately apparent that these new possessions must be connected, so soon as possible, with the line of Commonwealths on the west bank of the Mississippi by the Territorial organization of the country lying between. *The connection of California with the Mississippi valley.* Mr. Douglas had conceived this idea as far back as 1847, and had endeavored from that time forward to secure the attention of Congress for its realization. The seemingly more important questions involved in the Compromise Measures gave little room for the consideration of other subjects between 1848 and 1850. Now, however, that these questions had apparently received their final settlement, the moment seemed opportune for the solution of the problem of binding the Pacific slope with the settled country of the west valley of the Mississippi.

In the Congressional session of 1852–53, a bill passed the House of Representatives for organizing the region lying between Missouri and the Rocky Mountains, and between the latitudes thirty-six degrees, thirty minutes, and forty-three degrees, into the Territory of Nebraska. *Nebraska.* A vote upon the measure was, however, not reached in the Senate before the close of the session.

During the consideration of the bill in the House, Mr. Howe, of Pennsylvania, asked Mr. Giddings, of Ohio, who was a member of the committee on Territories, from which the bill had come, why there was no clause in the bill prohibiting slavery. Mr. Giddings replied that the Act of 1820 did that for all of this territory. Whereupon Mr. Howe used these significant words: "I should like to know of the gentleman of Ohio, if he has not some recollection of a compromise made since that time." Mr. Giddings quietly replied: "That does not affect this question."

During the discussion of the bill in the Senate, Mr. Atchison, of Missouri, said that one of his objections to the organization of this Territory was that Missouri would be surrounded on three sides by free soil, into which the slaves of the citizens of Missouri could easily escape, but that, as he could see no prospect of a repeal of the Act of 1820 making this region free soil, he would not be willing to delay the organization of the Territory on that account.

There is no explanation of the language used by these three gentlemen, except that Mr. Howe had conceived that, in some way or other, the Measures of 1850 had modified the Act of 1820 prohibiting slavery in the Louisiana territory above thirty-six degrees and thirty minutes, and that Mr. Giddings and Mr. Atchison had never thought of such a thing.

On December 14th, 1853, Mr. Dodge, of Iowa, introduced a bill into the Senate for the organization of Nebraska Territory. It was referred to the committee on Territories, of which Mr. Douglas was chairman.

On January 4th, 1854, Mr. Douglas presented a bill from the committee, with a special report, in which latter document the principles of the laws of the United States in respect to slavery in the Territories, as understood by the committee, or rather as Mr. Douglas under-

REPEAL OF THE MISSOURI COMPROMISE 383

stood them, were stated. The report was a more important document than the bill, since the bill, drawn in vague terms upon this subject, was to be interpreted by the principles declared in the report. The first paragraph of the report read:

<small>Mr. Douglas' Nebraska bill and report.</small>

"The principal amendments which your committee deem it their duty to commend to the favorable action of the Senate, in a special report, are those in which the principles established by the Compromise Measures of 1850, so far as they are applicable to Territorial organization, are proposed to be affirmed and carried into practical operation within the limits of the new Territory." The report then declares these principles to be: "That all questions pertaining to slavery in the Territories, and in the new States to be formed therefrom, are to be left to the decision of the people residing therein, by their appropriate representatives, to be chosen by them for that purpose: That all cases involving title to slaves, and questions of personal freedom, are to be referred to the adjudication of the local tribunals, with the right of appeal to the Supreme Court of the United States: That the provisions of the Constitution of the United States, in respect to fugitives from service, are to be carried into faithful execution in all the organized Territories the same as in the States."

These were most astonishing and confusing propositions in a variety of respects. In the first place, the claim that the Compromise Acts of 1850 contained any general principles of Territorial organization in respect to slavery, which were applicable to any other Territories than those organized under these Acts, was a surprising assumption. It was an induction from one precedent when there were half a dozen precedents against it. The fact was that the Acts of 1850 only set up a rule for a single case, a rule patched

<small>The surprising assumptions in the report.</small>

up by compromise, and not derived from any general principle. This claim was also, if admitted, highly confusing. Was it a principle of the Constitution, and therefore supreme over all Congressional policies in the case? Or was it simply a principle of Congressional policy? If the former, then it had already rendered the prohibition upon slavery in the Louisiana territory, by the Act of 1820, nugatory. If it was the latter, then it would require a new act of Congress to apply it to any other Territory than Utah and New Mexico. In the second place, the statement, also contained in the report, that there was a pronounced conflict of opinion in the country upon the question of the constitutional validity of the Act of 1820, prohibiting slavery in the Louisiana territory above thirty-six degrees and thirty minutes, was equally surprising. Nobody had heard the noise of any such conflict. The fact is, that conflict was yet to be aroused. And, lastly, it was most highly surprising and confusing that the attempt to rouse this conflict should proceed from the bosom of the party which had won its splendid victory under the peace issue upon the subject of slavery, and should be inaugurated by a member of that party from the North.

What was, or what could have been, Mr. Douglas' purpose? It is held by most historians that it was simply a reckless and dishonest bid for Southern support, in his ambitious plans to gain the presidency. Most of Mr. Douglas' political opponents at the time believed that he was animated solely by that desire. His character was, according to their view, that of a scheming politician, who would sacrifice anything and anybody for his own advancement. While we can understand this radical estimate of him by those with whom he was in daily conflict, it does seem that the historians, with his subsequent career before them, might

*Mr. Douglas' purpose.*

suspect, at least, that some conviction of the rightfulness of his views may have aided in moving him to the position which he took. Mr. Douglas was a Western Democrat; that is, he was a radical Democrat. He had, therefore, an exaggerated notion of the virtues of the people, and of the importance of local autonomy. He resented the idea that the sturdy adventurers who accomplished the first settlement of a Western Territory were not as fully capable of local self-government, from the very outset, as the "effeminate" inhabitants of an Eastern Commonwealth. He repudiated the notion that they needed any pupilage from the general Government in the management of public affairs. He was not alone in such views. It is safe to say that the mass of the people in his section held the same views at that time. They have not progressed much beyond them now. Is it not, then, fair to say that Mr. Douglas, in all probability, really believed that the reference of the questions in regard to slavery to the residents of each Territory, as well as to those of each "State," was the true principle of the political science of the Republic, and the true policy of its legislation? If his convictions and his ambition went hand in hand, and if his convictions were not the product of his ambition, should he be so harshly criticised for declaring them? It is true that his announcement of them filled the land with clamor and angry dispute, and that their adoption by Congress led to violence, bloodshed, and war; but can we conclude that he had any conception whatsoever that this could be the result of them? Is it not far more probable that he thought the quiet of the country would be confirmed and forever established by their general acceptance? There is certainly ground for this view of his motives. It is certainly very improbable that there was ever any balancing, in his mind, of risks to his country's peace and safety against his ambition for the presidency. It is much more probable that he believed his principles, without his presidency, would contribute, in high degree, to the peace and welfare of his country, but that, taken together with his presidency, they would shed untold blessings upon the land. This is no unusual psychology. It is decidedly common.

Mr. Douglas did not, however, insert his doctrine of popular sovereignty in the Territories, and his dictum as to the repeal of the slavery prohibition in the Act of 1820 by the principles of the Acts of 1850, in the bill. Possibly he thought it unnecessary. Possibly he did not venture to do so. Possibly he did intend to leave things in such an ambiguous shape that one interpretation might be put upon them in one section, and a somewhat different one in another. He would hardly have been an American politician if he had not, at some time or other in his life, practised something of this kind. This is what they call feeling the public pulse, which is a main point in the practice of democratic statesmanship. It is not particularly edifying to the academic statesman, but it is business, and Americans are a business people. Mr. Douglas simply modelled the bill after the Utah and New Mexico bills, in respect to slavery, that is, he made no mention of the subject in that part of the bill which provided for the Territorial period, but added a clause which read: "When admitted as a State, the said Territory, or any portion of the same, shall be received into the Union, with or without slavery, as its Constitution may prescribe at the time of its admission."

*The doctrines of the report at first not inserted in the bill.*

Taken apart from the report, the bill might be interpreted as not in conflict with the Act of 1820, but taken with the report, it meant the repeal of the Act of 1820, and the attribution of all power over the question of

# REPEAL OF THE MISSOURI COMPROMISE 387

slavery in the Territory to those who might squat upon its soil. Of course it was entirely within the power of Congress to repeal the Act of 1820. The restraints resting upon Congress in regard to this matter were moral, not legal. If Congress would, nevertheless, do it, it must do it in the form of a statute, and not in that of a report doubting the constitutionality of the Act, or even declaring it unconstitutional. It was entirely natural that the demand should be made for clearing the bill of its ambiguities.

*The report and bill together in conflict with the Act of 1820.*

Before the demand came, however, the committee itself did something in this direction. When the bill was printed, on January 7th, it contained twenty sections. On the 10th, a revised edition of it appeared, which contained twenty-one sections. The last section was the dictum of the report in regard to the principles of the Measures of 1850 upon the subject of slavery in the Territories. The committee explained that it had been left out of the first draft by a clerical error. This change did not, however, clear the bill of all ambiguity. The added provision was declaratory only, and did not expressly repeal the Act of 1820.

*The new section.*

At length, on the 16th, Mr. Dixon, of Kentucky, gave notice to the Senate that he should move, as an amendment to the bill, a provision expressly repealing the Act of 1820 in so far as it prohibited slavery in any of the Territories of the United States.

*Mr. Dixon's proposed amendment.*

In a letter of May 17th, 1873, to Mr. Gideon Welles, Mr. Montgomery Blair wrote of Mr. Seward: "I shall never forget how shocked I was at his telling me that he was the man who put Archy Dixon, the Whig Senator from Kentucky in 1854, up to moving the repeal of the

Missouri compromise, as an amendment to Douglas' first Kansas [Nebraska?] bill, and had himself forced the repeal by that movement, and had thus brought to life the Republican party. Dixon was to out-Herod Herod at the South, and he was to out-Herod Herod at the North."

<small>Mr. Blair's letter in reference to Mr. Seward's connection with Dixon's proposition.</small>

If this be true, it was a most reprehensible trick of unscrupulous politics. Mr. Seward scoffed at the doctrine of "popular sovereignty" in the Territories as arrant nonsense, and knew that the assertion of any such doctrine as a principle of the law of the country in respect to Territorial organization would rouse the North to angry and bitter resistance. What he did, he did with his eyes open. His vision did not probably reach so far as to civil war, but he knew that the risks of another slavery agitation were very grave. Neither could the ambiguity in Mr. Douglas' bill, and the necessity for relieving it of this obscurity, palliate such an offense. If he desired to make Mr. Douglas' bill entirely plain he should have done this, not by holding out a temptation to the South to enter upon a new course of slavery extension, but by an amendment asserting the continuing validity of the slavery prohibition in the Act of 1820. Mr. Sumner did this very thing on the next day. It was, however, too late to chain the spirit which Dixon's fatal move had loosed.

It is said that Mr. Douglas was surprised and disconcerted by Mr. Dixon's notice, and endeavored to dissuade him from carrying out his expressed intention, but was finally convinced by Mr. Dixon that the proposed amendment was only the fair and honest statement of constitutional principles, and of the legal results of the Compromise of 1850, and only made distinct and express what was unclear, though implied, in the bill.

<small>Douglas and Dixon.</small>

# REPEAL OF THE MISSOURI COMPROMISE 389

On the 23rd, Mr. Douglas brought in a new bill, and offered it as a substitute for the original bill. The new bill contained a clause declaring that that part of the Act of 1820 prohibiting slavery in the Louisiana territory above thirty-six degrees and thirty minutes was inoperative, being contrary to, and superseded by, the principles of the legislation of 1850. Mr. Douglas' new bill changed the southern boundary from thirty-six degrees and thirty minutes to thirty-seven degrees, made the northern boundary run up to the forty-ninth parallel west of Minnesota Territory, and cut this vast domain of nearly five hundred thousand square miles in area into two Territories by the fortieth parallel of latitude, the one to the north of it to be called Nebraska, and the one to the south of it Kansas. Mr. Dixon immediately expressed himself as satisfied with the provisions of the new bill, and said that they fulfilled the purposes of the amendment which he had intended to offer, and that he should, therefore, withhold the same. The Senate agreed to take up the bill on the following Monday.

*Mr. Douglas' new bill.*

On the same day that Mr. Douglas presented this second bill, there appeared in the *National Era*, the Abolition journal at Washington, and in several New York City papers, the noted address, signed by Messrs. Chase, Sumner, Wade, Smith, and De Witt, in which the Douglas bill was denounced in the most trenchant language as "a gross violation of a sacred pledge, as a criminal betrayal of precious rights, as a part and parcel of an atrocious plot to exclude from a vast unoccupied region immigrants from the Old World and free laborers from our own States, and convert it into a dreary region of despotism inhabited by masters and slaves." The contents of this celebrated paper constituted, it may be said, the

*The Free-soil protest against the bill.*

first draft of the creed of the party to be founded on the doctrine of resistance to slavery extension, the Republican party. The propositions contained in it drove Mr. Douglas to a fierce diatribe against their authors, in which he included an elaborate argument in defence of his dictum, that the Measures of 1850 had rendered the slavery prohibition in the Act of 1820 inoperative. He contended that the fact that Congress had, in the joint resolution admitting Texas, provided that in Texan territory north of the line of thirty-six degrees and thirty minutes slavery should be prohibited, proved that Congress and the people of the United States understood the legislation of 1820 to mean that the line of thirty-six degrees and thirty minutes was to be run through any and all territory that might be subsequently acquired by the United States; that the refusal of Congress to do this in regard to the territory acquired from Mexico had made the establishment of a new principle in regard to slavery in the Territories necessary; that that principle, as established by the legislation of 1850, was the neutrality of Congress in the question, and the right of the residents in each Territory to settle the question for themselves; and that this new principle had superseded the old principle and rendered all legislation under the old principle inoperative.

*Mr. Douglas' reply to the address.*

Such jurisprudence in respect to the effect upon each other of statutes relating to different and distinct Territories had never been heard before, and it was easy to show it to be a tissue of sophistries from beginning to end. It was entirely evident that Mr. Douglas and his committee shrank from proposing a bare and bald repeal of the slavery prohibition in the Act of 1820, and sought to avoid the responsibility of doing so under the convenient claim that it had already been repealed. But

# REPEAL OF THE MISSOURI COMPROMISE 391

Mr. Chase was determined to make them take this responsibility, and to expose their fallacies in their attempts to escape it. On February 3rd, Mr. Chase moved to remove from the bill the words referring to the Measures of 1850, and their effect upon the Act of 1820, and make the bill simply repeal the slavery prohibition of the Act of 1820, in so far as it applied to the Territories to be organized by the bill. Mr. Chase supported his amendment in a powerful speech, in which he demonstrated most clearly the fallacy and the duplicity of the doctrine which held that the legislation of 1850 in regard to Utah and New Mexico had repealed the legislation of 1820 in regard to the Louisiana territory north of thirty-six degrees and thirty minutes. Both he and his colleague, Mr. Wade, went, however, too far in denouncing the subterfuge as a conspiracy between the Southerners and the friends of Douglas to extend slavery. It was especially imprudent, to say the least, in Mr. Wade to do so. The Southern Whigs were highly incensed at the charge of conspiring with Northern Democrats, made by one of their own party, and they repudiated the accusation with great earnestness. Besides this, the Douglas idea of "popular sovereignty," or, as we now call it, home rule, in the Territories, had won many adherents. There is no question that a great many men, in both the North and the South, now began to feel that Mr. Douglas had discovered the true principle in regard to slavery in the Territories. Mr. Chase's amendment was lost by a vote of thirty to thirteen. The thirteen voting in favor of the amendment were all from the North. Of those voting against it, ten were from the North, and twenty from the South. Nineteen Senators, ten of whom were from the South, did not vote at all. The

*[margin notes: Mr. Chase's amendment to the bill. The Southern Whigs aroused by Mr. Wade's accusations. The Douglas doctrine convincing to many.]*

vote meant that the large majority of those voting held that, in some way or other, the legislation of 1850 had repealed the slavery prohibition in the legislation of 1820. This was execrable jurisprudence, and even Mr. Cass, who was really the father of the idea of home rule in the Territories, dissented from it, and voted for Mr. Chase's amendment.

*Mr. Chase's amendment lost.*

In spite of this support by the majority, Mr. Douglas was apparently disquieted by the attitude of Mr. Cass, and by the arguments against the correctness of his doctrine. He, himself, now moved to strike out of the bill the words: "which was superseded by the principles of the legislation of 1850, commonly called the Compromise Measures, and is hereby declared inoperative," and to insert instead thereof the words: "which being inconsistent with the principle of non-intervention by Congress with slavery in the States and Territories, as recognized by the legislation of 1850, commonly called the Compromise Measures, is hereby declared inoperative and void, it being the true intent and meaning of this Act not to legislate slavery into any Territory or State, nor exclude it therefrom, but to leave the people thereof perfectly free to form and regulate their domestic institutions in their own way, subject only to the Constitution of the United States."

*Mr. Douglas' last change in the wording of the clause.*

In a most able argument, remarkable both for its strong logic and its admirable temper, Mr. Everett demonstrated the weakness of Mr. Douglas' proposition in its last form, the declaration of inconsistency between the legislation of 1820 and that of 1850. He showed conclusively that, in place of an inconsistency, here were simply two policies in reference to different Territories, in which different conditions and relations obtained. He predicted that the

*Mr. Everett's views.*

insistence upon the same policy for all the Territories would lead to the struggle for determining whether they should be all slave or all free, and he demonstrated that "popular sovereignty" in the Territories was an illusion, since Congress could not by any act of its own divest itself of its duty, laid upon it by the Constitution, to legislate for the Territories. Mr. Everett was a member of the committee on Territories, from which the bill had proceeded, and his views should, on this account, have possessed an added weight.

Mr. Houston, of Texas, another member of the committee, now declared himself against the bill, on the ground, among other reasons, that it would reopen the slavery question by the destruction of one of the great measures upon which the settlement of that question rested. *Mr. Houston's opposition to the bill.*

It was furthermore suspected that Mr. Bell, of Tennessee, another member of the committee, was opposed to the bill. This suspicion turned out to be true. The bill can hardly be regarded therefore as having been reported by the committee at all. *Mr. Bell's attitude toward the bill.* The committee consisted of six Senators, and it was at last found that it had, at no time, received the support of more than three. Of these three, two were from the North, Douglas, of Illinois, and Jones, of Iowa, and one was from the South, Johnson, of Arkansas.

The vote upon this amendment was taken on February 15th. Thirty-five Senators voted for it, and ten against it. Of those voting for it, twenty-four were from the North and eleven from the South. Of those voting against it, nine were from the North and one, Mr. Houston, was from the South. *Mr. Douglas' amendment passed by the Senate.* Mr. Bell voted for the amendment for the reason, as he afterwards explained, that he thought Mr. Douglas ought to be allowed to perfect his bill.

Mr. Chase now suspected that there might be some catch concealed in the last words of the amendment just adopted. These words, it will be remembered, were: "subject only to the Constitution of the United States." Mr. Chase, therefore, moved to add the words: "under which the people of the Territory, through their appropriate representatives, may, if they see fit, prohibit the existence of slavery therein." Mr. Chase now put the home rule principle in regard to slavery in the Territories to the test, for if the people of a Territory could not, under the Constitution of the United States, prohibit slavery in the Territories, then was the Douglas doctrine a mere deception, a mere jugglery of words. Mr. Chase put his proposition, however, in a form which appeared one-sided, and Mr. Badger, of North Carolina, the best constitutional lawyer from the South in the Senate, contended that Mr. Chase's amendment would have the effect of denying to the Territories the power to admit slavery, and thus destroy, from that side, the home rule principle of the bill. To remedy this defect, Mr. Pratt moved to amend Mr. Chase's proposition so as to make it read that the people might introduce or prohibit slavery in the Territories. But this was an amendment to Mr. Chase's amendment to Mr. Douglas' amendment, and was held to be unparliamentary, unless Mr. Chase would accept it, and incorporate it into his amendment. This he refused to do, on the ground, first, that he did not believe that the Territories could, under the Constitution, introduce slavery, and, second, on the ground that the union of his proposition and that of Mr. Pratt in a single amendment would unite those who did not believe that the people of a Territory could introduce slavery with those who did not believe they could prohibit slavery against the entire amendment, and probably defeat it, while, if the two propositions could be voted on separately, they would both probably pass, and the bill would be cleared of all ambiguity.

Mr. Chase's attitude toward Mr. Pratt's motion compelled the Senate to vote upon his proposition separately, and the amendment was lost by a vote of thirty-six to ten. *Mr. Chase's amendment lost.*

Just before the close of the debate on Mr. Chase's motion, Mr. Walker, of Wisconsin, startled the Senate by the declaration that the repeal of the Act of 1820 prohibiting slavery would revive the old French law legitimizing slavery in all of the territory acquired from France. *Mr. Badger's amendment.* Both Mr. Benjamin and Mr. Badger said it would not have that effect, but on different grounds. In order to quiet apprehension on this point, and remove the difficulty out of the way of the passage of the bill, Mr. Badger gave notice that so soon as the vote should be taken on Mr. Chase's motion, he should move an amendment to the bill providing that "nothing contained in this Act shall be construed to revive or put in force any law or regulation, which may have existed prior to 1820, either protecting, establishing, prohibiting, or abolishing slavery." After the vote upon Mr. Chase's motion, Mr. Badger offered this amendment, and it was voted, without debate, by a very large majority.

Mr. Chase now turned his assaults upon other points of the bill. Mr. Douglas had been impressed by the taunts of the opponents of the bill that home rule was to be granted to the people of the Territories only upon the subject of *Mr. Chase's third amendment.* slavery, but that they were to continue in all other respects subject to the control of the general Government, and he now moved to strike out the veto power of Congress over Territorial legislation, in the cases in hand, and to so modify the usual veto power of the Territorial governors as to allow a two-thirds majority of the Territorial legislatures to overcome it. These propositions were voted without debate. Whereupon Mr. Chase moved that the governors, secretaries, and judges of the two Territories be elected by the people instead of being appointed by the President. This was logical, but it made the "squatter-sovereignty" doctrine ridiculous. It was, therefore, rejected with a considerable show of spirit.

Mr. Chase now moved that the whole country should be organized as one Territory instead of two. He seemed *Mr. Chase's fourth amendment.* to anticipate that if two should be established at the same time, the slaveholders would claim one. This proved to be a correct suspicion. It was subsequently declared throughout the South that the purpose in forming two Territories was to give one to the North and the other to the South. And when the North made the fight for Kansas, it was really felt in the South by the mass of the people that a tacit agreement had been violated. The Senators in favor of the bill had now come to think that Mr. Chase was simply endeavoring to discredit the bill, and they quickly voted this motion down by a large majority.

Down to this juncture, the bill had been considered in the Senate as a committee of the Whole. It was now *Mr. Bell's argument against the bill.* reported to the Senate as amended by this committee, and, on March 3rd, it came to the vote upon its final passage. It was at this point that Mr. Bell revealed his opposition to the bill, and made his great argument, the greatest effort of his long and useful life, against it. The speech was chiefly a logical and an eloquent elaboration of the three propositions, that popular sovereignty could not be established in the Territories by an Act of Congress, that the passage of the bill before the Senate attempting it would produce a vast development of the anti-slavery sentiment at the North, and that no practical benefits whatsoever could accrue to the South by the repeal of the restriction upon slavery extension in the Act of 1820. But the Southerners would not listen to these words of wisdom from their own greatest colleague.

Mr. Douglas is generally represented as having closed the debate, although Mr. Houston spoke briefly after him in opposition to the measure. Mr. Douglas' argument was masterful from every point of view but the highest. His chief proposition was, that, when his committee were charged with the duty of framing the bill, they were forced to choose between the principle of Congressional intervention in the Territories, in the matter of slavery, on the one hand, the principle of 1820, the principle which had, for thirty years, filled the land with agitation and conflict, and had been a standing menace to the existence of the Union, and the principle of Congressional non-intervention, on the other hand, the principle of the Measures of 1850, the principle which had tranquillized the country and cemented anew the Union, the principle which both of the two great political parties had unequivocally approved in their platforms of 1852, and which the people of the whole country had just as unequivocally approved in the elections of 1852. And his conclusion from this proposition was, that, as servants of the people who had established this principle of Congressional non-intervention, his committee were morally obligated to make it the principle of the bill presented by them for the organization of the new Territories, and that whoever arraigned him and his committee for so doing virtually arraigned the people of the United States. It was a

*Mr. Douglas' final argument.*

most excellent and refined bit of demagogy, and it fell upon an audience whose mental *niveau* was not quite high enough to distinguish between it and sound reasoning. He enforced this argument by another piece of catching demagogism, which, though not quite so refined, was equally effective. It was the proud and boastful assertion that American citizens were capable of self-government anywhere, whether in "States" or Territories, and under all conditions, whether aided by long established customs, or without any such guides to steady them in their progress. It was evident that his opponents preferred to avoid this point, and that he was sure he had them upon it. He was so thoroughly democratic in his own feelings that he entertained no doubt as to the triumph of his argument when stated in this form.

A few minutes before five o'clock on the morning of March 4th, after a continuous session of seventeen hours, the vote upon the bill was taken, resulting in thirty-seven voices in its favor and fourteen against it. Eleven Senators had not voted. Of these, three sent word that, if they could have been present, they would have voted for the bill, and one that he would have voted against it. There were also two vacancies at the moment, one in the Vermont delegation, and one in that of North Carolina. This reduced the number of those who actually refrained from voting, though present, to five. These gentlemen were Mr. Everett, of Massachusetts, Mr. Wright, of New Jersey, Mr. Cooper, of Pennsylvania, Mr. Clayton, of Delaware, and Mr. Pearce, of Maryland, all Whigs with the exception of Mr. Wright.

*The passage of the Kansas-Nebraska bill by the Senate.*

Counting the names of those who announced how they would have voted had they been able to be present, and considering the Commonwealths in whose delegations there were vacancies as represented fully by the one member from each, we may say that, in the Senate, New Hampshire, Michigan, Indiana, Illinois, Iowa, California, Virginia, Kentucky, Missouri, North Carolina, Arkansas, South Carolina, Georgia, Alabama, Mississippi, Florida, and Louisiana voted for the bill; that Maine, Vermont, Rhode Island, New York, Ohio, and Wisconsin voted against the bill; that Connecticut, Tennessee, and Texas were divided; and that Massachusetts, New Jersey, Pennsylvania, Delaware, and Maryland were doubtful. Not a single Northern Whig voted for the bill, and only two Northern Whigs failed to vote against it. One Southern Whig, Mr. Bell, voted against it, and two Southern Whigs, Mr. Clayton and Mr. Pearce, failed to vote for it. Every Southern Democrat, except only Mr. Houston, voted for the bill, while, even if we count Mr. Chase and Mr. Sumner as Democrats, only six Northern Democrats voted against it. The bill may thus be fairly considered to have been a Western and Southern measure, and a Democratic measure. The Western Democracy, with its crude and radical notions about local self-government, invited the South into a position which turned out to be a snare and a pitfall. It is not meant by this that the Western Democracy was insincere, but only that it was crude and vulgarly over self-confident. And it is not meant that the South was insincere, but only too eager to vindicate its honor and dignity, by obliterating the inequality with the North in regard to the common territory of the Union, under which it fancied it had suffered since the restriction placed upon slavery extension by the Act of 1820.

*Analysis of the vote upon the bill.*

If the bill had been subjected to the plebiscite on February 1st, it is very probable that the people in the Northern Commonwealths would have sustained the positions taken by their respective Senators. Had this been done on March 1st, it is probable that this would not have been the case in some of the Northern Commonwealths, whose Senators voted for the measure. And had it been done on April 1st, it is practically certain that it would not have been. After February 1st, there was developed throughout the North a very strong opposition to the bill among the people. The most influential newspapers denounced it. Numerous meetings, largely attended, protested against it. The legislatures of several of the Commonwealths passed resolutions condemning it. And the clergy generally arraigned it as immoral, inhuman, and irreligious. The movements against it seem to have been spontaneous and to have been connected with each other only by the common sentiment against the extension of slavery. It is, however, probable that the Address to the people, issued by Mr. Chase and his Free-soil friends in the latter part of January, furnished the necessary excitant. The Address seems to have been the text from which most of these articles, protests, memorials, speeches, and sermons were drawn. When the bill was sent to the House of Representatives, it was thus evident to all impartial observers that its growing unpopularity at the North would be a very great obstacle to its passage by the House. Its friends felt that they must get it through speedily or see it lost altogether.

*Development of popular opposition to the bill.*

Already, on January 31st, Mr. Richardson, of Illinois, Mr. Douglas' lieutenant in the House of Representatives, had reported from the House committee on Territories a bill for the organization of the Territories of Kansas and Nebraska, which was the same in substance and language as that reported by Mr. Douglas to the Senate. It had been discussed a little in the committee of the Whole House, but had slumbered there after February 15th.

# REPEAL OF THE MISSOURI COMPROMISE 401

On March 7th, the Senate bill was sent into the House for concurrence. It was taken up for consideration on the twenty-first, and, after some parliamentary passes, was referred to the House committee on Territories.

*The Kansas-Nebraska bill in the House.*

Some of the historians teach that this would have been the end of the bill, except for the interference of President Pierce and his two most trusted advisers, Mr. Caleb Cushing and Mr. Jefferson Davis. Mr. Davis relates his connection with the matter in his own book. He says that, on Sunday morning, January 22nd, gentlemen from the two Congressional committees on Territories called at his house and asked his aid in obtaining an interview with the President; that he went with them to the executive mansion, and secured for them the desired access to the President; that the President listened patiently to the reading of the bill for organizing Kansas and Nebraska; and that the President decided that the bill "rested upon sound constitutional principles, and recognized in it only a return to that rule which had been infringed by the Compromise of 1820, and the restoration of which had been foreshadowed by the legislation of 1850." Mr. Davis furthermore specifically denies that the measure was inspired by President Pierce or any member of his Cabinet. Of course, though not inspired, it may have been aided on the way of its passage through Congress by the Administration. The proof upon which these historians chiefly rely, in their assertion that it was so aided, was the fact that the editorials in the Washington *Union* supported the bill, and the claim that this paper was the organ of the Administration. But Mr. Sidney Webster, President Pierce's private secretary at the time, has recently declared that the Washington *Union* was not President

*The relation of the Administration to the bill.*

26

Pierce's organ in the Kansas-Nebraska matter, or in any other matter; that President Pierce had no organ.

The character of President Pierce was that of a punctilious gentleman. Mr. Davis resembled him much in this general trait. In fact, it was said to have been this likeness which drew them so closely together in their friendship for each other. Men of such character are not inclined to meddle, and a strong positive evidence is necessary to substantiate any such charge against them. There is no doubt that the President's view of the doctrine of the bill was well known. There is no doubt that there were members of Congress who made a chief point of coinciding with the Administration upon every subject, and who thought that such servility would give weight to their recommendations for official positions. And there is no doubt that the President appointed some persons to office recommended by such members. But no satisfactory evidence has been as yet produced to prove that President Pierce gave or promised any patronage to any member for supporting the bill, or withheld any to punish any member for not supporting it. In fact, the President's attitude toward the two factions of the Democratic party in New York in the matter of appointments, making selections from both in almost equal numbers, without regard to the Free-soil sentiments of the "Softs," manifests a quite different spirit from that with which these historians represent him to have been animated in meddling with the passage of the Kansas-Nebraska bill.

*President Pierce and Mr. Davis.*

And, finally, the inconsistency which these historians find between the President's message of December preceding and his attitude toward the Kansas-Nebraska bill can be so explained as to appear a perfect consistency. What the President said in his message was that the acquiescence of distinguished citizens in the Compromise Measures of 1850 had given renewed vigor to our institutions, and restored a sense of repose and security to the public mind throughout the Union, and that this repose should suffer no shock during his official term. If, now, we consider these measures of 1850 as containing the principle of home rule in the Territories in regard to the question of slavery, and if we attribute the repose of the public mind upon this subject to that principle, would it not be maintaining that repose to apply this principle in the organization of the new Territories, and would it not be destructive of that repose to undertake to settle the slavery question in the new Territories by an act of Congress, either original or confirmatory? This view is certainly intelligible. It was professed and advanced by all the supporters of the bill. It was unquestionably the view which the President took of the matter. It proved to be an erroneous view, but the views which mortal men hold, and conscientiously hold, are very frequently erroneous.

*The President's consistency.*

The Senate bill slept in the committee of the Whole of the House of Representatives from March 21st until May 8th. During this period its friends were undoubtedly working for it, and its opponents against it. By the latter date the leaders in favor of the bill knew that they had a reliable majority in the House, and, on that day, Mr. Richardson moved that the House go into committee of the Whole, for the purpose of taking up the House Kansas-Nebraska bill for consideration. After much parliamentary fencing, this was accomplished. Mr. Richardson then proposed to substitute the Senate bill, shorn of the provision in it confining suffrage and office-holding in these Territories

*The bill taken up in the committee of the Whole of the House of Representatives.*

to American citizens, for the House bill. The opponents of the bill now entered upon a course of obstruction, and, although there was a safe majority of about twenty in favor of the bill, they prevented such a vote being taken in the committee of the Whole, as would bring the matter to a crisis, for about two weeks. By this time Mr. Richardson seems to have been completely demoralized, and Mr. Alexander H. Stephens came forward and took the management of the bill into his own hands. He moved to strike out the enacting clause of the House bill. According to the rules of the House, this motion took the precedence of all motions to amend, and the effect of it would be, if passed, equivalent to the rejection of the bill, upon the happening of which the committee must rise and report its action to the House. The House could then refuse to concur with the report of the committee of the Whole, upon the happening of which Mr. Richardson could then offer the Senate bill, as a substitute, in the House, and in the House the obstructive tactics of the opposition could be dealt with as they could not be in the committee of the Whole. Mr. Stephens explained his tactics to the committee, in order that the friends of the bill might know how to vote. The opponents of the bill called this procedure a new "gag," but Mr. Stephens remained firm, and drove the Senate bill in this manner through the House by a vote of one hundred and thirteen to one hundred. The Senate concurred in the omission of the provision limiting suffrage and office-holding in the Territories to American citizens; and the President signed the bill, on May 30th.

*Mr. A. H. Stephens' management of the bill.*

*The bill passed and signed by the President.*

Eighty-seven members from the North, of whom forty-five were Whigs, counting the Free-soilers as Whigs, and forty-two of whom were Democrats, voted against

REPEAL OF THE MISSOURI COMPROMISE 405

the bill; while only forty-four members from the North, all Democrats, voted for it. Sixty-nine members from the South, of whom fifty-seven were Democrats and twelve were Whigs, voted for the bill; while seven Whigs and two Democrats from the South voted against it.

*Analysis of the vote on the bill in the House.*

These figures pretty well disposed of the claim that the bill was a tender from the North to the South. It was simply a Western and Southern Democratic measure. Taken together with the vote in the Senate, these figures also showed that the Whig party was a party opposed to slavery extension, unanimously so in the North, and in some degree in the South. They revealed that the Whig party in the North was to be merged in a Northern party with the Free-soil element of the Democratic party, and was to be overwhelmed in the South by the union of the pro-slavery-extension Whigs with the Democrats. They indicated that one sectional party was soon to hold the majority in the North, and another in the South; and gave thus the fearful warning that the North was, at last, to be arrayed against the South upon the subject which was of greater interest to the South, in the minds of the slaveholders, than the Union itself.

*What the figures taught.*

From the point of view of the present, we are compelled to regard the passage of the Kansas-Nebraska Act as probably the greatest error which the Congress of the United States ever committed, and the arguments by which it was supported as among the most specious fallacies that have ever misled the minds of men. We must take this ground, unless we assume that we could not have solved the slavery problem in any other way than we did, and at any less cost. If we make this assumption, we may then consider this Act as providential, in

*The Kansas-Nebraska Act a stupendous fallacy.*

that it precipitated a crisis, which was bound to come, and which would only have been made more terrible by delay. While, however, we of the succeeding generation may explain the place of this Act in our history in this way, no considerations of this kind can justify the men who produced it, and placed it upon the statute-book. That God should "make the wrath of man to praise him" does not excuse the wrath of man.

# CHAPTER XX.

## THE STRUGGLE FOR KANSAS

Eli Thayer and His Emigrant Aid Scheme—Reports in Regard to
its Character and Purposes—The Missouri "Border Ruffian"
of 1854—Nebraska for the North and Kansas for the South—
General Atchison—Dr. Charles Robinson—The First Party of
Emigrants—The Platte County "Self-defensive Association"—
The Founding of Lawrence—First Invasion of the Missourians—Governor A. H. Reeder—The Second Invasion of the
Missourians and the Election of the Delegate to Congress—The
Indignation of the North—The Republican Party—The Third
Invasion of the Missourians—Governor Reeder and the Territorial Elections—The Organization of the First Legislature of
Kansas Territory—The Topeka Constitution—The Removal of
Governor Reeder; and His Election as Congressional Delegate
—Establishment of the "Free-state" Government—The First
Violence—The "Free-state" Government and the Administration—The New Governor, Shannon, and the "Law and Order" Party—John Brown—The President's Proclamation—
The Congressional Committee to the Territory—Application for
Admission—The "Treason Indictments"—The Sacking of
Lawrence—The Attack on Senator Sumner—The Pottawattomie Massacres—The Battle at Black Jack—The Governor's
Proclamation, Enforced by United States Soldiers—The Passage of the Bill for the Admission of Kansas by the House—
Dispersal of the "Free-state" Legislature by Colonel Sumner
—The "Free-state" Directory—The Treaty of August 17th—
The New Invasion from Missouri—General Smith's Attitude
Toward Invaders—The failure of "Popular Sovereignty" in
the Territories—The New Governor Establishes Peace by
Means of the Army of the United States—The Judicial Contribution to Kansas History.

THE passage of the Kansas-Nebraska Act, the purchase of nearly fifty thousand square miles of territory from Mexico on the Southern boundary of New Mexico, and the issue of a manifesto from Ostend by the Ministers of the United States to Great Britain, France, and Spain, Messrs. Buchanan, Mason, and Soulé, advising the acquisition of Cuba by the United States, together with the preparation of filibustering expeditions in the South for the execution of this and similar designs, all coming within the same year, 1854, seemed to be sufficient evidence of a fixed plan among the slaveholders for the extension of slavery and the increase of the number of slaveholding Commonwealths in the Union, and roused the people of the North to an appreciation of the impending danger and to extraordinary exertions for meeting the same and warding it off.

During the debate upon the Kansas-Nebraska bill in Congress, it does not seem to have been generally appreciated that it might, after all, turn out to be a Free-soil measure, and that the question whether it would be such or not in a specific case resolved itself into the problem of immigration. There lived, however, in the town of Worcester, Mass., a shrewd, far seeing business man, with whose shrewdness, however, ideality and patriotism were mingled in an uncommon degree, who immediately comprehended the situation from this point of view. This man was the now well known and universally honored Eli Thayer. Before the Kansas-Nebraska bill had become law, the idea in his mind had ripened into a wide-reaching plan. This plan was the organization of an emigrant aid society, with an immense capital, the purpose of which should be to foster emigration from the Northern Commonwealths and the European states into the Territories and the slaveholding Commonwealths of the Union, to the end that a Free-soil population should gain control of them, and prohibit or abolish slavery in them by their own local acts. Mr. Thayer reasoned with himself that masters would be very timid about immigrating into a Territory with their slaves until the question should be determined whether slavery should have a legal existence in the Territory, while men without such impediments would go boldly forward and occupy the country, and vote the free status for the Territory; and again, that with only about one-fourth of the white population of the slaveholding Commonwealths pecuniarily interested in slavery, the immigration of a few thousand active anti-slavery men into these would finally turn the balance at the polls against the further existence of the institution in the slaveholding Commonwealths themselves. The plan was so comprehensive that most of Mr. Thayer's friends thought it visionary, and he modified it, after having obtained his charter from the legislature of Massachusetts, limiting it to the settlement of the Territories, and especially to that of Kansas Territory, by anti-slavery men. The organization, as thus finally effected, counted among its directors some of the purest, most patriotic, and most capable men of the country—Mr. A. A. Lawrence, Dr. Samuel Cabot, Mr. John Lowell, Mr. Moses H. Grinnell, Rev. Edward E. Hale, Rev. Horace Bushnell, Professor Benjamin Silliman, and others of the like fame and fortune. The way in which they proposed to accomplish their purpose was by lessening the hardships of the journey to the distant country, and the hardships of life in the new country. They proposed to organize the emigrants into companies, procure transportation for them at the most favorable rates, build hotels, boarding-houses, mills, school-houses, churches—in a word to send capital in advance of population, in order to attract a good, law-abiding population by planting for them the advantages and conveniences of civilization in the new country. It was a noble scheme, and none the less so because of the idea of making it pay ultimately as a business venture.

It cannot be said that it was a movement entirely new in American history, although this was charged by many of the politicians, both of the North and of the South. A number of the American colonies were originally planted under the auspices of corporations in the motherland, and others were formed by companies of immigrants for the purpose of securing more freedom than the Old World afforded. It is difficult to see how any objection could have been found to such an association, animated with such motives and purposes, and operating through such means, and yet it was charged, even by Northern men, with the responsibility for all the outrages perpetrated in Kansas during the stormy period of 1855-56. Even the President of the United States denounced it with great severity.

*Not an entirely new thing in American history.*

*Denunciations of it as an odious innovation.*

The view held by the President and his friends, both of the North and of the South, was that no aid should be allowed to be given, and no incentive offered, by any person or organization to any other person, to go to, and settle in, the common Territories of the Union, but that every emigrant should go entirely upon his own impulse, and be sustained entirely by his own means. This they regarded as the only natural and fair method for carrying into effect the principle of popular sovereignty in the Territories. Such a view was a perfect travesty of popular liberty, and manifests the tyranny which slavery was imposing upon the minds of freemen.

Mr. Thayer's company was never organized under its original charter, but under a charter obtained in 1855. During the period when the counter movements, to be described, were set on foot against it in Missouri, it had no corporate existence at all, but was a movement conducted by three private gentlemen, Mr. Thayer, Mr. Lawrence, and Mr. J. M. S. Williams. Moreover, the establishments which they founded in Kansas were open to use by immigrants from any and every part of the Union, or of the world, without distinction. Such was the organization which was made the justification, or better the subterfuge, for excesses, which had never before been committed in the history of the building of the Commonwealths of the Union.

*The organization of Mr. Thayer's company.*

During the early summer of 1854, exaggerated and false reports in regard to the character, purposes, and means of the proposed Emigrant Aid Company were circulated through Missouri and the entire South. It was said that an organization, chartered by the legislature of Massachusetts, possessing an immense capital, was preparing to abolitionize Kansas by means of military colonies, recruited from the slums of the Eastern cities, and planted in Kansas with all the munitions of war, to be used not only when necessary for their own defence, but for keeping out immigrants from the South. The notorious B. F. Stringfellow, co-editor with one Kelly of the *Squatter Sovereign*, a paper published at Atchison, which professed to be the organ of the Washington Government in western Missouri, rang the changes upon these misrepresentations in his newspaper, and advised that the emigrants sent out by the Aid Society be met with the weapons of their choice, which he charged were those of violence.

*Reports in regard to its character and purposes.*

The population of western Missouri was then such as to receive ready impression from such representations, and respond heartily to such counsel. This region was then the frontier between civilization and savagery, and into it had gathered a horde of desperate characters, vulgar, fearless, brutal, without respect for civilization or reverence for God, usually inflamed with whiskey and stained with tobacco, gambling by day and jayhawking by night, always ready for any adventure which promised fun, blood, or booty. It is true that they had no special interest in slavery. They were simply the ready material out of which the slaveholders of Missouri might recruit their mercenaries for any villainous work which might be found necessary. Such was the Missouri "border ruffian" of 1854. It must not be understood that western Missouri contained no other sort of people. There were many generous-hearted, fair-minded, upright men there, among both the slaveholders and the non-slaveholders, who would no sooner have done wrong than suffered wrong. Most of them felt, however, that Kansas for the South and slavery, and Nebraska for the North, was the fair thing, the only fair thing, the thing understood and intended in the organization of the two Territories by one Act, and that any attempt on the part of the North to make Kansas a non-slaveholding Territory was a breach of faith, which ought to be resisted by the South, and especially by Missouri.

General D. R. Atchison was such a man, and such was his view of the case. He was, at the time, the leading man of western Missouri, had represented Missouri in the Senate of the United States, and had been president *pro tem.* of the Senate. His opinion and his advice naturally determined the course which the people of western Missouri would pursue toward Kansas. In justice to his memory, however, it must be said that, while he was resolved to make Kansas a slaveholding Territory, and then a slaveholding Commonwealth, his presence and counsel exerted a moderating influence upon his fierce and reckless followers. He

# THE STRUGGLE FOR KANSAS 413

left Washington soon after the passage of the Kansas-Nebraska Act, and repaired to the scene of the coming conflict, for the purpose of organizing and conducting his forces.

In June of 1854, Mr. Thayer, Mr. Lawrence, and Mr. Williams invited Dr. Charles Robinson, of Fitchburg, Mass., to meet them in council, in regard to the projects of the Emigrant Aid Company. Dr. Robinson was a prominent "forty-niner," and the leader of the California squatters in the war against the Sutter land claims. He was shrewd, calm, courageous, and full of expedients. These qualities, together with his large experience in organizing the forces of an embryonic Commonwealth, fitted him exactly for the work which Mr. Thayer and his colleagues were seeking to accomplish. Dr. Robinson was not an Abolitionist, and neither was Thayer, Lawrence, nor Williams. They were simply working to prevent the extension of slavery. They were all Whigs or Free-soil Democrats. They were thus by their moderation in principles and their conservatism in character admirably fitted to undertake the great work of making Kansas a free Commonwealth.

*Dr. Charles Robinson.*

The conference resulted in the sending of Dr. Robinson to the front to inspect the Territory of Kansas and make arrangements for settlements. Accompanied by Mr. C. H. Branscomb, a young lawyer, of Holyoke, Mass., he started for Kansas in the last days of June, 1854. They went by way of St. Louis and Kansas City. When they arrived in Missouri they found the excitement in reference to the reported doings of the Emigrant Aid Company already at a high pitch. They heard threats that no anti-slavery man would be allowed to settle in Kansas, and they heard of rewards offered for the head of Eli Thayer. They found also that a goodly number of pro-slavery Missourians had already

*Mr. C. H. Branscomb.*

immigrated into the Territory, had held a popular convention or assembly at Salt Creek Valley, at which they had declared slavery to be an existing institution in the Territory, and called upon its friends to aid in its firmer establishment and its wider extension.

From Kansas City Mr. Branscomb proceeded alone up the Kansas River to Fort Riley, while Dr. Robinson went up the Missouri to Fort Leavenworth.

*Dr. Robinson and Mr. Branscomb in Kansas.*

The Doctor found surveyors laying off a town near Fort Leavenworth, despite the fact that the Government at Washington had not yet opened the country for purchase. He immediately returned to Kansas City, where he received a letter from Boston informing him that the first party of emigrants was on the eve of starting for Kansas, and instructing him to join them at St. Louis. Upon meeting them at St. Louis, a letter was handed him asking for his immediate presence in Boston. He wrote to Mr. Branscomb to join the party at Kansas City and lead them to a settlement, while he himself hurried to Boston.

Mr. Branscomb and a Colonel Blood, of Wisconsin, who had also been sent out by Mr. Lawrence, met the emigrants at Kansas City, and, after a good deal of deliberation, led them to the spot on the Kansas River, above the confluence of the Wakarusa with the Kansas, on which the town of Lawrence was afterward built.

*The first party of emigrants.*

A few days before this first party of emigrants had arrived from the East, a meeting of residents of Platte County in Missouri took place at Weston, and, under the lead of B. F. Stringfellow, an organization was formed, which called itself the "Platte County Self-defensive Association," with the declared purpose of aiding in the removal of all persons from the soil of Kansas who might go there through

*The "Platte County self-defensive association."*

the aid or protection or guidance of emigrant aid societies in the North. Other such associations were formed in other localities of western Missouri, and before the autumn of 1854 had hardly opened, from five to ten thousand persons, mostly desperate and reckless characters, were organized in the border counties of western Missouri, and ready to invade Kansas for the purpose of protecting the settlers in the Territory from Missouri and the South generally in the exclusive possession of the Territory.

In September, the little party of about thirty men, who had pitched their tents upon the site of the present city of Lawrence, were joined by Dr. Robinson and S. C. Pomeroy, with the second party from the East, numbering some two hundred men. *The founding of Lawrence.* Upon the arrival of these the work of laying out and building the town was begun, and the place was named, in honor of the strong financial supporter of the Emigrant Aid enterprise, Lawrence.

When the first party arrived at the site they found it occupied by a single settler, named Stearns. Mr. Branscomb immediately purchased Stearns' claim and improvements for the company. The Missourians had, however, rushed into the Territory, at the earliest moment after the passage of the organic Act, and marked all the best lands as taken, leaving very little for bona fide settlers. As the result of this procedure, another claimant to the site of Lawrence soon appeared, one John Baldwin, and ordered the Yankees to decamp. Robinson proposed that each settler be left in possession until some authorized tribunal could pass upon the claims, and declared that his party would hold possession until removed by a legal act. *First invasion of the Missourians.* Baldwin and his party rejected the proposition, and summoned their Missouri friends to assist them. Some came, but not enough to overcome the Yankees. The Yankees stood firm and the Missourians retired, declaring that they would come again, and breathing out threats of war and bloodshed upon their return. This was October 6th, 1854, and such was the first invasion of the Missourians.

On the next day, the Governor of the Territory, the President's representative, the Hon. A. H. Reeder, of Pennsylvania, arrived at Fort Leavenworth, and began his régime in the Territory. From this time forward the history of the Territory is the resultant of four elemental forces in contact with each other — the general Government, the pro-slavery inhabitants, the anti-slavery inhabitants, and the Missourians.

*Governor A. H. Reeder.*

Governor Reeder was a genial, intelligent, upright man, a good lawyer and a fine orator. He was a Union-loving Democrat, and a firm believer in the doctrine of home rule in the Territories. He declared that he would maintain peace and order in the Territory, and immediately set out on a tour of inspection through the Territory. After having finished this, he caused the Territory to be districted, and ordered the election of a delegate to Congress.

There is little question that at the moment a majority of the bona fide settlers in the Territory were pro-slavery, and would have elected the delegate to Congress without any outside aid, but the pro-slavery men in Kansas and Missouri had become excited by the rumors of the vast schemes in the East for planting anti-slavery military colonies in the Territories, and also in the slave-holding Commonwealths, and were in no state of mind to think quietly and act calmly. They felt that they must make sure of all of the elements of government in

*The second invasion of the Missourians and the election of the delegate to Congress.*

# THE STRUGGLE FOR KANSAS

Kansas at the outset. The Missourians consequently committed the fatal and unnecessary blunder of going over into Kansas, to the number of some seventeen hundred or more, and voting for the pro-slavery candidate for Congress, J. W. Whitfield, who was thus elected by a large majority. Without the vote of the Missourians, Whitfield had still a substantial majority, but this travesty of the principle of home rule in the Territories, this pollution of republican principles at the very fountain-head, roused the North to the highest pitch of indignation.

This election took place on November 29th, 1854. Had it occurred before the Congressional elections of that year, it would most probably have caused a much more rapid development of the Republican party than happened, and the election of the Republican candidate for the presidency two years later. *The indignation of the North.* As it was, the struggle over the Kansas-Nebraska bill, and its final passage, had started the amalgamation of the Northern Whigs, the Free-soilers, and the Northern Democrats who opposed the repeal of the Missouri Compromise, into the Republican party, and had, in the Congressional elections of 1854, been the chief cause in changing a Democratic majority of more than eighty in the House of Representatives into a minority by more than seventy.

Of course the disintegration of the two old parties would, under ordinary conditions, proceed slowly. The members of neither were willing to enter the organization, or bear the name, of the other. *The Republican party.* As the Northern Whigs had unanimously opposed the repeal of the restriction of 1820 upon slavery in the Territories, it was not unnatural that they should at first feel that they were already the anti-slavery-extension party, and that all persons holding to that principle should be willing to march under their banner. Some of the more liberal minds among them in the Northwest, especially in Wisconsin and Michigan, had, already in the summer of 1854, joined with the Free-soilers, and the Democrats who opposed the repeal of the Missouri Compromise, to form a new party, under a new name, the Republican party, which, indeed, had no other principle than that already represented by the Northern Whigs, but which did not repel the Democrats by requiring them to desert to their old enemy. The great majority of both Whigs and Democrats were, however, rather waiting to see how home rule in the Territories would work, and were in the meantime busying themselves, in large degree, with other questions, chief among which was the question whether the country ought not to be preserved against foreign Roman Catholic immigration, the question which gave rise to the short-lived Know-nothing party, with its principle of America for Americans, the only real service of which movement was the aid which it lent to the dissolution of the Whig party, and to the preparation of the way for the union of the Northern Whigs with the anti-slavery-extension elements of the other parties into the Republican party.

The interference of the Missourians in the first election in Kansas, demonstrating the impracticability of "popular sovereignty" in the Territories, was the very thing necessary to hasten the development of the Republican party, but it came too late to influence the elections of 1854, and the shock which it caused lost some of the sharpness of its effect before the autumn of 1856.

The Congress to which Whitfield presented his credentials was the one whose House of Representatives had been chosen in 1852. His claim to his seat was at first not resisted, and the first step in the programme for making Kansas a slaveholding Territory was thus successful.

# THE STRUGGLE FOR KANSAS 419

Of far more importance, however, than the election of the delegate to Congress was the election of the members of the first Territorial legislature, since, according to the principle of "popular sovereignty" in the Territories, it would have the power probably of determining primarily the legality or illegality of slavery in Kansas.

*The Territorial legislature.*

In February of 1855, the Territorial authorities took a census of the inhabitants of the Territory, and it was estimated that there were between eight and nine thousand bona fide settlers in the Territory, about three thousand of whom were voters. It was also found that about four-sevenths of the legal voters had emigrated from the South. It is not probable, however, that all of these were pro-slavery men.

March 13th following was the day appointed for the election. All through the month the Missourians of the border counties were assembling in their "Blue Lodges," arming, organizing and drilling. On the day of the election some four or five thousand of them marched, fully armed, to the voting places in the more eastern districts of the Territory, and compelled the acceptance of their ballots by the regular judges of the elections, or by judges appointed by themselves. About six thousand three hundred votes were cast at this election, and it was estimated that three-fourths of them were cast by the Missouri invaders. Some of them pretended to be residents of the Territory, but most of those who thought it necessary to justify the procedure at all claimed that the Emigrant Aid Company had sent out men for the sole purpose of voting, and that their own action was retaliatory. The invasion was a notoriously public deed. The Missourians came in companies, with music and banners, and made no attempt at concealment. The

*The third invasion of the Missourians.*

Governor of the Territory resided, at the time, near the Missouri border, and probably had ocular proof of the outrage. The anti-slavery men thought that he would set the entire election aside. He did call for protests, and appointed April 5th as the time for hearing the same and canvassing the returns.

When the day arrived protests had been received from only six or seven of the eighteen election districts, and affected the elections of not more than three of the thirteen persons returned as elected to the upper house, and of not more than nine of the twenty-six persons returned as elected to the lower house, of the Territorial legislature.

Dr. Robinson and the anti-slavery men who had gathered about the Governor as a sort of body-guard wanted the Governor to declare the entire election null and void, but the Governor was a good lawyer, and he quickly determined that he could not pronounce an election null and void in a district from which no charges of fraud were presented, on account of fraud charged in some other district, and that he could not refuse his certificate to any one elected on the face of the returns, if nobody disputed the regularity of his election. Upon examining the disputed cases he decided to refuse his certificate to eight of the twelve persons chosen on the face of the disputed returns. Thirty-one members were thus duly qualified to take their seats, and new elections for eight seats were ordered. Of these thirty-one, twenty-eight were counted as pro-slavery men, a large majority in both houses.

*Governor Reeder and the Territorial elections.*

Dr. Robinson and the anti-slavery men found great fault with the Governor, and charged him with being frightened out of his original purpose to set the entire election aside, but it is difficult to see how he could have done this without protests against the return of each

## THE STRUGGLE FOR KANSAS

and every person. It would certainly have been an arbitrary procedure to have done so. If the anti-slavery men were not brave enough to protest, it certainly did not become them to taunt the Governor with backing down, when they gave him nothing upon which to base the refusal to issue his certificates.

The 22nd day of the following month (May) was appointed for holding the elections for the seats declared unfilled by the Governor. The anti-slavery candidates were elected to all of them. The pro-slavery men ignored the election. This meant that those holding the Governor's certificate by virtue of this election would be rejected by the legislature itself, and those returned as elected at the first election would be seated, under the power of the legislature to determine finally upon the legitimacy of its members. This happened as soon as the legislature assembled and organized itself in the first days of July. *The new elections to the legislative seats unfilled at the first elections.*

The legislature as thus organized contained only a single anti-slavery man, a Mr. Houston, and he voluntarily vacated his seat a few weeks later in great disgust. From a technical point of view this legislature was a legitimate body, but from a moral and a political point of view it did not represent the people of the Territory. It represented simply the pro-slavery party, and used its powers in utter disregard of justice and right reason. *The organization of the first legislature of Kansas Territory.*

The great problem for the anti-slavery men now was to repudiate the jurisdiction of this legislature without rebelling against the general Government and its agent in the Territory, the Governor. Dr. Robinson had had the experience in California of aiding to make a Commonwealth in the Union, without the transitional period of Territor-  *The problem for the anti-slavery men. Dr. Robinson's plan.*

ial organization. He now applied this experience to the solution of the Kansas question.

The idea of Dr. Robinson and his colleagues was, to hold a convention of the people of the Territory for the purpose of framing an organic statute for Commonwealth government, which, after adoption by the people, should be sent to Congress, with a petition for the admission of Kansas into the Union as a Commonwealth. They proposed in the meantime to get on without any Territorial government as best they could.

Their idea was, in the second place, to ignore the Territorial government altogether as bogus, but to yield obedience to the officials of the general Government in the Territory. This distinction might be made, so far as the Territorial legislature was concerned, upon the "popular sovereignty" principle. The difficulty was in applying it to the Governor and the Territorial judges appointed by the President. To distinguish between their functions in such a way as to deny their authority when administering the acts of the Territorial legislature, and yield to it when administering the acts of Congress in the Territory, was certainly a very delicate procedure, if possible at all. Such distinctions would have to be very clearly understood, and very correctly applied in each case, in order to avoid the charge of rebellion and treason.

Had the Governor remained true to the legislature it is possible that this plan of rebellion against the Territorial government might have been suppressed at the outset, but such was not to be the course of history. He called the legislature to assemble at Pawnee on July 2nd. It remained in session there only four days. It did little more than unseat the persons holding the Governor's certificate by virtue of the second election, and seat

Conflict between the Governor and the Territorial legislature.

## THE STRUGGLE FOR KANSAS

those to whom he had denied his certificate on account of fraud at the first election. It then adjourned itself to Shawnee Mission, a place nearer the Missouri border. The Governor denied the power of the legislature to do this, since by the Act organizing the Territory, the legislature must first meet at the time and place appointed by the Governor, and was vested by the Act with power, thereafter, only over the time of commencing its regular sessions. The Governor vetoed the proposition of the legislature to change its place of meeting. The legislature passed the project over his veto, and removed to Shawnee Mission; after which the Governor broke off all official connection with it. There is little doubt that the pro-slavery legislature wanted to be where it could be easily supported by the Missourians, and that the Governor considered this a menace to his own independence, and an outrage upon the people of Kansas, and upon the principle of "popular sovereignty" in the Territories.

The attitude now assumed by the Governor toward the legislature at Shawnee Mission was a great encouragement to the anti-slavery men. Dr. Robinson had already sent to Mr. Thayer for Sharpe's rifles, and, at the time of the Governor's quarrel with the legislature, a sufficient number of these had arrived to furnish almost every anti-slavery man with a good outfit. *Sharpe's rifles.*

Dr. Robinson had, at the same time, overcome the attempts of James S. Lane to separate the anti-slavery men into parties, by the organization of a Democratic party in Kansas. In a powerful speech at Lawrence, on July 4th, 1855, the Doctor convinced his hearers of the necessity for all anti-slavery men standing together until Kansas should be admitted into the Union as a non-slavehold- *Factional movements among the anti-slavery men suppressed.*

ing Commonwealth. It was in this address that the Doctor repudiated the existing legislature as a Missouri institution, advising resistance to the execution of its acts, and made his noted declaration, that, if slavery in Missouri was impossible with freedom in Kansas, then slavery in Missouri must die in order that freedom in Kansas might live.

These bold utterances startled the North and the South, the people of Kansas and, especially, the people of Missouri. This speech, together with the letter of M. F. Conway to Governor Reeder, resigning his seat in the legislature and repudiating that body "as derogatory to the respectability of popular government and insulting to the virtue and intelligence of the age," set the "Free-state" scheme in motion.

*Excitement in Missouri and throughout the country over the "Free-state" movement.*

The enactments of the Territorial legislature greatly aided the movement by demonstrating to the people what they had to expect from the dominance of that body. They made the decoying, or aiding therein, of a slave away from his master in the Territory grand larceny, punishable by death. They made the decoying into Kansas of any slave away from his master in any other place, for the purpose of effecting his freedom, grand larceny, punishable by death. And they made the denial of the right to hold slaves in Kansas, either by word of mouth or in writing or printing, a felony, punishable by imprisonment at hard labor for not less than two years.

*The enactments of the Territorial legislature.*

When the knowledge of this infamous legislation spread throughout the North, it roused that section of the country to new efforts for peopling Kansas with anti-slavery men, who would rescue the Territory from the reign of such laws and such law-makers. The necessary reinforcements

*The North aroused by this legislation.*

were being assembled in the North when the creation of the "Free-state" government was begun.

A series of conventions, beginning with the convention at Lawrence on August 14th, and culminating with that assembled at Topeka on the 23rd day of October, 1855, consolidated the anti-slavery men in the Territory into the "Free-state" party, constructed a temporary election machinery, and produced, finally, a proposed Commonwealth constitution, which, in addition to the provisions for the structure of a Commonwealth government for Kansas, contained a clause prohibiting slavery in Kansas after July 4th, 1857, and excluding negroes from residence in Kansas after that date. *The Topeka constitution.*

In the meantime Governor Reeder had been removed by the President from the governorship of the Territory, and the Secretary of the Territory, one Daniel Woodson, a pro-slavery man, had become acting Governor for the time being. Ex-Governor Reeder now went over to the anti-slavery men, and was chosen by them on October 9th, at the same election at which the delegates to the Topeka convention were chosen, as delegate to Congress. Over twenty-seven hundred votes were cast at this election. *The removal of Governor Reeder; and his election as Congressional delegate.*

On December 15th, the Topeka constitution was submitted to the suffrages of the people. Seventeen hundred and thirty-one votes were cast in favor of its adoption, and forty-six votes against it. The pro-slavery men took no part in the voting. It is probable, however, that a majority of the legal voters in Kansas ratified this constitution. On January 5th, 1856, the elections for the legislative members and officials of the government provided by this constitution were held, and Dr. Robinson was chosen Governor. *The ratification of the Topeka constitution; and the establishment of the "Free-state" government.*

It was at this election that the conflict of arms between the "Free-state" government and the Territorial government began. A Territorial military company, called the Kickapoo Rangers, threatened to interfere with the elections at the town of Easton. A captain, R. P. Brown, organized a company of "Free-state" men at Leavenworth, and went to Easton to protect the ballot box. As the evening drew on a fight ensued, in which a Territorial man was killed. The next day the Leavenworth company was attacked, on their return, by the Kickapoo company, and Captain Brown was taken prisoner. Some movements were in progress for trying him, when one of the ruffians put an end to the matter by striking him on the head with a hatchet.

*The first violence.*

Two local governments of Kansas were now in existence. One, the Territorial, had been recognized as legitimate by the Washington Government. What, then, was the other? Was it a body of insurrectionists? If so, must the general Government suppress it? And, if the general Government must suppress it, must it do so at once, or should it wait until the insurrectionists should undertake to exercise some governmental power? These were knotty problems for the Administration at Washington, but they were problems which had to be solved. From the inaction of the Washington authorities we must conclude that the prevailing view with them was that the new government in Kansas must do something before it could be dealt with.

*The "Free-state" government and the Administration.*

The "Free-state" legislature met March 4th, 1856. It prepared a memorial to Congress, praying for the entrance of Kansas as a Commonwealth into the Union, under the Topeka constitution. It elected Reeder and Lane United States Senators. It appointed a committee to put the legisla-

*The acts of the "Free-state" legislature.*

tive business into shape for the next session. And it passed a few laws.

None of these acts were treasonable. Treason, by the Constitution, is levying war against the United States or any of the "States," or adhering to those who are doing so, giving them aid and comfort; and levying war has been defined by the Supreme Court to be the actual assembly of armed men for the treasonable purpose. Not even the voluntary submission to the laws passed by the "Free-state" legislature was treason or rebellion. The danger point would be reached when the "Free-state" government should undertake to enforce its laws, or should interpose armed resistance to the enforcement of the laws of the United States, or of the acts of the Territorial government, which government had been recognized as legitimate by the general Government, which was, in fact, but the local agent of the general Government.

Governor Robinson understood the situation. In his message to the legislature he recommended "no course to be taken in opposition to the general Government, or to the Territorial government, while it shall remain with the sanction of Congress." *Governor Robinson's message.*

In the midst of these movements by the "Free-state" men, the pro-slavery men organized themselves more closely for aggressive action. The new Governor appointed by the President, Wilson Shannon, ex-Governor of Ohio, a man of intelligence and high character, arrived at Shawnee Mission on September 3rd, 1855. The pro-slavery men did not like his appointment. They wanted the acting Governor, Woodson, to be made Governor. However, they received the new Governor with much pomp and ceremony, and succeeded in imposing upon him, at the outset, their view of the situation. On *The new Governor, Shannon, and the "law and order" party.*

November 14th, they held a pro-slavery convention at Leavenworth. They called it an assembly of "the lovers of law and order." The Governor presided over it, and made a rather violent speech, in which he declared that the Territorial government had the support of the Administration at Washington. The practical work of this convention was the organization of the "law and order" party; that is, the party for enforcing the acts and authority of the Territorial government.

Naturally a dispute about a land claim furnished the occasion for trying the powers of the Territorial government. *The attempt to enforce the Territorial laws upon the "Free-state" men.* In the course of this quarrel, which took place in the latter part of November, 1855, a pro-slavery man, named Coleman, killed a "Free-state" man, named Dow. The friends of Dow gathered about the spot where his dead body was found, and indulged in threats of vengeance. Among them was one Jacob Branson, who uttered threats against one Buckley, as the instigator of the murder of his friend. Buckley secured a peace warrant against Branson, and put it in the hands of one S. J. Jones, the sheriff, under the Territorial government, of Douglas County. The arrest of Branson under this warrant inaugurated the contest for imposing the authority of the Territorial government upon the "Free-state" men.

Sheriff Jones arrested Branson, and started for Lecompton with him, by way of Lawrence. His purpose *The Branson rescue.* in going through the head-quarters of the "Free-state" men was undoubtedly to tempt them to the rescue of Branson. But Branson was rescued several miles away from Lawrence by a company of "Free-state" men, under the lead of a Captain Abbott. This party, however, immediately repaired to Lawrence, while the sheriff went to Franklin, and from this place summoned his Missouri friends to his aid, and then reported his trouble to the Governor, and asked for his support.

The Governor immediately ordered the officers of the Territorial militia to collect the forces, and march to Lawrence. Although the sheriff asked for three thousand men, not one hundred residents of the Territory answered the call of the militia officers; but a great horde came from Missouri. By December 5th, 1855, more than a thousand Missourians had arrived, and had encamped upon the Wakarusa, a few miles to the east of Lawrence. General Atchison was with them. *The advance of the Missourians on Lawrence.*

Naturally the people of Lawrence were much excited, and set about preparing for defence. They constructed several small forts, and organized a military force of some six or seven hundred men, pretty well armed and equipped. They stood a very good chance to win in the trial of battle, but they resolved, most wisely, to rely upon the justice of their cause more than upon the power of their arms.

The committee of safety, which was directing matters in Lawrence, sent commissioners to Governor Shannon to enlighten him, from the point of view of the "Free-state" men, in regard to the situation. They made their way to Shawnee Mission, where they were coldly received by the Governor, who charged the "Free-state" men with rebellion against his government. The commissioners disputed his charge, told him that nobody in Lawrence had had anything to do with the rescue of Branson, that his rescuers had been warned out of the town as soon as they came into it, and had obeyed the warning, and gave him the committee's message demanding his protection against the invaders. *Lawrence's demand of protection from Governor Shannon.*

The Governor was somewhat staggered by these statements, and decided to go to Lawrence himself, and examine affairs on the spot. This was just what the "Free-state" men wanted. He arrived in Lawrence on December 7th. Dr. Robinson and Colonel Lane immediately stated the situation and the views of the "Free-state" men to him. The Governor saw, at once, that they were in the right, and could not be attacked. He recognized, at once, that his task was to send the Missourians out of the Territory. He entered into a sort of written agreement with the citizens of Lawrence, in which the people of Lawrence pledged themselves not to resist the legal service of any criminal process, but to aid in the execution of the laws, when called on by proper authority, and the Governor declared that he had no authority to call upon non-residents of Kansas to aid him in the execution of the laws, had not done so, and would not do so. The last clause provided that nothing in the agreement should be taken as a recognition of the validity of the acts of the Territorial legislature by the "Free-state" men.

*Shannon at Lawrence, and his agreement with the "Free-state" men.*

The Governor felt that he would have difficulty in reconciling the Missourians to his agreement, and insisted that Dr. Robinson and Colonel Lane should accompany him to Franklin, and aid him in his task. The calm statements of the Governor and of Dr. Robinson prevailed, and the Missourians saw the error into which they had been betrayed by the inconsiderate pro-slavery zeal of Sheriff Jones. General Atchison told his followers plainly that Dr. Robinson's position was impregnable, and that if they should persist in an attack upon Lawrence, contrary to the Governor's orders, they were only a mob. He added, that such a movement was not only without show of legality, but would ruin the Democratic

THE STRUGGLE FOR KANSAS 431

party, and cause the election of an Abolitionist President the next year. By these efforts and representations on the part of the Governor, Dr. Robinson, and General Atchison, the Missourians were induced to break camp and turn their faces homeward. *The retreat of the Missourians.*

At the moment of this victory of the "Free-state" men, won by moral forces and diplomatic address, appeared the Loki of Kansas "Free-state" history, John Brown. He mounted a box in one of the streets of Lawrence, railed and ranted against the settlement which had been reached, and breathed out words of slaughter and pillage, until some man of common sense pulled him down, and stopped his murderous canting babble. *John Brown.*

The Governor reported the affair to the President, expressed to him his forebodings as to the future, and suggested that he be allowed to call upon the United States troops stationed at Fort Leavenworth at his discretion, as a call for the militia would only end in a party struggle. This communication seems to have opened the eyes of the President, for the first time, to the true situation. *Shannon's report to the President.*

The "Free-state" men now addressed the President and demanded his protection against another invasion from Missouri, which they claimed was in preparation. On January 23rd, 1856, the leaders at Lawrence telegraphed the President that the outrage was on the point of consummation, and besought the President to issue his proclamation, at once, forbidding the invasion. At the same time, they informed certain members of Congress and the Governors of certain Northern Commonwealths of the impending danger; and they sent commissioners into the Northern Commonwealths to inform the people of the *The appeal of the "Free-state" men to the President.*

North in regard to the situation in Kansas, and to appeal to them to emigrate thither in sufficient numbers to save the Territory against the pro-slavery movement.

The agitation became now so general throughout the country, that the President felt constrained to interfere.

*The President's proclamation.*
On February 11th, he issued his proclamation, in which he warned all persons concerned that "an attempted insurrection" in the Territory of Kansas or "an aggressive intrusion into the same" would be resisted by the employment of the United States troops in Kansas, as well as the local militia; and called upon all good citizens outside of Kansas to abstain from intermeddling with the local affairs of the Territory, and upon all good citizens in Kansas to render obedience to the laws.

The "Free-state" men did not regard the proclamation as particularly friendly to them. While it forbade

*The situation made more embarrassing for the "Free-state" men.*
invasion, it commanded obedience to the existing Territorial government within. They were afraid that they would not be allowed to organize their "Free-state" government, created by the Topeka constitution. But, as we have seen, the day came and went for this, without any interference on the part of the President or the Governor against the movement, although the President had authorized the Governor to call upon the United States troops at Fort Leavenworth at his discretion. Under these circumstances it was certainly the part of wisdom for the "Free-state" men to do nothing superfluous or sensational in the organization of the new government, and to delay operations under it for the time being. The question of the recognition of the "Free-state" movement was before Congress, under the issue of the contest between Whitfield and Reeder for the seat in the House of Representatives. The policy, therefore,

## THE STRUGGLE FOR KANSAS

of representing the organization of the new government as tentative, and as conditioned upon the presumption of Congressional recognition, and as holding its powers in abeyance until that recognition should be secured, was wise and necessary.

The discussion of Kansas affairs in the House of Representatives revolved about the question of the admission of Whitfield or Reeder from the middle of February to March 19th, 1856, when it was voted to send a special committee of investigation to the Territory. *The Congressional committee to the Territory.* The gentlemen selected were Mr. Howard, of Michigan, Mr. Sherman, of Ohio, and Mr. Oliver, of Missouri. They proceeded to the Territory and opened their investigations about the middle of April.

A week before this, the memorial from the "Free-state" legislature praying for the admission of Kansas, as a Commonwealth, under the Topeka constitution, was presented in both Houses of Congress, and placed upon the calendar in each. *Application for admission.* The slavery question was herewith again before Congress in both principle and detail. The measure which was intended to put its discussion out of the halls of Congress had thus, in less than two years, proved itself an utter fiasco.

In the Territory the pro-slavery men pursued their policy of bringing the "Free-state" men into conflict with the general Government. The "Free-state" men sought just as diligently to avoid it. Both sides recognized this as the crucial test. *Sheriff Jones again at Lawrence; and the attempts to assassinate him.* By the middle of April, some of the men who participated in the rescue of Branson had made their way back to Lawrence, and Sheriff Jones laid his plans for arresting them. On April 19th, he rode into Lawrence and served a writ upon S. N. Wood, but the crowd jostled them apart, and Wood escaped. The

28

Sheriff returned on the next day with more writs, and undertook to arrest S. F. Tappan. Tappan resisted and struck the Sheriff. Jones went at once to the Governor, and the Governor gave him a detachment of United States soldiers. With these he returned to Lawrence, but they could find no one for whom the Sheriff had a writ. The party pitched tent at Lawrence to spend the night. After darkness came on, some wretch, then unknown to the "Free-state" leaders, approached the tent and shot the Sheriff, wounding him dangerously. This was an almost irreparable blow to the "Free-state" cause. The very thing which the "Free-state" leaders had sought most earnestly to avoid had been thrust upon them by the criminal deed of some meddlesome crank. The "Free-state" men recognized at once the seriousness of the situation, and, on the morning following the event, held a meeting, at which the outrage was repudiated and denounced, and a reward of five hundred dollars offered for the apprehension of the criminal. Colonel Sumner, the commander of the United States troops in Kansas, wrote to Dr. Robinson, urging him to use every effort to move the citizens of Lawrence to bring the assassin to justice, as his act would be charged by the pro-slavery men upon the whole community. The Doctor replied at once that the community repudiated the foul deed, and would certainly bring the guilty party to justice if he could be found. There was no municipal government in Lawrence at the time, and Dr. Robinson acted, in his reply to Colonel Sumner, as a sort of self-constituted representative of the citizens. He certainly represented the views of the large majority of them, but there were some who, at the time, knew who the guilty person was, and gave no sign which would aid in his discovery.

*The outrage repudiated by the "Free-state" men.*

The Sheriff's wound was not fatal, but it was reported that he was dead, and the Missourians began to organize for another invasion. Before they were ready, the Territorial judiciary came to their assistance. Chief Justice Lecompte charged the Grand Jury of Douglas County, in the early part of May, that resistance to the Territorial laws was high treason against the United States, and that entering into combinations for the purpose of making such resistance was constructive treason, and instructed the body to find true bills against all persons guilty of such offences. This was a most astounding piece of jurisprudence. It looked like nothing but a trick to deprive the "Free state" men of their leaders, since one arrested for treason was considered as not having the privilege of bail.

*Judge Lecompte's charge to the Grand Jury.*

The Grand Jury found indictments against nine or ten persons, among them Robinson, Reeder, and Lane, and also against two newspapers published in Lawrence, and the Emigrant Aid Company's hotel there. The indictments were put in the hands of the United States Marshal for the Territory, J. B. Donaldson. On May 11th, Donaldson issued a proclamation, declaring that the service of these writs by his deputy had been resisted in Lawrence, and calling "the law-abiding citizens of the Territory to appear at Lecompton, as soon as possible, and in numbers sufficient for the proper execution of the law." As a matter of fact, only Reeder had resisted service, and had succeeded in escaping. All the others, except Lane and Wood, were taken into custody without difficulty. Reeder's justification was that he was at the moment in attendance, as a witness, upon the Congressional committee sent to the Territory, and was, therefore, legally exempt from arrest at the time.

*The "treason indictments."*

## 436  THE MIDDLE PERIOD

The Marshal did not publish his proclamation in Lawrence, but a copy of it fell into the hands of a Lawrence citizen, who hastened to make known to the people the peril which was impending. The citizens already knew of forces being organized, both in the Territory and in Missouri, against Lawrence, and had demanded the Governor's protection against them. The Governor had replied that he knew of no force near or approaching Lawrence, except the posse under the orders of the United States Marshal and the Sheriff of Douglas County, who had writs to serve in Lawrence, and that he should not interfere.

*The Marshal's proclamation in Lawrence.*

The citizens of Lawrence now held a meeting and passed formal resolutions, declaring that the charges contained in the Marshal's proclamation were untrue, and that the citizens were not only ready to acquiesce in the service of any judicial writs against them by the United States Marshal, but to furnish him a posse, if required, to aid him in the discharge of his duty. And after receiving the Governor's reply, they appealed to the Marshal, asking him to state his demands, promising not to resist the service of his processes, but to aid him in the discharge of his legal duties, and praying his protection against the lawless bands collecting about their town for the purpose of its destruction.

*The action of the citizens of Lawrence.*

The Marshal replied in a flippant and sarcastic manner, saying that his correspondents must be strangers in Lawrence if they were ignorant of the demands against the citizens of the town, referring in exaggerated language to the shooting of Jones, and Reeder's resistance to his deputy, and to the military organization and equipment of the people of Lawrence, and declaring that he should execute all processes in his hands in his own time and way.

*The Marshal's reply.*

Three days later, on May 17th, the citizens communicated again with the Marshal, calling his attention to the depredations committed by the bands around Lawrence, asking if he was responsible for these bodies, and demanding protection from him against them. At the same time, the managers of the hotel appealed to the Governor to protect their property, and carried with them an offer from the citizens to give up their arms to Colonel Sumner, if he would station a detachment of United States soldiers in the town for their protection.

*Appeal of the citizens to the Marshal and the Governor.*

The Marshal and the Governor thought favorably of this proposition. They were willing to guarantee the safety of the citizens and their individual property, but they thought they must consult with the captains of the squads composing the posse before they could give such assurances in regard to the hotel and the printing offices. These persons were found to be determined on the destruction of the printing offices, certainly, and of the hotel, probably. Colonel Titus, of Florida, declared that the South Carolina boys in the posse would be satisfied with nothing short of the destruction of the printing offices.

*The hotel and the printing offices.*

The hotel managers and the representatives of the citizens turned again to the Governor and implored him to send the United States soldiers for the protection of the town, but he again refused to interfere; and, finally, when they said to him that they feared the citizens would be compelled to defend themselves by armed power, and precipitate the horrors of civil war, he answered angrily, while striding out of their presence: "War then it is, by God!"

On the morning of the 21st, the Marshal's armed force appeared upon one of the heights overlooking the town, displaying first a white flag, then a red one, and, lastly,

the flag of the United States. The Deputy-marshal then entered the town with a small posse, and called the man-
*The sacking of Lawrence.* agers of the hotel and several of the citizens to join his posse and assist him in the service of his writs. They obeyed, and two persons were arrested. The Deputy, with his force and his prisoners, returned to the camp. Colonel C. W. Topliff, a prominent citizen, went with them, bearing a communication from the committee of safety of Lawrence to the Marshal, in which the promise of obedience to his processes was again made, and his protection claimed.

It was hoped that the crisis was now passed. The Marshal dismissed his posse. But the Sheriff immediately reorganized the bands as *his* posse. This was most ominous of evil. The Sheriff was burning with passion for personal revenge. In the middle of the afternoon (May 21st), he rode into the town at the head of his army, and, in spite of every plea and remonstrance, caused the contents of the printing offices to be scattered through the streets and the hotel to be burned, and allowed the pillage, and even the burning, of private houses.

The atrocious and disgraceful deed of sacking Lawrence was denounced by many of the persons who had
*Repudiation of the deed by Atchison and others.* joined the Marshal's posse. General Atchison tried to prevent the Sheriff from thus wreaking his vengeance, and denounced his deed afterward. Jackson, the leader of the Georgians, and Buford, the captain of the Alabama squad, also denounced the vile procedure, and declared that they had not come to Kansas to destroy property.

Atchison knew well enough that a great blow had been given to the prospects of the Democratic party in the now approaching presidential election. What, then, must have been his despair upon learning that an attack, even more outrageous than the sacking of Lawrence, had been made, at the same time, upon the defender of "Free-state" Kansas in the Senate chamber at Washington?

The debate on the bills for the admission of "Free-state" Kansas had progressed from day to day, in both Houses of Congress, with increasing earnestness and excitement. At length, on May 19th and 20th, Mr. Sumner delivered his fierce philippic on the "Crime against Kansas." It was not only an unvarnished statement of the case from the Abolitionist point of view, but it was a personal arraignment of several of the Senators. The attack contained in it upon Senator Butler, of South Carolina, a gentleman of great refinement and politeness, and much honored and esteemed by his associates, was especially coarse and brutal. Almost all the Senators felt the attack to be more than a discourtesy. Senator Butler was in ill health and was absent from his seat, both of which circumstances made the affair all the more exasperating. For two days the Capital rang with denunciations of the insulting speech, when Preston S. Brooks, a nephew of Senator Butler, and a member of the House of Representatives, demanded and took satisfaction of Mr. Sumner for the attack upon his kinsman. Had he carried out his purpose in a brave and manly way, he would have been generally applauded for it, but being no match physically for Sumner, Brooks had recourse to a method which stamped him as a coward, and his attack upon Sumner as a brutal outrage. He entered the Senate chamber on May 22nd, after the adjournment of the body, and approaching Mr. Sumner, who was seated and bending over his desk, charged him with libel on South Carolina and her sons, and struck him with a cane upon the head

*The attack on Senator Sumner.*

until the Senator became helpless and unconscious. With this, Sumner's outrage upon Butler was entirely lost sight of in Brooks's far more brutal outrage upon Sumner.

The cowardly deed was looked upon everywhere in the North as the fit companion-piece to the sacking of Lawrence. The indignation of the North was roused to the highest pitch, and it seemed as if the elections of 1856 must bring the anti-slavery party into the seats of power.

But just at this most critical juncture, when everything depended on calmness and moderation on the part of the "Free-state" men to secure immediate victory, and when immediate victory, thus pursued, was, so far as human eye can discern, within their grasp, an outrage was perpetrated by a gang of men, or rather fiends, who claimed some sort of relation to the "Free-state" party, which so far overshadowed in cruel atrocity all that had gone before as to produce a revulsion of feeling most damaging to the "Free-state" cause. On May 23rd, John Brown, with six or seven others, all, except two, members of his own family, went to the settlement about Dutch Henry's Crossing on the Pottawattomie Creek, and, on the night of the 24th, took five men, innocent of anything which could even justify arrest by proper authorities, from their cabins, and murdered them, cutting and slashing their bodies with cutlasses, until their savage thirst for blood was partially satiated. So barbarously atrocious was the deed, so calculated to rouse the sentiment of the whole country against the "Free-state" cause in Kansas, that the Republican members of the Congressional committee of investigation in the Territory refused to make the event a part of their inquiry. The Democratic member, Mr. Oliver, investigated it, and reported it to Congress and to the public.

# THE STRUGGLE FOR KANSAS

No sane mind can find the slightest justification, excuse, or palliation for this atrocious crime. It was murder, pure and simple. And when we consider the purpose for which, as well as the mind with which, it was committed, it became, in addition to common crime, also public crime of the most grievous nature. Dr. Robinson says it was done for the purpose of involving the North and the South in war against each other. Thus to the murderous mind was added the seditious purpose. Some men have professed to find virtue in this noxious compound, but such minds have lost their moorings, and are roaming without star or compass over the border lands between reason and insanity. To murder, Brown and his vile brood added robbery; but this was so slight a crime in comparison with the other that it may be passed without further notice.

The inhabitants of the region were thrown into the greatest consternation and excitement. The pro-slavery and the anti-slavery men assembled together, denounced the horrible deed as foulest murder, and resolved to act together as men of reason and common sense for the maintenance of peace and order and the suppression of crime. *The excitement produced by them.*

For a few days it was not known who the authors of these murders were, but suspicion soon pointed to Brown and his gang, and steps were taken to procure warrants for their arrest. The Governor, also, sent down a body of troops to the scene of the massacre. The troops were volunteers, chiefly Missourians, commanded by a Captain Pate. Pate's force met Brown's at Black Jack, and Brown captured Pate and his men. This was June 2nd. With nothing to hinder him for the moment, Brown now robbed and pillaged all around. By the 3rd, however, the Missourians, led by Whitfield, were rallying to the aid of their pro-slavery friends in *The battle at Black Jack.*

Kansas, and by the 5th, battle was impending between the Missourians and the "Free-state" men, who had gathered in the neighborhood of the excitement. The
*The Governor's proclamation, enforced by United States soldiers.* Governor had at last comprehended the serious character of the situation. He issued his proclamation warning invaders to retire, and commanding armed and illegal organizations to disperse. And he sent Colonel Sumner with a company of regular cavalry to the scene of action.

Sumner rescued Pate and his men, dispersed Brown's gang, and ordered the Missourians to get out of Kansas. He did not arrest Brown, because he had no warrant for his apprehension, and did not know, at the time, that he was the author of the Pottawattomie murders. Sumner remained a fortnight or more in southern Kansas until the excitement was somewhat spent, and then returned to Fort Leavenworth. Brown disappeared, and a measure of peace was momentarily restored.

The Pottawattomie murders, and the robberies succeeding them, had, however, greatly damaged the "Free-
*The "Free-state" cause greatly injured by Brown's deeds.* state" cause. The great advantage which had accrued to it through the sacking of Lawrence and the outrage upon Senator Sumner was now largely lost again. Still, emigration from the Northern Commonwealths to Kansas continued in great activity, and the House of Representatives at Washington was steadily advancing toward the passage of the resolution for the admission of "Free-state" Kansas into the Union, although the flight of
*The passage of the bill for the admission of Kansas by the House.* its committee of investigation from the Territory, in consequence of the excitement following the murders on the Pottawattomie, and the two reports which its members made of the situation in Kansas, exercised an unfavorable influence on the movement. The House passed the bill,

# THE STRUGGLE FOR KANSAS

however, on July 3rd, by a majority of two votes, but it would admit neither of the claimants to a seat in the House.

On the other hand, Colonel Sumner, while personally in sympathy with the "Free-state" cause, felt it to be his official duty to disperse the "Free-state" legislature which assembled at Topeka on July 4th. The President and the Secretary of War, Mr. Jefferson Davis, subsequently disapproved of this act, and denied that the authority for it was either expressed or implied in any of their instructions to Colonel Sumner. The Colonel thought the contrary, and felt that the unpopularity of the procedure throughout the North had caused the President and the Secretary to disavow a responsibility for it which was rightfully their own. A careful reading of the dispatches leads to the conclusion that the Colonel did exceed his powers. He was, doubtless, led to do so unconsciously by the violent deeds of men professing connection with the "Free-state" party. The misunderstanding led finally to the retirement of Colonel Sumner from the command of the United States forces in Kansas, and the assignment of General P. F. Smith to that duty.

*Dispersal of the "Free-state" legislature by Colonel Sumner.*

After the dispersion of the "Free-state" legislature, the "Free-state" men, who were gathered in Lawrence, held a convention, and elected a committee, whose duty it should be to look after the interests of the people. This committee selected from among its members a sub-committee of five, and transferred all of its powers and duties to this sub-committee. The "Free-state" government had now become a directorial board of five persons, chief among whom were William Hutchinson and James Blood. The seat of this Directory was Lawrence.

*The "Free-state" Directory.*

The Directory organized a strong military force under the command of Colonel Walker. This force attacked and broke up three pro-slavery bands during the month of August, the last one at Fort Titus, near Lecompton, and commanded by the noted Colonel Titus himself. Titus and his men were captured.

*The organization of the "Free-state" military.*

The Governor now became alarmed for his own safety. Accompanied by Major Sedgwick, he went to Lawrence, on August 17th, and concluded with the Directory the noted agreement of that date, the terms of which were, that the "Freestate" men should keep the arms which they had captured from the pro-slavery bands; that the howitzer taken from Lawrence should be returned to the town; that all persons arrested by the United States Marshal, under charge of participating in the attack upon the pro-slavery band at Franklin, should be delivered unharmed to the Directory; that the Governor should disband the Territorial militia, order all bands of armed men to disperse, and command all armed bands of non-residents to leave the Territory. The Directory engaged, upon its side, to release Titus and his men. The Governor virtually surrendered to the Directory. He then returned to Lecompton, resigned his office, and made his way back to Ohio.

*The Treaty of August 17th.*

*Resignation of Shannon.*

Secretary Woodson was now again in the Governor's chair, and this, of itself, was notice to the Missourians to come on. They had already gathered on the border. On August 25th, Woodson published a proclamation, in which he declared the Territory to be "in a state of open insurrection and rebellion," called "upon all law-abiding citizens of the Territory to rally to the support of their country and its laws," and commanded "all officers,

*Woodson's proclamation, and the new invasion from Missouri.*

civil and military, and all other citizens of the Territory, to aid and assist by all means in their power in putting down the insurrectionists."

The Missourians took this as an invitation to advance. They entered the Territory again, on the 29th, and pitched their camp on Bull Creek. Atchison was in command. On the 13th, a detachment of them attacked and destroyed Ossawattomie. About a dozen men were killed in the fight.

General Smith now issued instructions that the United States troops should not "interfere with persons who may have come from a distance to give protection to their friends or others, and who may be behaving themselves in a peaceable and lawful manner." This attitude seemed at first view to be friendly to the pro-slavery men; but the friends of the "Free-state" men were now pouring into the Territory by way of Iowa and Nebraska, and Smith's order worked ultimately to their advantage. Unquestionably the General intended to be impartial. *General Smith's attitude toward invaders.*

The attack on Ossawattomie roused the "Free-state" men to new exertions. Three hundred of them, commanded by Lane, advanced upon the camp at Bull Creek. The two forces drew up in battle array, but, after a slight skirmish, they both drew off. *Marching and countermarching.*

Acting Governor Woodson now ordered Colonel Cooke to attack Topeka with United States troops, but the Colonel refused to obey the order, and General Smith sustained him.

The "Free-state" men now planned an attack upon Lecompton. They moved in two separate columns, one commanded by Harvey and the other by Lane. The attack was to be made on September 4th, but the failure of Lane's column to arrive until the 5th enabled the

United States soldiers to reach the town first. When the "Free-state" men learned that the regulars were in the town, they returned to Lawrence.

The Missourians were now roused to serious and decided action. An army of some three thousand of them had gathered on the border, and was on the point of marching in for the purpose of destroying every "Free-state" settlement in the Territory. Only one thing could now save the Territory from thoroughgoing and relentless civil war, and that was the interference of the United States army. The fiasco of "popular sovereignty" in the Territories was at last complete. The general Government must assume control.

*The failure of "Popular Sovereignty" in the Territories.*

The President's eyes had at last been opened to the fact, that if he allowed things to drift any farther in Kansas, the Republicans would win the presidential election in November. He, therefore, resolved to put the government of the Territory into impartial hands. He ordered the United States Marshal to release Robinson and his colleagues; appointed J. W. Geary, of Pennsylvania, a man of strong character, Governor of the Territory; and authorized Geary to call the United States troops to his assistance. Geary arrived at Lecompton on September 10th. On the 12th, he went to Lawrence, and, after promising the "Free-state" men protection against the Missourians, returned to Lecompton. On the 14th, the force advancing on Lawrence arrived in the neighborhood of the town. Word was immediately sent to the Governor. The Governor summoned a detachment of United States soldiers, and set out for the scene of action. On the morning of the 15th, he met the army of Missourians and interposed the United States army between

*Release of the "treason prisoners," and appointment of Geary.*

*The new Governor establishes peace by means of the army of the United States.*

them and Lawrence. The Governor informed the Missouri leaders that they must leave the Territory. They dared not put themselves in an attitude of hostility to the military power of the Union, and quickly retreated back to Missouri. With this the warfare inaugurated by the murders on the Pottawattomie ended. The Governor had at last brought peace to the distracted Territory, but at the expense of the principle of home rule in the Territory, and upon the point of the sword of the Union.

The establishment of order in Kansas saved the Democratic party, according to the general opinion, from the threatened defeat in the November election, and made Buchanan, instead of Frémont, President. After the danger was over, the Administration became less hearty in its support of Geary; and when Geary virtually espoused the "Free-state" cause, as he did during the winter of 1856–57, the Administration became largely estranged from him. He resigned in disgust on the day of Buchanan's inauguration to power.

*Geary and the Administration.*

The next contribution to the history of the struggle for Kansas was to come from an entirely new quarter. The new President indicated, in his inaugural, whence it was to come, if not what it was to be. He said: "A difference of opinion has arisen in regard to the point of time when the people of a Territory shall decide this question"—the question of slavery—"for themselves. This is, happily, a matter of but little practical importance. Besides it is a judicial question, which legitimately belongs to the Supreme Court of the United States, before whom it is now pending, and will, it is understood, be speedily and finally settled." The President referred to the Dred Scott case, which had been twice argued before the

*The judicial contribution to Kansas history.*

Supreme Court, and decision upon which, it was understood, would be published to the world in a few days. We must, therefore, break the thread of Kansas history here for a moment, and trace the history of this case down to the point where it becomes connected with the further history of the Territory.

## CHAPTER XXI.

### THE DRED SCOTT CASE

The Origin of the Dred Scott Case—Two Dred Scott Cases—The Facts of the Cases—The Case in the Missouri Courts—The Case in the United States Courts—The Case a Genuine Proceeding—The Decision by the Supreme Court of the United States—The Dissenting Opinion of Mr. Justice Curtis—Criticism of the Court's Opinion—The Obiter Dictum—The Chief Justice and the President—Justice Curtis' Dissent Continued—The Printing and Distribution of the Decision and the Dissenting Opinion—The Doctrine of Popular Sovereignty in the Territories Overthrown by the Opinion of the Court.

THE time has come when the correct story of the Dred Scott case may be told, and should be told. The author of this volume has been so fortunate as to obtain from A. C. Crane, Esq., of St. Louis, an account of the early history of the case, which is entirely original and authentic. Mr. Crane was, at the time that the case was brought in the Circuit Court of the United States, a clerk in the law office of the great lawyer who espoused Dred Scott's case, and who freely gave his legal services to the work of securing the negro's freedom, Roswell M. Field. Mr. Field was a native of Vermont, and a strong anti-slavery man. He was utterly incapable of any collusion with slaveholders for the getting up of a case, through which the Supreme Court of the United States might be brought to support the cause of slavery in the Territories, the purpose charged by many of the anti-slavery

*The origin of the Dred Scott case.*

men of the North for which this case was created. Mr. Crane most emphatically declares that Mr. Field was influenced to undertake the case only by humanitarian motives of the highest order.

There were, indeed, two Dred Scott cases, one in the courts of Missouri, and one in the United States courts, but they had no connection with each other. The case decided by the Supreme Court of the United States originated in the Circuit Court of the United States, and did not come up on a writ of error from the Missouri court.

*Two Dred Scott cases.*

The facts in the two cases were, however, the same. One Dr. Emerson, the owner of Dred Scott, had taken Dred, as his slave, into Illinois, a Commonwealth in which slavery was forbidden, and then into the Louisiana territory above the latitude thirty-six degrees and thirty minutes, where slavery was prohibited by the Congressional Act of 1820; had allowed Dred to marry in the free territory; had purchased the woman he married from an army officer at a post within the same; and had taken Dred back to Missouri, with his wife and a child born to them on free territory, and held them as slaves in Missouri. Dr. Emerson's return to Missouri was in 1838. In 1844 the Doctor died, leaving Dred and his wife and child to Mrs. Emerson. According to the statement of facts recited by the Chief Justice of the United States, Dr. Emerson sold Dred and his family to a Mr. Sandford, a citizen of New York, the defendant in the case before the Supreme Court, but Mr. Crane says that Dr. Emerson's will, in the Probate Office at St. Louis, shows that Dred and his family belonged to the Doctor at the time of the latter's death, and that Dred told him that such was the case. Mr. Crane also says that Dred told him that, after the Doctor's death, Mrs.

*The facts of the cases.*

# THE DRED SCOTT CASE 451

Emerson hired him out to different persons, and that he became dissatisfied with this treatment, and resolved to sue for his freedom.

This first suit was brought in one of the inferior courts of Missouri, and was decided in Dred's favor. Mrs. Emerson appealed the case to the supreme court of Missouri, and two of the three judges upon that bench held that the condition of slavery reattached to the negro upon his being brought back into Missouri, and reversed the decision of the lower court. *The case in the Missouri courts.*

While the case in the Missouri courts was in progress Mrs. Emerson made over the control of the Scotts to a relative of hers, a Mr. Sandford, then a citizen of New York, who hired them out to residents of Missouri. It was then, and for this reason, that Dred appealed to Roswell M. Field for his powerful aid in bringing suit against Sandford in the Courts of the United States.

The case in the Circuit Court of the United States was begun before the case in the Missouri court was concluded. The defendant in the Circuit Court of the United States first pleaded that Dred was not a citizen of Missouri, and could not be, since he was a negro and descended from slaves held in the United States, but the court overruled the plea, that is, decided that Dred Scott could be party in a suit in the courts of the United States. *The case in the United States courts.*

The evidence in the case consisted simply of a statement of facts agreed upon by the two parties. The pleas then put forward by the defendant in bar of the action were argued, on the basis of this statement, and the court ordered the jury to find for the defendant. Judgment was rendered in his favor in the month of April, 1854.

Mr. Field then carried the case to the Supreme Court

of the United States, upon a writ of error, and secured the services of his friend, the Hon. Montgomery Blair, for the negro. Mr. Blair undertook the management of the case at Washington, and, like Mr. Field, gave his time and labor without pecuniary reward. The court costs incurred by Dred in both cases were paid by Taylor Blow, son of the man who sold Dred to Doctor Emerson.

There is certainly not the slightest evidence in this history of the case that the case was anything but a genuine proceeding from beginning to end, conducted by anti-slavery men, for the purpose of securing the freedom of an intelligent and worthy African, who had been taken voluntarily by his master upon free soil, and had thus been made, by the principles of the common law, a free man.

*The case a genuine proceeding.*

The case was argued twice with great learning before the Supreme Court, and the decision finally reached was virtually acquiesced in by seven of the nine Justices, although Justice Nelson did not give his assent to any part of the opinion except that which decided that, on the return of Dred to Missouri with his master, any effect upon his slavery, which the taking of him into Illinois and the Louisiana territory above the latitude thirty-six degrees and thirty minutes might have had, disappeared. This seemed to Justice Nelson sufficient to the decision of the case, and he was unwilling to go farther, but some of his brethren, especially Justice Wayne, thought that the entire record of the case in the Circuit Court was brought up for examination by the Supreme Court, and that the Supreme Court ought to decide every point contained in the record. Justice Nelson had been, at first, selected by his colleagues to write the opinion, and it is thought that this attitude of his was what moved the Chief Justice to write the opinion himself.

*The decision by the Supreme Court of the United States.*

## THE DRED SCOTT CASE 453

Justice Catron also thought that there was nothing before the Supreme Court but the question whether, after the return of the Scotts to Missouri, their temporary sojourn on free territory could be held to have worked their emancipation. Justice Catron presided at the trial in the Circuit Court and ruled, as we have seen, in favor of Dred Scott on the point of his having a standing in the United States Courts, and the Justice thought that Scott could not bring up to the Supreme Court, on a writ of error, a point decided in his favor in the court below.

The Chief Justice, Mr. Taney, held that there were two leading questions presented by the record from the Circuit Court. The first was the question whether the Circuit Court had jurisdiction over the case, and the second was whether the judgment it gave was correct or erroneous.

The Chief Justice was right in holding that the writ of error brought up the entire record for examination by the Supreme Court, but it was not necessary that the Supreme Court should include every point of the record in its decision. And he was certainly wrong when he extended, as is now generally conceded he did, the opinion of the court beyond the points in the record of the case in the Circuit Court. The form of the judgment pronounced by the Chief Justice as the opinion of the Court, that is, of the majority of the Justices, was that the Circuit Court did not have jurisdiction of the case, since the Scotts were not citizens of Missouri, in the meaning of the Constitution of the United States, and that the judgment of the Circuit Court for the defendant must, therefore, be set aside, and a mandate be issued, directing the suit to be dismissed by the Circuit Court for want of jurisdiction. The Chief Justice undertook to sustain his opinion by a long argument, the principal propositions of which were, that negroes descended from negro slaves held in this country were not citizens in any of the "States" of the Union at the time of the formation of the Constitution of 1787; that by that Constitution the "States" transferred all power to make new classes of persons citizens to the Congress of the United States, and limited the power of Congress in this respect to the naturalization of persons born outside of the dominion of the United States; and that, consequently, negroes born of negro slave parents in the United States were not only not citizens of any of the "States" at the time of the formation of the Constitution of 1787, but could not be made such, either by the "States" or by Congress, subsequent to the adoption of that Constitution.

In his powerful dissenting opinion, Mr. Justice Curtis demolished this argument completely, by simply showing from the statute books and the judicial decisions of several of the "States" that, at the time of the formation of the Constitution of 1787, negroes descended from Africans, who had been held as slaves in the country, were citizens, even to the point of possessing the suffrage, in several of the "States" of the Union. The great argument of the Chief Justice turned out to be only a political essay, without fact, law, or jurisprudence to sustain it. Mr. Justice Curtis, therefore, held that, as nothing against Dred Scott's citizenship had been alleged by the defendant in the Circuit Court, except that he was a negro, and descended from negroes who had been held as slaves in this country, the jurisdiction assumed by the Circuit Court ought to be sustained by the Supreme Court.

*The dissenting opinion of Mr. Justice Curtis.*

But if the opinion of the Court should be accepted as correct upon this point, it is difficult to see why the opinion should not have ended with the decision upon

THE DRED SCOTT CASE          455

this point. Nothing further was necessary in the determination of the case. And it is certainly most difficult to see what connection the Act of 1820, prohibiting slavery in the Louisiana territory, north of the latitude thirty-six degrees and thirty minutes, had with the case. No decision upon that point was rendered by the Circuit Court, whose record the Supreme Court was reviewing.

*Criticism of the Court's opinion.*

If the Supreme Court had confirmed the jurisdiction of the Circuit Court in the case, and had then ruled that the Circuit Court was in error in holding that slavery reattached to the Scotts by Missouri law, upon their return to Missouri, even if they had been made free by their temporary sojourn upon free soil, probably the Supreme Court should have decided the question as to what effect that sojourn may have had, and, in this way, included the question of the constitutionality of the slavery prohibition clause in the Act of 1820. But the majority of the Supreme Court approved the view of the Circuit Court upon this point.

There is little doubt that the majority of the Justices thought that a declaration from the Supreme Court in regard to the mooted question of slavery in the Territories would aid in bringing quiet to the country, and that they had persuaded themselves that it was necessary to the decision of the point in issue. But they were certainly in error, as to the first consideration, and it is difficult to see that they were not as to the second.

The Chief Justice advanced to his conclusion in this part of the opinion through a most labored argument. He started with the dictum that there was no clause in the Constitution which gave Congress any power over territory acquired subsequently to the adoption of the Constitution, interpreting the provision which vests in Congress "the power to make

*The obiter dictum.*

all needful rules and regulations concerning the territory and other property of the United States," as applying only to territory held by the United States at the time of the adoption of the Constitution. He then founded the power to govern the territory subsequently acquired upon the right to acquire territory; and declared that in governing such territory, or providing for its government, Congress was limited by all those provisions of the Constitution which protect private rights against governmental power. He claimed, finally, that that one of these provisions which ordains that no person shall be deprived of life, liberty, or property without due process of law protected property in slaves, taken into the Territories by their masters, against both the power of Congress and of the agents of Congress in the Territories, the Territorial governments, to free them. The conclusion from this reasoning was that anybody could take slaves into a Territory of the United States, and hold them there in slavery, no matter what might be the disposition of Congress or of the Territorial government in regard to the subject, and that the question whether slavery was to be permanently established in a Territory or not could not be determined until the Territory should become a "State," and then only by an act of the "State."

This was the point which the Kansas-Nebraska Act had not covered, and which the President said, in his inaugural address, would be decided in the forthcoming opinion on the Dred Scott case.

The Chief Justice and the President.

The opinion was pronounced several days after the inaugural, and it was later charged by Mr. Seward, and intimated by Mr. Lincoln, and believed by a large number of persons, that the Chief Justice imparted the opinion of the Court to the President before it was pronounced. But this point, though not necessarily involved in the case, had been argued by counsel, and the newspapers had declared that it would be decided, and both Mr. Buchanan and Mr. Taney were men of the highest personal and official integrity, and possessed the most delicate sense of the requirements and proprieties of the great stations which they occupied. It is almost certain that the charge was an unfounded suspicion. The prevalence of the suspicion was, however, an ominous sign of the danger impending over the land.

Justice Curtis found no more difficulty in controverting these propositions than those upon the first point treated in the opinion of the Chief Justice. He first referred to the undoubted facts that not all the territory claimed by the several "States" had been ceded to the United States at the time that the Constitution of 1787 was adopted, but that it was expected that what remained would soon be so ceded, and that therefore the clause vesting in Congress "the power to make all needful rules and regulations concerning the territory of the United States" must have been framed with these future acquisitions in view, and intended to apply to them also. He then demanded to know why, if the Court could derive the power of Congress to govern territory acquired from foreign states from a right which is not expressed in the Constitution, but is itself implied, the right to acquire, should it hesitate to derive it from a power in respect to the territory of the United States which is expressed in the Constitution. He contended that until Congress or the Territorial legislature had legalized slavery in a Territory, no one could be said to be deprived of his property in slaves in the given Territory, either by a Congressional act forbidding the existence of such property, or by the failure of Congress or the Territorial

*Justice Curtis's dissent continued.*

legislature to enact laws for the security of such property. He repudiated the idea that a holder of slaves could take the law of the place from which he emigrated, securing such property, into a Territory with him as a monstrosity in jurisprudence, since it would introduce into a given Territory as many slave codes as there were slaveholding Commonwealths represented therein by their slaveholding emigrants, and he indicated, finally, that the reasoning of the Court must reach ultimately the proposition that Congress was required by the Constitution to establish slavery in every Territory of the Union, and consequently to make every new "State" a slaveholding "State."

The slaveholders and the Douglas Democrats of the North were in high glee over the decision, and hardly stopped to read the powerful dissenting opinion which had shattered it to atoms. They caused thousands upon thousands of copies of the decision to be printed and distributed among the masses of the people. The Free-soilers did the same thing with the opinion of Justice Curtis. It was not many weeks before it became entirely manifest that the cause of slavery had lost immensely by the decision, and the cause of free-soilism had gained in the same degree. Justice Curtis had demonstrated that the decision had cast the responsibility for the further extension of slavery upon the nation, and the nation now began to show its resolution to meet its responsibility by acquitting itself of any participation in this great wrong, in the only manner now left to it, that is, by preventing it. The nation could no longer deceive itself with the idea that it could stand neutral. The Court had actually swept away the dogma of "popular sovereignty" in the Territories. The nation must now

*The printing and distribution of the decision and the dissenting opinion.*

*The doctrine of popular sovereignty in the Territories overthrown by the opinion of the Court.*

neither prohibit, nor allow the Territorial governments to prohibit, slavery within the Territories, as the decision would have it, or the nation must itself prohibit it, as the dissenting opinion would have it. When these alternatives were distinctly recognized as necessary and exhaustive, it did not take the nation long to decide which course it must pursue.

# CHAPTER XXII.

## THE STRUGGLE FOR KANSAS CONCLUDED

The Lecompton Convention Ordered—Robert J. Walker and F. P. Stanton—Stanton and the "Free-state" Men—Walker's Address—The "Free-state" Legislature and Mass-meeting—The Plan to Capture the Territorial Legislature by the "Free-state" Men—The "Free-state" Men in Majority in the Territorial Legislature—The Lecompton Convention—The Lecompton Constitution—Only the Slavery Article to be Submitted Fully to the People—Protest of the "Free-state" Men—The Extra Session of the New Territorial Legislature—Stanton Removed—Lecompton Constitution With Slavery Adopted—The "Free-state" Men Capture the Lecompton Government and Reject the Lecompton Constitution—Denver Advises the President Against the Admission of Kansas Under the Lecompton Instrument—The President's Message of February 2nd (1858)—The Passage of the Lecompton Bill by the Senate—The Rejection of the Bill by the House—The English Bill—The Rejection of the Lecompton Constitution by the People of Kansas—A Fourth Government for Kansas—The Struggle for Kansas Closed—Dr. Robinson—The General Government—Mr. Jefferson Davis—The Beginning of Error and Wrong—Brown's Atrocities—The Forerunners of War.

ACCORDING to the dictum of the Court in the great case reviewed in the preceding chapter, slave property was lawful in Kansas during the Territorial period, and could be first dealt with by the constitutional convention, which should prepare the organic law for Kansas as a Commonwealth of the Union.

# THE STRUGGLE FOR KANSAS CONCLUDED 461

Already before the promulgation of the decision, the Territorial legislature had provided for the holding of the constitutional convention at Lecompton, and for the election of the delegates thereto. This election was appointed for June 15th, 1857.

*The Lecompton convention ordered.*

It was certain that the "Free-State" men now outnumbered the pro-slavery men, and that upon a fair census, registration, and distribution of seats, and with a fair election and count, they would be able to secure the majority in the convention. But could they consistently participate in an election ordered by, and under the control of, the Territorial government? Many of them felt that they could not. Others, however, were inclined to do so, if the regulations were impartial. They examined the provisions made by the Territorial legislature for the machinery of the registration and the election, and found that they were grossly favorable to the pro-slavery party. They also found that the legislature had made no provision for submitting the constitution which might be framed to the vote of the people.

While the "Free-state" men were deliberating upon this matter, the new Territorial officials appointed by the new President appeared. President Buchanan had selected Robert J. Walker, of Mississippi, to be Governor, and F. P. Stanton, of Tennessee, to be Secretary, of the Territory. Both of these men were capable, honest, and resolute. Walker was a shrewd politician, indeed, but he was fair-minded and faithful to his plighted word. Stanton arrived on the scene about the middle of April. Walker came a month later. Stanton, therefore, was Acting Governor during the first month of his residence in the Territory.

*Robert J. Walker, and F. P. Stanton.*

Stanton went to Lawrence, on the 24th, and urged the

"Free-state" men to take part in the approaching election. He had, however, already apportioned the representation in the convention on the basis of the existing census. It was evident that he was unaware that this was unjust to the "Free-state" men. Seeing this, the "Free-state" men made a counter proposition for a new census and apportionment, and for an impartial control of the elections. Stanton did not think he had the power to conclude an agreement with them on this basis, and the negotiations fell through.

*Stanton and the "Free-state" men.*

The new Governor now arrived, and bent all his energies to induce the "Free-state" men to participate in the election. He issued an address, in which he solemnly declared that he would secure honest elections and returns, and pledged himself that the constitution, which the convention might form, should be submitted to the people for ratification or rejection. He also threatened that he would enforce the laws of the Territory. His idea seems to have been to create an Administration party, which would win a majority of the seats in the convention and make Kansas a Democratic non-slaveholding Commonwealth. The pro-slavery men discovered the plan at once, and accused the Governor of leaning toward the "Free-state" party.

*Walker's address.*

The "Free-state" men were not yet, however, ready to trust the Governor. They thought it wisest to maintain their own organization, and make the Governor feel their power. On June 9th, the "Free-state" legislature assembled, to provide for the election of successors to the existing members and officials. Along with it was convoked a sort of mass-meeting of citizens. The legislature was at first without a quorum, and never had an honest quorum.

*The "Free-state" legislature and mass-meeting.*

This fact was sedulously concealed from the Governor, while the orators at the mass-meeting raised enough dust and smoke to cover up the real condition of affairs. They made the place fairly blue with their bluster and their threats, and the little Governor was greatly impressed by the apparent seriousness of the situation.

By this time, however, the "Free-state" men had become considerably discouraged in regard to the admission of Kansas into the Union under the Topeka constitution. The Senate had given the application the cold shoulder, and had, apparently, laid it aside permanently. The prevarications of Lane were said to have produced this result. As matters now stood, Robinson and the more conservative men of the "Free-state" party began to consider the advisability of attempting to capture the Territorial legislature, by participating in the election of members, which was to take place in the following October. They felt certain that upon a true census and a fair apportionment, and with an honest election, they could win a majority of the seats in the legislature, and would then be in a position to nullify the work of the Lecompton convention, which, on account of the abstention of the "Free-state" men from the election of the delegates, would be packed with pro-slavery representatives.

*The plan to capture the Territorial legislature by the "Free-state" men.*

The matter of first importance was to obtain a true census. Senator Wilson, of Massachusetts, was at the moment in Lawrence, conferring with Robinson and his friends concerning the state of affairs, and he strongly advised these gentlemen to take a correct census under the auspices of the "Free-state" government, and to nominate candidates for seats in the Territorial legislature, and elect them. He felt so decidedly about the matter that he offered to secure the funds necessary to defray the expenses of taking the new census.

Robinson and his friends were now convinced that this was the wise course, but they knew that it would be difficult to persuade the radical elements in their party to go with them. The mass-meeting at Topeka of June 9th had voted to stick to the "Free-state" government, and a convention of the "Free-state" men had assembled on July 15th to provide for its continuance. This convention, after nominating candidates for the legislative seats and for the offices, and resolving to adhere to the "Free-state" government, recommended the people to assemble in mass convention, at Grasshopper Falls, on the 26th of the following August, to take action in regard to the participation of the "Free-state" men in the October election of members of the Territorial legislature, since Governor Walker had declared that this election would be held under the laws of Congress, and not under the acts of the Territorial legislature, and had pledged himself to secure an honest election. It was evident from this that the conservative element in the "Free-state" party had won the day.

Before the day appointed for the Grasshopper Falls convention had arrived, the new census had been completed under the direction of the "Free-state" government, and it was morally certain that the "Free-state" men could elect a majority of the members of the new Territorial legislature. When the convention assembled, it therefore resolved, by a large majority, that the "Free-state" men should participate in the October election, warning the people, however, of the seriousness of the undertaking, and cautioning them against over-confidence in success.

The Lecompton convention assembled on the seventh day of September, and, after organizing, adjourned to October 19th, as if to await the result of the election of the members of the Territorial legislature.

# THE STRUGGLE FOR KANSAS CONCLUDED 465

This election came off on October 5th. The Governor remained true to his pledge of protecting the ballot-box. The presence of United States soldiers discouraged any movements from Missouri, and peace reigned at the polls. The returns from the counties of McGee and Johnson were, however, so manipulated by the pro-slavery election officers as to give the majority of the seats in the legislature to the pro-slavery party. These returns, as well as those from the other counties, were, however, to be canvassed finally by the Governor and Secretary. The "Free-state" men now demanded of them the fulfilment of their pledge of pure elections. The "Free-state" men had their newly taken census, and they convinced the Governor and Secretary that about ten times as many votes had been returned from these localities as there were residents in them. Walker and Stanton threw out the fraudulent returns, and gave, thus, the Territorial legislature to the "Free-state" men.

*The "Free-state" men in majority in the Territorial legislature.*

Two days before the Governor announced his intention of purging the returns of the frauds committed by the pro-slavery men in regard to them, and while the excitement about them was intense, it was suddenly discovered by the conservative "Free-state" men that Lane was working up a conspiracy for using violence against the members of the Lecompton convention. He, as commander-in-chief, had ordered the "Free-state" forces to assemble in Lawrence on October 19th for that purpose. The conservative men at once set themselves against this movement, and after a serious struggle happily won the day. They appointed a mass-meeting of the party at Lecompton for the following week, as much to protect the members of the convention against any sudden attack by

*The Lecompton convention.*

Lane and his reckless adherents as to watch their constitution-framing work. Before the meeting took place the Governor had announced the rejection of the fraudulent returns, and had thus deprived the "Free-state" men of all excuse for violence. Some boisterous speeches were, nevertheless, indulged in at the meeting, but the convention was allowed to complete its work in peace.

The convention framed an instrument after the Missouri model, and incorporated in it an article guaranteeing the property in slaves already within the Territory. The convention then framed an independent provision in regard to slavery as a permanent institution of the new Commonwealth. This provision alone was to be fully submitted to the vote of the people. The people must take the Lecompton constitution with slavery as a permanent institution, or the Lecompton constitution without slavery as a permanent institution but containing a guarantee of the slave property already in the Territory. The day appointed by the convention for the voters to signify their approval or disapproval of the provision in regard to slavery as a permanent institution was December 21st, 1857, and the day designated for the election of members and officers under the new constitution was January 4th following.

*The Lecompton constitution.*

*Only the Slavery article to be submitted fully to the people.*

The "Free-state" men regarded this submission of only a single article of the constitution to popular vote as a fraud upon the principle of "popular sovereignty," and demanded of Stanton, who was then discharging the Governor's duties, in the temporary absence of the latter, that the Governor's pledge as to the full submission of the proposed constitution to the people at the polls should be redeemed. Stanton bravely resolved to keep the Governor's word of

*Protest of the "Free-state" men.*

# THE STRUGGLE FOR KANSAS CONCLUDED 467

honor, although he believed it would cost him his position.

What the "Free-state" men asked of him was to convene at once the new Territorial legislature, in which the "Free-state" men now had a majority of the seats, for the purpose of giving it the opportunity to order the full submission of the Lecompton constitution to the suffrages of the people. Stanton yielded to their request, and called the legislature to meet at Lecompton on December 7th. This body at once resolved to submit the proposed constitution fully and in all its parts to the people, to be adopted or rejected by them at their pleasure, and appointed the 4th day of the following January as the time for taking the vote. *The extra session of the new Territorial legislature.*

Stanton was immediately removed from office by the Administration, and General John W. Denver, of Virginia, at the moment Indian Commissioner, was assigned to the duties of Acting Governor in the Territory. *Stanton removed.*

The "Free-state" men resolved to take no part in voting upon the slavery article of the Lecompton constitution, since they must take this constitution either with or without slavery as a permanent institution, and could not vote against the constitution as a whole. Consequently the Lecompton constitution with slavery as a permanent institution was, so far as the returns of the voting on December 21st were concerned, adopted. According to these returns, six thousand two hundred and sixty-six votes were cast for it. Of these, nearly three thousand were afterward shown to be fraudulent. Between five and six hundred votes were cast for this constitution without slavery as a permanent institution. None were counted against it *in toto*. That is to say, out of a vot-  *Lecompton constitution with slavery adopted.*

ing population of about fifteen thousand, less than four thousand were in favor of this constitution in either form.

The more prudent of the "Free-state" men now thought, however, that it would be wise to participate in the election of members and officers of the Lecompton "State" government on the day fixed by the Lecompton constitution, January 4th, 1858. They were to vote fully at that time, as we have seen, upon the Lecompton constitution, by order of the Territorial legislature, now in their hands. They felt certain of defeating the constitution, and they knew that they could win in the election of the officers and members. They nominated a ticket with G. W. Smith at its head, as their candidate for Governor.

On January 4th, more than ten thousand votes were cast against the Lecompton constitution entire, and only about one hundred and fifty votes were cast in its favor. The "Free-state" men also elected their candidates for the offices and seats in the government created by the Lecompton constitution.

*The "Free-state" men capture the Lecompton government and reject the Lecompton constitution.*

The "Free-state" men now had possession of the Topeka "Free-state" government, of the Territorial legislature, and of the Lecompton "State" government, and had rejected the Lecompton constitution by an undoubted majority of the suffrages of the citizens of Kansas.

As yet the Lecompton constitution had not been presented by the President to Congress, and Acting Governor Denver hastened to give him a truthful statement of the condition of affairs in the Territory, and to urge him not to recommend to Congress the admission of Kansas under this constitution, but to suggest to that body the passage simply of an enabling

*Denver advises the President against the admission of Kansas under the Lecompton instrument.*

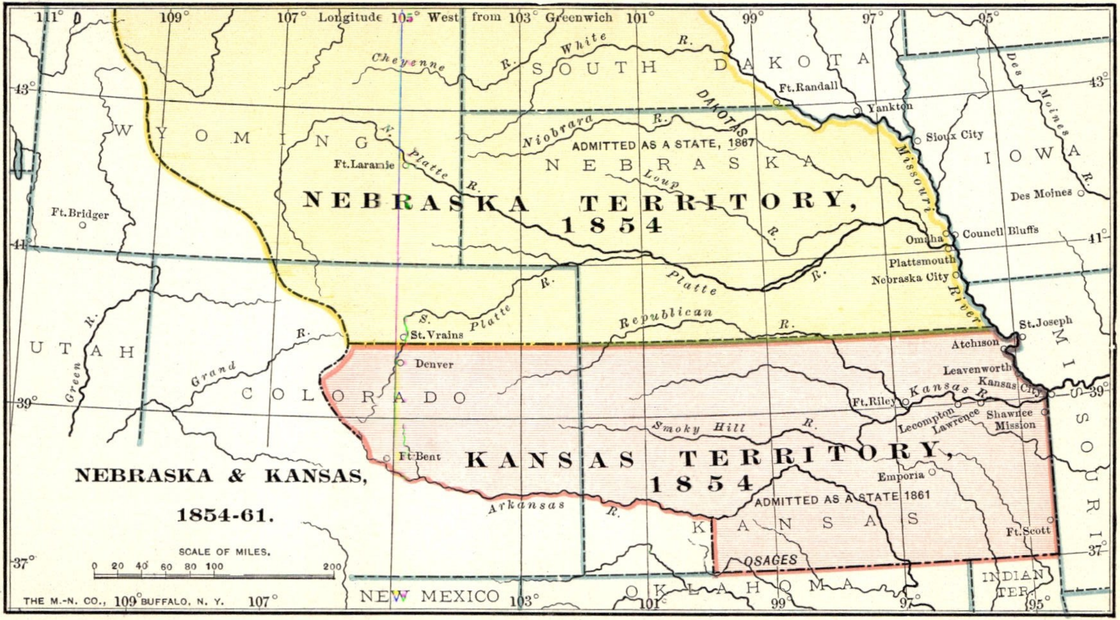
NEBRASKA & KANSAS,
1854-61.
NEBRASKA TERRITORY, 1854
KANSAS TERRITORY, 1854
ADMITTED AS A STATE, 1867
ADMITTED AS A STATE 1861
NEBRASKA
KANSAS
SOUTH DAKOTA
DAKOTAS
WYOMING
UTAH
COLORADO
IOWA
MISSOURI
OKLAHOMA
NEW MEXICO
INDIAN TER.
OSAGES
Longitude 105° West from 103° Greenwich
111° 109° 107° 101° 99° 97° 95°
43° 41° 39° 37°
White R.
Cheyenne R.
Niobrara R.
Loup R.
N. Platte R.
Platte R.
S. Platte R.
Republican R.
Smoky Hill R.
Kansas R.
Arkansas R.
Grand R.
Green R.
Missouri River
Des Moines R.
Ft.Randall
Yankton
Sioux City
Des Moines
Council Bluffs
Omaha
Plattsmouth
Nebraska City
St.Joseph
Atchison
Leavenworth
Kansas City
Ft.Riley
Lecompton
Lawrence
Shawnee Mission
Emporia
Ft.Scott
Ft.Laramie
Ft.Bridger
St.Vrains
Denver
Ft.Bent
SCALE OF MILES.
0 20 40 60 80 100 200
THE M.-N. CO., BUFFALO, N. Y.

# THE STRUGGLE FOR KANSAS CONCLUDED

act, under which the people of Kansas might begin again the work of forming a Commonwealth constitution.

But the President did not heed this wise warning. On February 2nd, 1858, he sent the Lecompton constitution, with the provision making slavery a permanent institution in Kansas, to Congress, and recommended the admission of the distracted Territory into the Union, as a "State," under it. *The President's message of February 2nd (1858).* His line of argument was that every step in the procedure of framing and adopting this constitution had been regularly and legally taken, and that all the voters could have participated in the work if they had chosen to do so. He claimed that the act of the Territorial legislature, after it came under the control of the "Free-state" men, in ordering another vote, and a different sort of vote, upon the constitution, than and from that appointed and required by the convention, was irregular; and he undertook to comfort the "Free-state" men with the suggestion that, Kansas once admitted, they could change its constitution to suit themselves, if they were really in majority.

The President's argument carried the Senate with him despite the powerful opposition of Mr. Douglas, who bravely antagonized the Administration, and held firmly that his great principle of "popular sovereignty" required the unreserved submission of every part of the constitution to the free suffrages of the people, in order to establish its validity. *The passage of the Lecompton bill by the Senate.* He declared that unless this should be done Congress could not know whether the people of Kansas had made a constitution or not, and that without that knowledge the admission of Kansas under the constitution before the Senate was tantamount to making a constitution for Kansas by Congressional act. The honest and manly stand taken by Mr. Douglas upon this great subject certainly presents him in the rôle of a patriotic statesman, rather than in his usual character of the shrewd politician.

The Senate passed the Lecompton bill on March 23rd, 1858, by a substantial majority, but the House promptly rejected it. The House passed a measure, instead, for referring the Lecompton constitution back to the people of Kansas, who should vote freely upon it in all its parts, and for admitting Kansas, without further Congressional action, under this constitution, if it should receive the popular ratification; but the Senate rejected this substitute for its bill.

*The rejection of the bill by the House.*

The matter was then sent to a conference committee of the two Houses. After long deliberation a measure was matured by this committee which appeared to deal with a subsidiary question only, but which, by some sort of an understanding, was held to give the people of Kansas the chance to reject the Lecompton constitution *in toto* at the polls. The measure is known as the English bill from its projector, Mr. W. H. English, a member of the conference committee from the House of Representatives. It provided for a reduction of the land grants from twenty-three millions of acres, asked for by Kansas under the Lecompton constitution, to about four millions of acres, and proposed the submission of this change to a vote of the people of Kansas. If the people adopted the change, they would be considered as having adopted the Lecompton constitution *in toto*. If, on the other hand, they rejected this change, they would be considered as having rejected this constitution *in toto*.

*The English bill.*

# THE STRUGGLE FOR KANSAS CONCLUDED 471

The English bill was agreed to by both Houses; and on August 2nd, 1858, the people of Kansas voted upon the measure. They rejected it, and with it the Lecompton constitution, by a vote of more than eleven thousand in a total vote of about thirteen thousand. *The rejection of the Lecompton constitution by the people of Kansas.*

In the meantime, fearing that Congress might pass the bill for admitting Kansas under the Lecompton constitution, the Territorial legislature, now in the hands of the "Free-state" men, passed a bill ordering a new constitutional convention. The bill was passed within a few days of the end of the session, and Governor Denver, thinking that Kansas had about enough governments already, pocketed the measure. The convention was, however, held, and a constitution was framed and submitted to the people which received some three thousand votes in favor of its adoption, while none were cast against it. Officers were chosen under it, and thus a fourth government for Kansas was created. All of these governments were now, however, in the hands of the conservative men of the "Free-state" party. *A fourth government for Kansas.*

With the rejection of the Lecompton constitution by the people of Kansas, on August 2nd, the struggle for Kansas was closed. It was to be a non-slaveholding Commonwealth and a Republican Commonwealth. The record of this struggle is certainly one of the most remarkable chapters in the history of the United States. There is much to admire in it, much to be ashamed of, and much to be repudiated as foul and devilish. The prudence, moderation, tact, and bravery of Dr. Robinson and his friends have rarely been excelled by the statesmen and diplomatists of the New World or of the Old. They were placed in a most trying situation *The struggle for Kansas closed. Dr. Robinson.*

both by their foes and by those who, professing to be their friends, endangered the cause more by violent and brutal deeds than did their open enemies. Their triumph over all these difficulties is a marvel of shrewd, honest, and conservative management, which may well serve as one of the best object-lessons of our history for succeeding generations.

The attitude of the general Government was also honorable and praiseworthy. It did its best to hold the balance even and impartial between the contending forces. It sent out intelligent, honest, and resolute men as Governors; and it used the army to maintain the peace, and protect person and property from violence. Even President Pierce's Secretary of War, Mr. Jefferson Davis, who was considered the very high-priest of the slavery interest, sent a military commander, Colonel E. V. Sumner, to Kansas, whom he knew to be in sympathy with Free-soil principles, and instructed him only to do what was just between all parties; and when Colonel Sumner, fearing that, from personal sympathy with the cause of the "Free-state" men, he might unconsciously act too favorably toward them, really went farther than his duty required against them, in dispersing their legislature, Mr. Davis expressed the opinion that the United States forces ought not to have interfered with the "Free-state" government until it had undertaken to execute some of its measures. It was said at the time that Mr. Davis' quasi disavowal of Colonel Sumner's act was caused by its unpopularity throughout the North; but Mr. Davis was not to any such degree sensitive to Northern opinion. Personally and officially Mr. Davis was a remarkably upright man, and was accustomed to take counsel chiefly of his own judgment and conscience, and to disturb himself very little about the views of

## THE STRUGGLE FOR KANSAS CONCLUDED 473

others concerning his duties and acts. Governor Robinson has recently testified to the impartial attitude of the military power of the United States in Kansas, and has declared that "had it not been for the officers of the United States army, the 'Free-state' struggle would have ended in disaster on more than one occasion."

Error began, unquestionably, with the repeal of the Act prohibiting slavery in the Louisiana territory above thirty-six degrees and thirty minutes north latitude, and wrong began, just as unquestionably, with the incursion of the Missourians, and their fraudulent voting at the Territorial election in March of 1855. A bogus legislature was thus thrust upon Kansas Territory at the outset. It was a political outrage of the first degree, and it would have justified rebellion against the execution of the enactments of this body. But it does not excuse, or even palliate, the criminal atrocities inaugurated by John Brown at Dutch Henry's Crossing, and the wild reign of murder and robbery which followed in their train. All this was common crime of the blackest and most villainous sort, and the men who engaged in it were cutthroats and highwaymen, who took advantage of the confusion in Kansas to prosecute their nefarious work. *[The beginning of error and wrong. Brown's atrocities.]*

It is often said that the Civil War began in Kansas, and simply spread from there over the country. It is true that violence began there, and in its degeneration into savagery developed those devilish dispositions that carried murder and robbery into Virginia, and thereby helped mightily to create that intensely hostile feeling between the North and the South which resulted in Civil War, but we affront good morals and common sense when we dignify those Kansas atrocities by the title of war; and we obliterate moral distinctions when we attempt to justify them by the end which their authors professed to have in view, the extermination of African slavery throughout the country. Such deeds are not means to anything except the establishment of the reign of hell on earth, and the maudlin adoration sometimes accorded their doers is evidence of an unbalanced moral sense. It is a source of congratulation that the juristic sense of the last decades of the nineteenth century refuses to place the crank who kills or robs for what he considers, or professes to consider, the welfare of society under any other class than that of the most dangerous criminals. It remains for the ethical sense of the twentieth century to sweep the hero-worship too often accorded such characters out of the world's literature.

But if the murders, and robberies, and arson committed in Kansas were not war, they were the forerunners of war. The last expedient which the minds of men could invent for putting the slavery question in the position of a purely local matter had been tried, and had utterly and miserably failed. The nation must now settle the question, by peaceable means if it could, but if it could not, then by force. The record of its attempts, first upon the one line, and then upon the other, will be the chief subject of the next and last volume of this series.

*The forerunners of war.*

# APPENDIX I.

## THE ELECTORAL VOTE IN DETAIL,
### 1820–1856.

#### Electoral Vote in 1820.

| States. | President. James Monroe, of Virginia. | John Quincy Adams, of Massachusetts. | Vice-President. Daniel D. Tompkins, of New York. | Richard Stockton, of New Jersey. | Daniel Rodney, of Delaware. | Richard Rush, of Pennsylvania. | Robert G. Harper, of Maryland. |
|---|---|---|---|---|---|---|---|
| Alabama | 3 | .. | 3 | .. | .. | .. | .. |
| Connecticut | 9 | .. | 9 | .. | .. | .. | .. |
| Delaware | 4 | .. | .. | .. | 4 | .. | .. |
| Georgia | 8 | .. | 8 | .. | .. | .. | .. |
| Illinois | 3 | .. | 3 | .. | .. | .. | .. |
| Indiana | 3 | .. | 3 | .. | .. | .. | .. |
| Kentucky | 12 | .. | 12 | .. | .. | .. | .. |
| Louisiana | 3 | .. | 3 | .. | .. | .. | .. |
| Maine | 9 | .. | 9 | .. | .. | .. | .. |
| Maryland | 11 | .. | 10 | .. | .. | .. | 1 |
| Massachusetts | 15 | .. | 7 | 8 | .. | .. | .. |
| Mississippi | 2 | .. | 2 | .. | .. | .. | .. |
| Missouri* | 3 | .. | 3 | .. | .. | .. | .. |
| New Hampshire | 7 | 1 | 7 | .. | .. | 1 | .. |
| New Jersey | 8 | .. | 8 | .. | .. | .. | .. |
| New York | 29 | .. | 29 | .. | .. | .. | .. |
| North Carolina | 15 | .. | 15 | .. | .. | .. | .. |
| Ohio | 8 | .. | 8 | .. | .. | .. | .. |
| Pennsylvania | 24 | .. | 24 | .. | .. | .. | .. |
| Rhode Island | 4 | .. | 4 | .. | .. | .. | .. |
| South Carolina | 11 | .. | 11 | .. | .. | .. | .. |
| Tennessee | 7 | .. | 7 | .. | .. | .. | .. |
| Vermont | 8 | .. | 8 | .. | .. | .. | .. |
| Virginia | 25 | .. | 25 | .. | .. | .. | .. |
| Total | 231 | 1 | 218 | 8 | 4 | 1 | 1 |

* Missouri was not formally admitted as a state until August. 1821

## Electoral Vote in 1824.

| STATES. | President. Andrew Jackson, of Tennessee. | President. John Quincy Adams, of Massachusetts. | President. William H. Crawford, of Georgia. | President. Henry Clay, of Kentucky. | Vice-President. John C. Calhoun, of South Carolina. | Vice-President. Nathan Sanford, of New York. | Vice-President. Henry Clay, of Kentucky. | Vice-President. Andrew Jackson, of Tennessee. | Vice-President. Martin Van Buren, of New York. | Vice-President. Nathaniel Macon, of North Carolina. | Vacancies. |
|---|---|---|---|---|---|---|---|---|---|---|---|
| Alabama | 5 | .. | .. | .. | 5 | .. | .. | .. | .. | .. | .. |
| Connecticut | .. | 8 | .. | .. | .. | .. | .. | 8 | .. | .. | .. |
| Delaware | .. | 1 | 2 | .. | 1 | .. | 2 | .. | .. | .. | .. |
| Georgia | .. | .. | 9 | .. | .. | .. | .. | .. | 9 | .. | .. |
| Illinois | 2 | 1 | .. | .. | 3 | .. | .. | .. | .. | .. | .. |
| Indiana | 5 | .. | .. | .. | 5 | .. | .. | .. | .. | .. | .. |
| Kentucky | .. | .. | .. | 14 | 7 | 7 | .. | .. | .. | .. | .. |
| Louisiana | 3 | 2 | .. | .. | 5 | .. | .. | .. | .. | .. | .. |
| Maine | .. | 9 | .. | .. | 9 | .. | .. | .. | .. | .. | .. |
| Maryland | 7 | 3 | 1 | .. | 10 | .. | .. | 1 | .. | .. | .. |
| Massachusetts | .. | 15 | .. | .. | 15 | .. | .. | .. | .. | .. | .. |
| Mississippi | 3 | .. | .. | .. | 3 | .. | .. | .. | .. | .. | .. |
| Missouri | .. | .. | .. | 3 | .. | .. | .. | 3 | .. | .. | .. |
| New Hampshire | .. | 8 | .. | .. | 7 | .. | .. | 1 | .. | .. | .. |
| New Jersey | 8 | .. | .. | .. | 8 | .. | .. | .. | .. | .. | .. |
| New York | 1 | 26 | 5 | 4 | 29 | 7 | .. | .. | .. | .. | .. |
| North Carolina | 15 | .. | .. | .. | 15 | .. | .. | .. | .. | .. | .. |
| Ohio | .. | .. | .. | 16 | .. | 16 | .. | .. | .. | .. | .. |
| Pennsylvania | 28 | .. | .. | .. | 28 | .. | .. | .. | .. | .. | .. |
| Rhode Island | .. | 4 | .. | .. | 3 | .. | .. | .. | .. | .. | 1 |
| South Carolina | 11 | .. | .. | .. | 11 | .. | .. | .. | .. | .. | .. |
| Tennessee | 11 | .. | .. | .. | 11 | .. | .. | .. | .. | .. | .. |
| Vermont | .. | 7 | .. | .. | 7 | .. | .. | .. | .. | .. | .. |
| Virginia | .. | .. | 24 | .. | .. | .. | .. | .. | .. | 24 | .. |
| Total | 99* | 84 | 41 | 37 | 182 | 30 | 2 | 13 | 9 | 24 | 1 |

* Since no President was elected, the House of Representatives proceeded to elect one, and John Quincy Adams was chosen on the first ballot, the vote standing Adams, 13 States; Jackson, 7 States; Crawford, 4 States.

## Electoral Vote in 1828.

| STATES. | President. Andrew Jackson, of Tennessee. | President. John Quincy Adams, of Massachusetts. | Vice-President. John C. Calhoun, of South Carolina. | Vice-President. Richard Rush, of Pennsylvania. | Vice-President. William Smith, of South Carolina. |
|---|---|---|---|---|---|
| Alabama | 5 | .. | 5 | .. | .. |
| Connecticut | .. | 8 | .. | 8 | .. |
| Delaware | .. | 3 | .. | 3 | .. |
| Georgia | 9 | .. | 2 | .. | 7 |
| Illinois | 3 | .. | 3 | .. | .. |
| Indiana | 5 | .. | 5 | .. | .. |
| Kentucky | 14 | .. | 14 | .. | .. |
| Louisiana | 5 | .. | 5 | .. | .. |
| Maine | 1 | 8 | 1 | 8 | .. |
| Maryland | 5 | 6 | 5 | 6 | .. |
| Massachusetts | .. | 15 | .. | 15 | .. |
| Mississippi | 3 | .. | 3 | .. | .. |
| Missouri | 3 | .. | 3 | .. | .. |
| New Hampshire | .. | 8 | .. | 8 | .. |
| New Jersey | .. | 8 | .. | 8 | .. |
| New York | 20 | 16 | 20 | 16 | .. |
| North Carolina | 15 | .. | 15 | .. | .. |
| Ohio | 16 | .. | 16 | .. | .. |
| Pennsylvania | 28 | .. | 28 | .. | .. |
| Rhode Island | .. | 4 | .. | 4 | .. |
| South Carolina | 11 | .. | 11 | .. | .. |
| Tennessee | 11 | .. | 11 | .. | .. |
| Vermont | .. | 7 | .. | 7 | .. |
| Virginia | 24 | .. | 24 | .. | .. |
| Total | 178 | 83 | 171 | 83 | 7 |

## Electoral Vote in 1832.

| STATES. | Andrew Jackson, of Tennessee. | Henry Clay, of Kentucky. | John Floyd, of Virginia. | William Wirt, of Maryland. | Vacancies. | Martin Van Buren, of New York | John Sergeant, of Pennsylvania. | William Wilkins, of Pennsylvania. | Henry Lee, of Massachusetts. | Amos Ellmaker, of Pennsylvania. |
|---|---|---|---|---|---|---|---|---|---|---|
| Alabama.......... | 7 | .. | .. | .. | .. | 7 | .. | .. | .. | .. |
| Connecticut .... | .. | 8 | .. | .. | .. | .. | 8 | .. | .. | .. |
| Delaware........ | .. | 3 | .. | .. | .. | .. | 3 | .. | .. | .. |
| Georgia.......... | 11 | .. | .. | .. | .. | 11 | .. | .. | .. | .. |
| Illinois ......... | 5 | .. | .. | .. | .. | 5 | .. | .. | .. | .. |
| Indiana......... | 9 | .. | .. | .. | .. | 9 | .. | .. | .. | .. |
| Kentucky ...... | .. | 15 | .. | .. | .. | .. | 15 | .. | .. | .. |
| Louisiana....... | 5 | .. | .. | .. | .. | 5 | .. | .. | .. | .. |
| Maine........... | 10 | .. | .. | .. | .. | 10 | .. | .. | .. | .. |
| Maryland....... | 3 | 5 | .. | .. | 2 | 3 | 5 | .. | .. | .. |
| Massachusetts... | .. | 14 | .. | .. | .. | .. | 14 | .. | .. | .. |
| Mississippi...... | 4 | .. | .. | .. | .. | 4 | .. | .. | .. | .. |
| Missouri......... | 4 | .. | .. | .. | .. | 4 | .. | .. | .. | .. |
| New Hampshire. | 7 | .. | .. | .. | .. | 7 | .. | .. | .. | .. |
| New Jersey..... | 8 | .. | .. | .. | .. | 8 | .. | .. | .. | .. |
| New York....... | 42 | .. | .. | .. | .. | 42 | .. | .. | .. | .. |
| North Carolina.. | 15 | .. | .. | .. | .. | 15 | .. | .. | .. | .. |
| Ohio............. | 21 | .. | .. | .. | .. | 21 | .. | .. | .. | .. |
| Pennsylvania ... | 30 | .. | .. | .. | .. | .. | .. | 30 | .. | .. |
| Rhode Island.... | .. | 4 | .. | .. | .. | .. | 4 | .. | .. | .. |
| South Carolina.. | .. | .. | 11 | .. | .. | .. | .. | .. | 11 | .. |
| Tennessee....... | 15 | .. | .. | .. | .. | 15 | .. | .. | .. | .. |
| Vermont........ | .. | .. | .. | 7 | .. | .. | .. | .. | .. | 7 |
| Virginia......... | 23 | .. | .. | .. | .. | 23 | .. | .. | .. | .. |
| Total ...... | 219 | 49 | 11 | 7 | 2 | 189 | 49 | 30 | 11 | 7 |

## APPENDIX

### Electoral Vote in 1836.

| STATES. | President. Martin Van Buren, of New York. | President. William Henry Harrison, of Ohio. | President. Hugh L. White, of Tennessee. | President. Daniel Webster, of Massachusetts. | President. Willie P. Mangum, of North Carolina. | Vice-President. Richard M. Johnson, of Kentucky. | Vice-President. Francis Granger, of New York. | Vice-President. John Tyler, of Virginia. | Vice-President. William Smith, of South Carolina. |
|---|---|---|---|---|---|---|---|---|---|
| Alabama | 7 | .. | .. | .. | .. | 7 | .. | .. | .. |
| Arkansas | 3 | .. | .. | .. | .. | 3 | .. | .. | .. |
| Connecticut | 8 | .. | .. | .. | .. | 8 | .. | .. | .. |
| Delaware | .. | 3 | .. | .. | .. | .. | 3 | .. | .. |
| Georgia | .. | .. | 11 | .. | .. | .. | .. | 11 | .. |
| Illinois | 5 | .. | .. | .. | .. | 5 | .. | .. | .. |
| Indiana | .. | 9 | .. | .. | .. | .. | 9 | .. | .. |
| Kentucky | .. | 15 | .. | .. | .. | .. | 15 | .. | .. |
| Louisiana | 5 | .. | .. | .. | .. | 5 | .. | .. | .. |
| Maine | 10 | .. | .. | .. | .. | 10 | .. | .. | .. |
| Maryland | .. | 10 | .. | .. | .. | .. | .. | 10 | .. |
| Massachusetts | .. | .. | .. | 14 | .. | .. | 14 | .. | .. |
| Michigan* | 3 | .. | .. | .. | .. | 3 | .. | .. | .. |
| Mississippi | 4 | .. | .. | .. | .. | 4 | .. | .. | .. |
| Missouri | 4 | .. | .. | .. | .. | 4 | .. | .. | .. |
| New Hampshire | 7 | .. | .. | .. | .. | 7 | .. | .. | .. |
| New Jersey | .. | 8 | .. | .. | .. | .. | 8 | .. | .. |
| New York | 42 | .. | .. | .. | .. | 42 | .. | .. | .. |
| North Carolina | 15 | .. | .. | .. | .. | 15 | .. | .. | .. |
| Ohio | .. | 21 | .. | .. | .. | .. | 21 | .. | .. |
| Pennsylvania | 30 | .. | .. | .. | .. | 30 | .. | .. | .. |
| Rhode Island | 4 | .. | .. | .. | .. | 4 | .. | .. | .. |
| South Carolina | .. | .. | .. | .. | 11 | .. | .. | 11 | .. |
| Tennessee | .. | .. | 15 | .. | .. | .. | .. | 15 | .. |
| Vermont | .. | 7 | .. | .. | .. | .. | 7 | .. | .. |
| Virginia | 23 | .. | .. | .. | .. | .. | .. | .. | 23 |
| Total | 167 | 73 | 26 | 14 | 11 | 144 | 77 | 47 | 23 |

* Michigan had not been formally admitted as a State at the time when the electors were chosen. When the votes were counted the President of the Senate declared Martin Van Buren elected President, no election for Vice-President. The Senate then elected a Vice-President, Richard M. Johnson receiving 33 votes and Francis Granger 16.

## Electoral Vote in 1840.

| States. | President. William Henry Harrison, of Ohio. | President. Martin Van Buren, of New York. | Vice-President. John Tyler, of Virginia. | Vice-President. Richard M. Johnson, of Kentucky. | Vice-President. Littleton W. Tazewell, of Virginia. | Vice-President. James K. Polk, of Tennessee. |
|---|---|---|---|---|---|---|
| Alabama | .. | 7 | .. | 7 | .. | .. |
| Arkansas | .. | 3 | .. | 3 | .. | .. |
| Connecticut | 8 | .. | 8 | .. | .. | .. |
| Delaware | 3 | .. | 3 | .. | .. | .. |
| Georgia | 11 | .. | 11 | .. | .. | .. |
| Illinois | .. | 5 | .. | 5 | .. | .. |
| Indiana | 9 | .. | 9 | .. | .. | .. |
| Kentucky | 15 | .. | 15 | .. | .. | .. |
| Louisiana | 5 | .. | 5 | .. | .. | .. |
| Maine | 10 | .. | 10 | .. | .. | .. |
| Maryland | 10 | .. | 10 | .. | .. | .. |
| Massachusetts | 14 | .. | 14 | .. | .. | .. |
| Michigan | 3 | .. | 3 | .. | .. | .. |
| Mississippi | 4 | .. | 4 | .. | .. | .. |
| Missouri | .. | 4 | .. | 4 | .. | .. |
| New Hampshire | .. | 7 | .. | 7 | .. | .. |
| New Jersey | 8 | .. | 8 | .. | .. | .. |
| New York | 42 | .. | 42 | .. | .. | .. |
| North Carolina | 15 | .. | 15 | .. | .. | .. |
| Ohio | 21 | .. | 21 | .. | .. | .. |
| Pennsylvania | 30 | .. | 30 | .. | .. | .. |
| Rhode Island | 4 | .. | 4 | .. | .. | .. |
| South Carolina | .. | 11 | .. | .. | 11 | .. |
| Tennessee | 15 | .. | 15 | .. | .. | .. |
| Vermont | 7 | .. | 7 | .. | .. | .. |
| Virginia | .. | 23 | .. | 22 | .. | 1 |
| Total | 234 | 60 | 234 | 48 | 11 | 1 |

## ELECTORAL VOTE IN 1844.

| STATES. | President. James K. Polk, of Tennessee. | President. Henry Clay, of Kentucky. | Vice-President. George M. Dallas, of Pennsylvania. | Vice-President. Theodore Frelinghuysen, of New Jersey. |
|---|---|---|---|---|
| Alabama | 9 | .. | 9 | .. |
| Arkansas | 3 | .. | 3 | .. |
| Connecticut | .. | 6 | .. | 6 |
| Delaware | .. | 3 | .. | 3 |
| Georgia | 10 | .. | 10 | .. |
| Illinois | 9 | .. | 9 | .. |
| Indiana | 12 | .. | 12 | .. |
| Kentucky | .. | 12 | .. | 12 |
| Louisiana | 6 | .. | 6 | .. |
| Maine | 9 | .. | 9 | .. |
| Maryland | .. | 8 | .. | 8 |
| Massachusetts | .. | 12 | .. | 12 |
| Michigan | 5 | .. | 5 | .. |
| Mississippi | 6 | .. | 6 | .. |
| Missouri | 7 | .. | 7 | .. |
| New Hampshire | 6 | .. | 6 | .. |
| New Jersey | .. | 7 | .. | 7 |
| New York | 36 | .. | 36 | .. |
| North Carolina | .. | 11 | .. | 11 |
| Ohio | .. | 23 | .. | 23 |
| Pennsylvania | 26 | .. | 26 | .. |
| Rhode Island | .. | 4 | .. | 4 |
| South Carolina | 9 | .. | 9 | .. |
| Tennessee | .. | 13 | .. | 13 |
| Vermont | .. | 6 | .. | 6 |
| Virginia | 17 | .. | 17 | .. |
| Total | 170 | 105 | 170 | 105 |

## Electoral Vote in 1848.

| States. | Zachary Taylor, of Louisiana. | Lewis Cass, of Michigan. | Millard Fillmore, of New York. | William O. Butler, of Kentucky. |
|---|---|---|---|---|
| Alabama | .. | 9 | .. | 9 |
| Arkansas | .. | 3 | .. | 3 |
| Connecticut | 6 | .. | 6 | .. |
| Delaware | 3 | .. | 3 | .. |
| Florida | 3 | .. | 3 | .. |
| Georgia | 10 | .. | 10 | .. |
| Illinois | .. | 9 | .. | 9 |
| Indiana | .. | 12 | .. | 12 |
| Iowa | .. | 4 | .. | 4 |
| Kentucky | 12 | .. | 12 | .. |
| Louisiana | 6 | .. | 6 | .. |
| Maine | .. | 9 | .. | 9 |
| Maryland | 8 | .. | 8 | .. |
| Massachusetts | 12 | .. | 12 | .. |
| Michigan | .. | 5 | .. | 5 |
| Mississippi | .. | 6 | .. | 6 |
| Missouri | .. | 7 | .. | 7 |
| New Hampshire | .. | 6 | .. | 6 |
| New Jersey | 7 | .. | 7 | .. |
| New York | 36 | .. | 36 | .. |
| North Carolina | 11 | .. | 11 | .. |
| Ohio | .. | 23 | .. | 23 |
| Pennsylvania | 26 | .. | 26 | .. |
| Rhode Island | 4 | .. | 4 | .. |
| South Carolina | .. | 9 | .. | 9 |
| Tennessee | 13 | .. | 13 | .. |
| Texas | .. | 4 | .. | 4 |
| Vermont | 6 | .. | 6 | .. |
| Virginia | .. | 17 | .. | 17 |
| Wisconsin | .. | 4 | .. | 4 |
| Total | 163 | 127 | 163 | 127 |

## Electoral Vote in 1852.

| STATES. | President. Franklin Pierce, of New Hampshire. | President. Winfield Scott, of Virginia. | Vice-President. William Rufus King, of Alabama. | Vice-President. William A. Graham, of North Carolina. |
|---|---|---|---|---|
| Alabama | 9 | .. | 9 | .. |
| Arkansas | 4 | .. | 4 | .. |
| California | 4 | .. | 4 | .. |
| Connecticut | 6 | .. | 6 | .. |
| Delaware | 3 | .. | 3 | .. |
| Florida | 3 | .. | 3 | .. |
| Georgia | 10 | .. | 10 | .. |
| Illinois | 11 | .. | 11 | .. |
| Indiana | 13 | .. | 13 | .. |
| Iowa | 4 | .. | 4 | .. |
| Kentucky | .. | 12 | .. | 12 |
| Louisiana | 6 | .. | 6 | .. |
| Maine | 8 | .. | 8 | .. |
| Maryland | 8 | .. | 8 | .. |
| Massachusetts | .. | 13 | .. | 13 |
| Michigan | 6 | .. | 6 | .. |
| Mississippi | 7 | .. | 7 | .. |
| Missouri | 9 | .. | 9 | .. |
| New Hampshire | 5 | .. | 5 | .. |
| New Jersey | 7 | .. | 7 | .. |
| New York | 35 | .. | 35 | .. |
| North Carolina | 10 | .. | 10 | .. |
| Ohio | 23 | .. | 23 | .. |
| Pennsylvania | 27 | .. | 27 | .. |
| Rhode Island | 4 | .. | 4 | .. |
| South Carolina | 8 | .. | 8 | .. |
| Tennessee | .. | 12 | .. | 12 |
| Texas | 4 | .. | 4 | .. |
| Vermont | .. | 5 | .. | 5 |
| Virginia | 15 | .. | 15 | .. |
| Wisconsin | 5 | .. | 5 | .. |
| Total | 254 | 42 | 254 | 42 |

## ELECTORAL VOTE IN 1856.

| STATES. | President. James Buchanan, of Pennsylvania. | President. John C. Frémont, of California. | President. Millard Fillmore, of New York. | Vice-President. J. C. Breckinridge, of Kentucky. | Vice-President. William L. Dayton, of New Jersey. | Vice-President. A. J. Donelson, of Tennessee. |
|---|---|---|---|---|---|---|
| Alabama | 9 | .. | .. | 9 | .. | .. |
| Arkansas | 4 | .. | .. | 4 | .. | .. |
| California | 4 | .. | .. | 4 | .. | .. |
| Connecticut | .. | 6 | .. | .. | 6 | .. |
| Delaware | 3 | .. | .. | 3 | .. | .. |
| Florida | 3 | .. | .. | 3 | .. | .. |
| Georgia | 10 | .. | .. | 10 | .. | .. |
| Illinois | 11 | .. | .. | 11 | .. | .. |
| Indiana | 13 | .. | .. | 13 | .. | .. |
| Iowa | .. | 4 | .. | .. | 4 | .. |
| Kentucky | 12 | .. | .. | 12 | .. | .. |
| Louisiana | 6 | .. | .. | 6 | .. | .. |
| Maine | .. | 8 | .. | .. | 8 | .. |
| Maryland | .. | .. | 8 | .. | .. | 8 |
| Massachusetts | .. | 13 | .. | .. | 13 | .. |
| Michigan | .. | 6 | .. | .. | 6 | .. |
| Mississippi | 7 | .. | .. | 7 | .. | .. |
| Missouri | 9 | .. | .. | 9 | .. | .. |
| New Hampshire | .. | 5 | .. | .. | 5 | .. |
| New Jersey | 7 | .. | . | 7 | .. | .. |
| New York | .. | 35 | .. | .. | 35 | .. |
| North Carolina | 10 | .. | .. | 10 | .. | .. |
| Ohio | .. | 23 | .. | .. | 23 | .. |
| Pennsylvania | 27 | .. | .. | 27 | .. | .. |
| Rhode Island | .. | 4 | .. | .. | 4 | .. |
| South Carolina | 8 | .. | .. | 8 | .. | .. |
| Tennessee | 12 | .. | .. | 12 | .. | .. |
| Texas | 4 | .. | .. | 4 | .. | .. |
| Vermont | .. | 5 | .. | .. | 5 | .. |
| Virginia | 15 | .. | .. | 15 | .. | .. |
| Wisconsin | .. | 5 | .. | .. | 5 | .. |
| Total | 174 | 114 | 8 | 174 | 114 | 8 |

# APPENDIX II.

## THE CABINETS OF MONROE, ADAMS, JACKSON, VAN BUREN, HARRISON, TYLER, POLK, TAYLOR, FILLMORE, PIERCE, AND BUCHANAN—1816–1858.

### THE SECRETARIES OF STATE.

Department created by Act of Congress, September 15, 1789.

| NAME. | STATE. | FROM |
|---|---|---|
| John Quincy Adams | Mass | March 5, 1817. |
| Henry Clay | Ky | March 7, 1825. |
| James A. Hamilton | N. Y | March 4, 1829, *ad int.* |
| Martin Van Buren | N. Y | March 6, 1829. |
| Edward Livingston | La | May 24, 1831. |
| Louis McLane | Del | May 29, 1833. |
| John Forsyth | Ga | June 27, 1834. |
| J. L. Martin | N. C | March 3, 1841, *ad int.* |
| Daniel Webster | Mass | March 5, 1841. |
| Hugh S. Legaré | S. C | May 9, 1843, *ad int.* |
| Abel P. Upshur | Va | June 24, 1843, *ad int.* |
| Abel P. Upshur | Va | July 24, 1843. |
| John Nelson | Md | February 29, 1844, *ad int.* |
| John C. Calhoun | S. C | March 6, 1844. |
| James Buchanan | Penna | March 6, 1845. |
| John M. Clayton | Del | March 7, 1849. |
| Daniel Webster | Mass | July 22, 1850. |
| Charles M. Conrad | La | September 2, 1852, *ad int.* |
| Edward Everett | Mass | November 6, 1852. |
| William Hunter | R. I | March 3, 1853, *ad int.* |
| William L. Marcy | N. Y | March 7, 1853. |
| Lewis Cass | Mich | March 6, 1857. |

## The Secretaries of the Treasury.

Department created by Act of Congress, September 2, 1789.

| Name. | State. | From |
|---|---|---|
| William H. Crawford | Ga. | October 22, 1816. |
| Samuel L. Southard | N. J. | March 7, 1825, *ad int.* |
| Richard Rush | Penna. | March 7, 1825. |
| Samuel D. Ingham | Penna. | March 6, 1829. |
| Asbury Dickins | N. C. | June 21, 1831, *ad int.* |
| Louis McLane | Del. | August 8, 1831. |
| William J. Duane | Penna. | May 29, 1833. |
| Roger B. Taney | Md. | September 23, 1833. |
| McClintock Young | Md. | June 25, 1834, *ad int.* |
| Levi Woodbury | N. H. | June 27, 1834. |
| McClintock Young | Md. | March 3, 1841, *ad int.* |
| Thomas Ewing | Ohio. | March 5, 1841. |
| McClintock Young | Md. | September 13, 1841, *ad int.* |
| Walter Forward | Penna. | September 13, 1841. |
| McClintock Young | Md. | March 1, 1843, *ad int.* |
| John C. Spencer | N. Y. | March 3, 1843. |
| McClintock Young | Md. | May 2, 1844, *ad int.* |
| George M. Bibb | Ky. | June 15, 1844. |
| Robert J. Walker | Miss. | March 6, 1845. |
| McClintock Young | Md. | March 6, 1849, *ad int.* |
| William M. Meredith | Penna. | March 8, 1849. |
| Thomas Corwin | Ohio. | July 23, 1850. |
| James Guthrie | Ky. | March 7, 1853. |
| Howell Cobb | Ga. | March 6, 1857. |

## The Secretaries of War.

Department created by Act of Congress, August 7, 1789.

| Name. | State. | From |
|---|---|---|
| Isaac Shelby | Ky. | March 5, 1817. |
| George Graham | Va. | April 7, 1817, *ad int.* |
| John C. Calhoun | S. C. | October 8, 1817. |
| James Barbour | Va. | March 7, 1825. |
| Samuel L. Southard | N. J. | May 26, 1828, *ad int.* |
| Peter B. Porter | N. Y. | May 26, 1828. |
| John H. Eaton | Tenn. | March 9, 1829. |
| Philip G. Randolph | Va. | June 18, 1831, *ad int.* |
| Roger B. Taney | Md. | July 21, 1831, *ad int.* |

## APPENDIX

### THE SECRETARIES OF WAR.—*Continued*.

| NAME. | STATE. | FROM |
|---|---|---|
| Lewis Cass | Ohio | August 1, 1831. |
| Benjamin F. Butler | N. Y | October 25, 1836, *ad int*. |
| Joel R. Poinsett | S. C | March 7, 1837. |
| John Bell | Tenn | March 5, 1841. |
| John McLean | Ohio | September 13, 1841. |
| John C. Spencer | N. Y | October 12, 1841. |
| James M Porter | Penna | March 8, 1843. |
| William Wilkins | Penna | February 15, 1844. |
| William L. Marcy | N. Y | March 5, 1845. |
| George W. Crawford | Ga | March 8, 1849. |
| Winfield Scott | Va | July 23, 1850, *ad int*. |
| Charles M. Conrad | La | August 15, 1850. |
| Jefferson Davis | Miss | March 7, 1853. |
| Samuel Cooper | N. Y | March 3, 1857, *ad int*. |
| John B. Floyd | Va | March 6, 1857. |

### THE SECRETARIES OF THE NAVY.

Department created by Act of Congress, April 30, 1798.

| NAME. | STATE. | FROM |
|---|---|---|
| Benjamin W. Crowninshield | Mass | December 19, 1814. |
| Smith Thompson | N. Y | November 9, 1818. |
| John Rodgers | Md | September 1, 1823, *ad int*. |
| Samuel L. Southard | N. J | September 16, 1823. |
| John Branch | N. C | March 9, 1829. |
| Levi Woodbury | N. H | May 23, 1831. |
| Mahlon Dickerson | N. J | June 30, 1834. |
| James K. Paulding | N. Y | June 25, 1838. |
| George E. Badger | N. C | March 5, 1841. |
| Abel P. Upshur | Va | September 13, 1841. |
| David Henshaw | Mass | July 24, 1843. |
| Thomas W. Gilmer | Va | February 15, 1844. |
| John Y. Mason | Va | March 14, 1844. |
| George Bancroft | Mass | March 10, 1845. |
| John Y. Mason | Va | September 9, 1846. |
| William B. Preston | Va | March 8, 1849. |
| William A. Graham | N. C | July 22, 1850. |
| John P. Kennedy | Md | July 22, 1852. |
| James C. Dobbin | N. C | March 7, 1853. |
| Isaac Toucey | Conn | March 6, 1857. |

## The Secretaries of the Interior.

Department created by Act of Congress, March 3, 1849.

| Name. | State. | From |
|---|---|---|
| Thomas Ewing............ | Ohio ... | March 8, 1849. |
| Thomas M. T. McKennan.. | Penna .. | August 15, 1850. |
| Alexander H. H. Stuart.... | Va ..... | September 12, 1850.] |
| Robert McClelland........ | Mich ... | March 7, 1853. |
| Jacob Thompson.......... | Miss. ... | March 6, 1857. |

## The Attorneys-General.

Duties prescribed by the Judiciary Act of September 24, 1789. Department reorganized in 1870.

| Name. | State. | From |
|---|---|---|
| Richard Rush............. | Penna... | February 10, 1814. |
| William Wirt............. | Va ..... | November 3, 1817. |
| John M. Berrien.......... | Ga ..... | March 9, 1829. |
| Roger B. Taney........... | Md..... | July 20, 1831. |
| Benjamin F. Butler....... | N. Y... | November 15, 1833. |
| Felix Grundy............. | Tenn ... | July 5, 1838. |
| Henry D. Gilpin.......... | Penna... | July 11, 1840. |
| John J. Crittenden........ | Ky ..... | March 5, 1841. |
| Hugh S. Legaré........... | S. C.... | September 13, 1841. |
| John Nelson.............. | Md..... | July 1, 1843. |
| John Y. Mason............ | Va...... | March 6, 1845. |
| Nathan Clifford........... | Me .... | October 17, 1846. |
| Isaac Toucey...... ....... | Conn ... | June 21, 1848. |
| Reverdy Johnson.......... | Md..... | March 8, 1849. |
| John J. Crittenden........ | Ky ..... | July 22, 1850. |
| Caleb Cushing............ | Mass.... | March 7, 1853. |
| Jeremiah S. Black......... | Penna... | March 6, 1857. |

## The Postmasters-General.

A Bureau of the Treasury until 1829. Made a Cabinet office in that year.

| Name. | State. | From |
|---|---|---|
| Return J. Meigs, Jr. | Ohio | March 17, 1814. |
| John McLean | Ohio | June 26, 1823. |
| William T. Barry | Ky | March 9, 1829. |
| Amos Kendall | Ky | March 1, 1835. |
| John M. Niles | Conn | May 19, 1840. |
| Francis Granger | N. Y. | March 6, 1841. |
| Charles A. Wickliffe | Ky | September 13, 1841. |
| Cave Johnson | Tenn | March 6, 1845. |
| Jacob Collamer | Vt | March 8, 1849. |
| Nathan K. Hall | N. Y | July 23, 1850. |
| Samuel D. Hubbard | Conn | August 31, 1852. |
| James Campbell | Penna | March 7, 1853. |
| Aaron V. Brown | Tenn | March 6, 1857. |

# CHRONOLOGY

Territory of Missouri erected......................June 4, 1812
Treaty of Fort Jackson.........................August 10, 1814
Treaty of Ghent signed.......................December 24, 1814
Commonwealth of Indiana admitted .........December 11, 1816
Madison's veto of internal improvements bill......March 3, 1817
Attack on Fowltown........................November 21, 1817
Commonwealth of Mississippi admitted.......December 10, 1817
Jackson's "Rhea" letter to Monroe.............January 6, 1818
Execution of Ambrister and Arbuthnot...........April 29, 1818
Convention with Great Britain as to Oregon ....October 20, 1818
Commonwealth of Illinois admitted ...........December 3, 1818
Tallmadge amendment offered.................February 13, 1819
Treaty with Spain as to Florida...............February 22, 1819
Decision in McCulloch vs. Maryland...................... 1819
Commonwealth of Alabama admitted.........December 14, 1819
Thomas amendment offered ....................February 3, 1820
Maine bill approved..............................March 3, 1820
First Missouri bill approved......................March 6, 1820
Commonwealth of Maine admitted..... .........March 15, 1820
Report of Clay's Committee of Thirteen.......February 10, 1821
Second Missouri bill approved ....................March 2, 1821
Jackson, as Governor, takes command in Florida...July 17, 1821
Commonwealth of Missouri admitted............August 10, 1821
Congress of Verona ....................October–December, 1822
Monroe's veto of internal improvements bill.........May 4, 1822
Clay nominated for presidency by the Kentucky legislature.
                                        November 18, 1822
"Monroe Doctrine" announced...............December 2, 1823
Congressional caucus nominates Crawford.....February 14, 1824
Harrisburg convention............................March 4, 1824
Jackson's "Coleman Letter"....................April 26, 1824
Presidential election in House of Representatives.....Feb. 9, 1825

Indian Springs convention .................... February 12, 1825
Mexico-Columbia treaty ..................... September 25, 1825
The Creek treaty ............................... January, 1826
Abduction of Morgan ................... September 11, 12, 1826
Protectionist convention at Harrisburg ............ July 30, 1827
Treaty with Great Britain ....................... August 6, 1827
Tariff bill approved ............................. May 19, 1828
The "South Carolina Exposition" published .............. 1828
Hayne's speech on Foote's resolution ........... January 19, 1830
Webster's reply to Hayne ..................... January 26, 1830
Jackson's speech on the Union ................... April 13, 1830
Veto of the Maysville Road bill ................... May 27, 1830
Publication of the "Liberator" begun .......... January 1, 1831
"Address to the People of South Carolina" published ....
July 26, 1831
The Southampton massacre ....................... August, 1831
Anti-Masonic convention at Baltimore ....... September 26, 1831
National Republican convention at Baltimore.. December 12, 1831
New England Anti-Slavery Society formed ...... January 6, 1832
Bank of the United States asks re-charter ........ January 9, 1832
National Democratic convention at Baltimore ...... May 21, 1832
Calhoun's letter to Governor Hamilton .......... August 28, 1832
South Carolina convention meets at Columbia.. November 19, 1832
Ordinance of nullification ................... November 24, 1832
President Jackson's nullification proclamation.. December 10, 1832
Clay proposes compromise tariff .............. February 12, 1833
The "Force Bill" approved ...................... March 2, 1833
Compromise tariff bill approved .................. March 2, 1833
Re-assembling of the South Carolina convention.. March 11, 1833
The "Paper read in the Cabinet" ............ September 18, 1833
Removal of the deposits ordered ............. September 26, 1833
American Anti-Slavery Society formed .......... December, 1833
Van Buren nominated by Baltimore convention .... May 20, 1835
Charleston, S. C., post-office robbed ............... July 29, 1835
Provisional declaration of Texan independence.. November 7, 1835
Meeting of Texas convention ..................... March 1, 1836
Declaration of Texan independence ............... March 2, 1836
The Alamo massacre ........................... March 6, 1836
Battle of San Jacinto .......................... April 21, 1836
House adopts the "gag" resolution ................ May 26, 1836
Commonwealth of Arkansas admitted ............ June 15, 1836

# CHRONOLOGY 493

The "Specie Circular"..............................July 11, 1836
Senate passes the "expunging resolution"......January 16, 1837
Commonwealth of Michigan admitted..........January 26, 1837
Financial panic begins.............................April, 1837
Murder of Lovejoy ..........................November 7, 1837
Harrisburg "harmony" convention............September 4, 1839
Whig convention at Harrisburg................December 4, 1839
Democratic-Republican convention at Baltimore.....May 5, 1840
Independent Treasury bill approved.................July 4, 1840
Death of President Harrison ......................April 4, 1841
The Ashburton treaty ...........................August 9, 1842
Veto of National Bank bill.....................August 16, 1842
Second bank bill vetoed......................September 9, 1842
Abolition convention at Buffalo.................August 30, 1843
Whitman's party reaches the Columbia.........September 5, 1843
Whig convention at Baltimore .......................May 1, 1844
Democratic convention at Baltimore...............May 27, 1844
Commonwealth of Florida admitted...............March 3, 1845
Polk's message on Oregon.....................December 2, 1845
Commonwealth of Texas admitted.............December 29, 1845
Mexicans cross the Nueces.......................April 23, 1846
Arista notifies Taylor of beginning of hostilities....April 24, 1846
Battle of Palo Alto................................May 8, 1846
Congress declares war begun by Mexico........May 12, 13, 1846
Treaty with Great Britain as to Oregon............June 15, 1846
Kearny takes Santa Fé.........................August 18, 1846
Battle of Monterey .......................September 21–23, 1846
Commonwealth of Iowa admitted..............December 28, 1846
Battle of Buena Vista......................February 22, 23, 1847
Capture of Vera Cruz.......................March 27–29, 1847
Battle of Cerro Gordo. ..........................April 18, 1847
Battle of Chapultepec....................September 12, 13, 1847
Treaty of Guadalupe Hidalgo .................February 2, 1848
Democratic convention at Baltimore...............May 22, 1848
Special message on Oregon......................May 29, 1848
Commonwealth of Wisconsin admitted............May 29, 1848
Abolition convention at Rochester..................June 2, 1848
Whig convention at Philadelphia ..................June 7, 1848
Special message on California and New Mexico .....July 6, 1848
Free-soil convention at Buffalo..................August 9, 1858
Territory of Oregon organized...................August 14, 1848

California convention at Monterey............September 1, 1849
Clay proposes his compromise.................January 29, 1850
Calhoun's last speech.........................March 4, 1850
Webster's speech on the Constitution.............March 7, 1850
Death of Calhoun.... ........................March 31, 1850
Clayton-Bulwer treaty...........................April 19, 1850
Clay reports on the compromise.....................May 8, 1850
Death of President Taylor.........................July 9, 1850
Commonwealth of California admitted........September 9, 1850
President's message on the fugitive slave law..February 21, 1851
The "Jerry rescue"..............................October, 1851
Democratic convention at Baltimore................June 1, 1852
Whig convention at Baltimore....................June 16, 1852
Death of Clay....................................June 29, 1852
Free-soil Democratic convention at Pittsburg....August 11, 1852
Death of Webster...............................October 23, 1852
The Gadsden treaty..........................December 30, 1853
Douglas reports on Nebraska....................January 4, 1854
Kansas-Nebraska bill approved....................May 30, 1854
Salt Creek Valley convention.....................June 10, 1854
The Ostend manifesto..........................October 18, 1854
Congressional election in Kansas..............November 29, 1854
Territorial election in Kansas....................March 30, 1855
Kansas legislature meets at Pawnee..................July 2, 1855
Robinson's speech at Lawrence.....................July 4, 1855
Convention at Lawrence, Kansas................August 14, 1855
Convention at Big Springs, Kansas...........September 5, 1855
Convention at Topeka, Kansas..............September 19, 1855
Convention at Topeka, Kansas............. ....October 23, 1855
Popular vote on the Topeka constitution......December 15, 1855
Robinson elected governor of Kansas............January 5, 1856
President's proclamation on Kansas...........February 11, 1856
Kansas Free-state legislature meets................March 4, 1856
Philadelphia convention of the "American party". Feb. 22, 1856
Congressional committee begins sessions at Kansas City.....
April 14, 1856
Sumner's speech on the "Crime against Kansas".May 19, 20, 1856
The sack of Lawrence............................May 21, 1856
Brooks's attack on Sumner.......................May 22, 1856
Massacre at Dutch Henry's Crossing...............May 24, 1856
Affair at Black Jack..............................June 2, 1856

# CHRONOLOGY 495

A.D.

Democratic national convention at Cincinnati........June 2, 1856
Republican national convention at Philadelphia....June 17, 1856
Assault on Sheriff Jones..........................June 23, 1856
House Committee reports on Kansas.................July 1, 1856
Dispersal of Free-state legislature at Topeka.....July 4, 1856
Oliver makes minority report on Kansas............July 11, 1856
Treaty at Lawrence..............................August 17, 1856
Woodson's proclamation in Kansas................August 25, 1856
Destruction of Ossawattomie.....................August 29, 1856
Whig convention at Baltimore.................September 17, 1856
Free-state legislature dispersed at Topeka.......January 6, 1857
Territorial legislature meets at Lecompton......January 12, 1857
Dred Scott decision...............................March 6, 1857
Election of Lecompton constitutional convention...June 15, 1857
Meeting of Free-state convention at Topeka........July 15, 1857
Convention at Lecompton, Kansas..............September 7, 1857
Free-state election in Kansas....................October 5, 1857
Convention at Lecompton, Kansas.................October 19, 1857
Mass-meeting at Lawrence, Kansas..............December 2, 1857
Kansas legislature meets at Lecompton..........December 7, 1857
Pro-slavery vote on the Lecompton constitution.December 21, 1857
Free-state vote on the Lecompton constitution...January 4, 1858
Buchanan's message on Kansas..................February 2, 1858
Commonwealth of Minnesota admitted..............May 11, 1858
Vote in Kansas on the English bill propositions...August 2, 1858
Commonwealth of Oregon admitted............February 14, 1859

# BIBLIOGRAPHY

This bibliography must not be taken as containing the material used in the preparation of this volume, but as a list of good books recommended to the general reader, which treat of, or touch upon, the subjects considered. Only a few of the books in this list have been consulted by the author in the preparation of this work. As indicated in the preface, the author has endeavored, in all cases, to go back to original matter, which is usually disconnected and fragmentary, and practically inaccessible to the general reader.

## LIST OF TITLES

*The alphabetical arrangement is, in most instances, based upon the names of authors or editors.*

Adams, C. F.: Railroads; their origin and problems. New York, 1878.

Adams, H.: Life of Albert Gallatin. Philadelphia, 1879.

Adams, H.: History of the United States. 9 vols. New York, 1889–91.

Adams, H.: John Randolph. Boston, 1882.

Adams, J. Q.: Memoirs; Comprising Parts of His Diary from 1795 to 1848. 12 vols. Philadelphia, 1874–77.

Alfriend, F. H.: Life of Jefferson Davis. Cincinnati, 1868.

Baker, G. E. [Ed.]: Works of William H. Seward. 5 vols. New York, 1853–54.

Bancroft, H. H.: Arizona and New Mexico, 1530-1888. San Francisco, 1889.

Bancroft, H. H.: History of California. 7 vols. San Francisco, 1884-90.

Bancroft, H. H.: North Mexican States and Texas, 1531-1889. 2 vols. San Francisco, 1884.

Bancroft, H. H.: Oregon, 1834-1888. 2 vols. San Francisco, 1886-88.

Barrows, W.: Oregon: The Struggle for Possession. Boston, 1883.

Benton, T. H.: Thirty Years' View; or, History of the Working of the American Government for Thirty Years, from 1820 to 1850. 2 vols. New York, 1854-56.

Birney, W.: James G. Birney and His Times. New York, 1890.

Blaine, J. G.: Twenty Years of Congress (1860-80). 2 vols. Norwich, 1884-86.

Bolles, A. S.: The Financial History of the United States. 3 vols. New York, 1879-86.

Bolles, A. S.: Industrial History of the United States. Norwich, 1878.

Bourne, E. G.: History of the Surplus Revenue of 1837. New York, 1885.

Bruce, H.: Life of General Houston. New York, 1891.

Bryce, J.: The American Commonwealth. 2 vols. New York, 1895.

Cairnes, J. E.: Slave Power: Its Character, Career, and Probable Designs. New York, 1862.

Calhoun, J. C.: Works. 6 vols. New York, 1853-55.

Carr, L.: Missouri, a Bone of Contention. Boston, 1888.

Channing, E.: The United States of America, 1765-1865. New York, 1896.

Choate, R.: Works, with a Memoir by S. G. Brown. 2 vols. Boston, 1862.

Chase, L. B.: History of the Polk Administration. New York, 1850.

Cobb, T. R. R.: Historical Sketch of Slavery. Philadelphia, 1858.

Cobb, T. R. R.: Enquiry into the Law of Negro Slavery in the United States. Philadelphia, 1858.

Colton, C. [Ed.]: Works of Henry Clay. 6 vols. New York, 1857.

Colton, C.: Life and Times of Henry Clay. 2 vols. New York, 1846.

Colton, C. [Ed.]: Private Correspondence of Henry Clay. New York, 1855.

Colton, C.: The Last Seven Years of the Life of Henry Clay. New York, 1856.

Cooper, T.: Lectures on the Elements of Political Economy. Columbia, 1826.

Curtis, G. T.: Constitutional History of the United States. 2 vols. New York, 1889, 1896.

Curtis, G. T.: Life of James Buchanan. 2 vols. New York, 1883.

Curtis, G. T.: Life of Daniel Webster. 2 vols. New York, 1870.

Davis, J.: The Rise and Fall of the Confederate Government. 2 vols. New York, 1881.

Davis, V. H.: Jefferson Davis, ex-President of the Confederate States. 2 vols. New York, 1890.

Douglass, F.: Life and Times. Written by himself. Hartford, 1881.

Draper, J. W.: History of the American Civil War. 3 vols. New York, 1867-70.

Dunbar, C. F.: Laws of the United States relating to currency, finance and banking from 1789 to 1891. Boston, 1893.

Frémont, J. C.: Memoirs of My Life. Chicago, 1887.

Frothingham, O. B.: Gerrit Smith; A Biography. New York, 1879.

Frothingham, O. B.: Theodore Parker; A Biography. Boston, 1874.

Gannett, H.: Boundaries of the United States, and of the several States and Territories. Washington, 1885.

Giddings, J. R.: Speeches in Congress. Boston, 1853.

Gillet, R. H.: Democracy in the United States. New York, 1868.

Gilman, D. C.: James Monroe in his Relation to the Public Service. Boston, 1883.

Greeley, H.: The American Conflict. 2 vols. Hartford, 1864-67.

Greeley, H.: Recollections of a Busy Life. New York, 1868.

Greeley, H.: History of the Struggle for Slavery Extension or Restriction in the United States. New York, 1856.

Hall, B. F.: The Republican Party, 1796-1832. New York, 1856.

Hammond, J. D.: The History of Political Parties in the State of New York. 4th edit. 2 vols. Cooperstown, 1846.

Hay, J.: see Nicolay, J. G.

Helper, H. R.: Impending Crisis of the South, and how to meet it. New York, 1857.

Hildreth, R.: The History of the United States. 6 vols. New York, 1851-56.

Holst, H. E. von: The Constitutional History of the United States. 8 vols. Chicago, 1876-92.

Holst, H. E. von: John Brown. Boston, 1888.

Holst, H. E. von: John C. Calhoun. Boston, 1882.

Hurd, J. C.: Law of Freedom and Bondage in the United States. 2 vols. Boston, 1858-62.

Jay, W.: Miscellaneous writings on slavery. Boston, 1853.

Jay, W.: Review of the Causes and Consequences of the Mexican War. Boston, 1849.

Jenkins, J. S.: History of Political Parties in the State of New York. Auburn, 1846.

Jenkins, J. S.: Life of James K. Polk. Auburn, 1850.

Johnson, O.: William Lloyd Garrison and his Times. Boston, 1880.

Johnston, A.: History of American Politics. New York, 1880.

Johnston, A. [Ed.]: Representative American Orations. 3 vols. New York, 1884.

Julian, G. W.: Life of Joshua R. Giddings. Chicago, 1892.

Kapp, F.: Die Sklaverei in den Vereinigten Staaten. Hamburg, 1861.

Kinley, D.: History, Organization, and Influence of the Independent Treasury of the United States. New York, 1893.

Knox, J. J.: United States Notes. New York, 1888.

Lalor, J. J.: Cyclopædia of Political Science, Political Economy, and of the Political History of the United States. 3 vols. Chicago, 1881-84.

Lodge, H. C.: Daniel Webster. Boston, 1883.

Lyman, T.: Diplomacy of the United States. Boston, 1826.

Mackenzie, W. L.: Life and Times of M. Van Buren. Boston, 1846.

McLaughlin, A. C.: Lewis Cass. Boston, 1891.

McCulloch, H.: Men and Measures of Half a Century. New York, 1888.

Mallory, D.: Life and Speeches of Henry Clay. 2 vols. New York, 1843.

May, S. J.: Memoirs: Consisting of Autobiography and Selections from his Diary and Correspondence. Boston, 1873.

May, S. J.: Some Recollections of our Anti-Slavery Conflict. Boston, 1869.

Morse, J. T., Jr.: Abraham Lincoln. 2 vols. Boston, 1893.

Morse, J. T., Jr.: John Quincy Adams. Boston, 1882.

# BIBLIOGRAPHY

Nicolay, J. G. and Hay, J.: Abraham Lincoln: A History. 10 vols. New York, 1890.

Nicolay, J. G. and Hay, J. [Eds.]: Complete Works of Abraham Lincoln. 2 vols. New York, 1894.

Nixon, O. W.: How Marcus Whitman Saved Oregon. Chicago, 1895.

Ormsby, R. McK.: History of the Whig Party. Boston, 1860.

Parker, J.: Personal Liberty Laws. Boston, 1861.

Parton, J.: General Jackson. New York, 1893.

Parton, J.: Life of Andrew Jackson. 3 vols. Boston, 1883.

Phillips, W.: Conquest of Kansas. Boston, 1856.

Phillips, W.: Speeches, Lectures, and Letters. Boston, 1863.

Pierce, E. L.: Memoir and Letters of Charles Sumner. 4 vols. Boston, 1893.

Pike, J. S.: First Blows of the Civil War. New York, 1879.

Pollard, E. A.: The Lost Cause. New York, 1868.

Quincy, E.: Life of Josiah Quincy. Boston, 1867.

Quincy, J.: Memoirs of the Life of John Quincy Adams. Boston, 1858.

Redpath, J.: Public Life of Capt. John Brown. Boston, 1860.

Rhodes, J. F.: History of the United States from the Compromise of 1850. 3 vols. New York, 1893-95.

Robinson, C.: The Kansas Conflict. New York, 1892.

Robinson, S. T. L.: Kansas, Its Interior and its Exterior Life. Boston, 1856.

Roosevelt, T.: Thomas Hart Benton. Boston, 1887.

Royce, J.: California from the Conquest in 1846 to the Second Vigilance Committee in San Francisco. Boston, 1886.

Schouler, J.: History of the United States Under the Constitution. 5 vols. New York, 1893.

Schurz, C.: Life of Henry Clay. 2 vols. Boston, 1887.

Schuyler, E.: American Diplomacy. New York, 1886.

Seward, W. H.: Autobiography, from 1801 to 1834, with a Memoir of His Life. New York, 1877.

Seward, W. H.: Life and Public Services of John Quincy Adams. Auburn, 1849.

Shepard, E. M.: Martin Van Buren. Boston, 1888.

Smith, W. L. G.: Fifty Years of Public Life; the Life and Times of Lewis Cass. New York, 1856.

Spring, L. W.: Kansas; the Prelude to the War for the Union. Boston, 1885.

# BIBLIOGRAPHY

Stanwood, E.: A History of Presidential Elections. Boston, 1892.

Stephens, A. H.: A Constitutional View of the Late War between the States. 2 vols. Philadelphia, 1868-70.

Stickney, W. [Ed.]: Autobiography of Amos Kendall. Boston, 1872.

Story, W. W.: Life and Letters of Joseph Story. 2 vols. Boston, 1851.

Story, W. W. [Ed.]: Miscellaneous Writings of Joseph Story. Boston, 1835.

Strohm, I. [Ed.]: Speeches of Thomas Corwin. Dayton, 1859.

Sumner, C.: Works. 15 vols. Boston, 1870-83.

Sumner, W. G.: Andrew Jackson as a Public Man. Boston, 1882.

Sumner, W. G.: History of American Currency. New York, 1884.

Taussig, F. W.: State Papers and Speeches on the Tariff. Cambridge, 1893.

Taussig, F. W.: Tariff History of the United States, 1789-1888. New York, 1888.

Thayer, E.: History of the Kansas Crusade. New York, 1889.

Tyler, L. G.: Letters and Times of the Tylers. 2 vols. Richmond, 1884.

Tyler, S.: Memoir of R. B. Taney. Baltimore, 1872.

Van Buren, M.: Inquiry into the Origin and Growth of Political Parties in the United States. New York, 1867.

Webster, D.: Works. 6 vols. Boston, 1851.

Webster, F. [Ed.]: Private Correspondence of Daniel Webster. 2 vols. Boston, 1857.

Williams, A. M.: Sam Houston and the War of Independence in Texas. Boston, 1893.

Williams, E.: The Statesman's Manual. 4 vols. New York, 1849.

Wilson, H.: History of the Rise and Fall of the Slave Power in America. 3 vols. Boston, 1872-77.

Wilson, W.: Division and Reunion, 1829-1889. New York, 1893.

Wise, H. A.: Seven Decades of the Union. Philadelphia, 1876.

Woodbury, L.: Writings, Political, Judicial, and Literary. 3 vols. Boston, 1852.

Yoakum, H. K.: History of Texas, from its First Settlement in 1685, to its Annexation to the United States in 1846. 2 vols. New York, 1856.

# INDEX

Material in the Appendices is not included in this Index

ABBOTT, J. B., leader of "Free-state" Company, 428

Abolition, 242 et seq.; relation to Revolution of 1830, 244, 245; its philosophy, 245; the opposite theory, 245; the true philosophy of history, 245, 246; the beginning of abolition, 246 (see Garrison, William Lloyd); possible ways of attacking slavery, 248; charges as to Southampton massacre, 249; denials by abolitionist historians, 249; abolitionist methods, 249, 250; killing of Lovejoy, 250; significance of abolition movement, 250, 251; its growth, 251; the moderates, 251; petitions for abolition in District of Columbia, 251, 252; position of Adams, 252, 253; Quaker petition, 253; position of Mason and Adams, 253; more petitions, 253 (see Petition, right of); Dickson presents petitions, 254; his controversy with Chinn, 254; the Fairfield petitions, 254; excitement begun by Slade's motion, 254; Polk's ruling, 255; action on Jackson's petitions, 255 et seq.; assumption as to ethical position, 265; attitude of Calhoun and Rives, 267, 268; the Vermont petition, 269; the Calhoun resolutions, 269; use of mails, 270 et seq. (see Mail, United States); significance of the contests over petitions and the mails, 274–277; result of struggle over petitions, 296; demands of Clay, 319; criticism of Clay as to annexation, 320; candidacy of Birney, 320; position on Polk's first message, 324, 325; as to war with Mexico, 330, 331; attitude on Texan boundary, 355; attitude to fugitive slave law of 1793, 355; attitude to Clay's proposals, 357; Webster's Seventh of March speech, 359; effect of propaganda, 366; nomination of Hale for presidency, 377; the *National Era* address, 389; effect of the address, 400; as to leaders of Emigrant Aid Company, 413; relation of Kansas affairs to presidential nominee, 431; point of view of the "Crime against Kansas," 439

Abolitionists, *see* Abolition

Adams, John Quincy, relation to Jackson, 34–36; opinion of treaty with Spain, 36; negotiations with Spain, 37, 38; effect of Seminole War, 38; declaration to Tuyl, 124, 125; qualification as presidential candidate in 1824, 132–136; electoral vote of 1824, 136, 137; supported in House by Clay, 141; the Kremer charge, 141; elected president, 142; offers State Department to Clay, 142, 143; threats of opposition, 142, 143; no proof of bargain with Clay, 143; opposition to Administration organized, 144–146; relation to Panama Congress, 148, 149; nominates commissioners to the Congress, 149; nomination confirmed, 150; relation to Spain's colonies, 152, 153; as to internal improvements, 155, 156; message of December, 1826, 157; appropriations approved for internal improvements, 169; chairman of committee, 184; reports tariff bill, 185; bill passed, 186; report on Bank, 191; relation to Bank history, 192; representations from Creek chiefs, 212; orders Gaines to Georgia, 213; controversy with Troup, 213, 214; steps to carry out agreement of 1826, 214; defiance of Georgia, 214; submits matter to Congress, 215; refers Cherokee affair to Jackson, 215, 216; view of Indian titles, 217; principles of administration reviewed by Supreme Court, 219; relation to Cabinet intrigue against Jackson, 220; as to authorship of Jacksonian principles, 240; presents abolition petitions, 252; his position on abolition, 252, 253; prevents debate on abolition petitions, 253; compared with Slade, 254; opinion as to procedure on petitions, 256; appeal for right of petition, 257; presents petition on abolition, 258, 259; his belief as to the right involved, 259; effort at settlement, 260; affair of February 6, 1837, 262; address on annexation, 303

"Address on the Relations of the States and Federal Government," 179

"Address to the People of South Carolina," 179

Admiralty jurisdiction, proposal to decrease that of federal courts, 109

Africa, 41

Alabama, Commonwealth of, in process of creation, 62; slavery allowed, 63; Indian problem in Jackson's message of 1829, 216, 217; Alabama letter of Clay, 319, 320; vote on Kansas-Nebraska bill, 399; Buford's men in Kansas, 438

Alamo atrocities, 293, 294

Albany Regency, The, 133; in election of 1824, 137

Alien and Sedition Laws, 173

Alleghanies, The, 116, 129, 139, 163, 193

Ambrister, Robert C., 32, 36

Amelia Island, 30, 31

America for Americans, principle of, 418

American Anti-Slavery Society, formed, 251

American Board of Missions, sends out Whitman, 315

American Society for Emancipation, 62

"American System," The, 178, 189 (*see* Clay, H.)

Ampudia, Pedro de, demands Taylor's withdrawal, 329

Anderson, Richard Clough, Jr., nominated commissioner to Panama Congress, 149; nomination confirmed, 150

Appalachicola River, The, 21, 22, 25, 26, 31

Arbuthnot, Alexander, 32, 36

Archer, William S., opposition to Texas treaty, 308, 309; his doctrine adopted by Tyler, 309; report on Texas resolution, 322, 323

Arista, Mariana, notifies Taylor of beginning of hostilities, 329

Arkansas, Commonwealth of, admitted, 290; vote on Kansas-Nebraska bill, 399

Arkansas, Territory of, 88

Arkansas River, the, 33

Army of the United States, legislation upon, 13, 14; troops in Florida, 24 *et seq.* (*see* Mexico, and Kansas, Territory of); as to South Carolina, 230

Ashburton, Alexander Baring, first Baron, negotiations with Webster, 314

Ashburton Treaty, 303

Asia, California the road to, 332

Astor, John Jacob, understanding with the Government, 313

Astoria, founded, 312, 313

Atchison, Missouri, place of publication of *Squatter Sovereign*, 411

Atchison, David R., criticism of organization of Nebraska Territory, 382; his record and influence, 412, 413; on the Wakarusa, 429; agrees with Robinson, 430; causes Missourians to withdraw, 431; repudiates the sacking of Lawrence, 438; in command at Bull Creek, 445

Austin, Moses, secures Texan grant from Mexico, 291

Austin, Stephen Fuller, colonizes grant in Texas, 291

Austria, in Holy Alliance, 123


BADGER, GEORGE EDMUND, contention as to Chase's amendment, 394; offers amendment, 395

Baldwin, John, claims site of Lawrence, 415

Baltimore, Maryland, petition for

# INDEX 505

abolition, 252; Hamlet case, 367; conventions of 1852, 376

Baltimore & Ohio railroad, system begun, 169

Bank of the United States, bill for its creation, 3; Calhoun's argument, 4, 5, 6; Clay's early view, 4; Webster's objections, 6; Clay's support, 6, 7; modified bill passed by House, 7, 8; attitude of Barbour, Bibb, Taylor, Wells, 8; passed by Senate, 8; bill of 1816 a Southern and national measure, 8, 14; bank bill under comparison, 15, 16; Jackson's message of 1829, 190; later interpretations of Jackson's attack, 191, 192; the troubles in New Hampshire, 191; the opposition of principle, 192, 193; origin of opposition to "money power," 193, 194; origin of "State's rights" opposition to Bank, 194; tax on branches in Ohio and Maryland, 194; the results, 195; relation to "relief party" in Kentucky, 195, 196; Benton's attack, 196; his resolution defeated, 196; attitude of Benton, 197; and of Jackson, 197, 198; Bank supported by committees, 198; Jackson's message of December, 1830, 198, 199; relation of question to slavery, 198; relation to politics, 198; Jackson's second attack, 198, 199; Benton's resolution of 1831, 199, 200; Jackson's message of 1831, 200; the Bank question before the people, 200, 201; advice of Clay and Webster, 201; petition for recharter, 201; relation of Bank question to question of Jackson's election, 201; action by the Senate, 201, 202; Clayton committee report in House, 202; McDuffie's report on Bank, 202; House passes the Senate bill, 202; veto by Jackson, 202; analysis of his message, 202-206; interpretation of the message, 206-209; the principles of Jackson ratified by the people, 209; effect on Jackson's views of election on Bank issue, 279; control of deposits, 279; removal of McLane and Duane, 280; deposits suspended by Taney, 280; Taney's contention, 280, 281; Senate's resolutions of censure, 281; attitude of Benton, 281; Jackson successful in all points, 282; result of removal of deposits, 283; enforcement and effect of Act of June 23, 283, 284; Bank bills vetoed by Tyler, 286

Barbour, James, supports bank bill, 8; proposes union of Maine and Missouri bills, 82; position on Maine-Missouri bill, 83; on conference committee, 88; letter to Troup, 212, 213; controversy with Troup, 213

Barbour, Philip Pendleton, in Missouri bill debate, 70; opposes tariff bill of 1824, 113, 114

Beaufort, South Carolina, instructions to collector, 230

Beecher, Henry Ward, opposes fugitive slave law, 368

Behring's Strait, 123

Belgium, recognizes Texan independence, 304

Bell, John, report on President's powers, 235; proposition as to California and New Mexico, 359; its reference, 359, 360; on Committee of Thirteen, 360; attitude to Kansas-Nebraska bill and to Douglas's amendment, 393; speech against the bill, 396, 397; vote on the bill, 399

Bell, P. H., extends jurisdiction of Texas, 362, 363

Benton, Thomas Hart, attacks the Bank, 196; resolution defeated, 196; becomes Jackson's lieutenant, 197; resolution against the Bank, 199; his resolution not accepted, 200; attack on practices of Bank, 201; opinion on use of Government deposits by the Bank, 205; defends Jackson against censure of Senate, 281; criticism of Texas treaty, 308; changes vote, 347; opposition to Foote's motion, 360; offers to cudgel Foote, 360

Berrien, John McPherson, opinion of Indian agreement of 1826, 214; report on Calhoun's proposition, 349, 350; views on slavery in Mexican acquisition, 351, 352; on Committee of Thirteen, 360

Bibb, William Wyatt, supports bank bill, 8

Biddle, Nicholas, beginning of bank

## INDEX

trouble, 191; management of bank, 195

Birney, James G., effect of Clay's Alabama letter, 320

Bishop of London, 44

Black Jack, Brown captures Pate at, 441

Blair, Montgomery, letter to Welles on Seward, 387, 388

Blood, James, at Kansas City, and at site of Lawrence, 414; in "Free-State" directory, 443

Bloomfield, Joseph, voting, 73

Blow, Taylor, connection with Dred Scott case, 452

"Blue Lodges," in Missouri, 419

Body of Liberties, Massachusetts, 41

Bonaparte, Napoleon, relation to slavery in Louisiana, 54, 55; commercial system, 123; relation to Holy Alliance, 123

Boon, Ratliff, in House proceedings, 254

Boston, Massachusetts, beginning of Abolition, 246; meetings on fugitive slave law, 367; the Crafts case, 368; the Shadrach case, 370; the Sims case, 372, 373; Kansas emigrants departing, 414

Boston and Albany railroad, survey begun, 169

Branscomb, Charles H., goes to Kansas, 413, 414; at the site of Lawrence, 414; buys claim of Stearns, 415

Branson, Jacob, threatens Buckley, 428; arrested by Sheriff Jones, 428; rescued by "Free State" men, 428, 429; charges as to the rescue, 429; effort to arrest participants in rescue, 433

Bright, Jesse D., motion as to Territorial governments, 346; on Committee of Thirteen, 360

Brooks, Preston Smith, assault upon Sumner, 439, 440; effect of assault modified by Pottawattomie massacre, 442

Brown *vs.* Maryland [12 Wheaton, 419], 195, 198

Brown, John, appears at Lawrence, 431; the Pottawattomie massacre, 440; the massacre characterized, 441; captures Pate at Black Jack, 441; dispersal of the gang and disappearance of Brown, 442; effect of massacre, 442; his work characterized, 473, 474

Brown, Mary, arrest of Hamlet, 367

Brown, R. P., organizes company of "Free-state" men, 426; captured and murdered, 426

Buchanan, James, position upon tariff bill of 1827, 158, 159; attitude to fugitive slave law, 368; candidate for presidential nomination, 376; the Ostend manifesto, 408; relation of his election to events in Kansas, 447; inaugural address quoted, 447; charge as to improper official conduct, 458; appoints Walker and Stanton to office in Kansas, 461; special message of February 2, 1858, 469

Buckley, ——, secures peace warrant against Branson, 428

Buenos Ayres, 30

Buffalo, New York, Free-soil convention, 347

Buford, Jefferson, repudiates sacking of Lawrence, 438

Bull Creek, Kansas, Missourians encamped on, 445; skirmish at, 445

Burrill, James, Jr., position on Maine-Missouri bill, 83

Burt, Armistead, moves amendment to Douglas's bill, 341

Bushnell, Horace, member of Emigrant Aid Society, 409

Bustamente, Anastasio, decree on immigration, 291

Butler, Andrew Pickens, contention as to fugitive slave law, 371; minority report on president's powers, 372; in debate on Foote's resolutions, 374; attacked by Sumner, 439

CABOT, SAMUEL, member of Emigrant Aid Society, 409

Calhoun, John Caldwell, 2; committee service, 3; argument for the bank, 4–6; chief author of bank bill, 8; speech on tariff bill, 10–12; on internal improvements, 14–16; views rejected by Madison, 17; relation to Jackson, 34, 35; effect of Seminole War, 38; as to relation between protection and slavery, 109; bill for internal improvements vetoed, 1817, 116, 117; qualifications as presidential candidate in 1824, 133, 134; as to vice-

# INDEX 507

presidency, 138; elected vice-president, 142, 143; relation to administration, 143; relation to Adams's administration, 144, 146; elected vice-president, 163, 164; political scientist of slavery, 173; publishes "South Carolina Exposition," "Address on Relation of States and Federal Government," and "Address to the People of South Carolina," 179; his argument, 180, 181; his doctrine of nullification, 189; relation to Jackson and Seminole War, 220; the Forsyth letter, 220; hostility of Jackson and Calhoun, 220, 221; his letter to Governor Hamilton, 221; his theory of nullification reproduced, 223; resigns vice-presidency and becomes Senator, 224; opinion on the position of South Carolina, 226, 227; statement in Senate as to South Carolina's acts, 232, 233; opinion of the "Force Bill," 234; attitude to Clay's compromise tariff, 236; attitude to the Wilkins "Force Bill," 236; argument answered by Webster, 237; attitude to Clay's bill, 237; motive in course on nullification, 238; restatement of Jefferson's principles, 239; opinion of slavery cited, 253; antedated by Hammond, 255; contention as to petitions, 264; view of slavery, 265–268; resolutions of December 27, 1837, 269; fallacy of his position, 270; makes committee report, with bills, on use of mails, 273, 274; his plan defeated, 274; views on recognition of Texas, 295, 296; view on annexation of Texas, 301; his views expressed by Wise, 302; again Secretary of State, 307; notifies Texas of proposal to move forces, 307; view of constitutional position of Texas, 308; adopts idea of Archer as to annexation, 309; views as to method of annexation, 321; characterization of his views on annexation, 323, 324; attitude to Mexican War, 330; views as to slavery in Territories, 344, 345; his last speech, 358; his death, 360; views on fugitive slave laws, 367

California, as to Congress of Verona, 124; occupied by Kearny, 332; importance of its occupation, 332; importance of Buena Vista, 333; about to be transferred, 334; acquisition in view, 337; in negotiations, 337 (*see* Upper California); Polk's message of July 6, 1848, 345, 346; motions of Bright and Clayton, 346; the Clayton bill, 346, 347; Polk's message of December, 1848, 348; gold and silver discoveries, 348; Douglas's bill, 349; Smith's bill, 349; Berrien's report, 349, 350; new bill by Douglas, 350; motion by Walker, 350, 351; proceedings in Congress, 351; views of Berrien and Webster, 351, 352; failure of Congress to act, 352; effect of discoveries, 352, 353; plan of Taylor, 353; the Monterey Convention, 353; Taylor's message of December 4, 1849, 353, 354; Foote's bill, 354; Clay's plan, 355, 356; objections of Southerners, 356; attitude of abolitionists, 357; application for admission, 357; consideration begun, 357, 358; Calhoun's last speech, 358; Webster's Seventh of March speech, 359; Bell's proposition, 359; report of Committee on Territories, 360; Committee of Thirteen, 360; Clay's report, 360–362; passage of bill for admission, 363, 364; vote on Kansas-Nebraska bill, 399; Robinson in, 413; Sutter land troubles, 413; Robinson's experience in, applied to Kansas, 421, 422

Cambreleng, Churchill C., opposes tariff bill of 1824, 113

Canada, 21, 370, 374

Canning, George, proposal to Rush, 125; declaration to Polignac, 125

Cape Breton, 21

Capulets, tomb of the, 351

Cass, Lewis, opposes Upham's amendment, 336; views on relation of slavery and Mexican War, 338; Presidential nominee, 345; letter to Nicholson, 345; on Committee of Thirteen, 360; attitude to fugitive slave law, 368; candidate for Presidential nomination, 376; attitude to Chase and Douglas, 392

Castle Pinckney, becomes seat of custom-house for Charleston dis-

## 508   INDEX

trict, 230; Congress notified of change, 232

Catron, John, opinion on Dred Scott case, 453

Cerro Gordo, battle of, 333

Channing, William Ellery, opposition to fugitive slave law, 373

Chapultepec, battle of, 338

Charleston, South Carolina, Government in control of anti-nullifiers, 181; nullifiers elect mayor, 182; test of tariff law, 182; Scott ordered to, 230; instructions to collectors, 230; removal of customhouse, 230; Congress notified, 232; post-office robbed, 271; committee of public safety elected, 271; postmaster communicates with New York postmaster, 271; the position of Postmaster-General Kendall, 271, 272

Chase, Salmon Portland, contention as to fugitive slave law, 371; signs *National Era* address, 389; moves amendment to Kansas-Nebraska bill, 391; speech in Senate, 391; proposes further amendment, 394; contention with Pratt, 394, 395; proposes third amendment, 395, 396; proposes fourth amendment, 396; vote on Kansas-Nebraska bill, 399; effect of *National Era* address, 400

Chattahoochee River, the, 211, 214

Cheever, George Burrell, opposes fugitive slave law, 368

Cherokee Nation vs. Georgia [5 Peters, 1], 218

Cherokees, brought under criminal jurisdiction of Georgia, 215; appeal to President, 215, 216; Jackson's reply, 216; Cherokees refuse offers for cession of claims, 216; the question in Jackson's message of 1829, 216, 217; different views of Indian land titles, 217, 218; Cherokee lands incorporated by Commonwealth of Georgia, 218; the Cherokee nation case, 218; the case of Worcester against Georgia, 218, 219

Cherubusco, battle of, 334

Cheves, Langdon, management of bank, 195

Chihuahua, captured by Doniphan, 332

Chili, treaty of 1823 with Columbia, 147

Chillicothe, O., bank trouble, 195

Chinn, Joseph W., resents Dickson's attack, 254

Choate, Rufus, attitude to fugitive slave law, 368

Christian baptism, relation to slavery, 44

Clark, George Rogers, sent out by Jefferson, 312

Clay, Henry, views on the bank in 1812, 4; Speaker of House, 6; support of bank bill, 6, 7; on tariff bill, 10; relation to Jackson, 34, 35; opinion of treaty with Spain, 36, 38; suggests union of Maine and Missouri bills, 77; plan of Clay, 100; report of Committee of Thirteen, 100, 101; first plan defeated, 101; conference committee and its report on Missouri, 101, 102; plan accepted, 102, 103; supports tariff bill of 1824, 112, 113; opposed by Barbour, Cambreleng and Webster, 113, 114; efforts with reference to "Monroe Doctrine," 128; qualifications as presidential candidate in 1824, 134–136; electoral vote of 1824, 137; in control of situation, 140, 141; supports Adams, 141; the Kremer charge, 141; offer of secretaryship of state, 142, 143; opposition threatened, 142, 143; Clay accepts office, 143; no proof of corruption, 143; opposition in Senate to his appointment, 144; approached by ministers of Mexico and Columbia, 147; negotiations, 148, 149; negotiations with Czar of Russia and with Spanish-American colonies, 152, 153; his "American System" anticipated by Jackson, 172; resolution on tariff, 186; speech on the "American System," 187; bill reported and tabled, 188; his ideas used, 188; nominated for presidency in 1831, 201; advice to Bank party, 201; proposes compromise tariff, 235; his purposes, 235, 236; attitude of Calhoun, 236; his bill amended and passed by both Houses, 237, 238; signed by President, 238; motive in course on nullification, 238; opinion of Jacksonian principles,

240; criticises Calhoun's bill as to use of mails, 274; his followers called Whigs, 282; dropped by Whigs, 286; reports resolution on Texas, 295; nominated for presidency, 309; letter of April, 310; election an apparent certainty, 319; demands of abolitionists, 319; the *National Intelligencer* letter, 319, 320; effect of the Alabama letter, 320; presidential election of 1844, 320; the Alabama letter, 329; plan as to California, New Mexico and Texas, 355, 356; objections of Southerners, 356, 357; agrees to Douglas's motion, 357; relations with Foote, 357, 358; debate on Clay's resolutions, 358, 359; their reference, 360; chairman of Committee of Thirteen, 360; Clay's report, 360–362; results of debates, 362; passage of bills separately, 363, 364; attitude to fugitive slave law, 368; motion on Shadrach case, 370; motion on President's message, 371; death, 377

Clayton, John Middleton, secures appointment of committee on Bank, 202; makes committee report against Bank, 202; motion as to Territorial government, 346; reports bill, 346, 347; not voting on Kansas-Nebraska bill, 398, 399

Clemens, Jeremiah, in debate on Foote's resolution, 374, 375

Clinton, De Witt, qualifications as presidential candidate in 1824, 132

Coahuila-Texas, a province and Commonwealth of Mexico, 291; local government, 291; resistance to Santa Anna, 292; Texans in control, 292, 293; war begun by Mexicans, 293; declaration of independence, 293. *See* Texas

Cobb, Thomas A., relation to Jackson, 34, 35

Coleman, L. H., letter from Jackson, 138

Coleman, F. N., murders Dow, 428

Columbia, treaties with Chili, Mexico, Peru, and Central America, 147

Colorado River, 291

Columbia, South Carolina, convention of 1827, 159, 160

Columbia River, 123; sources discovered, 312, 314, 316, 318, 324, 325

Committee on Commerce of the House of Representatives, 185

Committee on District of Columbia of House of Representatives, 252, 253, 254, 257

Committee on the District of Columbia of the Senate, 253

Committee on Finance of the Senate, 198, 199

Committee on Foreign Affairs of the House of Representatives, 321

Committee on Foreign Relations of the Senate, 150, 295, 308, 322

Committee on the Judiciary of the House of Representatives, 232, 235, 369

Committee on the Judiciary of the Senate, 82, 83, 84, 87, 232, 233, 341, 343, 349, 363, 371, 372

Committee on Manufactures of the House of Representatives, 110, 112, 158, 160, 172, 174, 175, 184, 185

Committee on Manufactures of the Senate, 188

Committee on Territories of the House of Representatives, 340, 382, 400, 401

Committee on Territories of the Senate, 349, 363, 382, 401

Committee on Ways and Means of the House of Representatives, 9, 10, 110, 172, 174, 185, 198, 231, 351

Compromise Measures of 1850, in Fillmore's message, 368, 369; in Fillmore's message of December 2, 1851, 374; memorials on finality, 375; Democratic platform of 1852, 376; Whig platform of 1852, 376; unity of Whig party imperilled, 376, 377; effect of election of 1852, 377; situation in December, 1852, 381; the Howe-Giddings colloquy, 381, 382; interpretation of the compromise, 382; the Douglas report on Nebraska, 383–387; dictum of the committee, 387; claim of Dixon, 388; as to Kansas-Nebraska bill, 389; dictum of Douglas, 390; the amendment of Chase, 391; the amendment of Douglas, 392; views of Everett, 392, 393 (*see* Kansas, Territory of, and Nebraska, Territory of); effect of acquiescence, 403

Concord, New Hampshire, 191

Confederation of Spanish-American States, plan initiated, 147; proposed congress and relations of United States, 147 *et seq.*

Congress of the Confederation, lack of power over slavery, 48; passed Ordinance of 1787, 48; power in the case, 49

Congress, Continental, forbids importation of slaves, 48

Congress of the United States, Acts of the Fourteenth, 1, 2; Congress of 1801 and 1815, 3; power over Bank, 4, 5; early action on tariff, 8; meeting in December, 1815, 9; vote as to tariff, 9; acts of the Fourteenth, 12-14; discussion of its powers by Calhoun, 13, 14; powers discussed by Monroe, 15; pay of members, 16; passage of internal improvements bill, 16; acts as to Florida, 24, 25; acts of 1811 as to Florida, 30; limitation as to slavery, 50; abolition of slave trade, 51; division of Louisiana territory, 55, 56; power over Territories, 63; power to erect Commonwealths, 64; attitude to slavery, 65; debate on powers of Congress, 67 *et seq.*; annals of, 74; powers discussed by Taylor, 79, 80, and by Holmes, 80, 81, and by McLane, 81, 82; Pinckney's argument on powers of, 84-87; conference committee on Missouri, 88, 89; interpretation of Act of Congress, 89; significance of the Compromise, 90-95; powers considered by Lowndes, 96; Sergeant on power of creating Commonwealths, 96, 97; course of Congress considered, 97, 98; oath of members, 98; second conference committee on Missouri, 101-103; significance of the compromise, 104; doctrine of its control of commerce, 110; conference committee on tariff, 114, 115; early practice as to internal improvements, 116, 117; vote on internal improvements bill of 1822, 118; Monroe on the powers of, 120, 121; power over expenditures, 121; act of April 30, 1824, 122; inaction upon "Monroe Doctrine," 128; Calhoun a member of, 133; joint session for count of electoral votes, 141, 142; as to power over roads, 155; Act of April 30, 1824, 155, 156; memorials to, 158; attitude of South Carolina to, 159 *et seq.;* passes Maysville Road bill, 167; appropriations for internal improvements, 169; as to powers of, 170; attitude to tariff, 178; Calhoun's attitude to. 179; control of courts by, 180; President's message before, 184; conference committee on tariff, 188; attitude to the planters, 189; decision on Bank Act of, 195; relation to President as to legislation, 206, 207; as a nominating body, 208; failure to override Jackson's veto, 209; inaction as to Indian problem, 215; Jackson's message to, 216; ten years' struggle of South in, 221 , its acts nullified, 222; Jackson's messages on South Carolina, 231, 232; abolition petitions to, 251, 252; abolition petitions before, 253; recommendations of Jackson, 272, 273; argument as to power over mails. 273 *et seq.;* conflict with President over Bank, 279 *et seq.;* passage of Independent Treasury bill, 285, 286; erection of new Commonwealths, 290; President's message on Texas, 298; action of Congress, 298-300; effect of its action, 300; address of certain Whig members, 303; message of Tyler to, 305; affairs of Texas, 306 *et seq. ;* Tyler's message of December, 1844, 320, 321; competency as to matters of treaty, 322; Polk's message on Oregon, 324; action as to Oregon, 325, 326; power over Texan boundary, 328; Act as to Corpus Christi, 329-331; Polk's message on Mexican War, 330; action on war, 331; Polk's message to, August 8, 1846, 334; consent to acquisition of California and New Mexico, 337; Polk's message on Trist, 338; as to attitude to Missouri Compromise, 341; special message on Oregon, 344; discussion of powers of, 344; Cass on policy of, 345; special message of July 6, 1848, to, 345, 346; as to power in Territories, 347; attitude to slavery, 348; Taylor's message of December 4, 1849, 353, 354; action on new Territories, 353 *et seq.;* Fillmore's message of August 6, 1850, 362; completion of compro-

# INDEX

mise measure, 363, 364; Fillmore's message of December, 1850, 368; petitions on fugitive slave law, 369; Fillmore's message of December 2, 1851, 374; Fillmore's message of December 6, 1852, 380; action on organization of Kansas and Nebraska, 381 *et seq.;* Kansas election for delegate to, 416, 417; Whitfield in, 418; as to powers in Kansas, 422; memorial from Kansas, 426; [Kansas question before, 432; slavery question before, 433; laws of, in Kansas, 464; President's message of February 2, 1858, 469

Connecticut, Commonwealth of, 13; legislation on slavery, 48; in election of 1824, 142; resolution on independence of Texas, 290; vote on Kansas-Nebraska bill, 399

Constitution of the Confederation, 48; relation to Ordinance of 1787, 48, 49

Constitution of the United States of America, the, as to Bank, 5; as cited by Calhoun, 13; as interpreted by Monroe, 17; relative to parties, 17, 18; slavery in, 49, 50; interpreted with reference to national character of slavery, 59; the control of slavery, 62, 65; powers of Congress, 63, 64; test of the Tallmadge amendment, 66 *et seq.;* Taylor as to powers of Congress, 79; Holmes' speech, 80, 81; McLane's argument, 81, 82; limitations on new Commonwealths, 85; as to restriction on Commonwealths, 89; significance of the first Missouri Compromise, 90–95; as cited by Lowndes, 97; cited by Sergeant, 97; extent of its protection, 98, 99; second Missouri compromise, 102, 103; significance of the compromise, 104, 106; as to fourteenth amendment, 105; Taylor's interpretation of, 119; Monroe's interpretation of, 120, 121; development of the particularistic interpretation, 122; as construed by Adams, and Clay, 146; as to international status of slavery, 151; amendment proposed, 155; reaction as to interpretation of, 156; as interpreted by Buchanan, 159; amendment suggested by Jackson, 167, 168; as interpreted by Taylor, 168, 169; as interpreted by McDuffie, 173, 174; as interpreted by Calhoun, 178–181; regard for processes of, 181; as interpreted by Calhoun, 183; as to origin of revenue bill, 188; political science of, 192, 193; decision as to constitutionality of Bank Act, 195; as construed by Jackson, 199; Jackson on operation of, 205, 206; effect of his Bank veto, 207–209; as cited| by Jackson, 216, 217; the Cherokee nation case, 218; case of Worcester vs. Georgia, 218, 219; powers conferred on President by, 220; as interpreted in the Nullification Ordinance, 222; as construed by the nullifiers, 227; as interpreted in Jackson's proclamation, 229; as expounded by Calhoun, 236; as explained by Webster, 237; effect of events of 1832 and 1833 on, 238–241; as to control of civil status, 247, 248; attitude of Garrison to, 248; guarantees as to right of petition, 255, 256; in Calhoun's argument, 273; provision as to treaties, 305; nature of war according to, 306; as to treaty-making powers, 307, 308; as to annexation of Texas, 321; as to procedure on treaties, 324; as interpreted by Rhett, 342; as to Oregon bill, 343; compromises of, 348; as to extension of its effect, 350; amendment suggested by Calhoun, 358; Webster on the, 359; effect of formation of, 366; as to fugitive slaves, 366, 367; as interpreted by Fillmore, 370; as interpreted by Butler, 372; as cited by Fillmore, 374; in Douglas's report, 383, 392; as viewed by Everett, 393; in Chase's amendment, 394; treason, as defined by, 427; the Dred Scott case, 449 *et seq.*

Continental Congress. *See* Congress, Continental

Contreras, battle of, 334

Convention, Federal Constitutional, of 1787, attitude to slavery, 49, 50

Convention. *See* Treaty

Conway, M. F., letter to Governor Reeder, 424

Cooke, P. St. George, ordered to at-

# INDEX

tack Topeka, 445; refuses to obey, 445

Cooper, James, on committee of Thirteen, 360; not voting on Kansas-Nebraska bill, 398

Cooper, Thomas, speech at Columbia, 159; his life and views, 173; his relation to slavery and to McDuffie, 173

Corpus Christi, made port of delivery, 329; advance of Taylor, 329

Cos, Martin Perfectos de, attacks Gonzales, 293; driven from Texas, 294

Cotton, relation to slavery, 52, 53; exportation reduced, 54

Crafts, Ellen, escape, 368

Crafts, William, escape, 368

Cramer, John, motion in House, 254

Crane, A. C., statement as to Dred Scott case, 449, 450

Crawford, William Harris, relation to Jackson, 34, 35; opinion of treaty with Spain, 36; effect of Seminole War, 38; qualifications as presidential candidate in 1824, 132, 133, 136, 141; electoral vote of 1824, 137; relation to Adams' administration, 144–146; relation to Jackson and the Seminole War, 220

Creeks, the, 26, 29; Council of 1824, 212; Indian Springs convention, 212; its repudiation, 212; resistance to Georgia, 212; protest to general government, 212, 213; controversy as to Creek lands, 213, 214; new agreement of 1826 as to lands, 214; agreement repudiated by Georgia, 214

"Crime against Kansas," the, delivered, 439

Cuba, in the Spanish-American troubles, 152–154; the Ostend manifesto, 408

Cumberland Road, built, 116; bill of 1822, 118; analysis of vote, 118, 119; attitude of East and West, 119, 120

Curtis, Benjamin Robbins, opinion on Dred Scott case, 454, 457, 458

Curtis, George Ticknor, attitude to fugitive slave law, 368; in Shadrach case, 370; connection with Sims case, 373

Cushing, Caleb, relation to Kansas-Nebraska bill, 401

Customs Act, of 1789, 8; of 1812, 9

DAGGETT, DAVID, voting, 74

Dallas, Alexander James, presents Bank memorial, 201; on Senate committee, 201; reports Bank bill, 201

Davis, Jefferson, views as to slavery in Territories, 344, 345; moves amendment to Oregon bill, 344; effect of his action, 345; attitude to Clay's proposal, 357; views on fugitive slave law, 367; contention as to fugitive slave law, 371; relation to Kansas-Nebraska bill, 401, 402; disapproves Col. Sumner's course, 443; attitude to Kansas affairs, 472, 473

De Bree, John, owner of Shadrach, 370

Declaration of Independence, the, 70, 92, 94, 193, 229, 245

Delaware, Commonwealth of, 8; legislation on slavery, 48; in election of 1828, 163; vote on Kansas-Nebraska bill, 399

Democratic party, appearance, 38, 104; principles, 104; circumstances of its appearance, 146; party nomenclature, 162, 163; demands of 1828, 163; the making of its creed, 165; divisions of the party and policies of each, 165; origin and influence, 193, 194; radical development in Kentucky, 195, 196; attack of western element upon privilege, 196; Jackson becomes leader, 196, 197; opposes Gordon's proposal as to independent treasury, 285; supports Independent Treasury Bill of 1840, 285; relation to the questions of slavery and territorial extension, 287, 288; nominates Polk for presidency, 309; the platform, 309, 316; views of the union of Texas and Oregon in platform, 317; Thompson's opinion, 317; characterization the work of the Democrats, 317; platform of 1844, 318; attitude to Wilmot proviso, 338; platform of 1848 as to slavery in Territories, 344, 345; the Clayton committee, 346; election of 1848, 348, 349; convention of 1852, 376;

INDEX 513

electior of 1852, 377; controversy on Kansas-Nebraska bill, 391; vote on Kansas-Nebraska bill, 399; attitude of Pierce to New York factions, 404; vote in House on Kansas-Nebraska bill, 404, 405; meaning of the vote, 405, 406; as to leaders of Emigrant Aid Company, 413; effect of Kansas struggle, 417; relation to rise of Republican party, 418; Lane's effort at organization in Kansas, 423; relation of Kansas affairs to national party organization, 430, 431; effect on party prospects of sacking of Lawrence, 438; as to effect of events in Kansas, 447; effect of Dred Scott decision, 458; plan as to Democracy in Kansas, 462

Denver, John W., appointed Acting-Governor of Kansas Territory, 467; his report to the President, 468, 469; pockets bill for constitutional convention, 471

Deseret, Foote's bill, 354

Des Moines River, the, Falls of, 66

De Witt, Alexander, signs *National Era* address, 389

Dickerson, Mahlon, reports tariff bill in Senate. 188

Dickinson, Daniel Stevens, on Committee of Thirteen, 360

Dickson, John, presents abolition petitions, 254; controversy with Chinn, 254

District of Columbia, adoption of Maryland laws, 51; exclusive government vested in central Government, 247, 248; petitions for abolition of slavery in, 251, 252; report on slavery in District, 253; disposal of Quaker petitions, 253; more petitions in House, 254; contest begins, 254; petitions presented by Dickson and Fairfield, 254; the Dickson-Chinn controversy, 254; Slade's motion, 254; Granger's intimation, 257; the demand of Wise, 257, 258 (*see* Petition, Right of); Pinckney resolutions quoted, 261; re-enacted, 262; Vermont petition, 265, 269; effort of Calhoun as to slavery in the District, 268; recurrence of the slavery question, 355; Clay's plan, 356; attitude of Southerners, 357; attitude of abolitionists, 357; Clay's report, 362; bill passed, 364. *See* Washington, D. C.

Dixon, Archibald, proposes amendment to Nebraska bill, 387; Blair's letter on Dixon, 387, 388; attitude of Douglas, 388

Dodge, Augustus Cæsar, introduces bill on Nebraska, 382

Donaldson, J. B., proclamation as to resistance to service of writs, 435; dealings with citizens of Lawrence, 436, 437; appears with force before Lawrence, 437; dismisses posse, 438; the sacking of Lawrence, 438

Doniphan, Alexander William, captures Chihuahua, 332

Douglas, Stephen Arnold, attitude to Wilmot proviso, 338; presents bill on Oregon in House, 340, 341; presents bill in Senate on Oregon, 343; moves amendment, 347; changes vote, 347; reports bill, 349; Berrien's adverse report, 349, 350; new bill on Territories, 350; motion as to California, 357; attitude to fugitive slave law, 368; candidate for presidential nomination, 376; early plans for organization of territory west of the Mississippi, 381; presents bill and report on Nebraska, 382, 383; consideration of report and its author, 383–387; attitude to Dixon, 388; presents new bill on Nebraska and Kansas, 389; *National Era* address, 389, 390; Douglas's reply, 390; charged with conspiracy, 391; his principle as to slavery in Territories, 391; amendment to bill, 392; vote on his amendment, 393; debate on further amendments, 394–397; proposes amendment, 395, 396; final argument on Kansas-Nebraska bill, 397, 398; substance of bill reported in House bill, 400; Douglas's bill in House, 401, 403; effect of Dred Scott decision on Douglas Democrats, 458; opposition to Buchanan, 469, 470

Douglas county, Kansas, Sheriff Jones of, 428; charge of Chief Justice Lecompte, 435; indictment by Grand Jury, 435

Dow, C. M., murdered by Coleman, 428

## INDEX

Downs, Solomon W., on committee of Thirteen, 360
Drayton, William, relation to nullification, 181
Dred Scott vs. Sandford [19 Howard, 293], 447, 449 et seq.
Duane, William John, removed from head of Treasury Department, 280
Dutch Traders, at Jamestown, 39
Dutch Henry's Crossing, massacre at, 440; the massacre characterized, 441; and denounced by settlers, 441; effect of massacre, 442; the work characterized, 473, 474

EAST FLORIDA, 21
Eaton, John Henry, as to Bank trouble, 192
Easton, Kansas, election trouble at, 426
Election, presidential, of 1820, 129; of 1824, 130-137; in House of Representatives, 140-142; of 1828, 163, 164; of 1832, 189, 190 et seq.; of 1836, 283; of 1840, 286; of 1844, 320; of 1848, 349; of 1852, 377; of 1856, relation to election of Whitfield in Kansas, 417; indications as to election of 1856, 440; of 1856, as related to affairs in Kansas, 446, 447
Electoral Colleges, 50
Ellis, Powhatan, ordered to make final demand on Mexican Government, 299
El Paso, 361
Emancipation, early schemes for, 243, 245
Embargo, of 1807, 54
Emerson, Dr., owner of Dred Scott, 450; his will, 450
Emerson, Irene, owner of Dred Scott, 450; sells him to Sandford, 451
Emigrant Aid Company, misrepresentations as to, 411; conference with Robinson, 413; excitement occasioned in Missouri, 413; claims as to its purpose, 419; indictment against hotel in Lawrence, 435
England, 21, 45, 368
English, William Hayden, bill on Kansas, 470, 471
Erie Canal, 132
Eustis, William, efforts for admission of Missouri, 100
Everett, Edward, reply to McDuffie, 176; speech on Kansas-Nebraska bill, 392, 393; not voting on Kansas-Nebraska bill, 398
Ewing, Thomas, on Bank Committee of Senate, 201

FAIRFIELD, JOHN, presents abolition petition, 254
Federal Party, 12, 104; extinction, 129; its errors, 129; effects of War of 1812, 130; principles on which it lost power, 239
Field, Roswell M., connection with Dred Scott case, 449, 452
Fillmore, Millard, becomes President, 360; message on Texas, 360; message of December, 1850, 368, 369; opposition of Giddings, 369; message on Shadrach case, 370, 371; report on President's powers, 372; message of December 2, 1851, 374; contest in Whig Convention of 1852, 376; message of December 6, 1852, 380, 381
Fitchburg, Massachusetts, home of Charles Robinson, 413
Flint River, 22
Florida, its acquisition, 19-38; treaty of Florida Seminoles, 290; constitution formed, 290; admitted as Commonwealth, 290; vote on Kansas-Nebraska bill, 390
Floyd, John, message on Southampton massacre, 249
Foote, Henry Stuart, bill for Territories, 354; criticises Clay, 357, 358; motion on Bell's resolutions, 359; accepts amendment, 360; draws pistol on Benton, 360; introduces finality resolutions, 374; passed by Senate and rejected by Senate, 375
"Force Bill," the. See Wilkins, William
Foreign affairs, relation to party development, 122; the Holy Alliance, 123-125; the "Monroe Doctrine," 125-128; significance of the diplomatic questions, 129; success of Van Buren, 164. See Committee on Foreign Relations
Forsyth, John, letter as to intrigue against Jackson, 220; letter from Morfit, 296, 297
Fort Brown, attempt at relief, 329
Fort Jackson, treaty of, 26, 29
Fort Leavenworth, Robinson at, 414;

arrival of Governor Reeder, 416; Governor authorized to call troops from, 432; Sumner returns to, 442

Fort Monroe, transfer of artillery, 230

Fort Moultrie, transfer of artillery, 230

Fort Riley, Branscomb at, 414

Fort Scott, 31

Fort Titus, Kansas conflict at, 444

Fowltown, destroyed, 28, 29

France, 21, 22, 23, 24; abolition of slavery, 54; gets Louisiana territory, 54, 65; in Holy Alliance, 123; relation to Congress of Verona, 124; boundary dispute with Spain, 290; recognizes Texan independence, 304; cedes Louisiana to United States, 312, 318, 395. *See* Treaty

Francis, Indian priest, 26

Franklin, Kansas, Jones goes to, 428; Lane and Robinson accompany Shannon to, 430, 431; as to treaty of August 17, 444

Free-Soil party, Buffalo convention of 1848, 347; nomination and platform, 347, 348; nomination of Hale, 377; the *National Era* address, 389; its effect, 400; vote in House on Kansas-Nebraska bill, 404, 405; meaning of the vote, 405, 406; appearance of Eli Thayer, 408, 409; as to leaders of Emigrant Aid Company, 413; effect of Kansas struggle, 417; relation of Free-soil party to rise of Republican party, 418; effect of Dred Scott decision, 458

Frémont, John Charles, effect of events in Kansas on his candidacy in 1856, 447

French Republic, the, 23

Fugitive slave law, passed by Congress, 51; law of 1850, 363, 364 (*see* also Slavery); law of 1850 makes slavery a national matter, 366; its further effect, 366, 367; views of Calhoun, Davis, and Rhett, 367; the Hamlet case, 367; efforts at repeal of law, 367, 368; the Crafts case, 368; the "Underground" established, 368; attitude of the lawyers, 368; Fillmore's message of December, 1850, 368, 369; Fillmore's message, 369; motion of Giddings, 369; petitions for repeal, 369, 370; the Shadrach case, 370; Fillmore's message, 370, 371; debate on Clay's motion, 371; report on powers of President, 371, 372; the Sims case, 372, 373; Boston meetings, 373; leaders of opinion, 373; the "Jerry rescue," 373, 374; Fillmore's message of December 2, 1851, 374; debate on Foote's finality resolutions, 374, 375; the result, 375; petitions for repeal, 375; Whig convention of 1852, 376; attack by Sumner, 377; effect of election of 1852, 377; various policies as to slavery, 377–379

Fuller, Timothy, in Missouri bill debate, 68

"Fundamentals," Massachusetts, 41

Furness, William Henry, opposes fugitive slave law, 368

GAINES, EDMUND PENDLETON, in Florida, 28, 30, 31; ordered to Georgia, 213; authorized to advance into Texas, 289

Garland, James, reply to Slade, 258

Garrison, William Lloyd, beginning of abolition, 246; estimate, 246; the constitutional situation, 246–248; attack on the Constitution, 248; publishes the *Liberator*, 251; compared with moderates, 251; opposition to fugitive slave law, 373

Geary, John White, appointed governor of Kansas with authority over troops, 446; at Lecompton and Lawrence, 446; enforces withdrawal of Missourians, 446, 447; his resignation, 447

Geography, relation to political development, 20

Georgetown, South Carolina, instructions to collector, 230

Georgia, Commonwealth of, 8, 26, 27, 28, 33; slavery prohibited, 43; conditional cession of western lands, 50, 56; attitude to internal improvements bill of 1817, 118; attitude to internal improvements bill of 1822, 119; stock held in United States Bank, 203; nullification in Georgia, 210; conditional cession of lands of 1802, 211; the attempt to erect an Indian State, 211; problem of land titles in Georgia, 211, 212; legislature memorializes for quieting of Indian claims, 212; the Indian Springs convention, 212; its repudiation, 212; the attempt to survey the lands, 212; Barbour's letter to Troup, 212, 213; quieting of Indian titles by agreement of 1826, 214; Georgia repudiates the agreement, 214; defiance of central Government, 214, 215; President refers matter to Congress, 215; Congress fails to act, 215; legislature extends criminal jurisdiction over Cherokees, 215; Jackson's opinion of Georgia's position, 216; obstinacy of the Cherokees, 216; the question in Jackson's message of 1829, 216, 217; opinions of Indian titles, 217; the solution in Georgia, 217, 218; legislature incorporates Cherokee lands in the Commonwealth, 218; the Cherokee Nation case, 218; the case of Worcester against Georgia, 218, 219; failure to execute decision, 219, 220; convention in, 375; vote in Kansas-Nebraska bill, 399; Jackson's Georgians in Kansas, 438

Ghent, treaty of, 9, 26

Giddings, Joshua Reed, denounces Fillmore and Webster, 369; colloquy with Howe, 381, 382

Glascock, Thomas, attitude on procedure as to petitions, 259

Goliad, atrocities, 293

Gonzales, attacked, 293

Gordon, William F., proposal as to independent treasury, 285; relation of parties to its rejection, 285

Gorham, Benjamin, attitude to tariff bill of 1823, 111; reply to McDuffie, 176

Gorostiza, Manuel Eduardo de, leaves Washington, 299

Granger, Francis, claim as to District of Columbia, 257

Grasshopper Falls, Kansas, convention at, 464

Great Britain, treaty of 1763, 21, 23; treaty of 1783, 22; war of United States with, 24; treaty of 1814, 26; Nicholls's proposition to, 27; Indian allies of, 29; relations with United States as to slaves, 58, 59; claims in North Pacific, 123; relation to Holy Alliance, 123, 124; proposal as to Holy Alliance, 125; Canning's declaration, 125; diplomatic relations, 287; Ashburton Treaty, 303; recognizes Texan independence, 304; as mediator between Mexico and Texas, 304; the London letter of British plans, 304; claims to Oregon, 311; Nootka Convention, 311, 312; effect of war with Spain, 312; Treaty of Utrecht, 312; claim of United States, 312, 313; treaty of 1818 with United States, 313; effect of treaty of 1819 between United States and Spain, 313; agreement of 1828 with United States, 314; in Ashburton-Webster negotiations, 314; ignorance as to Oregon, 314, 315; the work of Whitman, 315, 316; Democratic platform of 1844, 316; negotiations as to Oregon, 321; statement of negotiations in Polk's first message, 324; his recommendations, 324; action of Congress, April, 1846, 325, 326; treaty of June, 1846, 326; possibility of holding California, 332; result of treaty with, 339; United States minister to, 408

Great lakes, 325

Greeley, Horace, views on election of 1844, 320

Grimke, Thomas Smith, relation to nullification, 181

Grinnell, Moses H., member of Emigrant Aid Society, 409

Guadalupe Hidalgo, treaty of, terms, 336; ratified by Senate, 339

HALE, EDWARD EVERETT, member of Emigrant Aid Society, 409

Hale, John Parker, moves amendment to Oregon Bill, 344; effect of his action, 345; contention as to fugitive slave law, 371; presents petitions for repeal of fugitive slave law, 375; nominated for presidency, 377; popular vote compared with Van Buren's in 1848, 377

Hamilton, James, the Calhoun letter, 221; calls special meeting of legislature, 221; chairman of nullification convention, 221; sends ordinance of nullification to legislature, 224

Hamlet, James, arrest, 367

Hamlin, Hannibal, presents petition in Senate, 370

Hammond, James Hamilton, motion not to receive abolition petitions, 255; wrangle over his two motions, 256

Harrisburg, Penn., convention of 1824, 139

Harrison, William Henry, voting, 73; nominated for presidency, 286; succeeded, on his death, by Tyler, 286

Harvey, James Madison, commands column of "Free-state" force, 445

Hayne, Robert Young, theory on tariff, 114; view of slave labor, 161; view repeated by McDuffie, 177; Calhoun and the Webster debate, 179; criticism of Clay's resolution on tariff, 187, and amendment of it, 188; on Bank committee of Senate, 201; his inaugural as governor of South Carolina, 224

Hayti, its affairs mentioned by Salazar, 151; consideration of its example in the United States, 152; isolated, 154

Hegel, Georg Wilhelm Friedrich, cited on human purpose, 243, 244

Heister, William, presents abolition petition, 253

Herrera, José Joaquin de, refuses to receive Slidell, 328; gives way to Paredes, 328

Hill, Isaac, in Bank trouble, 191

Hillards, the, in Crafts case, 368

Hillis Hajo, 32

Himallemico, 32

Holmes, John, voting, 73; presents Maine petition for admission, 77; reports bill, 77; speech on Missouri, 80, 81; on conference committee, 88

Holy Alliance, formation, 123; relation to England, 124; Congress of Verona, 124; Canning's declaration to Polignac, 125; the "Monroe Doctrine," 125-128; relation to Spain's colonies, 153, 154

Holst, Hermann Edouard von, opinions reviewed, 27; opinion of Jackson's veto message considered, 206, 207

Holyoke, Massachusetts, residence of Branscomb, 413

Home Government [of England], as to baptism of slaves, 44

Hopkinson, Joseph, committee service, 3

House of Representatives, of the United States, action on Madison's message, 3; Clay, Speaker of, 6; passage of Bank bill, 7, 8; reference of tariff matters, 9; debate on tariff, 10-12; passage of tariff bill, 12; debate on internal improvements, 13, 14; pay of members, 16; passage of internal improvements bill, 18; second passage of internal improvements bill, 18; vote on censure of Jackson, 35, 36; representation in, 63; petitions from Missouri, 66; debate on the Tallmadge amendment, 66 *et seq.;* passage of Tallmadge amendment and Missouri bill, 73; disagreement with Senate, 74; petition from Maine referred, 75; Maine bill passed by House, 75; Missouri bill and Taylor's amendment, 78-80; Holmes's speech, 80, 81; McLane's speech, 81, 82; Pinkney's speech on powers of Congress, 84-87; disagreement with Senate, 88; conference committee, 88-89; significance of the compromise, 90-95; Missouri constitution considered, 95, 96; report of Lowndes, 96; speech of Sergeant, 96, 97; consideration of the question, 97, 98; defeat of the Lowndes bill, 99; tables Senate bill, 99; Clay's proposals, 100; report of committee of thirteen, 100, 101; defeat of the bill and amendment, 101; second conference committee, 101, 103; plan to limit membership, 109; reference of Monroe's recommendations, 110; tariff bill of 1823, 110, 111; tariff bill of 1824, 112; Clay's argument, 112, 113; replies to Clay, 113, 114; conclusion in conference committee, 114, 115; early votes on internal improvements, 117; vote on internal improvements bill of 1822, 117, 118, 119, 120; Monroe's letter on internal improvements, 120, 121; vote on vetoed bill, 121; Clay, Speaker of, 134; election of President in, 140-142; memorials on tariff, 158; tariff bill passed, 159; tariff bill reported, 160; vote on tariff bill, 162; vote on vetoed Maysville road bill, 168; question as to reference of President's message, 172-174; tariff bill before House, 174, 175; McDuffie's argument, 175,176, 177; reference of President's message, 184, 185; tariff bill before, 185, 186; tariff bill passed, 186; refusal to concur with Senate, 188; conference committee, 188; report on the Bank, 198; relation of members of constituencies, 200; reports on Bank, 202; bill for re-charter passed, 202; Jackson on duty of members, 206; early control of presidential elections, 208; action on President's message, 231, 232; bill reported on President's powers, 235; claim as to origin of tariff bills, 236; passage of tariff bill and "Force Bill," 237; abolition petitions in, 252; report on petitions, 253; more petitions referred, 253; action on Dickson's motion, 254; conflict over right of petition, 254 *et seq.*; adoption of the Pinckney resolutions, 261; further work of Adams and Slade, 262; rule of January 8, 1840, 263; Gordon's amendment in, 285; resolutions as to recognition of Texan independence, 296; contingent action as to Texan independence, 299, 300; effect of action, 300; Wise's speech in, 302; Tyler's message on Texan treaty, 309; action on annexation of Texas, 321, 322; action on admission of Texas, 322; concurrence with Senate's action on Texas, 323; McKay's bill, 335; the Wilmot proviso, 335, 336; Oregon bill in, 341; action on Oregon bills, 343; rejects Clayton bill, 347; final agreement with Senate, 347; action on erection of California and New Mexico, 349 *et seq.*; completion of compromise measures, 363, 364; action on President's message, 369; passage of finality resolutions, 375; action on organization of Kansas and Nebraska, 381 *et seq.*; contest for seat in, 432; appointment of committee of investigation for Kansas affairs, 433; memorials from Kansas, 433; bill for admission of Kansas, 442, 443; action on Kansas, 470. *See* Congress of the United States

Houston, Samuel, leader of Texans, 293; Benton's description, 293, 294; his early record, 294; San Jacinto and the presidency of Texas, 294; sends special envoy to Washington, 306; promise of Murphy disavowed, 307; changes vote, 347; speech on Kansas-Nebraska bill, 393; vote on Douglas's amendment, 393; speech on the bill, 397; vote on Kansas - Nebraska bill, 399

Houston, S. D., withdraws from Kansas Territorial legislature, 421

Howard, William A., on committee for Kansas investigation, 433

Howe, John W., discussion with Giddings, 381, 382

Hudson Bay Company, agents in Oregon, 314; relation to policy of Great Britain, 314; representations as to Oregon, 314, 315

Hunt, Memucan, proposes Texan annexation to Van Buren, 301

Hutchinson, William, in "Free-state" directory of Kansas, 443

IBERVILLE RIVER, the, 21, 22

Illinois, Commonwealth of, slavery forbidden, 62, 63; condition on erection, 68, 69, 71; vote on Kansas-Nebraska bill, 399; as to Dred Scott case, 450

Independent treasury, Van Buren's message of September 4, 1837, 284, 285; Gordon's proposal, 285; attitude of the parties, 285; Act of July 4, 1840, 285; party contest over the bill, 285, 286

Indian Springs, Convention at, 212

Indiana, Commonwealth of, slavery forbidden, 62, 63; condition on erection, 68, 69, 71; vote on Kansas-Nebraska bill, 399

Indiana, Territory of, relation to slavery, 51; jurisdiction over part of Louisiana Territory, 55

Ingersoll, Joseph R., claim as to District of Columbia, 257; reports joint resolution on Texas, 321

Ingham, Samuel D., in debate, 10; position upon tariff bill of 1827, 158; as to Bank trouble, 191

Internal improvements, bill present-

# INDEX 519

ed, 14; Calhoun's speech, 15, 16; bill passed, 16; President's veto, 17; Madison's earlier recommendations, 17; failure to overcome veto, 18; development in theory, 116–119; the Act of 1806, 116; Calhoun's bill of 1817 vetoed by Madison, 116, 117; analysis of vote, 117, 118; Cumberland road bill of 1822, 118; analysis of vote, 118, 119; Taylor's position, 119; attitude of East and West, 119, 120; Monroe's veto, 120, and message, 120, 121; vote on vetoed bill, 121; Act of April, 1824, 122; relation to foreign affairs, 122; significance of the questions, 129; Adams's first message, 155; Van Buren's opposition, 155; relation to political divisions, 156; practical difficulties, 156, 157; Jackson's views in 1829, 167; passage of Maysville road bill, 167; the veto, 167, 168; vote on vetoed bill, 168; analysis of vote, 168; significance of veto, 169; appropriations approved by Adams and Jackson, 169; relation to private enterprise, 169, 170; relation to slavery, 170; Jackson's message of December, 1830, 178; Jackson's message of December, 1831, 184

Iowa, Commonwealth of, admitted, 290; memorial of legislature on finality resolutions, 375; vote on Kansas-Nebraska bill, 399

Jackson, Andrew, in Florida, 24, 25, 28, 30, 31, 32, 33; attempt at censure, 34, 35, 36; vindicated, 36; Territorial governor of Florida, 38; effect of Seminole War, 38; qualifications as presidential candidate in 1824, 135, 136, 139, 141; electoral vote of 1824, 136, 137; the Coleman letter, 138; opposition to Adams threatened, 142, 143, and begun, 144, 146; elected President, 163, 164; makes Van Buren secretary of state, 164; vigorous foreign policy, 164; first annual message, 166, 167; vetoes Maysville road bill, 167, 168; significance of the veto, 169; appropriations approved by Adams and Jackson, 169; message of December, 1829, as to tariff, 171, 172; its reference, 172; message of December, 1830, 178; message of December, 1831, 184; message of December, 1829, 190; later interpretations of his attack on Bank, 191, 192; relation to "relief party" in Kentucky, 196; leader of Democratic party, 196, 197; attitude to Bank, 197, 198; his views opposed by committees, 198; message of December, 1830, 198, 199; his message of December, 1831, 200; puts the Bank question before the people, 200; relation of Bank question to question of Jackson's election, 201; effect of his veto of Bank bill, 202; analysis of his message, 202–206; opinion of von Holst on the veto message considered, 206, 207, the message interpreted, 206–209; relation of Congress to his election as President, 207; the people accept the principles of Jacksonian democracy 209; opinion of Georgia's claims, 216; reply to Cherokees, 216; message of December, 1829, 216, 217; different opinions of Indian titles, 217; failure to execute decision of Supreme Court, 219, 220; view on South Carolina's opinion of tariff, 220; supposition as to Cabinet intrigue of 1819, 220; the Forsyth letter, 220; hostility of Jackson and Calhoun, 220, 221; message of December, 1832, 228; proclamation of December 10, 1832, 228–230; active military preparations, 230, 231; instructions to collectors, 230; instructions to Scott, 230, 231; popular approval of Jackson's course, 231; attitude of Congress, 231; Hayne's proclamation, 232; Jackson's message of January, 1833, 232; Bell's report on President's powers, 235; signs Compromise Tariff, and "Force Bill," 238; motive in course on nullification, 238; significance of his doctrines, 239, 240; as to responsibility for Jacksonian principles, 240; message of 1835 as to use of mails, 272, 273; decides to destroy the Bank, 279; power of removal, 279; removal of McLane and Duane, 280; the work of Taney, 280; consideration of the proper exercise of power, 280; censured by Senate, 281; Benton begins effort at removal of censure, 281; his contest successful, 282; tendency of government to his day, 282; his successor, 284; sends Morfit to Texas, 296; message of December 21, 1836, on Texas, 298; special message as to reprisals, 298; authorizes Gaines to advance into Texas, 298; orders Ellis to make demands on Mexico, 299; satisfaction not given, 299; special message of February 6, 1837, 299; request for unusual powers not granted by Congress, 299; recognizes Texas and her agent, 300; ends diplomatic relations with Mexico, 301

Jackson, William, presents abolition petition, 255

Jackson, Zadock, repudiates sacking of Lawrence, 438

Jalapa, captured by Scott, 333

Jamestown, slaves introduced at, 40

Janus, gates open, 260

Jefferson, Thomas, 2, 3; relation to French philosophy, 129; share of Congress in his election as President, 207; principles restated by Calhoun, 239; tendency of government from his day, 282; sends out Lewis and Clark, 312; view as to extent of Louisiana, 312

Johnson, Robert Ward, position on Kansas-Nebraska bill, 393

Johnson, William, relation to nullification, 181

Johnson County, Kansas, contested election, 465

Johnston, Josiah S., on bank committee of Senate, 201

Jones, George Wallace, position on Kansas-Nebraska bill, 393

Jones, John W., reply to Adams on right of petition, 257

Jones, Samuel J., as sheriff, arrests Branson, 428; rescue of Branson, 428; goes to Franklin and calls help from Missouri, 428, 429; his error recognized, 430; serves writ on Wood, 433; tries to arrest Tappan, 434; attempt to assassinate, 434; Donaldson's reference to the shooting, 436; the sacking of Lawrence, 438

KANSAS CITY, Mo., 316; Branscomb and Robinson at, 413, 414

Kansas, Territory of, bill for organization of, 389; the abolition protest, 389, 390; reply of Douglas, 390; amendment of Chase, 391, 392; position of Wade, 391; amendment of Douglas, 392; views of Everett, 392, 393; speech of Houston, 393; position of Bell and the committee, 393; vote on the amendment, 393; Chase's amendment, 394, 395; Pratt's amendment, 394; Walker's declaration and Badger's amendment, 395; Chase's third amendment, 395, 396; Douglas's amendment, 395, 396; Chase's fourth amendment, 396; speech of Bell against bill, 396, 397; speech of Houston, 397; final argument of Douglas, 397, 398; vote on bill in Senate, 398; analysis of vote, 398, 399; rise of popular opposition, 399, 400; the Richardson bill, 400; the Senate bill in the House, 401; position of Cushing, Davis, and Pierce, 401-403; action in House, 403; management of bill by Stephens, 404; bill signed by President, 404; analysis of vote, 404, 405; meaning of the vote, 405, 406; relation of Act to slavery, 407, 408; the struggle for Kansas, 407 et seq.; the plan of Thayer and his associates, 409; organization of the society, 409, 410; opposition, 410; incorporation of the society, 410, 411; misrepresentations to Emigrant Aid Company, 411; considered as of the South, 412; influence of Atchison, 412, 413; expedition of Robinson and Branscomb, 413, 414; "Platte County Self-defensive Association," 414, 415; the founding of Lawrence, 415; trouble over contesting claimants, 415, 416; arrival of Governor Reeder, 416; election of Whitfield, 417; effect on Republican party of interference of Missourians in Kansas, 418; significance of the seating of Whitfield, 418; census of Kansas, 419; interference of Missourians in election of first Territorial legislature, 419, 420; action on contested election cases, 420; supplementary elections, 421; first Territorial legislature, 421; Robinson's plan for anti-slavery party, 421, 422; legislature meets at Pawnee, 422; pro-slavery members seated, 422, 423; trouble over adjournment to Shawnee Mission, 423; arrival of Sharpe's rifles, 423; Lane's faction checked by Robinson's Lawrence speech, 423, 424; Robinson's declaration as to slavery, 424; Conway's letter to Reeder, 424; beginning of the "Free-state" movement, 424; legislation upon slavery, 424; its effect on the North, 424, 425; the Lawrence and Topeka conventions, 425; the adoption of the Topeka constitution, 425; removal of Governor Reeder, 425; Woodson Acting-Governor, 425; election of Reeder as Congressional delegate, 425; election of Robinson as Governor, 425; conflicts between "Free-state" and Territorial Governments, 426; petition for admission and election of Senators by "Free-state" party, 426, 427; characterization of "Free-state" acts, 427; Robinson's message to legislature, 427; arrival of Governor Shannon, 427; the Leavenworth convention, 428; conflict between the two governments, 428; the Branson rescue, 428, 429; invasion of Missourians, 429; Lawrence committee meet Governor Shannon, 429; Shannon goes to Lawrence, 430; agreement of Shannon with citizens of Lawrence, 430; Lane, Robinson, and Shannon at Franklin, 430; Atchison and the withdrawal of the Missourians, 430, 431; appearance of John Brown, 431; Shannon's report to President, 431; appeal of leaders at Lawrence, 431; the President's proclamation, 432; attitude of "Free-state" party to proclamation, 432; difficulty of the situation, 432, 433; organization under Topeka constitution, 432; contest for seat in House of Representatives, 432, 433; House appoints committee of investigation, 433; application for admission under Topeka constitution, 433; work of Jones and attempt to assassinate him, 433, 434; the assault repudiated by the "Free-state" party, 434; letters of Robinson and Sumner, 434; Lecompte's charge to grand jury, 435; the "treason indictments," 435; Donaldson's proclamation, 435, 436; dealings of citizens of Lawrence with Shannon and Donaldson, 436, 437; the sacking of Lawrence, 438; repudiation by Atchison and others, 438; the "Crime against Kansas," 439; the attack on Sumner, 439, 440; the Pottawattomie massacres, 440; attitude of the Congressional committee, 440; characterization of the massacre, 441; denunciation by settlers, 441; Brown and Pate at Black Jack, 441; Shannon's proclamation and the work of the troops, 442; effect of massacre on "Free-state" cause, 442, 443; committee report and bill in House, 442, 443; dispersal of legislature at Topeka, 443; Smith succeeds Sumner, 443; the Lawrence convention and the directory, 443; "Free-state" military force organized and in conflict, 444; capture of Titus, 444; treaty of August 17, at Lawrence, 444; resignation of Shannon, 444, Woodson again Acting-Governor, 444; proclamation of August 25, 444; Missourians under Atchison in camp on Bull Creek, 445; destruction of Ossawattomie, 445; Smith's orders as to invaders, 445; Lane leads in skirmish at Bull Creek, 445; Woodson's order and Cooke's refusal to attack Topeka, 445; failure of plan to attack Lecompton, 445, 446; active steps by President, 446; actions of Geary, 446; retirement of the Missourians, 446, 447; resignation of Geary, 446; effect of events on presidential election, 447; Buchanan's inaugural address, 447, 448; plan for convention at Lecompton, 461; Walker and Stanton in charge, 461; negotiations of Stanton with "Free-state" men, 461, 462; address by Walker, 462, the party situation, 462; the "Free-state" legislature, 462; the "Free-state" mass-meeting, 463; chances of the Topeka constitution, 463; Robinson's plan to capture Territorial government, 463; Wilson's advice, 463; the Topeka mass-meeting, 464; the Grasshopper Falls convention, 464; census completed, 464; Lecompton convention assembles, 464; the election of October 5, 465; contests in McGee and Johnson counties, 465; Lane's conspiracy and its failure, 465, 466; mass-meeting and convention at Lecompton, 465, 466; the Lecompton constitution, 466; "Free-state" demands on Stanton, 466, 467; constitution to be submitted in full, 467; Stanton removed, 467; Denver appointed Acting-Governor, 467; Lecompton Constitution accepted in election of December 21, 467; Lecompton Constitution rejected in election of January 4, 1858, 468; "Free-state" men in control of three Governments in Kansas, 468; Denver's report to the President, 468, 469; President submits Lecompton constitution to Congress, 469; attitude of Douglas, 469, 470; Lecompton bill passed by Senate and rejected by House, 470; the House proposal rejected, 470; the English bill, 470, 471; the proposals rejected in Kansas, 471; a fourth government erected, 471; close of the struggle, 471; characterization of the leaders, 471, 472; attitude of the general government, of Davis, and of Sumner, 472, 473; Act of 1854 the beginning of error, Missourians the beginners of wrong, 473; characterization of John Brown's work, 473, 474; relation of events in Kansas to Civil War, 473, 474. *See* Nebraska, Territory of

Kansas-Nebraska bill, 343, 456 (*see* Kansas, Territory of; and Nebraska, Territory of); effect of the Dred Scott dictum, 460

Kansas river, 66, 414

Kearny, Philip, ordered to occupy New Mexico, 331; orders to Doniphan, 332; occupies California, 332

Kelly, ——, Editor of *Squatter Sovereign*, 411

Kendall, Amos, instructions to New York postmaster, 271, 272

Kentucky, created Commonwealth with slavery, 50, 62, 63; attitude to tariff of 1824, 115; attitude to internal improvements bill of 1817, 118; attitude to internal improvements bill of 1822, 119; legislature nominates Clay for presidency, 136; attitude toward tariff bill of 1827, 158; relation to tariff of 1832, 188; relief measures for debtors, 195, 196; electoral vote in 1844, 320; views as to slave policy, 378; vote on Kansas-Nebraska bill, 399

Kickapoo Rangers, organized, 426; capture Captain Brown, 426

King, Rufus, voting, 74

King, William Rufus, states his creed on State sovereignty, 269, 270; on committee of Thirteen, 360

Kinsey, Charles, on conference committee, 88

Know Nothing party, 418

Kremer, George, charge against Adams and Clay, 141

LACOCK, ABNER, voting, 74

Lake of the Woods, 312, 313

Lane, James S., effort to organize Democratic party in Kansas, 423; elected Senator by "Free-state" party, 426; negotiations with Shannon, 430; at Franklin, 430; indictment against, 435; as to service of indictment, 435; in command of "Free-state" force, 435; failure to arrive at Lecompton for attack, 445, 446; result of his prevarications, 463; conspiracy against Lecompton convention, 465; thwarted, 465, 466

Lawrence, Amos Adams, member of Emigrant Aid Society, 409; his work, 411; conference with Robinson, 413; town named in honor of, 415

Lawrence, Kansas, site occupied, 411; town founded, 415; quarrels as to claims, 415, 416; Robinson's speech of July 4, 1855, 423; convention at, 425; the Branson rescue, 428; Missourians approach, 429; committee sent to Shannon, 429; Shannon goes to, 430; agreement of citizens with Governor Shannon, 430; appearance of John Brown, 431; appeal of citizens to President, 431; Jones serves writ on Wood, 433; trouble with Tappan, 434; attempt to assassinate Jones, 434; communica-

# INDEX

tions of Robinson and Sumner as to assault on Jones, 434; indictment against hotel and newspapers in, 435; Donaldson's proclamation, 435, 436; dealings of citizens with Shannon and Donaldson, 436, 437; Donaldson's force approaches the town, 437; sacking of the town, 438; repudiation of the deed, 438; effect of the sacking and of assault on Sumner, 440; effect of sacking modified by Pottawattomie massacre, 442; "Free-state" convention at, 443; treaty of August 17, 444; Geary at, 446; Stanton at, 461; Wilson meets Robinson at, 463; "Free-state" forces ordered to meet at, 465

Leavenworth, Kansas, "Free-state" company organized at, 426; convention at, 428

Lecompte, S. D., charge to grand jury of Douglas County, 435

Lecompton, Kansas, the Branson rescue, 428; citizens summoned to, by Donaldson, 435; conflict at Fort Titus, 444; failure of plan to attack Lecompton, 445, 446; Geary at, 446; plan for convention at, 461; as to work of convention, 463; convention assembles at, 464; Lane's conspiracy against convention at, 465; "Free-state" mass-meeting at, 465, 466; constitution formed at, 466; legislature meets at, 467. *See* Kansas

Lewis, Meriwether, sent out by Jefferson, 312; on the Columbia, 312

Lewis, William B., 33; the Coleman letter, 138

Lexington, Kentucky, 167

*Liberator, The*, publication begun, 251

Liberties, Body of, 41

Lincoln, Abraham, intimation as to official conduct of Taney, 456

Loki, the, of Kansas, appears, 431

London, 26, 33

London, Bishop of, as to baptism of slaves, 44

Loring, Charles Greeley, in Sims case, 372

Lorings, the, in Crafts case, 368

Louisiana, Commonwealth of, erected, 56; slavery in, 56, 62, 63, 65; condition on erection, 69, 71; relation to tariff of 1832, 188; vote on Kansas-Nebraska bill, 399

Louisiana territory, 20, 21, 22, 23, 24, 37; added to public domain, 51; slavery in, 54, 55, 56, 57; owned by France and Spain, 54; ceded to United States, 55; divided, 55; early ownership and division, 65; condition on cession to United States, 72; motion of Thomas as to slavery, 84; motion renewed, 87; carried, 88; conference report, 88; relation to Missouri bill, 92, 93; ceded to France, and to United States, 312; as to inclusion of Oregon, 312; cession of 1803, 318; effect of acquisition, 366; act of 1820, 382; as to the Douglas report on Nebraska, 384; as to repeal of Acts of 1820, 391; as to Dred Scott case, 450, 452

Louisiana, Territory of, organized, 56; name changed, 56. *See* Missouri, Territory of

Lovejoy, Owen, killed, 250

Lowell, John, member of Emigrant Aid Society, 409

Lowell, Massachusetts, meetings on fugitive slave law, 368

Lower California, 337

Lowndes, William, committee service, 9; on conference committee, 88; reports bill on Missouri, 95, 96; bill defeated, 99; relation of family to nullification, 181

Lundy, Benjamin, instigates abolition petition, 252

McCulloch *vs.* Maryland [4 Wheaton, 316], 205

McDuffie, George, opinion on slave labor, 161; chairman ways and means committee, 172; relation to Dr. Cooper, 173; contention as to origin of tariff bills, 173, 174; reports a tariff bill, 174; its terms and disposal, 174; forms economic basis of nullification, 175, 176, 177; opposition to tariff, 177; amendment lost, 177; as to bill of 1832, 185; tariff bills in House, 186; attitude to the Bank, 198; makes minority report in support of Bank, 202

McGee County, Kansas, contested election, 465

McGregor, Gregor, 30

McHenry, Jerry. rescue of, 373, 374
McKay, James J., introduces bill, 335
McLane, Louis, speech on Missouri, 81, 82; removed from head of Treasury Department, 280
McLean, John, voting, 73
Macon, Nathaniel, committee service, 3; position on Maine-Missouri bill, 83
Madison, James, his message of 1815, 2, 3; vetoes internal improvements bill, 17; earlier recommendations, 17; relation to Republican party, 17; relation to War of 1812, 17; as to relation between slavery and protection, 109; vetoes bill, 1817, for internal improvements, 116, 117; his views, 117
Mail, United States, effect of presence of abolition literature, 251; use by abolitionists, 270 *et seq.;* Charleston, South Carolina, post-office robbed, 271; request of Charleston postmaster to New York postmaster, 271; refusal to receive abolitionist documents in New York post-office, 271; Kendall's instructions to the postmasters, 271, 272; the question in Jackson's message, 272, 273; Calhoun's report and bill, 273, 274; criticism by Clay, 274; defeat of the bill, 274; Act of July 2, 1836, 274; significance of the contest, 274-277
Maine, Commonwealth of, constitution formed, 76; petition for admission, 77; bill introduced and passed by House, 77; bill in Senate, 82; connection with Missouri bill, 82, 83, 87; amended bill passed in Senate, 88; House disagrees, 88; conference committee report, 88, 89; bill approved by president, 89; significance of the controversy, 88, 90 *et seq.;* attitude to tariff of 1824, 114; attitude toward tariff of 1824, 115; attitude toward tariff bill of 1827, 158; in election of 1828, 164; vote on Kansas-Nebraska bill, 399
Mallary, Daniel, reports tariff bill of 1827, 158; opposes bill of 1828 as reported, 160, 161
Mangum, Willie Person, motion as to Clay's and Bell's resolutions, 360; on Committee of Thirteen, 360
Mann, Abijah, Jr., motion in House, 258
Mann, Horace, opposition to fugitive slave law, 373
Martin, Luther, letter to Maryland legislature, 49, 50
Maryland, Commonwealth of, 9; legislation on slavery, 48; Martin's letter to legislature, 49, 50; laws of, in District of Columbia, 51; domestic slave trade, 57, 58; relation to Cumberland road, 116; attitude to internal improvements bill of 1817, 118; attitude to internal improvements bill of 1822, 119, 120; in election of 1828, 163, 164; tax on Bank of the United States, 194; decision on the tax, 195; relation to slavery in District of Columbia, 253; vote on Kansas-Nebraska bill, 399
Mason, James Murray, reads Calhoun's speech, 358; on Committee of Thirteen, 360
Mason, Jeremiah, in Bank trouble, 191
Mason, John Young, calls yeas and nays, 253; yields to Adams, 253; the Ostend manifesto, 408
Mason, Jonathan, voting, 73
Mason and Dixon's Line, 163
Massachusetts, Commonwealth of, 13; slavery recognized, 41; slave laws, 46; substantial abolition of slavery, 48; separation of Maine, 76 *et seq.;* as a type, 86; as to citizenship law, 99; attitude to tariff bill of 1823, 111; and to that of 1824, 114; attitude toward tariff of 1824, 115; attitude toward tariff bill of 1827, 158; abolition petition in House, 255; laws on jails, 370; vote on Kansas-Nebraska bill, 399; legislature grants charter to Thayer's society, 409
Matamoras, concentration of Mexican troops at, 328; approach of Taylor, 329; occupied by Taylor, 331
Maurepas, Lake, 21, 23
May, Samuel Joseph, the "Jerry rescue," 374
Maysville road bill passed, 167; vetoed, 167, 168; vote on vetoed bill, 168; analysis of vote, 168

# INDEX

Mellen, Prentiss, position on Maine-Missouri bill, 83

Mexico, as to Congress of Verona, 124; treaty of 1825 with Colombia, 147; revolts from Spain, 291; the Austin grant, 291; establishment of federal government, 291; Bustamente's decree on immigration, 291; refuses to sell any Texan territory, 292; overthrow of federal government, 292; possibility of complications with, 296; minister leaves Washington, 298, 299; demand by Ellis, 299; full satisfaction refused, 299; impossibility of regaining Texas, 300; diplomatic relations with United States resumed, 301; the claims commission, 301, 302; Great Britain as mediator between Mexico and Texas, 304; threatens war on United States, 305; claims Texans are still rebels, 305; Benton's criticism of the Texas treaty, 308; relation of war to election of Polk, 320; threatens war, 320; Tyler's message of 1844, 320, 321; makes annexation of Mexico a casus belli, 327; envoy leaves Washington, 327; Slidell's mission, 327, 328; governments of Herrera and Paredes, 328; gathering of forces at Matamoras, 328; position of Mexico with reference to Texan boundary, 328; war with United States, 329–334; title between Nueces and Rio Grande, 330, 331; persistence of the Government, 332; Santa Anna again in control, 332; Polk's message of August 6, 1846, 334, 335; McKay's bill and the Wilmot proviso, 335–337; Polk's message of December, 1846, 335; the First embassy, 337; rejection of proposals, 337; the Mexican offer, 337; war resumed, 337, 338; treaty of Guadalupe Hidalgo, 338; result of treaty with, 339; proposal as to Mexican acquisitions, 341, 342, 349, 350; views of Berrien and Webster as to slavery in Mexican acquisitions, 351, 352; Foote's bill, 354; problem of Texan boundary, 354, 355; Clay's plan, 356; opposition of Southerners, 356; attitude of abolitionists, 357; relation of Mexican acquisition to slavery, 408

Mexico, City of, captured, 338

Mexico, Gulf of, 20, 21, 297, 307, 337, 363

Michigan, Commonwealth of, 290; electoral vote in 1844, 320; vote on Kansas-Nebraska bill, 399; early Republican party in, 418

Mississippi, Commonwealth of, created with slavery, 62, 63; legislature calls Nashville convention, 375; convention in, 375; vote on Kansas-Nebraska bill, 399

Mississippi River, the, 21, 22, 38, 66, 78, 290, 381

Missouri, Commonwealth of, 33; creation, 61–107; significance of the circumstance, 65; petition for erection, 66; memorial for erection, 66; the Tallmadge amendment, 66–73; bill for erection passed by House, 73; bill passes Senate without Tallmadge amendment, 74; disagreement, 74; question again presented, 74, 75; Taylor's plan, 75, 76, 78; Storrs's plan, 78; Taylor's motion and argument on it, 78 et seq.; Holmes's speech, 80, 81; McLane's speech, 81, 82; memorial for admission referred, 82; connection with Maine bill, 82, 83, 87; argument of Pinkney, 84–86; motion of Thomas, 84, 87, 88; amended bill carried in Senate, 88; House disagrees, 88; agreement of conference committee, 88, 89; report accepted, 89; bill signed by President, 89; consideration of the results, 90–95; proposed constitution before Congress, 95; the Lowndes bill, 95, 96; opposition of Sergeant, 96, 97; consideration of the situation, 97, 98, 99; defeat of Lowndes bill, 99; Smith bill passes Senate, 99; tabled by House, 99; efforts of Eustis, 100; Clay's plan, 100; report of Committee of Thirteen, 100, 101; plan defeated, 101; opposition of Tomlinson, 101; conference committee and its report, 101, 102; report attached, 102; resolution passed, 102, 103; effects of the compromise, 103–107; decision brings slavery into national politics, 108; attitude toward tariff of 1824, 115; attitude toward tariff bill of 1827, 158; relation to tariff of 1832, 188; admitted as Commonwealth, 289; line of compromise in Burt's amendment, 341, and in Douglas's amendment, 347; the compromise in connection with the Oregon bill, 348; views as to slavery policy, 378; bill to organize territory west of, 381; Atchison's objection to such organization, 382; Dixon and the repeal of the Compromise, 387, 388; vote on Kansas-Nebraska bill, 399; misrepresentations as to Emigrant Aid Company, 411; the "border ruffians," 411, 412; attitude to slavery in Kansas, 412; influence of Atchison, 412, 413; "Platte County Self-defensive Association," 414, 415; claimants to site of Lawrence, Kansas, 415, 416; interference in election of Whitfield in Kansas, 416, 417; relation of Missouri Compromise and Republican party, 417, 418; effect on Republican party of Missourian interference in Kansas, 418; organization in "Blue Lodges," 419; interference in Kansas Territorial election, 419, 420; Kansas legislature at Shawnee Mission, 423; Robinson's declaration as to slavery in, 424; Missourians summoned by Sheriff Jones, 429; Missourians on the Wakarusa, 429; attitude of Shannon toward Missourians, 430; influenced by Atchison to withdraw, 430, 431; claims of intended invasion, 431, 432; preparation for further invasion, 435, 436; volunteers under Pate, 441; dispersal of volunteers under Whitfield in Kansas, 441, 442; import of Woodson's accession to power, 444; Missourians on Bull Creek and at Ossawattomie, 445; new invasion of Kansas, 446; forced to retire by United States troops, 446, 447; as to Dred Scott case, 450-452; decision of Supreme Court of Missouri, 451; the Missourians the beginners of wrong, 473

Missouri, Territory of, organized, 56; slavery in, 56, 65

Missouri River, the, 66, 414

Mitchell, David B., 28, 29

Mobile, cession of river and port of, 21

Mohawk and Hudson railroad, begun, 169

Molino del Rey, battle of, 338

Monroe, James, relation to Jackson, 31, 34, 35; as to relation between protection and slavery, 110; messages of 1821 and 1822, 110; message of 1823, 111; veto of 1822, 120; message on internal improvements, 120, 121, 156; message of December, 1823, 125-128; electoral vote of 1820, 129; interpretation of message of 1823 by Spanish-Americans, 146, 147, 149; cabinet intrigue against Jackson, 220

"Monroe Doctrine," the, 125-128, 146

Monterey, captured by Taylor, 331, 332; Doniphan sent to, 332

Monterey, California, convention at, 343

Moors, 45

Morfit, Henry M., agent to Texas, 296; report to Forsyth, 296, 297

Murphy, W. S., letter from Upshur, 304; assurance to Texas of protection, 306; promise to Houston disavowed, 307

NAPOLEON. See Bonaparte

Napoleonic decrees, 54

Nashville convention, 375

National Assembly of France, 54

*National Era*, the, protest against Kansas-Nebraska bill, 389; effect of the address, 400

*National Intelligencer*, letter of Clay, 319, 320

National Republican party, the origin, 104; circumstance of appearance, 146; party nomenclature, 162, 163; insists on taking the Bank as a campaign issue, 200, 201; nominates Clay for presidency, 201; feeling toward Jackson, 202; its defeat in 1832, 202; basis of party action, 278, 279; known as Whig party, 281, 282. See Whig Party

Navy of the United States, legislation upon, 13, 14

Nebraska, Territory of, bill for organization passed by House, 381; the Howe-Giddings colloquy, 381, 382; speech of Atchison, 382; bill introduced by Dodge, 382; bill and report by Douglas, 382, 383;

consideration of the report and its author, 383-387; dictum of the committee, 387; Dixon's proposal, 387; Seward and Dixon, 387, 388; new bill presented by Douglas, 389; abolition protest in *National Era*, 389; reply of Douglas, 390; amendment of Chase, 391; position of Wade, 391; amendment of Douglas, 392; views of Everett, 392, 393; Houston's speech, 393; position of Bell and committee, 393; vote on amendment, 393; Chase's amendment, 394, 395; contention of Badger and Pratt, 394; declaration of Walker and Badger's amendment, 395; Chase's third amendment, 395, 396; Douglas's amendment, 395, 396; Chase's fourth amendment, 396; speech of Bell against bill, 396, 397; speech of Houston, 397; final argument of Douglas, 397, 398; vote in Senate on bill, 398; analysis of vote, 398, 399; rise of popular opposition, 399, 400; the Richardson bill, 400; Senate bill in House, 400; position of Cushing, Davis, and Pierce, 401-403; actions in House, 403; management of bill by Stephens, 404; bill signed by President, 404; analysis of vote, 404, 405; meaning of the vote, 405, 406; relation of Act to slavery, 407, 408; considered as of North, 412; immigrants to Kansas through, 445; the Act of 1854 the beginning of error, 473

Negro Fort, 28, 29

Negro labor, adapted to the South, 42

Negro slavery. *See* Slavery

Nelson, Samuel, position on Dred Scott case, 452

Nelson, John, Secretary of State, disavows Murphy's promise to Houston, 307; relation to Texas question, 307

New England, 7, 59; opposed to internal improvements bill of 1817, 117; attitude to improvements bill of 1822, 119; attitude upon Maysville road bill, 168; votes as to Pinckney resolution, 263

New England Anti-Slavery Society, formed, 251

New Hampshire, Commonwealth of, legislation on slavery, 48; attitude toward tariff of 1824, 115; in election of 1824, 142; vote on Kansas-Nebraska bill, 399

New Jersey, Commonwealth of, legislation on slavery, 48; attitude on Maysville road bill, 168; legislative memorial on finality resolutions, 375; vote on Kansas-Nebraska bill, 399

New Mexico, Kearny ordered to occupy, 331; importance of Buena Vista, 333; about to be transferred, 334; acquisition in view, 337; in negotiations, 337; treaty of Guadalupe Hidalgo, 338; Polk's message of July 6, 1848, 345, 346; motions of Bright and Clayton, 346; the Clayton bill, 346, 347; Polk's message of December, 1848, 348; Douglas's bill, 349; Smith's bill, 349; Berrien's report, 349, 350; new bill by Douglas, 350; motion of Walker, 350, 351; failure of Congress to act, 352; Taylor's message of December 4, 1849, 354; Foote's bill, 354, as to question of Texan frontier, 355, Clay's plan, 355, 356; Webster's Seventh of March Speech, 359; Bell's propositions, 359, 360; report from committee on Territories, 360; Committee of Thirteen, 360; Clay's report, 360, 361; encroachments of Bell, 362, 363; passage of bill for territorial organization, 363, 364; as to the Douglas report on Nebraska, 384; Chase on Act of 1850, 391

New York, Commonwealth of, legislation on slavery, 48; attitude to internal improvements bill of 1817, 118; attitude to internal improvements bill of 1822, 119; in election of 1824, 137; in election of 1828, 164; attitude on Maysville road bill, 168; electoral vote in 1844, 320; vote on Kansas-Nebraska bill, 399

New York Central Railroad, system begun, 169

New York City, attitude to tariff bill of 1823, 111; and to that of 1824, 114; attitude to tariff of 1824, 115; attitude toward tariff bill of 1827, 158; postmaster refuses to receive abolitionist documents, 271; the instructions from

Kendall, 271, 272; arrest of Hamlet, 367; meetings on fugitive slave law, 367; publication of protest against Kansas-Nebraska Act, 389

New York *Courier and Enquirer*, applies name to Whig Party, 282

Nicholls, Edward, 25, 26, 27, 28

Nicholls Fort, 27, 28

Nicholson, A. O. P., letter from Cass, 345

Niles, John Milton, presents memorial on Texas, 295

Nootka Convention, 311

North Carolina, Commonwealth of, conditional cession of western lands, 50, 56; attitude to internal improvements bill of 1817, 117, 118; attitude to internal improvements bill of 1822, 119; stock held in United States Bank, 203; electoral vote in 1844, 320; vacancy in Senate delegation, 398; vote on Kansas-Nebraska bill, 399

Northwest, the, attitude to internal improvements bill of 1817, 118; attitude to internal improvements bill of 1822, 119

Nueces, River, 300, 316, 329, 330, 337, 361

Nullification, origin, 169; economic basis, 175, 176, 177; attitude of South Carolina, 176; threatened by McDuffie, 177; Calhoun's publications, 179, and argument, 180, 181; parties in South Carolina, 181, 182; nullification or rebellion, 183, 184; Calhoun's theory, 189; in Georgia and South Carolina, 210; the South Carolina convention, 221; the Ordinance of Nullification, 222, 223; Ordinance sent to the legislature, 224; Hayne's attitude, 224; acts for enforcement of Ordinance, 224–226; views on the position of South Carolina, 226–228; South Carolina in Jackson's message of 1832, 228; Jackson's proclamation of December 10, 1832, 228–230; Jackson's message of January, 1833, 232; execution of Ordinance postponed, 235; character of nullification defined by Webster, 237; Ordinance of Nullification withdrawn, 238; motive of leaders in affairs of nullification, 238; nullification as represented by Amos Kendall, 272

OBREGON, PABLO, negotiations as to Panama Congress, 147, 148, 149

Ohio, Commonwealth of, slavery forbidden, 62, 63; condition on erection, 68, 69, 71; appropriation of enabling act, 116; tax on Bank of United States, 194; the result, 195; memorial on Texas, 296; vote on Kansas-Nebraska bill, 399

Ohio River, the, 48, 62, 63, 167

Oliver, Mordecai, on committee for Kansas investigation, 433; investigates Pottawattomie massacre, 440

Onis, Luis de, 37, 38

Orders in Council, British, 54

Ordinance of 1787, passed, 48; authority of the Congress, 49; restriction on slavery, 69; in Douglas's bill, 341; in the Smith bills, 349

Oregon, its "re-occupation" in the Democratic platform, 309; points in the question, 310; Oregon of the last century, 311; Spanish and English claims, 311; the Nootka Convention, 311, 312; effect of war between Spain and Great Britain, 312; ceded to France and to United States, 312; work of Lewis and Clark, 312; treaty of Utrecht, 312; Astoria founded, 312, 313; joint occupation agreement, 313; agreement of 1828, 314; effect of Whitman's work, 316; in platform of 1844, 318; effect of election of 1844, 320; Tyler's message of 1844, 321; Polk's first message, 324; his recommendations, 324; the question before Congress, 324; the action of Congress, 324, 325; treaty of June, 1846, 326; bill reported by, 340, 341; Thompson's amendment, 341; the Douglas bill, 341; defeat of Burt's amendment, 341; Wick's proposal, 341, 342; speech by Rhett, 342, 343; end of the second bill, 343; new bill by Douglas, 343; special message of Polk, 344; Hall's amendment, 344; views of Calhoun and Davis, 344; Davis moves amendment, 344; effect of Davis and Hale on action of Senate, 345; motions of Bright and Clayton, 346; the Clayton bill, 346, 347; the final settlement, 347; bill approved, 348

## INDEX

Orleans, Territory of, organized, 55; slavery in, 55; erected into Commonwealth, 56

Osceola, begins hostilities, 290; defeated, 290

Ossawattomie, Kansas, destroyed by Missourians, 445; effect of the attack, 445

Ostend, the manifesto from, 408

Otis, Harrison Gray, voting, 74; position on Maine-Missouri bill, 83

Oxford University, Professor Senior of, 186

PACIFIC OCEAN, claims in the north of various nations, 123, 311, 324, 325, 336, 341, 358, 375, 379, 381

Palo Alto, battle of, 330

Panama Congress, early negotiations, 147, 148, 149; commissioners of United States named, 149, 150; popular views of the movement, 150; analysis of vote in Senate, 150, 151; relation of vote to slavery, 151; nature of opposition, 153; adjournment of the congress, 153, 154; discussion of the results, 154, 155; effect of question on Republican party, 155

Paredes y Arrillago, Mariano. leader of military party, 328; overthrows Herrera, 328; refuses to receive Slidell, 328

Paris, treaty of. *See* Treaty

Parker, Severn E., on Conference Committee, 88

Parker, William, opposition to fugitive slave law, 373

Parkers, the, in Crafts case, 368

Parma, Duke of, 23

Parrot, John T., voting, 73

*Partus sequitur ventrem*, 43, 44, 45

Pate, H. C., captured at Black Jack by Brown, 441; rescued by Sumner, 442

Patton, John M., speaks in House, 259; conclusion from his position, 259

Pawnee, Kansas, legislature meets at, 422

Pearce, James Alfred, introduces bill on Texan boundary, 363; not voting on Kansas-Nebraska bill, 398, 399

Pennsylvania, Commonwealth of, 3; provision for gradual emancipation, 48; 62, 63; attitude to tariff bill of 1823, 111; relation to Cumberland Road, 116; attitude to internal improvements bill of 1817, 118; attitude to internal improvements bill of 1822, 119; conventions nominate Jackson for presidency, 136; in election of 1824, 137, 138, 139; attitude toward tariff bill of 1827, 158; in election of 1828, 162, 164; attitude to Maysville road bill, 168; petitions for abolition, 252, 253; memorial on Texas, 296; vote on Kansas-Nebraska bill, 399

Pennsylvania railroad, system begun, 169

Pensacola, 24, 25, 32

Perdido River, the, 21, 22, 23, 25

Perote, captured by Scott, 333

Peru, treaty of 1823 with Columbia, 147

Petition, Right of, early action on abolition petitions, 253; the Chinn-Dickson controversy, 254; Slade's motion, 254; Polk's ruling, 255; Jackson's petition and Hammond's motion, 255; relation of the Constitution to the right of petition, 255, 256; customary procedure before 1834, 256; wrangle over Hammond's two motions, 256; the final arrangement, 256; Adams's appeal for right of petition, 257; reply by Jones, 257; Granger's and Ingersoll's claim as to District of Columbia, 257; demand of Wise, 257, 258; Slade's declaration of war on slavery, 258; Garland's argument, 258; disposal of the question, 258; revived by Adams, 258, 259; ruling of Speaker, 259; Southern members take advanced ground, 259, 260; effort of Adams at peace, 260; decision on the fifty-fourth rule, 260; the contest precipitated, 260; Pinckney resolutions quoted, 261; the new rule of procedure, 261, 262; affair of February 6, 1837, 262; rule as to petition by slaves, quoted, 262; further attempt at agitation by Slade, 262; increase of petitions, 263; the standing rule of 1840, quoted, 263; effect of this step, 263, 264; disposal of the question by the Senate, 264, 265; the Vermont petition, 265–269;

530 INDEX

Petigru, James L., relation to nullification, 181

Phelps, Samuel Shethar, on Committee of Thirteen, 360

Philadelphia, Pa., constitutional convention at, 49

Phillips, Wendell, opposes fugitive slave law, 373

Philosophy of the eighteenth century, 47

Philosophy of 1776, 52

Pickering, Timothy, committee service, 3

Pierce, Franklin, nominated for presidency, 376; elected, 377; relation to Kansas-Nebraska bill, 401, 403; views of historians stated and considered, 401, 402; signs Kansas-Nebraska bill, 404; views on emigration to Territories, 410; appoints Shannon Governor of Kansas Territory, 427; Shannon's report to, 431; appeal from "Free-state" party in Kansas, 431; proclamation as to Kansas, 432; disapproves Col. Sumner's course, 443; takes active steps as to Kansas, 446

Pinckney, Henry Laurens, reports resolution on control of slavery, 261; resolution re-enacted, 262

Pinkney, William, argument on powers of Congress, 84-86; argument restated, 86, 87; effect of his argument, 87; on conference committee, 88

"Platte County Self-defensive Association," formed, 414, 415

Pleasants, James, committee service, 3

Poinsett, Joel Roberts, effort with reference to "Monroe Doctrine," 128

Point Isabel, base of supplies, 329

Polignac, Jules Auguste Armand Marie de, declaration of Canning, 125

Political philosophy, French, 129, 139, 193

Polk, James Knox, ruling as Speaker, 255; quoted, 256; confused rulings, 256; further ruling on procedure as to petitions, 259; con-

position of Calhoun, 279; disposal by Swift's motion, 270; significance of the contest, 274-277; result of the struggle, 296

clusion from his position, 259; decision on fifty-fourth rule, 260; nominated for presidency, 309; attitude of abolitionists, 320; elected President, 320; first annual message, 324; his recommendations, 324; the question before Congress, 325; the action of Congress, 325, 326; Polk's dealings with the Senate, 326; treaty of June, 1846, 326; overtures to Mexico, 327; the Slidell mission, 327, 328; duty as to Texan boundary, 329; orders to General Taylor, 329; message on Mexican War, 330; authorized to call for volunteers, 331; orders to Kearny, Sloat, Stockton, and Taylor, 331; message of August 6, 1846, 334; McKay's bill, 335; Wilmot's amendment, 335; Polk's message of December, 1846, 335; empowered tacitly to secure California and New Mexico, 337; the treaty offered through Trist, 337; rejected by Mexico, 337; recalls Trist, 338; message to Congress, 338; treaty of Guadalupe Hidalgo, 338; sends treaty to Senate, 339; special message on Oregon, 344; message on California and New Mexico, 345, 346; approves Oregon bill, 348; message on California and New Mexico, 348; effect of message on California, 352, 353

Pomeroy, S. C., at Lawrence, 415

Pontchartrain, Lake, 21, 23

Porto Rico, in Spanish-American troubles, 152, 153, 154

Portsmouth, New Hampshire, 191

Portugal, Clay's attitude to its colonies, 135

Pottawattomie Creek, massacre on, 440; the massacre characterized, 441; and denounced by the settlers, 441; effect of massacre, 442; end of fighting occasioned by massacre, 447

Potter, James, owner of Sims, 372

Pratt, Thomas George, contention as to amendment of Chase's amendment, 394, 395

Prigg vs. Pennsylvania [16 Peters, 539], 363

Protection, as regarded between 1815 and 1820, 109; as voiced by the House in 1822, 110; Monroe's messages of 1821 and 1822, 110; bill of 1823, 111; Monroe's message of 1823, 111; bill of 1824, 112. *See* Tariff

Prussia, King of, as arbiter for claims commission, 302

Prussia, in Holy Alliance, 123

Puebla, captured by Scott, 333

QUAKERS, petitions for abolition of slavery, 252, 253

Quincy, Edmund, opposition to fugitive slave law, 373

RAILROADS, begun in the United States, 169; relation to national improvements, 169, 170

Randolph, John, 11; opposition to tariff of 1816, 12

Rantoul, Robert, Jr., in Sims case, 372

Red River, the, 33

Reeder, Andrew H., arrives at Fort Leavenworth, 416; character and work, 416; action upon contested election cases, 420; criticism by Robinson, 420, 421; disregard of his certificates of election, 421, 422; attitude of anti-slavery party, 421; difficulties in treatment proposed by Robinson, 422; calls legislature to meet at Pawnee, 422; breaks with legislature over question of adjournment to Shawnee Mission, 423; letter from Conway, 424; removed from governorship of Kansas Territory, 425; elected Congressional delegate, 425; elected Senator by "Free-state" party, 426; contest for seat in House of Representatives, 432, 433; indictment against, 435; avoids arrest, 435; Donaldson's reference to his resistance, 436

Representatives, House of. *See* House of Representatives

[Jeffersonian] Republican Party, its nationalization, 1-18; 2; its principles in 1801 and 1816, 3; position on national bank, 4, 5; early principles, 17; division, 38, 103, 104, 115; absorption of Federal party, 129; effect of War of 1812, 130; nature of the struggle of 1824, 130; division of the party, 145 *et seq.*; effect of Panama Congress, 155; effect of tariff on division of party, 157; power of Congress in its régime, 207; principles on which it gained power, 239; effect of War of 1812, 239

Republican Party, brought to life, 388; creed in the *National Era* address, 390; effect of troubles in Kansas, 417; the union of the various elements, 417, 418; effect of interference of Missourians in Kansas, 418; as to possible effect of events in Kansas, 446; Kansas assured to the party, 471

Resaca de la Palma, battle of, 330

Revenue. *See* Tariff

Revolution of 1830, relation to abolition, 244

Revolution, the American, slave laws before, 46; effect upon slavery, 47, 80

Revolution, the French, 47

Rhea, John, 31

Rhett, Robert Barnwell, speech on control of Territories, 342, 343, 345; views adopted by Calhoun and Davis, 344; views on fugitive slave law, 367; contention as to fugitive slave law, 371; in debate on Foote's resolutions, 374

Rhode Island, Commonwealth of, 13; legislation on slavery, 48; vote on Kansas-Nebraska bill, 399

Richardson, William A., reports bill on Kansas and Nebraska, 400; motion in House, 403; yields management of Kansas-Nebraska bill to Stephens, 404

Riley, Bennett, calls California convention, 353

Rio del Norte River, 36

Rio Grande River, 297, 300, 305; Mexican troops on, 328; claimed by Texas a boundary, 328; scene of conflict, 329, 330, 331, 332; upper valley occupied by Doniphan, 332, 337, 338, 354, 361, 363

Rio Grande del Norte River, 290, 297

Rives, William Cabell, view of slavery, 265-267

Roberts, Jonathan, motion on Maine-Missouri bill, 82; position as to the bill, 83; moves to amend, 83

Robertson, George, committee service, 3

Robinson, Charles, conference with leaders of Emigrant Aid Company,

413; expedition to Missouri and Kansas, 413, 414; the founding of Lawrence, 415; criticism of Reeder's action on contested election cases, 420, 421; plan of procedure for anti-slavery party in Kansas, 421, 422; sends for Sharpe's rifles, 423; checks factions by the Lawrence speech, 423, 424; elected Governor of Kansas, 425; message to legislature, 427; negotiations with Shannon, 430; at Franklin, 430; communication with Sumner as to assault on Jones, 434; indictment against, 435; opinion as to purpose of Pottawattomie massacre, 441; his release ordered, 446; plan to capture Territorial government, 463; conference with Wilson, 463; difficulty of the situation, 464; his work characterized, 471, 472; his work quoted, 473

Rocky Mountains, 312, 313, 324, 325, 326, 381

Rush, Benjamin, proposal of Canning, 125

Russia, in the North Pacific, 123; edict as to northwest lands, 123; in Holy Alliance, 123, 124; Adams's statement to Tuyl, 124, 125; the Czar in negotiation with Clay, 152, 153

Russian American Company claims in North Pacific, 123

SABINE RIVER, the, 33, 36, 290

St. Augustine, 25

St. Ildefonso, treaty of, 22, 23, 24, 54, 312

St. Louis, 65; Branscomb and Robinson at, 413, 414

St. Mark's, 25, 32

St. Mary's River, the, 22, 30

Salazar, José Maria, negotiations as to Panama Congress, 147, 148, 149; cites Haytian affairs, 151

Salt Creek Valley, pro-slavery convention, 414

San Antonio, battle of, 334

Sandford, John F. A., owner of Dred Scott, 451; defendant in federal courts, 451 *et seq.*

San Diego, Cal., occupied by Kearny, 332

San Jacinto, battle of, 294, 295

San Jacinto River, 294

Santa Anna, Antonio Lopez de, establishes presidential government in Mexico, 292; opposition in Coahuila-Texas, 292; war of Texan independence, 293, 294; a prisoner, 297; in power again, 332; his plan of action, 332; battle of Buena Vista, 332, 333; battle of Cerro Gordo, 333; battles of Contreras, San Antonio and Cherubusco, 334

Savannah, Ga., 373

Scott, Dred, his case as referred to in Buchanan's inaugural address, 447, 448; origin of the case, 449, 450; facts of the case, 450, 451; decision of Missouri Supreme Court, 451; sold to Sandford, 451; judgment in Circuit Court, 451; case before Supreme Court, 451; opinion of Justice Nelson, 452; opinion of Justice Catron, 453; opinion of Chief Justice Taney, 453, 454; opinion of Justice Curtis, 454; criticism of the decision, 455; criticism of Taney's argument, 455, 456; relation of inaugural and decision, 456, 457; opinion of Justice Curtis, 457, 458; distribution of the opinions, 458; effect of the decision, 458, 459; effect of the dictum, 460

Scott, John, secures reference of Missouri memorials, 74

Scott, Martin, in Florida, 31

Scott, Winfield, ordered to Charleston, 330; his instructions, 330, 331; ordered against Vera Cruz, 332; captures Vera Cruz, 333; battle of Cerro Gordo, 333; captures Jalapa, Perote, Puebla, 333; effect of his successes, 337; Trist at his head-quarters, 337; battles of Molino del Rey and Chapultepec, 338; takes Mexico, 338; nominated for presidency, 376; defeated, 377

Sedgwick, Major, accompanies Shannon to Lawrence, 444

Seminole War, 28, 29, 33; results, 38; cabinet intrigue on conduct of war, 220

Seminoles, 32; treaty of 1832, 290; repudiate treaty and are expelled, 290

Senate of the United States, passage of Bank bill, 8; passage of tariff bill, 12; pay of members, 16; passage of internal improvements

## INDEX 533

bill, 16; action on censure of Jackson, 36; ratifies treaty of 1819, 36, 38; effect of method of representation in, 63; Missouri bill referred, 73; vote on Tallmadge amendment, 74; disagreement with House, 74; Clay's suggestion of effect, 75; Maine and Missouri bills in, 82, 83; the Thomas amendment, 84; Pinkney's speech, 84-87; Missouri - Maine bill, and Thomas amendment, 87, 88; the conference committee, 88, 89; significance of the compromise, 90-95; Missouri constitution considered, 95, 96; passage of Smith bill on Missouri, 99; bill defeated in House, 101; work of second conference committee, 101-103; plan to alter judicial system and limit number of Representatives, 109; conference committee on tariff, 114, 115; recommendation of Cumberland road, 116; vote on internal improvements bill of 1822, 118, 119; Clinton a member of, 132; Crawford a member of, 133; Clay a member of, 134; Jackson a member of, 136; opposition to Clay's appointment, 144; action on Panama mission, 149, 150; Van Buren's statement on action of, 153; Van Buren leader of opposition in, 155; action on tariff bill, 159, 160; passage of tariff bill, 162; South Carolina memorial in, 171; Clay's proposal as to tariff, 186; speeches of Clay and Hayne, 187; vote on House tariff bill, 188; conference committee, 188; Benton's attack on Bank, 196; report on the Bank, 198; Benton's resolution on the Bank, 199, 200; relation of members to constituencies, 200; memorial for recharter of Bank, 201; Benton's attack on Bank, 201; bill for recharter passed, 201, 202; Jackson on duty of members, 206; ratifies Indian Springs convention, 212; Calhoun takes Hayne's seat in, 224; Calhoun's statement in, 232, 233; "Force Bill" reported, 233, 234; Clay's proposition in, 235, 236; support of Calhoun, 236; passage of "Force Bill" and of tariff bill, 237; abolition petitions referred, 253; contest on right of petition, 264, 265; Calhoun's efforts as to policy of, 268; incident of the Vermont memorial, 269, 270; reference of President's message, 273; Connecticut memorial on Texas, 295; Clay resolutions adopted, 295; Calhoun's statement, 295, 296; the Walker resolution on Texas, 298, 299; action on President's message as to refusals, 298, 299; effect of action, 300; as to power over treaties, 307, 308; treaty with Texas, 308, 309; action as to Texas, 322, 323; action as to Oregon, 325, 326; bills on Mexico, and the Wilmot proviso, 335, 336; ratifies treaties with Mexico, 339; Oregon bill in, 341; action on Oregon bills, 343; debate on Oregon bill, 344; lack of result, 345; Bright and Clayton on Oregon, 346; passes Clayton bill, 347; final agreement with House, 347; action on erection of California and New Mexico, 349 et seq.; Calhoun's last speech, 358; Webster's Seventh of March speech, 359; action on Texan boundary, 363, 364; completion of compromise measures, 363, 364; action on Shadrach case, 370; action on President's powers, 371, 372; Foote's finality resolutions, 374, 375; petitions to, 375; action on organization of Kansas and Nebraska, 381 et seq.; Atchison, President pro tem., 412; memorials from Kansas, 433; speech on the "Crime against Kansas," 439; Brooks' assault, 439, 440; action on Kansas, 469, 470. See Congress of the United States

Senior, Nassau William, cited, 186
Sergeant, John, opposition to Lowndes's bill, 96, 97; nominated commissioner to Panama Congress, 149; nomination confirmed, 150
Sewall, Samuel E., in Sims case, 372
Seward, William Henry, presents petitions for repeal of fugitive slave law, 375; contest in convention of 1852, 376; relation to Dixon and Nebraska bill, 387, 388; charge as to official conduct of Taney, 456
Shadrach, escape to Canada, 370; Clay's motion and Fillmore's message, 370, 371

Shannon, Wilson, becomes Governor of Kansas Territory, 427; presides over Leavenworth convention, 428; orders to Territorial militia, 429; meets Lawrence committee at Shawnee Mission, 429; goes to Lawrence, 430; agreement with citizens of Lawrence, 430; treats with Missourians at Franklin, 430, 431; report to President, 431; gives troops to Sheriff Jones, 434; dealings with citizens of Lawrence, 436, 437; orders troops to the Pottawattomie, 441; his proclamation, 442; orders troops out under Sumner, 442; goes to Lawrence, 444; treaty of August 17, 444; resigns office, 444

Shaw, Henry, voting, 73

Shawnee Mission, Kansas, removal of legislature to, 423; arrival of Governor Shannon, 427; Lawrence committee at, 429

Sherman, John, on committee for Kansas investigation, 433

Shields, James, attitude to fugitive slave law, 368

Sierra Nevada Mountains, 349

Silliman, Benjamin, member of Emigrant Aid Society, 409

Silsbee, Nathaniel, attitude to tariff of 1828, 162

Sims, Thomas, arrest, 372; trial and rendition, 372, 373

Slade, William, motion to print abolition petitions, 254; compared with Adams, 254; Polk's ruling on his attempt to debate, 255; his motion tabled, 255; declares war on slavery, 258; his object, 259; further attempt at agitation, 262

Slave Code, Virginia code of 1705, 45

Slavery, beginnings in United States, 40; early view of system, 40; legal recognition, 41; prohibited in Georgia, 43; legislation in Virginia, 43; Virginia statute of 1662, 44, 45; relation to Christian baptism, 44; Virginia code of 1705, 45; legislation on public relations of slavery, 46; law of slavery before the Revolution, 46; substantially abolished in Massachusetts, 48; legislation in Rhode Island, Connecticut, New Hampshire, Pennsylvania, New York, New Jersey, Delaware, Maryland and Virginia, 48; letter of Luther Martin, 49, 50; in Constitution of 1787, 50; status in Georgia and North Carolina cessions and in Kentucky, 50, 51, 56; passage of fugitive slave law, 51; abolition of slave trade by Congress, 51; relation to cotton culture, 52, 53; in Louisiana territory, 54, 55, 57, 65, 72, 88; in Orleans Territory, 55; in Louisiana Territory, 55, 56; in Missouri Territory and Commonwealth of Missouri, 56, 65; effect of abolition of foreign slave-trade, 57; domestic slave-trade, 57, 58; relation of slavery to diplomacy, 58; international status, 59; relation of slavery to public policy, 60; status in various States, 62, 63; division of Congress on territorial basis as to slavery, 63; in the Territories, 63; in Northwest Territory, 69; in the Tallmadge amendment, 73; slavery in Territories, 75; Taylor's plan as to Missouri, 75, 76, 78; Storrs's plan as to Missouri, 78; Taylor's motion, 78 et seq.; motion of Thomas, 84, 87, 88; relation of slavery to Missouri struggle, 92, 93, 106, 107; status of slavery in 1776, 1787, 1820, 93; slavery in national politics after 1820, 108; relation of slavery to protection, 109, 110; relation of slavery to Panama Congress, 151; relation to tariff, 157; relation to Maysville road bill, 168; relation to internal improvements, to Missouri struggle, and to tariff of 1828, 170; view of Hayne and McDuffie, 177; relation to the Bank question, 198; effect of race domination, 244; as regarded before 1830, 244; humanitarianism of 1830, 244; the philosophy of abolition and of its opponents, 245; the true philosophy, 245, 246; slavery in the Constitution, 246–248; possible ways of attacking slavery, 248; Southampton insurrection, 248, 249; Floyd's message, 249 (see Petition, Right of); declaration of war by Slade, 258; the contest precipitated, 260; the Pinckney resolutions evoked, 261; relation to denial of

INDEX 535

right of petition, 263, 264; views of Rives, 265-267; views of Calhoun, 265-268; significance of the contest over petitions and the mails, 274-277; relation of Whig principles to slavery, 283; relation of Whig and Democratic parties to slavery extension, 287, 288; slavery in Florida constitution of 1838, 290; slavery in the Texas constitution of 1836, 294; relation of slavery to recognition of Texas, 296; relation of slavery to question of Texan annexation, 300, 301, 302; Clay's views of relation of slavery and annexation, 319; relation of slavery to Mexican War, 330, 331; the Wilmot proviso, 335, 336; Cass's view of relation of Mexican war and slavery, 338; Thompson's amendment, 341; Burt's motion as to the Wilmot proviso, 341, 342; meaning of Rhett's views, 343; views of Calhoun and Davis as to slavery in territories, 344; Democratic platform of 1848, 344, 345; Cass's letter to Nicholson, 345; Whig platform of 1848, 345; the Clayton bill, 346, 347; Free-soil platform of 1848, 347, 348; as to signature of Oregon bill, 348; Douglas's and Smith's bills, 349; Berrien's report, 349, 350; views of Berrien and Webster on slavery in Mexican acquisitions, 351, 352; Taylor's message of December 4, 1849, 354; indication of policy in the Foote bill, 354; relation of slavery to question of Texan boundary, 354, 355; question of slavery in District of Columbia, 355; Clay's plan of compromise, 355, 356; opposition of Southerners, 356, 357; attitude of Davis, and of abolitionists, 357; Calhoun's last speech, 358; Webster's Seventh of March speech, 359; Clay's report, 361, 362; the bills as adopted, 363, 364; slavery before and after 1850, 365-367; relation of parties to slavery question, 377; various policies as to slavery, 377-379; situation in December, 1852, 380, 381; Douglas's report on Nebraska, 382-387; dictum of the committee, 387; Dixon's motion, 387; dictum of Douglas as to act of 1820, 390; controversy on the Kansas-Nebraska bill, 390 *et seq.*; speech of Houston, 393; the *National Era* address, 399, 400; the struggle for Kansas, 407 *et seq.*; indications of plan for extension, 408; the question in Kansas, 412; Robinson's declaration as to slavery in Kansas and Missouri, 424; Kansas legislation on slavery, 424; its effect on the North, 424, 425; the Topeka constitution, 425; the Dred Scott case, 449-459; effect of the Dred Scott dictum, 460; further struggle in Kansas, 460-474; the Lecompton constitution, 467, 468. *See* Kansas, Territory of

Slaves, introduced at Jamestown, 40. *See* Slavery

Slidell, John, sent to Mexico, 327; refused audience, and leaves Mexico, 328; effect of his rejection, 329

Sloat, John Drake, ordered to Upper California, 331

Smith, Caleb B., reports bills on New Mexico and Upper California, 349

Smith, Gerrit, the "Jerry rescue," 374; signs *National Era* address, 389

Smith, Persifer Frazer, assigned to command in Kansas, 443; orders as to invaders of Kansas, 445; sustains Cooke in disobeying Woodson, 445

Smith, George W., candidate for Governor of Kansas, 468

Smith, William, reports Maine-Missouri bill, 82; position on the bill, 83; presents bill to Senate on Missouri, 99; bill passed by Senate and tabled by House, 99; presents protest as to tariff, 170

"Softs," the, attitude of Pierce, 402

Soulé, Pierre, the Ostend manifesto, 408

South Carolina, 8, 9; slave laws, 46; repeals law against slave importation, 51; as to citizenship law, 99; protest against tariff of 1824, 115, 116; attitude to internal improvements bill of 1817, 118; attitude to internal improvements bill of 1822, 119; in election of 1824, 137,

138; opposition to tariff bill of 1827, 159, 160; legislature protests against tariff of 1828, 170, 171, 174; attitude to Jackson's views, 172; relation to McDuffie bill of 1830, 174; attitude to McDuffie's argument, 176; attitude to Congress in 1830–31, 178; the tariff and Calhoun's work, 179, 181, 183; nullification or rebellion, 183; relation to Jackson's message of 1831, 184; stock held in United States Bank, 203; nullification earlier in Georgia, 210; relation to the Indian troubles in Georgia, 220; special meeting of legislature, 221; the nullification convention and its work, 221; the ordinance of nullification, 222; committee to the legislature, 223; addresses of the convention, 223, 224; Hamilton's message, 224; Hayne's inaugural, 224; the Replevin Act, 224–226; change of representation in Senate, 224; acts to enforce ordinance of nullification, 226; opinion of Calhoun and others as to position of South Carolina, 226–228; South Carolina in Jackson's message of 1832, 228; Jackson's proclamation of December 10, 1832, 228–230; active steps taken by Jackson, 230, 231; feeling of the other States, 231; Hayne's proclamation and the action of South Carolina, 232; Jackson's message of January, 1833, 232; Calhoun's statement in the Senate, 232, 233; the "Force Bill" reported, 233, 234; answers Replevin Act, 234; attitude of Calhoun, 234; postponement of execution of nullification ordinance, 235; Bell's report on President's powers, 235; Clay's proposals, 235, 236; attitude of Calhoun, 236, 237; attitude to Clay's bill, 237, 238; ordinance of nullification withdrawn, 238; motive of leaders in affairs of nullification, 238; effect of nullification considered, 238–241; opinion of Jacksonian principles, 240; convention in, 375; vote on Kansas-Nebraska bill, 399; demands of South Carolinians in Kansas, 437; the assault upon Sumner, 439

South Carolina College, 173

"South Carolina Exposition, The," 179

South Sea, the, 33

Southampton County, Virginia, slave insurrection, 248, 249; Floyd's message, 249; passed over, 250; effect on consideration of abolition petitions, 252

"Southern Address," the, 374

Spain, as to American possessions, 20, 21, 22, 23, 24, 25, 29, 30, 32, 33, 35, 36; cedes Louisiana territory, 54, 65; claims in North Pacific, 123; relation to colonies and to Congress of Verona, 124; attitude of Great Britain and United States as to her colonies, 125; the "Monroe Doctrine," 125–128; Clay's attitude to Spain's colonies, 135, 152, 153; trouble in the colonies, 147, 151–153; boundary disputes with France and United States, 290; treaty of 1819, 290; revolt of Mexico, 291; claim to Oregon, 311; the Nootka Convention, 311, 312; effect of war with Great Britain, 312; cedes Louisiana to France, 312; cedes Florida, 313; treaty of 1819, 318

Spalding, Henry Harmon, missionary to Oregon, 315

Spanish Government, 37

Spear, Samuel T., opposes fugitive slave law, 368

"Specie Circular," its results, 283

*Squatter Sovereign*, the, misrepresentations as to Emigrant Aid Company, 411

Stanton, F. P., appointed secretary of Kansas Territory, 461; as Acting Governor, negotiates with "Free-state" men, 461, 462; action on fraudulent elections, 465; demands of "Free-state men, 466, 467; calls legislature at Lecompton, 467; removed, 467

"States' rights" founder of party, 2; position of Webster, 6; early condition of party, 122; nucleus of party, 146; Calhoun's doctrine, 179 *et seq.;* as to the Bank, 194, 195; Benton's speech, 199; Troup's attitude, 213; Calhoun's position, 234, 236, 268, 269, 270; King's views, 269, 270; and *see* 3, 49, 109, 130, 136, 137, 159, 192, 215, 217, 274

Stearns, ——, sells rights to site of Lawrence, 415

Stephens, Alexander Hamilton, management of the Kansas-Nebraska bill, 404

Stockton, Robert Field, ordered to Upper California, 331

Storrs, Henry R., voting, 73; on Missouri affair, 78

Storrs, Richard Salter, opposes fugitive slave law, 368

Strange, Robert, motion in Senate, 270

Stringfellow, B. F., coeditor of *Squatter Sovereign*, 411; formation of "Platte County Self-defensive Association," 414

Sullivan, G., interview with Adams, 142, 143

Sumner, Edwin Vose, communication with Robinson as to assault on Jones, 434; conditional offer of Lawrence citizens to surrender arms to, 437; rescues Pate, 442; returns to Fort Leavenworth, 442; disperses legislature at Topeka, 443; his act disapproved, 443; retirement, 443; attitude to Kansas affairs, 472

Sumner, Charles, presents petitions for repeal of fugitive slave law, 375; speech on fugitive slave law, 377; effort to improve Nebraska bill, 388; signs *National Era* address, 389; vote on Kansas-Nebraska bill, 399; speech on the "Crime against Kansas," 439; assaulted by Brooks, 439, 440; effect of assault modified by Pottawattomie massacres, 442

Supreme Court of the United States, decisions by: Brown *vs.* Maryland, 195, 198; McCulloch *vs.* Maryland, 205; Cherokee Nation case, 218; Worcester *vs.* Georgia, 218, 219; *see also* 109, 207, 222, 229, 346, 348, 366, 383, 427, 447, 460; Prigg *vs.* Pennsylvania, 363; Dred Scott *vs.* Sandford, 447, 449, *et seq.*

Sutter land claims, war against, 413

Swift, Benjamin, presents abolition petition, 269; motion to lay on table, 270

Syracuse, New York, meetings on fugitive slave law, 368; the "Jerry rescue," 373, 374

Tacubaya, 153

Tait, Charles, report, 74

Tallmadge, James, 34; amendment to Missouri bill, 66-74; leader of restrictionists, 68

Taney, Roger Brooke, appointed secretary of the treasury, 280; ceases deposits in United States Bank, 280; the contention as to propriety and legality, 280, 281; criticism by the Senate, 281; opinion on Dred Scott case, 453, 454; criticism of his argument, 455, 456; charge as to divulging court secrets, 456, 457

Tappan, S. F., resists Sheriff Jones, 434

Tariff, bill of 1816, 3, 8, 9, 10; views of Clay, 10; speech of Calhoun, 10, 11, 12; passed by House and Senate, 12; attitude of Randolph and Telfair, and the New Englanders, 12; act under comparison, 15, 16; Monroe's messages of 1821 and 1822, 110; bill of 1823, 110, 111; failure of the bill, 111; Monroe's message of 1823, 111; bill of 1824, 112; support of Tod, 112, and of Clay, 112, 113; opposition of Webster, Cambreleng and Barbour, 113, 114; Hayne's theory, 114; modified bill passed by House, 114; House rejects Senate amendments, 114; conference committee, 114, 115; characterization of tariff of 1827, 115; attitude of various States toward tariff of 1824, 115; protest of South Carolina, 115, 116; significance of the question, 129; relation to slavery, 157; act of 1824 a failure, 157; memorials, 158; Mallary bill of 1827, 158; provisions, 158; attitude of the various sections, 158, 159; bill passed by House, 159; opposition of South Carolina, 159, 160; bill abandoned in Senate, 160; bill of 1828 reported, 160; its provisions, 160; opposed and modified, 160, 161; analysis of vote in House, 162; passed by Senate and approved, 162; relation to party lines, 162, 163; South Carolina protests against bill of 1828, 170, 171, 174; Jackson's message of December, 1829, 171, 172; its reception in South Carolina,

172; its reference, 172; question of origin of tariff bills, 173, 174; bill reported by McDuffie, 174; its terms and disposal, 174; manufactures committee bill, 175; argument of McDuffie, 175, 176, 177; passage of bills of 1830, 177, 178; Jackson's message of December, 1830, 178; the work of Calhoun, 179-181, 183; the law in court, 182, 183; Jackson's message of December, 1831, 184; two bills of 1832, 185; disposal in House, 186; Clay's resolution in Senate, 186, 187, 188; House bill in Senate, 188; amended and passed, 188; distribution of vote in Senate, 188; conference and bill becomes law, 188; its effect on the situation, 188, 189; proposal in address of South Carolina convention, 224; Jackson's message of December, 1832, 228; bill reported by Verplanck, 231, 232; discussion of Verplanck bill, 235; Clay proposes compromise tariff, 235; his purposes, 235, 236; attitude of Calhoun, 236; controversy over the bill, 236; Clay's bill amended and substituted for Verplanck's bill, 237; attitude of South Carolina, 238; President's approval, 238; result of modified bill of 1833, 283; tariff bills vetoed by Tyler, 286

Tassells, Cherokee Indian, executed, 218

Taylor, John, supports Bank bill, 8; presides over Columbia convention, 159

Taylor, John W., in Missouri bill debate, 68; plan as to Missouri, 75, 76, 78; new motion and argument, 78 *et seq.*; on conference committee, 88; attitude toward internal improvements bill of 1822, 119; vote upon Maysville road bill, 168

Taylor, Zachary, ordered to advance from Corpus Christi, 329; demand of Ampudia, 329; hostilities begun, 329; battles of Palo Alto and Resaca de la Palma, 329, 330; occupies Matamoras, 331; takes Monterey, 331, 332; battle of Buena Vista, 332, 333; battles of Contreras, San Antonio, and Cherubusco, 334; armistice, 334; presidential nominee, 345; elected President, 349; plan as to California, 353; message of December 4, 1849, 353, 354; special message under consideration, 357, 358; death, 362

Tehuantepec, Isthmus of, 337

Telfair, Thomas, opposition to tariff of 1816, 12

Tennessee, 31, 32, 35; created a Commonwealth, 51; with slavery, 62, 63; attitude to internal improvements bill of 1817, 118; attitude to internal improvements bill of 1822, 119; legislature nominates Jackson for the presidency, 136; electoral vote in 1844, 320; vote on Kansas-Nebraska bill, 399

Territorial extension, position of Whig and Democratic parties, 287, 288

Texas, early boundary dispute, 290; Austin grant, 291; efforts of United States to buy Texas, 292; declares independence, 293; the Mexicans defeated, 294; constitution formed and Houston elected President, 294; the Connecticut resolution, 295; the Senate's resolution, 295; Calhoun's position, 295, 296; House passes resolution, 296; Morfit's mission, 296-298; Jackson's message of December 21, 1836, 298; Walker's resolution, 298; Jackson's special message as to reprisals, 298; Walker resolution adopted, 299; Texas in diplomatic appropriation bill, 299; Jackson deals with agent of Texas, 300; Texan independence recognized, 300; the question of annexation, 300, 301; Wise's doctrine as to annexation, 302; Whig address on annexation, 303; negotiations of Upshur and Van Zandt, 304; independence recognized by Powers, 304; possibility of British interference, 304; relations to Mexico, 305, 306; proposal of annexation, 305; legal position, 306; Murphy's assurance to President of Texas, 306; Houston sends special envoy to Washington, 306; Murphy's assurance disavowed, 307; President's proposal to move forces, 307; Texas treaty sent to Senate, 307, 308;

## INDEX

President's view of constitutional position of Texas, 308; treaty rejected by Senate, 308; Benton's claim, 308; opposition of Archer, 308, 309; "reannexation" in the Democratic platform, 309; documents sent to House, 309, 310; in Democratic platform of 1844, 316, 317, 318; the Clay letters, 319; demands of abolitionists, 319; the *National Intelligencer* letter, 319, 320; relation to annexation of election of Polk, 320; Greeley's views as to triumph of annexation, 320; Tyler's message of 1844, 320, 321; Ingersoll reports joint resolution, 321; various views as to method of annexation, 321, 322; House passes enabling act, 322; the Archer report in the Senate, 322, 323; the Walker amendment, 323; measure signed by President, 323; Texas admitted, 323; annexation a casus belli for Mexico, 327; Texas congress of December, 1836, 328; the Rio Grande as boundary, 328; President's duty as to Texan boundary, 329; Congressional acts as to Corpus Christi, 329; importance of Buena Vista, 333; problem of Texan boundary, 354, 355; Clay's plan, 355, 356; opposition of Southerners, 356, 357; attitude of abolitionists, 357; Webster's Seventh of March speech, 359; Clay's report, 361; extension of jurisdiction by Bell, 362, 363; passage of bill as to Texan boundary, 363, 364; dictum of Douglas as to annexation of Texas, 390; vote on Kansas-Nebraska bill, 399. *See also* Coahuila-Texas

Thayer, Eli, beginning of his work, 408, 409; his reasoning, 409; organization effected, 409, 410; incorporation, 410, 411; conference with Robinson, 413; reward offered for his head, 413; sending of Sharpe's rifles, 423

Thomas, Jesse B., motion as to slavery, 84, 87, 88; on conference committee, 88

Thompson, James, moves amendment to Oregon bill, 341; amendment in Douglas bill, 341

Thompson, Waddy, as minister to Mexico receives threat of war, 305; opinion on slavery extension, 330

Titus, Colonel, in troubles at Lawrence, 437; captured, 444; his release promised, 444

Tod, John, reports tariff bill, 110; bill fails, 111; reports tariff bill of 1824, 112; supports the bill, 112

Tomlinson, Gideon, opposes report of Committee of Thirteen, 101

Topeka, Kansas, convention at, 425 (*see* Kansas, Territory of); legislature at, dispersed, 443; Cooke refuses to obey Woodson's order to attack Topeka, 445; mass-meeting at, 464

Topliff, C. W., dealings with Donaldson for Lawrence citizens, 438

Treaty of April 11, 1713 (Utrecht), 312

Treaty of 1762, between France and Spain, 21, 22, 23

Treaty of Paris, February 10, 1763, between France, Great Britain, and Spain, 20, 21, 22, 23

Treaty of Paris, September 3, 1783, 22

Treaty of 1790 (Nootka Convention), between Great Britain and Russia, 311

Treaty of 1800 (St. Ildefonso), between France and Spain, 22, 23, 24, 54, 312

Treaty of April 30, 1803, between France and the United States, 23, 24, 55, 57, 72, 312, 318

Treaty of Fort Jackson, 1814, 26, 29

Treaty of December 24, 1814, between Great Britain and the United States, 9, 26

[Convention] of October 20, 1818, between Great Britain and the United States, 313, 314

Treaty of February 22, 1819, between Spain and the United States, 33, 36, 37, 38, 290, 313, 318

Treaty of July 12, 1823, between Colombia and Peru, 147

Treaty of July 12, 1823, between Colombia and Chili, 147

Treaty of February 12, 1825, between United States and Creek Indians, 212, 214

Treaty of April 12, 1825, between Colombia and United Provinces of Central America, 147

Treaty of September 20, 1825, between Colombia and Mexico, 147

Treaty of January, 1826, between United States and Creek Indians, 214

[Convention] of August 6, 1827, between Great Britain and the United States, 314, 324

Treaty of 1832, between United States and Seminole Indians, 290

[Treaty] of April 11, 1839, between Mexico and the United States, 301

Treaty of August 9, 1842, between Great Britain and the United States, 303

Treaty of April 12, 1844, between Texas and the United States, 307, 308, 309

Treaty of June 15, 1846, between Great Britain and the United States, 326, 339

Treaty of February 2, 1848, between Mexico and the United States, 338, 339, 354, 355

Tremont Temple, fugitive slave law meetings, 373

Trist, Nicholas P., offers treaty to Mexico, 337; proposals rejected, 337; signs treaty of Guadalupe Hidalgo, 338; returns to Washington, 338, 339

Troup, George McIntosh, attempts survey of Creek land, 212; letter from Barbour, 212, 213; controversy with Barbour and Adams, 213, 214; repudiates agreement of 1826, 214; controversy with Administration as to surveys, 214, 215; his message to the legislature, 215

Tucker, George, committee service, 3

Turks, 45

Turner, Nat, leads slave insurrection, 249

Tuyl, Baron, declaration from Adams, 124, 125

Tyler, John, succeeds Harrison, 286; vetoes bank bills and tariff bills, 286; Cabinet resignations, 286, 287; friction with Whigs, 287; accession to presidency, 301; opens negotiations with Texas, 301; relation to annexation, 302; resignation of Webster, 303; makes Upshur secretary of state, 303, 304; the London story of interference in Texas, 304; attitude to Mexican threat of war, 305; relation to Texan negotiation, 307; as to defence of Texas, 307; sends treaty to Senate, 307, 308; view of constitutional position of Texas, 308; significance of Archer's criticism of annexation treaty, 309; sends Texas documents to House, 309, 310; relations with Whitman, 315, 316; message of 1844, 320, 321; views as to method of annexation, 321; signs measure for annexation of Texas, 323; characterization of his acts, 323, 324

"UNCLE TOM'S CABIN," 106

"Underground," the, established, 368. See Fugitive Slave Law

United Provinces of Central America, treaty of 1825, with Colombia, 147

United States Bank. See Bank of the United States

United States of America, the, effect of military statutes, 13; national spirit in, 19; territorial extension of, 20; independence recognized, 22; purchase of Louisiana, 23; claims on Florida, 23, 24; occupation of Florida, 24, 25; effect of treaty of Ghent, 26; affair at Nicholls Fort, 27, 28; character of Seminole War, 29, 30; relations with Spain as to occupation of Florida, 32, 33; treaty with Spain, 33, 36, 37, 38; transfer of Florida, 38; slavery in, 40, 50, 52, 53; treaty of 1803, 55; obligations to Georgia and North Carolina, 56, and to France, 57; attitude to slavery, 58, 59, 60, 62-65; debate on powers of general Government, 66 *et seq.;* Taylor's discussion of powers, 79, 80; federal system of 1820, 87; nature of the Union, 97; effect of second Missouri compromise, 103; significance of the compromise, 104-106; commercial position, 112, 113; foreign relations of, in 1822, 122; claims in the North Pacific, 123; relation to Spain's American possessions, 124 *et seq.;* attitude to Holy Alliance, 124 *et seq.;* relations with Spanish-American states, 146 *et seq.;* constitutional interpretation in the history of, 156; relations with Great Britain, 164; railroads in, 169; tariff the necessary policy of, 171; statistics from foreign trade of, 175, 176; meaning of the term, 180; regard for laws of, 181; danger of bank to, 202; Jackson's view considered, 203; as to veto power, 207; effect of Jackson's bank veto, 207-209; cession by Georgia to, 211; treaty with Creek Indians, 212; dispute as to title, 213; treaty with Creek Indians, 214; trouble with Georgia, 214 et seq. ; the issue as offered by South Carolina, 226; principle of the governmental system of, 227; the time for a revenue tariff, 228; Jackson on the character of the Union, 229; officers of, in South Carolina, 230; resistance to laws checked, 234; effect of events of 1832 and 1833, 238-241; development of national purposes, 243, 244; abolition and opinion of slavery in, 244; contest over use of mails of, 270 et seq. ; disputes as to deposits of, 280 et seq. ; treaty with Seminoles, 290; recognition of Spanish rights, 290; immigration into Texas from, forbidden, 291; attempts to purchase Texas, 292; importation of slaves into Texas from, allowed, 294; as to recognition of Texan independence by, 295, 296; Morfits report on Texas, 297; question of natural boundaries, 300, 301; annexation of Texas proposed, 301; diplomatic relations with Mexico, 301, 302; recognition of Texan independence by, 304; relations with Mexico and Texas, 305 et seq. ; as to admission of Texas, 310; purchase of Louisiana, 312; claims in Oregon, 312, 313; conventions with Great Britain, 313, 314; Oregon and Great Britain, 314 et seq.; as to claim on Texas and Oregon, 318; Clay's views as to policy of, 319, 320; relations with Mexico, 320, 321; as to annexation of Texas, 321; as to method of annexation to, 323, 324; claims to Oregon, 324 et seq. ; negotiations with Great Britain, 326; suspension of diplomatic relations with Mexico, 327; mission to Mexico, 328; question of the Texan frontier, 328, 329; relations with Mexico, 329 et seq. ; military power in California, 332; the Trist mission, 337, 338; treaty with Mexico, 338; Rhett on the nature of the union, 342, 343; extension of public law of, 352; relations to Cuba, 408; relation to affairs in Kansas, 445 et seq.

Upham, William, introduces amendment, 338; opposition of Cass and rejection, 338

Upper California, to be occupied to Sloat and Stockton, 331; treaty of Guadalupe Hidalgo, 338; Smith's bill, 349. See California

Upshur, Abel P., made secretary of state, 303, 304; negotiations with Van Zandt, 304; letter to Murphy, 304; formally proposed annexation, 305; demand from Van Zandt, 306; relation to Murphy's promise, 306; death, 306

Utah, Foote's bill for territorial organization, 254; report of committee on territories, 360; Committee of Thirteen, 360; Clay's report, 360, 361; bill as to Utah passed, 362; as to the Douglas report on Nebraska, 384; Chase on Act of 1850, 391

Utrecht, treaty of, 312

VAN BUREN, MARTIN, relation to Crawford, 133; attitude toward civil service reform, 133; in election of 1824, 137; attitude upon Panama Congress, 153; opposition to Adams on internal improvements, 155; share in election of 1828, 164; made secretary of state, 164; his success in diplomacy, 164; relation of Administration to the financial situation, 284; message of September 4, 1837, 284, 285; origin of independent treasury idea, 285; Van Buren's recommendation and the law of July 4, 1840, 285, 286; declines proposition of Texan annexation, 301; resumed diplomatic relations with Mexico, 301; treaty proclaimed, 301, 302; put aside by his party, 309; nominated for presidency, 347; popular vote in 1848 compared with that for Hale in 1852, 377

Vanderpoel, Aaron, motion in House, 255
Van Zandt, Isaac, negotiations with Upshur, 304; proposal of Upshur, 305; demand upon Upshur, 306
Venezuela, 30
Vera Cruz, campaign against, ordered, 332; captured by Scott, 333
Vermont, slavery forbidden, 62, 63; Rev. S. A. Worcester, of, 218; abolition petition, 265, 269; position of Calhoun, 270; disposal of Swift's motion, 270; vacancy in Senate delegation, 398; vote on Kansas-Nebraska bill, 399
Verona, Congress of, 124
Verplanck, Gulian Crommelin, reports tariff bill, 231, 232; bill discussed, 235; bill used in argument, 236; Clay's bill substituted for Verplanck's bill, 237
Virginia, Commonwealth of, 8, 41; legislation on slavery, 43; statute of 1662, 44, 45; slave code of 1705, 45; legislation on public elements of slavery, 46; forbids importation of slaves, 48; domestic slave-trade, 57, 58; as a type, 86; relation to Cumberland road, 116; attitude to internal improvements bill of 1817, 117; attitude to improvements bill of 1822, 119; stock held in United States Bank, 203; relation to slavery in District of Columbia, 253; anticipated by Connecticut in recognizing Texas, 295; views as to policies on slavery, 378; vote on Kansas-Nebraska bill, 399
"Virginia dynasty," the, extinct, 131
Vivês, Francisco D., 37

Wade, Edward, signs *National Era* address, 389; opposition to Douglas, 391
Wakarusa River, the, settlement near, 414; Missourians on, 429
Walker, Isaac P., motion as to Mexican acquisitions, 350, 351; declaration as to repeal of act of 1820, 395
Walker, Robert John, offers resolution as to Texas, 298; adopted, 299; offers amendment to Texas resolution, 323; appointed Governor of Kansas Territory, 461; his address, 462; party relations, 462; declaration as to law controlling territorial election, 464; action on fraudulent elections, 465
Walker, Samuel, in command of "Free-state" forces in Kansas, 444
Walla Walla, mission on the, 315, 316
War of 1812, 1, 5, 8, 9, 13, 17, 24, 25, 28, 29, 33, 54, 58, 59; effect upon political parties, 130; effect on Republican party, 239; as to Astoria, 313
War with Mexico, a result of social development, 277; relation of war to election of Polk, 320; details, 327 *et seq.;* the casus belli, 327; the concentration of forces, 328; point of conflict, 328, 329; beginning of hostilities, 329; battles of Palo Alto and Resaca de la Palma, 329, 330; attitude of parties to war, 330; character of war, 330, 331; Congress authorizes war, 331; occupation of New Mexico and Upper California, 331; capture of Monterey, 331, 332; seizure of California, 332; return of Santa Anna and plans against Vera Cruz, 332; battle of Buena Vista, 333, 333; capture of Vera Cruz, 333; battle of Cerro Gordo, 338; capture of Jalapa, Perote, and Puebla, 333; battles of Contreras, San Antonio, and Cherubusco, 334; armistice, 334; Cass's view of relation of the war and slavery, 338; battles of Molino del Rey and Chapultepec, 338; capture of Mexico, 338; opposition to the war, 338; treaty of Guadalupe Hidalgo, 338
War of 1861, an historical necessity, 65; a result of social development, 277; relation of events in Kansas to, 473, 474
War Department, 28, 30, 31, 32, 35
Warrenton, Virginia, 138
Washington, D. C., 2, 33, 124, 299, 300, 301, 302, 304, 307, 313, 315, 327, 330, 339, 375, 389, 401, 426, 428, 439
Washington Hall, fugitive slave law meetings, 373
Washington *Union*, the, relation to President Pierce, 401, 402
Webb, James Watson, applies name to Whig party, 281, 282

INDEX 543

Webster, Daniel, objection to Bank bill, 6; as to tariff bill, 12; qualifications as presidential candidate in 1824, 134, 136; attitude to tariff of 1828, 162; Calhoun and the Hayne debate, 179; relation to Jackson and the Bank, 191; advice to Bank party, 201; on Bank committee of Senate, 201; answers Calhoun's argument, 237; retires from Tyler's cabinet, 286, 287; New York speech on Texas, 301; checks annexation plans, 303; resigns from State Department, 303; the Ashburton treaty, 303; negotiation with Ashburton, 314; views on slavery in Mexican acquisitions, 351, 352; Seventh of March speech, 359; on Committee of Thirteen, 360; attitude to fugitive slave law, 368; denounced by Giddings, 369; contest in Whig convention of 1852, 376; death, 377

Webster, Sidney, statement as to position of Washington *Union*, 401, 402

Welles, Gideon, Blair to Welles on Seward, 387, 388

Wells, William, as to Bank bill, 8

West Florida, 21

Weston, Missouri, meeting of residents of Platte County, 414

Westport, Missouri, meeting of Whitman colonists, 316

Wheeling, West Virginia, 116

Whig party, appearance, 38, 104; acquisition of name, 279, 281, 282; significance of its composition and principles, 282, 283; relation to Gordon's independent treasury proposal, 285; opposes independent treasury bill of 1840, 285, 286; convention of 1839, 286; election of 1840, 286; Bank bill and tariff bill as party measures, 286; friction between Congress and President, 286, 287; relation of its principle to the new question of slavery and territorial extension, 287, 288; address on Texas annexation, 303; convention nominates Clay for presidency, 309; position on Polk's first message, 324, 325; attitude to Mexican War, 330; platform of 1848, 345; the Clayton bill, 346, 347; election of 1848, 348, 349; convention of 1852, 376; tendency to division of party, 376, 377; election of 1852, 377; controversy over Kansas-Nebraska bill, 391; vote on Kansas-Nebraska bill, 398, 399; vote in House on Kansas-Nebraska bill, 404, 405; meaning of the vote, 405, 406; as to leaders of Emigrant Aid Company, 413; effect of Kansas struggle, 417; tendency to dissolution, 417, 418

Whitfield, John W., elected to Congress in Kansas, 417; credentials accepted, 418; contest for seat in House of Representatives, 432, 433; leads Missourians in Kansas, 441

Whitman, Marcus, missionary to Oregon, 315; settlement, and visit to Tyler, 315; helped by the Administration, 315, 316; the Oregon colony, 315

Wick, William W., moves amendment, 341, 342

Wilkins, William, reports "Force Bill," 233, 234; bill used in argument, 236; attitude of Calhoun, 236; bill passed by Senate, 237; and by House, 237, 238; approved, 238; "Force Bill" considered, 240

Williams, J. M. S., in emigrant aid work, 411; conference with Robinson, 413

Wilmot, David, moves amendment, 335; passed by House, 335; no action in Senate, 336; amendment again passed by House, 336 (*see* Upham, William); motion for amendment of Wilmot proviso, 341, 342; the proviso and the Whig platform of 1848, 345; the proviso in Berrien's speech, 352; the proviso in abolitionist demands, 357

Wilson, Henry, meets Robinson at Lawrence, 463; urges new census for Kansas, 463

Wisconsin, Commonwealth of, vote on Kansas-Nebraska bill, 399; early Republican party in, 418

Wise, Henry A., demand as to District of Columbia, 257; doctrine on Texan annexation, 302; connection of speech with President's policy, 303

Witan, 262

Wood, S. N., Jones serves writ on,

433; as to "treason indictment," 435

Woodbury, Charles Levi, connection with Sims case, 373

Woodbury, Levi, beginning of Bank trouble, 191

Woodson, Daniel, Acting-Governor of Kansas Territory, 425; superseded by Shannon, 427; again Acting-Governor, 444; proclamation of August 25, 444, 445; orders Cooke to attack Topeka, 445

Worcester vs. Georgia [6 Peters, 515], 218, 219

Worcester, Samuel A., violation of Georgia statute, 218, 219; case of Worcester against Georgia, 219

Worcester, Massachusetts, home of Eli Thayer, 408

Wright, William, not voting on Kansas-Nebraska bill, 398

# THE AMERICAN HISTORY SERIES

"The 'American History Series,' now in the course of publication by the Scribners, constitutes one of the most valuable contributions as yet made to the connected history of the United States, and is certain to find a place in every city and town library, and among the prescribed text-books of our colleges and schools."—*The New York Sun.*

A series of seven volumes containing a connected history of the United States from the discovery of America to the present day. Divided into four distinct epochs, each of which is treated by a writer of eminence and of special authority in this field. The volumes are sold separately and each contains maps and plans.

The authorship represents the best scholarship of the times.

The literary value of each volume is noteworthy.

The student has here a comprehensive history prepared expressly for his use by men experienced in the needs and methods of class instruction.

The general reader finds what he is constantly seeking, an authentic account which he can read as he would a story and rely upon as an impartial recital of events.

The volumes are sold separately, enabling those interested in one distinct epoch to find what they wish without unnecessary expense.

*Sent, postpaid, at the given price. Correspondence in regard to class use particularly invited.*

"For practical service in the American college curriculum this Series thus far is admirably suited. Nothing better has yet been proposed as a plan of instruction in American history than these four books."—President JOHN FRANKLIN CROWELL, Trinity College, N. C.

OVER

# THE AMERICAN HISTORY SERIES

## THE COLONIAL ERA
### 1402-1756

By Rev. GEORGE P. FISHER, D.D., LL.D., Professor of Ecclesiastical History in Yale University. With 3 maps. 12mo, $1.00 *net*.

"We know of no other work which in the compass of a single volume offers so complete and satisfactory a conspectus of the subject, and we have therefore no hesitation in commending this book as particularly adapted to the needs of schools and colleges."—*N. Y. Sun*.

"Professor Fisher has given us a compact, suggestive and readable account of our colonial history—the best brief sketch of the period of which it treats."—*N.Y. Evening Post*.

"Professor Fisher's work shows the hand of a master still in its strength. He seems to have a positive genius for clear, compact, and readable condensation."—*The Critic*.

## THE FRENCH WAR AND THE REVOLUTION
### 1756-1783

By WILLIAM M. SLOANE, Ph.D., Professor of History in Columbia University. With maps. 12mo, $1.00 *net*.

"I have read very carefully, and with great interest and pleasure, Professor Sloane's book on 'The French War and the Revolution.' Being a field in which I have done special work, I have been gratified to find my own conclusions confirmed by a scholar so discriminating and so thorough. The book seems to me to furnish new and important help to the study and understanding of the great period of which it treats."—Professor MOSES COIT TYLER, Cornell University.

"Professor Sloane's sound judgment, his remarkable deductive powers, keen insight and tersely vigorous style well qualify him for the work he undertook and in which he is so happily successful."—*Boston Transcript*.

# THE AMERICAN HISTORY SERIES

# THE MAKING OF THE NATION
## 1783-1817

By General FRANCIS A. WALKER, President of the Massachusetts Institute of Technology. With maps. 12mo, $1.00 *net*.

"Nothing better has been written on American affairs in the era between the Presidency of Washington and that of Monroe."—*London Spectator*.

"We can not hesitate to commend this book as marked by a pure and lively style, a sound but chastened patriotism, and a recognition at once scholarly and practical of that transcendent idea, the 'Commonwealth of Nations.'"
—*The Nation*.

"The account is given in a remarkably interesting and almost dramatic manner, with absolute simplicity and directness, with good judgment and an unfailing sense of the relative value of things, which keeps the history in good historical perspective."—*The Independent*.

### Three Volumes by Prof. John W. Burgess of Columbia University

# THE MIDDLE PERIOD
## 1817-1860

By JOHN W. BURGESS, Ph.D., LL.D., Professor of Political Science and Constitutional Law in Columbia University. With maps. 12mo, $1.00 *net*.

"We believe that never before have these questions been so clearly presented for the use of the general reader as in the well-written and compact pages of this volume."
—*The Dial*.

"It may be said in closing that the book is written in a style at once lucid and picturesque, and while there is no attempt at dramatic expression the reader's interest is never allowed to lapse because of uninteresting methods of presenting facts."—*Brooklyn Eagle*.

"This fourth volume of the 'American History Series' is in point of excellence fully up to the high standard of the three remarkable preceding volumes."—*Chicago Tribune*.

# THE AMERICAN HISTORY SERIES

## THE CIVIL WAR AND THE CONSTITUTION

By JOHN W. BURGESS, Ph.D., LL.D., Professor of Political Science and Constitutional Law in Columbia University. With maps. 12mo, in two volumes, $2.00 *net*.

The fifth number in the "American History Series" will ably sustain the high reputation of the preceding issues. It covers the interesting and most important period of the Civil War and Reconstruction. It is eminently a constitutional history in its discussion of the points at issue in the light of public law and political science, but it is also a stirring and graphic account of the events of the war (in which the author was a participator). An especial feature of the book is its brilliant and searching portraiture of the great personalities concerned in the contest on both sides.

*IN PREPARATION*

## RECONSTRUCTION AND THE CONSTITUTION

By Prof. JOHN W. BURGESS, Professor of Political Science and Constitutional Law in Columbia University.

## CHARLES SCRIBNER'S SONS
PUBLISHERS

597-599 Fifth Avenue             New York